# Fodor's

# HONDURAS &
# THE BAY ISLANDS

1st Edition

Where to Stay and Eat
for All Budgets

Must-See Sights
and Local Secrets

Ratings You Can Trust

Fodor's Travel Publications   New York, Toronto, London, Sydney, Auckland
**www.fodors.com**

**FODOR'S HONDURAS & THE BAY ISLANDS**
**Editor:** Kelly Kealy

**Writers:** Maria Gallucci, Jeffrey Van Fleet

**Production Editor:** Evangelos Vasilakis
**Maps & Illustrations:** David Lindroth, *cartographer;* Bob Blake, Rebecca Baer, *map editors;* William Wu, *information graphics*
**Design:** Fabrizio La Rocca, *creative director;* Guido Caroti, Siobhan O'Hare, *art directors;* Tina Malaney, Chie Ushio, Ann McBride, Jessica Walsh, Nora Rosansky, *designers;* Melanie Marin, *senior picture editor*
**Cover Photo:** (Roatan marine park, Bay Islands) Stuart F. Westmorland/danitadelimont. com
**Production Manager:** Angela L. McLean

**SPECIAL SALES**
This book is available at special discounts for bulk purchases for sales promotions or premiums. Special editions, including personalized covers, excerpts of existing books, and corporate imprints, can be created in large quantities for special needs. For more information, write to Special Markets/Premium Sales, 1745 Broadway, MD 6-2, New York, NY 10019, or e-mail specialmarkets@randomhouse.com.

**AN IMPORTANT TIP & AN INVITATION**
Although all prices, opening times, and other details in this book are based on information supplied to us at press time, changes occur all the time in the travel world, and Fodor's cannot accept responsibility for facts that become outdated or for inadvertent errors or omissions. So **always confirm information when it matters,** especially if you're making a detour to visit a specific place. Your experiences—positive and negative—matter to us. If we have missed or misstated something, **please write to us.** Share your opinion instantly through our online feedback center at fodors.com/contact-us.

PRINTED IN THE UNITED STATES OF AMERICA

10 9 8 7 6 5 4 3 2 1

# Be a Fodor's Correspondent

Your opinion matters. It matters to us. It matters to your fellow Fodor's travelers, too. And we'd like to hear it. In fact, we need to hear it.

When you share your experiences and opinions, you become an active member of the Fodor's community. That means we'll not only use your feedback to make our books better, but we'll publish your names and comments whenever possible. Throughout our guides, look for "Word of Mouth," excerpts of your unvarnished feedback.

Here's how you can help improve Fodor's for all of us.

Tell us when we're right. We rely on local writers to give you an insider's perspective. But our writers and staff editors—who are the best in the business—depend on you. Your positive feedback is a vote to renew our recommendations for the next edition.

Tell us when we're wrong. We're proud that we update most of our guides every year. But we're not perfect. Things change. Hotels cut services. Museums change hours. Charming cafés lose charm. If our writer didn't quite capture the essence of a place, tell us how you'd do it differently. If any of our descriptions are inaccurate or inadequate, we'll incorporate your changes in the next edition and will correct factual errors at fodors.com immediately.

Tell us what to include. You probably have had fantastic travel experiences that aren't yet in Fodor's. Why not share them with a community of like-minded travelers? Maybe you chanced upon a beach or bistro or B&B that you don't want to keep to yourself. Tell us why we should include it. And share your discoveries and experiences with everyone directly at fodors.com. Your input may lead us to add a new listing or highlight a place we cover with a "Highly Recommended" star or with our highest rating, "Fodor's Choice."

How to reach us. Share your opinion instantly through our online feedback center at fodors.com/contact-us.

You and travelers like you are the heart of the Fodor's community. Make our community richer by sharing your experiences. Be a Fodor's correspondent.

Buen Viaje!

Tim Jarrell, Publisher

# CONTENTS

## MAPS

# ABOUT THIS BOOK

## Our Ratings

Sometimes you find terrific travel experiences and sometimes they just find you. But usually the burden is on you to select the right combination of experiences. That's where our ratings come in.

As travelers we've all discovered a place so wonderful that its worthiness is obvious. And sometimes that place is so unique that superlatives don't do it justice: you just have to be there to know. These sights, properties, and experiences get our highest rating, **Fodor's Choice,** indicated by orange stars throughout this book.

Black stars highlight sights and properties we deem **Highly Recommended,** places that our writers, editors, and readers praise again and again for consistency and excellence.

By default, there's another category: any place we include in this book is by definition worth your time, unless we say otherwise. And we will.

Disagree with any of our choices? Care to nominate a place or suggest that we rate one more highly? Visit our feedback center at www.fodors.com/feedback.

## Budget Well

Hotel and restaurant price categories from ¢ to $$$$ are defined in the opening pages of each chapter. For attractions, we always give standard adult admission fees; reductions are usually available for children, students, and senior citizens. Want to pay with plastic? **AE, D, DC, MC, V** following restaurant and hotel listings indicate whether American Express, Discover, Diners Club, MasterCard, and Visa are accepted.

## Restaurants

Unless we state otherwise, restaurants are open for lunch and dinner daily. We mention dress only when there's a specific requirement and reservations only when they're essential or not accepted—it's always best to book ahead.

## Hotels

Hotels have private bath, phone, and TV and operate on the European Plan (aka EP, meaning without meals), unless we specify that they use the Continental Plan (CP, with a Continental breakfast), Breakfast Plan (BP, with a full breakfast), or Modified American Plan (MAP, with breakfast and dinner), or are all-inclusive (AI, including all meals and most

activities). We always list facilities but not whether you'll be charged an extra fee to use them, so when pricing accommodations, find out what's included.

### Many Listings
★ Fodor's Choice
★ Highly recommended
⊠ Physical address
⊹ Directions or Map coordinates
⌂ Mailing address
☎ Telephone
🖷 Fax
⊕ On the Web
✉ E-mail
🎟 Admission fee
☉ Open/closed times
Ⓜ Metro stations
▭ Credit cards

### Hotels & Restaurants
🏨 Hotel
🛏 Number of rooms
♻ Facilities
🍴 Meal plans
✕ Restaurant
⌲ Reservations
🏛 Dress code
⚲ Smoking
🍷 BYOB

### Outdoors
⛳ Golf
⛺ Camping

### Other
☺ Family-friendly
⇨ See also
⊠ Branch address
☞ Take note

# 1

# Experience Honduras

"I spent six weeks backpacking La Ruta Maya, visiting well over 80 ruins both known and not-so-well known. I easily count Copán in my top three Maya sites."

—JODYxBUFFY

"One of my favorite first [dive experiences] was around the Bay Islands in Honduras. The currents are minimal, and under the water is amazing."

—cybor

# WHAT'S WHERE

*Numbers refer to chapters.*

**2 Tegucigalpa.** Honduras's capital sits off on its own in a mountain valley in the south central part of the country, slightly removed from the rest of what you want to see. For that reason, international visitors arrive and depart via one of Honduras's other main hubs (San Pedro Sula, Roatán, or La Ceiba), bypassing the capital entirely.

**3 Southern Honduras.** Easily accessible from Tegucigalpa but little known in tourist circles, the country's south is really two regions in one. Two colonial towns, Danlí and Yuscarán, hide themselves away in the hills east of the capital. Then the landscape tumbles down to the Pacific, with the hub city of Choluteca serving as a pit stop on the way to the beaches on Isla del Tigre in the Gulf of Fonseca.

**4 Western Honduras.** Here's the Honduras that everybody comes to see, thanks to the magnificent Mayan ruins of Copán near the Guatemalan border. The colonial cities of Gracias, Comayagua, and Santa Rosa de Copán are bonuses that more travelers are including in their visits. Lago de Yojoa, Honduras's largest natural lake, is a top bird-watching destination.

**5 The Caribbean Coast.** No actual highway hugs the entire length of Honduras's 700 km (420 mi) northern coast; instead you'll zigzag in and out among the Coast's party-centric hub cities. This is Honduras at its most ethnically diverse, where the country's dominant Latino way of doing things shares the stage with the coast's Afro-Caribbean Garífuna culture.

**7** **The Mosquitía.** The jungly northeast region of the country is Honduras at its wild and wooly best. The region's Reserva de la Biósfera del Río Plátano is the country's largest and most fabulous protected area and teems with plant and animal life. Enlist the help of a guide, pack your binoculars and some heavy-duty insect repellant, and prepare yourself for the biggest adventure Honduras has to offer.

**8** **Nicaragua.** The 1980s *did* perform an encore in Honduras's New York State–size southeastern neighbor, in the form of the leftist Sandinista government's return to power, but politics need not concern you during a visit here. The lovely colonial city of León, the hill country, and a few little-known beaches on the Pacific coast await you in Nicaragua's north.

**9** **El Salvador.** Forget those 1980s headlines. Densely populated El Salvador has plenty to offer you these days, and its compact size makes it an easy side trip from Honduras. The capital, San Salvador, is way more "big city" than anything Honduras could hope to have, but the soul of the country lies in its coffee-growing, artisan-creating villages.

**6** **Roatán and the Bay Islands.** The country's crown jewels are its trio of islands off the Caribbean coast. Roatán, long ago discovered but not overrun, envelops you in a low-key lifestyle that would make Jimmy Buffett proud. Utila is catching up as a favorite tropical destination, but least-visited Guanaja, the third Bay Island, is a place for you to plant your explorer's flag. Oh, and the islands are one of the world's foremost diving and snorkeling destinations, too.

# IF YOU LIKE

## A Reason to Celebrate

Honduras's festivals don't all have their roots in the country's Catholicism—just some of them do.

**Semana Santa, Comayagua, Santa Rosa de Copán, Tegucigalpa.** Holy Week is an excuse for most Hondurans to flee to the beach—you'll be surprised at how the country shuts down for seven days in March or April—but the faithful stay behind and pay homage to the somber and joyous events of the Christian calendar's most sacred week.

**Virgen de Suyapa, Tegucigalpa.** How many countries have a patron saint just 2½ inches tall? Each February, Hondurans flock to the capital from all over the country to pay homage to a small statue of the Virgin Mary that dates from 1747 and is said to have cured all manner of ills and contributed to the betterment of their health and welfare.

**Festival de San Isidro, La Ceiba, Caribbean.** Rather than try to compete with the pre-Lenten carnivals held elsewhere in Latin America, Honduras's equivalent takes place in May. The parades, music, and merrymaking of the country's biggest blowout of the year all cement La Ceiba's reputation as the country's party-hearty capital.

**Garífuna Day, Caribbean and Bay Islands.** The British exiled the indigenous-African mixed Garífuna to Roatán in 1797, following their revolt on the Caribbean island of Saint Vincent. Sounds like a tragic event to commemorate, right? The dancing and revelry will make you realize this April celebration is anything but.

## Chill-out Time on the Beach

Although Honduras boasts two coasts, almost everybody gravitates toward the longer Caribbean side and its white-sand beaches. The north-coast infrastructure is more developed, but that doesn't mean you can't find that perfect stretch of sand away from the crowds.

**West Bay, Roatán, Bay Islands.** Take a poll: This one out on the far end of the island likely wins as everybody's favorite beach in Honduras. How could it not be? The postcard-perfect white sand and turquoise water are the stuff that dreams are made of.

**Cayos Cochinos, Bay Islands.** There really are more than three Bay Islands. The term also encompasses the sprinkling of nearby keys, the so-called Hog Islands. Nearly all are uninhabited, and a beach excursion here from one of the big islands—Roatán, Utila, and Guanaja—is sure to give you that Robinson Crusoe experience.

**Punta Sal, Parque Nacional Jeanette Kawas, Caribbean.** The Caribbean-coast beaches at Tela are certainly beautiful, but a short boat ride away lies this white-sand strand inside a nearby national park with a forest of palm trees coming practically right up to the water's edge.

**Playa Negra, Isla del Tigre, Southern Honduras.** The Pacific coast doesn't get the press that the Caribbean side does. Never has, never will. But if you're down here in the southern part of the country, don't let that stop you from relaxing on the pretty black-sand beach—Playa Negra means "Black Beach"—On Honduras's Very Own Pacific Island.

## A Stroll Through the Colonial Past

Several cities and towns in Honduras are monuments to the country's proud pre-independence past. Credit Spain: It originally constructed the buildings that made up its settlements in Honduras in the 16th through 19th centuries, of course; and it is actively aiding Honduras in their restoration today. Yet these cities' colonial cores are not filled with stuffy museum-piece architecture. Centuries-old structures serve today as thriving parish churches, government buildings, offices, shops, and homes.

**Gracias, Western Honduras.** Utterly charming Gracias once served briefly as the capital of Spain's empire in Central America. Residents are working hard to maintain the legacy of those pre-independence glory days.

**Santa Rosa de Copán, Western Honduras.** The highlands' unofficial capital has taken active measures to maintain its colonial architecture with strict laws regarding maintenance and construction of buildings in its city center.

**Comayagua, Western Honduras.** Honduras's capital until 1880, Comayagua contains the country's largest repository of colonial architecture, and residents are engaged in the country's most active effort to preserve their heritage.

**Tegucigalpa.** Most of Honduras's sprawling capital is quite modern, but many of the buildings in the city center date from the colonial era. For a sense of the country's history, a visit to its capital—admittedly, the average tourist bypasses the place entirely—is a must.

## An Opportunity to Be Sustainable

*Sustainable* is the watchword in tourism these days. It encompasses the whole eco-tourism thing, yes, but it also takes into account the need for a business to be an integral part of its community—in other words, to have the chance to sustain itself. We wish there were many more such places, but the near total lack of chain hotels outside the two big cities does mean that by staying at most Honduran lodgings, you are helping provide employment for local people.

**The Lodge at Pico Bonito, Parque Nacional Pico Bonito, Caribbean.** Surprise! A stay in the wild can be surprisingly comfortable as a visit to one of the country's premier lodges can attest. And we say, so much the better when it's such an environmentally conscious place that repatriates its profits back to community projects.

**Casa del Árbol** and **Casa del Árbol Galerías, San Pedro Sula, Western Honduras.** Another surprise: You don't need to stay in the middle of the rain forest to be an environmentally conscious traveler. This pair of city hotels is reducing its carbon footprint with solar power, and has provided employment to a cadre of female Lenca artisans who helped decorate both places.

**Hacienda San Lucas, Copán Ruinas, Western Honduras.** This century-old ranch house outside of town uses solar power to minimize use of electricity. These folks also actively promote local indigenous Chortí culture in the form of employment and customs.

# HONDURAS TOP ATTRACTIONS

## Copán, Western Honduras

**(A)** What hasn't been said about this "Paris of the Mayan World" and its intricately carved stelae, monuments to its Mayan rulers? Easily accessed, tourist-friendly, and with a ton of related activities when you tire of looking at ruins, this is the country's top tourist attraction.

## Gracias, Western Honduras

**(B)** Cool, crisp Gracias was once the capital of Spain's entire Central American colony—but for only four years in the 16th century. Residents are busy restoring their community to the appearance it had during those glory days, and other than the addition of motor vehicles, they've been successful. It will always be the capital of the highland towns in our book.

## Lago de Yojoa, Western Honduras

**(C)** Part tropical lowland, part Honduran highland, the country's largest natural lake sits in a transition zone between north and south and between east and west that permits it to be a crossroads of biodiversity. In particular, bird watchers come here to spot 400 species of their favorite animal.

## Parque National La Tigra, Tegucigalpa

**(D)** You'd never know you were just a few miles north of the capital when you enter one of the world's most beautiful tracts of cloud forest. Its proximity to the city means that this protected area can be easily done as a day trip—best with the help of a guide—but if you're feeling intrepid, make it an overnight stay in the rustic accommodation within the park.

## Parque Nacional Pico Bonito, Caribbean

**(E)** One of Honduras's foremost national parks is easily visited from La Ceiba, but we like this protected area for the opportunity it offers to stay at its namesake lodge with its myriad eco-activities. And you'll love the sight of Pico Bonito itself,

a nearly 8,000-foot peak that turns a dreamy blue at dusk.

## Reserva de la Biósfera Río Plátano, La Mosquitía

(F) Few actually make it to Honduras's largest biological reserve—much planning is needed to get here—but make the effort and you will be richly rewarded with Honduras at its unspoiled best. The stories of the jungle, the plants, and the animals you see are guaranteed to wow the folks back home.

## Roatán, Utila, and Guanaja: the Bay Islands

(G) Who could ever truly decide which of the three Bay Islands is best? Roatán is developed, to be sure, but its selection of lodgings, restaurants, and sights means you're never at a loss for things to do. Up-and-coming Utila is a smaller version of its larger neighbor, and far more low-key—not that Roatán is ever frenzied. Guanaja really remains that get-away-from-it all tropical island. Each is fabulous in its own way.

## Valle de Ángeles, Tegucigalpa

(H) High in the hills just outside Tegucigalpa is the favorite weekend getaway for *capitalinos* (residents of Tegucigalpa, the capital), even if it's only for Sunday lunch. Do as they do: partake of the *típico* (traditional) food at the many eateries, shop for handicrafts, and bask in the cool, fresh, clear air, a welcome respite from the sometimes smoggy capital.

## Yuscarán, Southern Honduras

(I) Honduras's other colonial communities are bigger and better known, but cute, charming little Yuscarán is close enough to the capital to be easily visited if you're staying in this part of the country. And to top it off, it's home to Honduras's best-know distillery and you can see how the firewater *guaro* is made.

# TOP EXPERIENCES

**Ponder the mysteries of the Maya.**
Although historians know most of the background of the ancient city of Copán, a walk through its ruins in southwest Honduras is bound to raise more questions than answers: How could a people of a millennium ago have created the intricate stelae figures that populate the complex here? Are there ruins that are yet to be excavated? Oh, and what's going to happen when the Maya calendar comes to a scheduled end in December 2012? Should I put off my holiday shopping that year? After a visit to Copán, even the most no-nonsense curmudgeons find themselves deliberating the mysteries of the cosmos.

**Come face-to-face with an eagle ray.**
The Bay Islands are home to the second-largest barrier reef on the planet, one that also takes in Belize and Mexico, and are one of the world's great underwater destinations. Whether you're a finely tuned diver or haven't yet gotten your feet wet, rates here are reasonable for dive excursions, a beginner's course, or those "get acquainted" classes that won't certify you but will tease you with a diving sampling.

**Wolf down a baleada.**
Honduras's answer to Mexico's quesadilla is the ubiquitous *baleada*, and sampling one is a rite of passage into the fold of true Honduran travelers. Take a corn- or wheat-flour tortilla, fill with mashed black beans, and top with a dollop of sour cream. That's a baleada at its most basic, as it originated in La Ceiba. Dress them up with sliced tomatoes, cheese, sausage, chicken, pork, avocadoes, onions, peppers. . . . The variety is limited only by the number of people who make them and the part of the country you're in. Ever-present baleada ladies sell them on the street, but local sit-down restaurants all serve them, too, and that's probably a better bet.

**Observe Holy Week.**
You needn't be Catholic, or even Christian, to appreciate the pageantry of Honduras's *Semana Santa* processions the entire week preceding Easter. Most of the country flees to the beach for the week, but the faithful stay behind to reenact Jesus' last week on earth, with the biggest doings in Comayagua, Tegucigalpa, and Santa Rosa de Copán. Integral to the Good Friday observances are the *alfombras*, intricate street carpets made of colored sawdust. Why would townspeople put so much effort into creating something only to have it trampled by the processions in a matter of minutes? "What a question!" you'll likely get in response. They're sure to tell you it's in gratitude for some grace bestowed upon them.

**"Voluntour."**
You see them on flights to and from Honduras: groups of people wearing identical T-shirts, coming here to work on a development project, perhaps medical, perhaps educational in focus. Honduras is one of the hemisphere's premier destinations for a volunteer vacation. (A Google search of "HONDURAS VOLUNTEER" turns up 1.4 million entries and counting). Some of the groups are secular; others, religious in focus (hence the oft-used term "mission trip"). It's a way to make a difference—away from the glitzy tourist facade, the need is great here—and to give something back to Honduras.

**Look into the workings of a fine cigar.**
Yes, it is smoking—we know, we know—and we would never promote the activity. But cigars *are* one of Honduras's top exports, and tobacco has played a prominent role in engineering the country's

economy since colonial times when the Spanish established the Royal Tobacco Factory in the highlands. Manufacturers in Danlí and Santa Rosa de Copán are happy to show you how tobacco is cultivated, harvested, cured, and rolled into cigars that rank right up there in quality with the finest Cuban product.

### Dance the punta.

It's not reggae, or salsa, or hip-hop, but the *punta* music indigenous to the Caribbean coast's Garífuna people resembles all three. The name is thought to be a corruption of *bunda*, the word for "buttocks" in the Mandé language of West Africa, from where the music originated, and the name is apt. Can you remain stationary from the waist up while rotating your hips? If, yes, congratulations: You're a born punta dancer. If you're like the rest of us, probably not, but don't be shy about getting out on the dance floor and trying. Performers at shows always encourage audience participation.

### Add to your life list.

Those in the know in the birding community salivate at the mention of Honduras. As the meeting place of the Americas, Central America's narrow landmass funnels an incredible amount of biodiversity—Honduras alone logs 700 species of birds—into its territory. Lago de Yojoa, in the center of the country, is a crossroads of another type, where highlands and tropical lowlands meet. If you're diligent, you'll check off 400 species at the lake. The Mosquitía is home to a few hundred species, too, but you need not travel so far afield either: La Tigra and Cusuco national parks, just outside Tegucigalpa and San Pedro Sula respectively, are perfect venues if your time is limited.

### Veer around a Class III rapid.

Or if you're feeling particularly adventurous, try a IV or V. The easily accessible Río Cangrejal contains sectors of all three, and is close enough to La Ceiba or Pico Bonito National Park for you to be back at your hotel or lodge after a day of white-water rafting in time to establish bragging rights over dinner. The IIIs are really III-pluses on the Cangrejal, so inquire carefully before booking an excursion. Outfitters in this part of the country get high grades for safety and professionalism. Farther afield, the Río Plátano, in the reserve of the same name in the Mosquitía, needs to be a multiday affair because of its isolation, but that gives you ample opportunity to soak in the nature that you can't focus on while you negotiate that rapid.

### Aprender una lengua.

Learn a language—Spanish, of course. Honduras lacks the hordes who study Spanish in neighboring Guatemala, but that's a selling point for taking up the language here. (It means less temptation to lapse into English with all your classmates outside school.) Copán Ruinas, La Ceiba, Roatán, and Utila hold the bulk of the language schools. Morning might begin with you and your instructor, one-on-one—that's the structure for most beginning courses here—over a cup of coffee out on the school's patio, tackling conjugations with a few props to aid you. Bid farewell and move on to a café for the afternoon, notebook in hand to review your day's lessons. Evening means dinner with your host family and a chance to practice what you've learned. It's all about immersing yourself in the language.

# HONDURAS TODAY

## Government

Honduras is a multiparty democracy with an elected president and one-house congress, and is divided into 18 province-like divisions known as *departamentos* (departments), and 296 municipal entities called *municipios*. That said, what's on paper has differed from reality during much of its history.

The country has had an astonishing 67 presidents plus another six governing councils since 1839. From 1821 to 1839, when Honduras formed part of a larger Central American federation with Guatemala, El Salvador, Nicaragua, and Costa Rica, another 18 presidents ruled. June 2009 brought a painful reminder that military coups still do happen in Latin America, when leftist President Manuel Zelaya was bundled up in his pajamas and spirited out of the country by the army early one Sunday morning. (At the time of the coup and during its aftermath, visitors to Copán and the Bay Islands reported they barely knew anything was going on, though. Nearly all the footage that dominated international news came out of Tegucigalpa during those days.)

The *crisis political* that followed—that's the euphemistic term everybody here prefers to use—dried up investment and stagnated tourism for months. Free elections were held that November—that's when they had been scheduled anyway—and Honduras's temporary status as an international pariah ended, although a few holdout countries still refuse to recognize the new government. You'll still see the occasional rally in Tegucigalpa and San Pedro Sula in support of the now-exiled Zelaya, but most walk right on by without paying any attention, breathing a sigh of relief that the troubles of 2009 are over.

## Economy

You've heard the term *banana republic*? Honduras was the original, a 19th century nation beholden to one export crop and to the multinational corporations that called the shots and controlled its cultivation and export. Bananas are still an important sector of the country's economy and have made significant recovery following their near wipeout here during 1998's devastating Hurricane Mitch.

Coffee has overtaken bananas as Honduras's number-one agricultural export, however, with sugar, pineapples, mangoes, and cultivated shrimp also growing in importance. Honduras remains, unfortunately, a largely agrarian country dependent on products whose prices are set by the vagaries of the world market. That fact of life has meant a real rollercoaster ride for its economy through the years.

The country's *maquiladora* sector—where raw materials are temporarily imported for assembly in factories here and then re-exported as full-fledged products—remains strong. The majority of such firms are Asian owned. Critics decry the *maquila* system as keeping citizens penned to low-wage jobs, but pay is comparable, or better, than the typical Honduran earns elsewhere.

Hondurans living abroad send remittances of approximately $2 billion annually back home, contributing over one-fourth of the country's gross domestic product. Without the remittances, many families could not survive. Honduras is placing new hopes in international free-trade treaties. It and its Central American neighbors completed negotiations of an agreement with the United States in 2006 and with the European Union in 2010.

## Tourism

Visitor numbers in Honduras have been respectable through the years, thank you very much, considering it must compete with Guatemala and Costa Rica, the two tourism powerhouses in the isthmus. The Mayan ruins at Copán and the underwater wonders (and relaxed pace of life) of the Bay Islands have always been crowd pleasers. However, Honduras has struggled—not always successfully—to let visitors know that there's much more to the country than those two main hotspots.

The tourism ministry in the current administration has launched new campaigns to inform visitors about Lenca villages, colonial towns, and the natural wonders of the Lago de Yojoa and the Mosquitía. The industry has had success and achieved acclaim with its new international marketing slogan: "Honduras: the Central America you know, the country you'll love."

Tourists from other Central American countries, primarily El Salvador and Guatemala, contribute a plurality of visitor numbers, with the United States following in next place. The industry here is looking to promote itself more strongly to North America and Europe than it has done in the past. It has also forged alliances with its counterparts in other Central American countries, marketing the entire isthmus as a multinational tourist destination.

## Religion

Honduras's constitution guarantees complete religious freedom. No official statistics exist on how the country's population divides up into religious groups, and figures depend on who is doing the talking.

Honduras is a nominally Catholic nation, that historic bulwark of faith in Latin America, and Honduras's Catholicism took center stage in 2005 when Tegucigalpa's archbishop, the well-liked Cardinal Óscar Rodríguez, was seen as a strong candidate to succeed Pope John Paul II. The church's own sources cite the number at 81% of the population, but polls conducted by Gallup here suggest that the country is quite religiously diverse. The Catholic church may not have as strong a following as it claims, with just less than half the population identifying itself that way.

The explosive growth in the past three decades has been among the one-third of the population who belong to evangelical and Pentecostal groups. They hold services in small houses of worship, occasionally storefront churches, and with their revival-style singing, you'll always hear them before you see them. The remainder of the population belongs to several Protestant denominations, with Episcopalian, Lutheran, Methodist, Presbyterian, and Baptist churches represented here. Mormons, Seventh-day Adventists, and Jehovah's Witnesses have small but thriving communities here, too.

Tegucigalpa and San Pedro Sula each have a synagogue, with San Pedro also having the country's only mosque. Some 2% of Honduras's population is of Arab lineage—that's the highest figure of any country in the Western Hemisphere—descended from Palestinian merchants who migrated to Honduras in the early 20th century. The majority of Honduran Arabs are Palestinian Christians, however.

# GREAT ITINERARIES

Slightly smaller than the state of Ohio, Honduras is compact enough and easy enough to get around—mostly—so that any listing of itineraries can be broken apart and reassembled, mix-and-match style. The presence of four international airports and a good domestic air network means you can vary your arrival and departure points, too. (And, yes, there is more to the country than Copán and Roatán.) Note that there are no connecting agreements between the international airlines that serve Honduras and its domestic airlines, and same-day international-to-domestic flight itineraries (or vice versa) are not recommended.

## THE BIG TWO: COPÁN AND ROATÁN

### Day 1: Arrival in San Pedro Sula and Copán Ruinas

Arrive in San Pedro Sula. If your schedule permits it, taxi directly to the Gran Central Metropolitana, San Pedro's massive bus terminal just south of town, where you can catch a bus to the town of Copán Ruinas, about a three-hour ride. The bus company Hedman Alas also has transport from the airport with connections to its service to Copán Ruinas a few times a day. Arrive in Copán Ruinas late afternoon or evening. Check into your hotel. Twisted Tanya's or Jim's Pizza each offers reassuring surroundings after a long day of travel.

### Day 2: The Ruins of Copán

Remember, the difference: Copán Ruinas is the town; Copán is the complex of Mayan ruins. The early bird catches the worm, as the saying goes, and it catches the best time of day to visit the ruins here, too. Walk from town—it takes about 15 minutes—or take one of the fun, three-wheeled "tuk-tuk" vehicles that are the town's taxis. Be there when the gates open at 8 AM: it will be cooler—there's some shade but not as much as you'd like in such a tropical locale—and you'll be competing with fewer visitors. As the sun begins to rise in the sky (along with the temperatures), make your way to the on-site Museum of Maya Sculpture. The museum charges a separate admission, but the extra insight you gain is well worth it. Head back to town as noon approaches and treat yourself to a nice lunch after a morning of playing fantasy archaeologist. Take the afternoon to rest a bit, but remember that all those rest-of-Copán activities beckon and will easily fill this half day and all day tomorrow. One afternoon option is the Copán Coffee Tour, on which you'll learn about the life and times of Honduras's most important beverage. The afternoon tour leaves at 2 PM.

### Day 3: Copán Ruinas and Environs

The Enchanted Wings Butterfly Garden sits on the edge of town on the road to the Guatemalan border. An early-morning visit—the place opens at 8—lets you catch the most activity, your laminated identification card in hand to help identify butterfly species. Another type of flying animal holds court at the Macaw Mountain Bird Park about 10 minutes north of town. This bird-rescue center is a must for anyone visiting the area. Lunch here is proffered by the folks at the Twisted Tanya's restaurant in town and is just as yummy. Spend the afternoon at the Hacienda San Lucas, south of town. An L40 day pass lets nonguests in to use the facilities, and the zip-line canopy tour and the walk to the small Los Sapos archaeological site are crowd pleasers. Lunch or dinner here is the best of Honduran típico in the setting of a century-old ranch house.

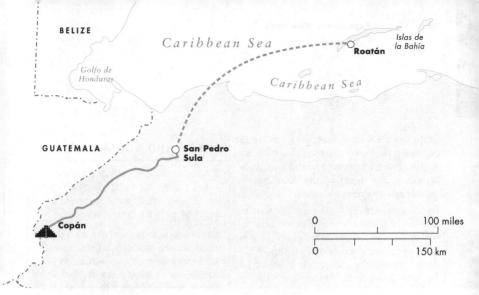

## Day 4: San Pedro Sula and Roatán

An early-morning bus—think Hedman Alas again—gets you back to San Pedro Sula in time to catch an afternoon flight to Roatán. Check into your hotel and treat yourself to a nice evening meal. Taxi drivers in Roatán have been known to overcharge visitors. Ask the folks at your hotel desk for a lay of the land and an idea of what taxi fares should be.

## Days 5 and 6: Roatán

Are two days enough for Roatán? Probably not, because a whirlwind of activities awaits. If you've never been scuba diving before, most dive operators offer a "get acquainted" course that won't certify you, but will give you a taste of diving and pique your underwater interest. Didn't come to Roatán for diving? That's cool, too. The same outfitters that organize scuba excursions—and they are numerous here—can also take you snorkeling. Back on land, you can choose from—take a deep breath—the Roatán Butterfly Garden, the dolphin shows at the Roatán Institute for Marine Sciences, the Tropical Treasures Bird Park, and the midday feedings of the namesake animals at Arch's Iguana and Marine Farm. And when all that wears you out, the white-sand beach at Half Moon Bay on the island's west end

will give you a new standard by which to measure all such strands of sand.

## Days 7 and 8: To San Pedro Sula and Departure

Catch an early-morning flight from Roatán back to San Pedro Sula. Check into your hotel—the city has a huge array of lodgings—and take time to browse the offerings in the Guamilito market, with one of the best selections of souvenirs in Honduras, just a few blocks north of the central park. Or if you're feeling more like being a mall rat after a week out-country, head for the massive Multiplaza or City Mall on the Circunvalación, the suburban ring road that surrounds the city. Enjoy a nice dinner at one of the city's many restaurants. Get to the airport in plenty of time your final day. Airlines recommend checking in three hours before departure.

## Alternatives

Some international flights to San Pedro Sula arrive too late for you to be able to head out to Copán Ruinas that same day. (You might not feel like a three-hour bus ride after a long day of flying either.) Also, many flights also depart San Pedro too early in the day to be arriving from another destination that same morning. That frequently makes San Pedro a first-night, last-night place to stay. If you can't get to Copán Ruinas that first night, head out early the next morning. You'll have an afternoon to partake of the non-ruins activities, and head to the ruins themselves early the next morning.

Renting a car and driving to Copán Ruinas is always an option, of course, but under no circumstances should you drive the route after dark. Portions of the road between the crossroads town of La Entrada and Copán Ruinas are winding and potholed. Sunset is between 5:30 and 6 PM year-round. If driving, always be at your destination before then. Bus drivers know the route well; it's fine to leave the driving to them, no matter what the time of day.

Roatán has Honduras's second busiest airport, and with its handful of international flights, it is possible to juggle the order around and begin and/or end this itinerary from there.

If diving is your draw to Roatán, you'll likely want more than two days there. If you're planning to take a dive course, you'll need at least three or four days.

## CARIBBEAN COAST

### Day 1: Arrival in La Ceiba

Disembarkation at La Ceiba's tiny airport is as much a breeze as the light winds that blow in off the sea here. Check into any of the town's fine lodgings—there's a good selection here—and prepare yourself for an evening of Honduras's best nightlife. Take in a Garífuna music performance, engage in an evening of dancing, or enjoy a beer at a quiet seaside bar. But as in any port city, don't walk the streets after dark. Take a taxi to and from instead.

---

**COPÁN AND ROATÁN TIPS**

1. When inquiring about transportation, always specify that you're going to "Copán Ruinas." The term *Copán* alone means different things to different Hondurans.

2. For comfort and punctuality, we recommend Hedman Alas for bus travel between San Pedro Sula and Copán Ruinas; the company offers three runs a day each way. It costs more but is still a bargain at L350 ($18) one way for the three-hour trip.

3. Landslides occasionally block the road between the crossroads town of La Entrada and Copán Ruinas during the worst of the rainy season (September and October) and can cause delays.

---

### Day 2: La Ceiba to Tela

An early-morning start gets you to Tela, a scant 60 km (37 mi) west of La Ceiba. As with most travel along the Caribbean coast, the road veers inland on the drive between the hub cities and does not hug the shore. No matter: the route takes you through forests and banana plantations that are lush, green, and scenic no matter what time of year you're here. (Rainfall along the coast is more evenly dispersed throughout the year.) If you got going early enough, you should have time to take in a boat tour at the nearby Jeanette Kawas National Park. (Early is best for spotting the park's population of howler and capuchin monkeys.) Take in the Lancetilla botanical gardens in the afternoon—they're the world's second-largest such facility, or the nearby, distinctive Garífuna village of Miami, which bears no resemblance to the metropolis in Florida.

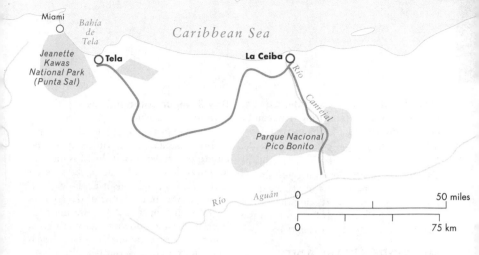

## Day 3: Parque Nacional Pico Bonito

It's back toward La Ceiba on your third day, but south of the city lies the expanse of one of Honduras's best-known national parks. *Pico Bonito* means "pretty peak," and this nearly 8,000-foot summit looms captivatingly over the park. A stay at the park's lodge is pricey, but it remains one of Honduras's top eco-experiences. The lodge employs top-notch guides who will take you along the park's trails, the most popular being the trek to the La Ruidosa ("the noisy one") waterfalls. Dinner at the lodge is informal and festive, and you can join in the conversation about what you spotted that day. Such discussions frequently go long into the evening, even though everybody knows they have to get up early for the next morning's nature outing.

## Day 4: Río Cangrejal

Take in the country's top white-water rafting experience on your fourth day. The Río Cangrejal offers Class III, IV, and V sectors with the option of half- or full-day excursions.

## Day 5: Departure

Pico Bonito is one of those "so close and yet so far" destinations. Even though you feel as if you're a million miles from anywhere, you're close enough to La Ceiba

---

### CARIBBEAN COAST TIPS

1. Nighttime and beaches never mix. All the daytime hubbub of the Caribbean beaches fizzles out once the sun goes down. Wandering deserted beaches at night spells trouble.

2. We fear Tela may be one of those "enjoy it now while you can" places. This sector of the coast is slated for major development, the so-called Tela Bay project, in coming years, with some predicting the area will become Honduras's very own Cancún. That might be stretching things, but this is the time to go.

---

that an early-morning departure from the park gets you back in time for a midday flight out.

### Alternatives

La Ceiba does receive a few international flights, making it entirely possible to begin and/or end this itinerary there. San Pedro Sula does give you a bigger variety of flights from the United States to choose from, however, and there are plenty of domestic flights between San Pedro and La Ceiba, too.

Rates at The Lodge at Pico Bonito start at $240 per night, to which you might say,

"Ouch!" All excursions in the park, as well as the Cangrejal rafting trip, can be done to and from La Ceiba as well.

Rafting the Río Cangrejal is not for everybody. The Class-III sectors could really be classified as III-plus, meaning you should have a bit of experience—or at least minimal fear—before undertaking the trip. A hike in the park to Pico Bonito itself is a nice alternative to the rafting trip.

# METROPOLITAN AND THE MOSQUITÍA

## Day 1: Arrival in Tegucigalpa

Arrive in Tegucigalpa—most international flights arrive midday—and taxi to your hotel. You may have time for an afternoon of sightseeing in the capital's historic downtown. The cathedral, the Dolores church, and the Museum of National Identity are must-sees if you have an interest in the history of this sometimes-complex country.

## Day 2: Valle de Ángeles and Tegucigalpa

The charming mountain town of Valle de Ángeles lies just under an hour east of the capital, and is a favorite day trip for visitor and resident alike. A few hours out here gives you an opportunity to grab lunch and browse the shops and stalls that populate the center of town. If you've not been able to shop elsewhere in Honduras, you'll still find souvenirs from around the country here. You'll appreciate long sleeves when you make the jaunt here; Valle lies about 1,000 feet higher than Tegucigalpa. Return to the capital in time for dinner.

## Day 3: Tegucigalpa to Brus Laguna and Raista

An early-morning flight to the airstrip in Brus Laguna takes you from the big city to the wilderness of the Mosquitía in about an hour. Grab one of the waiting water taxis to the Raista Ecolodge, rustic to be sure, but still one of the region's best lodging options. An afternoon of horseback riding down to the coast gives you an entirely different Caribbean beach experience than Honduras's glitzier sections of coast farther west will give you, and most people who visit here wouldn't trade the isolation for anything. Take in an evening Miskito-dancing performance around a campfire.

## Day 4: Raista and Belén

If you're up to it, grab an early-morning local water taxi west to Belén and the Laguna de Ibans. An all-day hike to the hamlet of Banaka takes you via rain forest, waterfalls, and ancient petroglyphs. Such an excursion is not for beginners, but does give you that day in the wilderness for which the Mosquitía is famous. An evening crocodile-caiman watch through the adjoining canals is always a crowd pleaser.

## Day 5: Brus Laguna to Tegucigalpa to Comayagua

Catch an early-morning flight back to Tegucigalpa. Taxi to the bus terminal in the neighborhood of Comayagüela to grab a bus to Comayagua. (Note the difference: Comayagüela is the sprawling working-class neighborhood adjoining downtown Tegucigalpa—only visit to catch a bus—and Comayagua is Honduras's first capital and one of its premier colonial cities—it is worth visiting.) Spend the remainder of the day visiting Comayagua's four anchor churches and

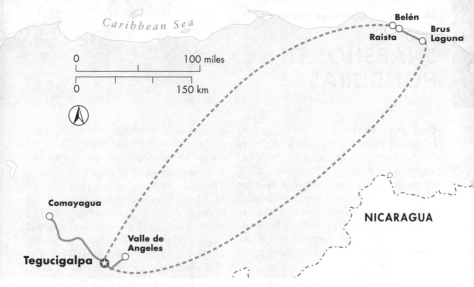

its wonderful Museum of Archaeology. The Hotel Colonial Casa Grande is the best lodging option, and dinner at Villa Real is the best dining choice for soaking in the town's colonial ambience.

### Day 6: Comayagua to Tegucigalpa

Catch a bus back to the capital. (Once again, don't linger upon arrival in the Comayagüela neighborhood of the city and head right to your hotel.) Spend your last full day shopping: Tegucigalpa is Honduras's shopping-mall central but plenty of crafts and souvenirs are yours in the shops downtown and adjoining Colonia Palmira.

### Day 7: Departure

Since most international flights depart the capital's Toncontín Airport at midday, you'll have a leisurely morning for breakfast at your hotel and a taxi to the airport.

### Alternatives

Valle de Ángeles is at its most lively on weekends; if you can juggle your itinerary around to be there on Saturday or Sunday, you'll get the best feel for how the capitalinos enjoy their favorite weekend destination.

It is possible to visit Comayagua as a long day trip from Tegucigalpa, but spending the night gives you more time to explore the town at your leisure.

---

### METROPOLITAN AND THE MOSQUITÍA TIPS

1. At Tegucigalpa's international airport, same-day connections are unrealistic; the capital is your first-night, last-night place to stay.

2. Comayagua's Museum of Colonial Religious Art was damaged in a 2009 fire, although most of its fabulous collection was saved. Reopening is scheduled for an unspecified future date; ask about its status while you're in town.

3. Concierge? Internet? Pool? Prepare to do without these during your time in the Mosquitía. It's no great loss, and they would interfere with the experience anyway.

---

Brus Laguna can be reached by plane from La Ceiba, making the Caribbean city an option for beginning or ending your Mosquitía adventure, too.

The day of hiking to Banaka could be replaced with a half-day basic jungle survival course offered by local guides. It's not that you actually need such skills to visit the Mosquitía, but could you ask for a more distinctive body of knowledge to take back home as a souvenir?

# SNAPSHOT OF HONDURAS

## The Hondureños

Honduras lacks the overwhelmingly visible indigenous cultures that populate neighboring Guatemala. Around 90% of the country's 7.5 million people are of mixed Spanish and indigenous descent and referred to as *mestizo*. Yet visits to several of Honduras's tourism hubs put you in contact with some of the ethnic groups that fall outside the stereotypical Latino orbit.

The largest purely indigenous group is the Lenca, some 300,000 strong who live in the southwest highlands in the territory centering around Gracias. The Lenca descended from peoples who migrated here thousands of years ago from what is now Colombia. They figure large in Honduras's history, having put up strong resistance to Spanish colonists—the country's currency takes its name from the martyred Lenca leader Lempira.

The few thousand Maya-descended Chortí who live in Honduras are in the region hugging the Guatemalan border, especially the area around Copán Ruinas. Most Chortí live across the border in Guatemala, where their language thrives, mostly due to that country's language revitalization efforts. Honduran Chortí are more likely to speak Spanish.

Arguably Honduras's most distinctive ethnic group is the Garífuna, a mixed African-indigenous people descended from exiles brought from the British Caribbean islands in the late 18th century. Today the Garífuna live on the Caribbean coast and Bay Islands, as well as in Belize, Guatemala, and Nicaragua. (Migration from Central America, mainly in the 1980s, means that, today, the United States contains the world's largest Garífuna population.) Music and dance traditions and the Garífuna language, called *Garinagu*, thrive, even if old-timers lament the creeping influence of Spanish, rap, and reggae.

## A Crumpled Piece of Paper

The story is likely apocryphal: One of Honduras's myriad presidents—nobody ever specifies which one—scrunched up a piece of paper for a visitor, undid it, and threw it on the desk, proclaiming, "There! That's what our country looks like." Picture Honduras as an inverted triangle: south to north, you'll see narrow Pacific plains at the lower apex, then mountains, followed by narrow Caribbean plains, and, of course, islands.

The defining element of Honduras's geography has always been its highlands—the term *mountains* is probably a stretch—technically several ranges rather than just one, covering 80% of its territory, but a historical barrier to transportation and development. Yet visit this part of Honduras and you'll never feel that you're in the sweltering tropics, part of the reason it provides a hospitable springlike climate where the majority of the country's population is content to live.

The northern Caribbean lowlands were once thought of as a malarial backwater. Then came the banana in the late 19th century. Combine a climate and terrain suitable for growing the new crop (and several others through the years) and easy port access to North America and Europe, and the region has been the engine that drives Honduras's economy ever since. (With no prominent port and mountains blocking the route north, the corresponding Pacific lowlands could never parlay its similar setting into the same prosperity.)

The narrow Caribbean lowlands do broaden extensively as they approach the Nicaraguan border. This is the famed

Mosquitía, swampy, forested, largely roadless, and not suited to agriculture, so tourism is the economic focus.

## Copán, Columbus, Coups, and Crops

Although Christopher Columbus gets credit for "discovering" Honduras during his fourth and final voyage to the New World in 1502, his landing at what is today Trujillo more accurately made him the country's first tourist. By that time, the region already had thriving indigenous communities—Chortí, Lenca, Miskito—who conducted commerce with other indigenous peoples throughout Mesoamerica. And, of course, the flourishing Mayan city of Copán had reached the peak of its civilization some 700 years before the arrival of Columbus. Subjugation and slavery followed, both sadly typical of Spain's reign in the Americas.

Spanish control was never strong on the Caribbean coast, and English settlers and pirates happily filled the void, especially in the Bay Islands. Today, the Caribbean coast still goes its own way as a result, often echoing the sounds of far-off Jamaica rather than the mestizo-dominated highlands. Honduras's history since independence has, at times, been a revolving door of presidents, several ousted in overthrows. (The most recent of these occurred, shockingly, in 2009, although the troubles are over as far as most of the population is concerned, and as far as any visitor need be concerned.)

The late 19th century saw the dominance of fruit, most notably bananas, in Honduras's economy. The near-absolute control exerted by the Standard Fruit Company on the country's economy and decision-making apparatus for the next half century gave rise to the term *banana republic* to describe Honduras. The rise of new crops shifted development from the highlands and its traditional reliance on mining and sustenance farming to large-scale agriculture in the Caribbean lowlands. Tegucigalpa remained the political center of the country—the capital had moved there from Comayagua in 1880—but the true growth would begin to occur in San Pedro Sula, La Ceiba, Puerto Cortés, and Trujillo, and that boom continues today.

## Care for the Environment (with Some Caveats)

There's good news and bad news, as they say, about the environment in Honduras. In spite of the country's reputation for being largely deforested, some 41% of the country's territory is still covered with forest, a figure comparable to that of environmental-darling Costa Rica. And one-third of the tree cover here is primary forest. While Honduras does receive accolades over that fact, much of the conservation has been passive rather than the result of anybody's active steps. Huge sections of the country, especially the east, are sparsely populated, meaning that no one troubles the forest there.

That said, the pressure is on, and is expected to increase in coming years. Illegal logging has been the biggest contributor to deforestation, and at an annual 2% growth rate, Honduras's population is increasing demand for space and agricultural use. All these factors chip away at the integrity of the borders of Honduras's two biosphere reserves and 20 national parks. Happily, the protected areas that show the greatest promise for tourism—La Tigra, Cusuco, Celaque, and Pico Bonito, for example—are the targets of the strongest efforts to keep reserves intact.

# KIDS AND FAMILIES

Honduras doesn't necessarily leap to mind when planning a vacation with the kids. (This isn't Orlando, after all.) It's not that the country is *un*friendly to children, but planning a vacation here with the kids does take some advance preparation. It's no surprise that Roatán and Copán Ruinas, Honduras's top two destinations for travelers in general, also have the jaguar's share of activities for kids. Here are kid-friendly activity suggestions for those locations and several others.

## A Honduras Kids' Top Ten

**Chiminike, Tegucigalpa.** Ever wanted to learn what causes flatulence? The capital's fun new children's museum will teach you this and a host of other offbeat tidbits of information and is guaranteed to put a smile on your child's—and your—face.

**Macaw Mountain Bird Park, Copán Ruinas.** This bird-rescue center outside of town is a crowd pleaser among kids of all ages. Macaws, toucans, and parrots dominate among the 20 or so species here. Also, these are fine, animal-loving people who do good work, and those are values worth instilling in anybody.

**Enchanted Wings Butterfly Garden, Copán Ruinas.** Butterflies flutter and flitter at this park on the edge of town. Take the guided tour, or grab one of the laminated cards illustrating the species that are here and try to identify as many as you can.

**Casa K'inich, Copán Ruinas.** Your kids can don a Mayan-noble costume, learn to count in the Chortí language, and pose as a stela sculpture at this in-town interactive educational center. It might help make a visit to the ruins themselves come alive for them.

**Arch's Iguana & Marine Farm, Roatán.** Although the typical Bay Island iguana ends up in somebody's stew, the 2,700 animals here roam freely for the rest of their natural days. Feeding time is early afternoon, the perfect time for a visit.

**Roatán Institute for Marine Sciences, Roatán.** This research center provides the country's ultimate dolphin-encounter experience, teaching kids to snorkel and become a "Dolphin Trainer for a Day." The dolphin shows themselves are free and a good bet if you're short on time.

**Gumbalimba Park, Roatán.** Roatán's version of a nature-themed amusement park lets your kids frolic with monkeys and parrots, explore a cave, and go for a horseback ride. If your schedule permits, make it an early-morning visit to beat the crowds.

**Garífuna shows, Caribbean and Bay Islands.** The spectacles are touristy, yes, but who wouldn't be mesmerized by the infectious punta music and colorful costumes? If your kids like to strut their stuff, tell them to be ready when the performers beckon audience members onto the dance floor.

**Hiking, La Mosquitia, Lago de Yojoa.** Guided nature walks at Honduras's remote locales can turn a "boring" eco-stay, where there's "nothing to do," into an informative, enlightening experience for your kids.

**Zip-Lining, Copán Ruinas, Roatán, Omoa, Cascadas de Pulhapanzak.** Is there any better way for your older kids to wow their friends back home than with tales of zipping through the rain forest canopy courtesy of a cable, a helmet, and a secure harness? Check ahead for age and size minimums; they vary by operator.

# CRUISING TO HONDURAS

Although Honduras counts two coastlines, only its Caribbean side hosts cruise ships, all on select Panama Canal, Western Caribbean, and Central America itineraries of various companies. Nearly all of them call at Roatán in the Bay Islands.

Carnival opened its own cruise terminal in 2010 at Mahogany Bay near Dixon Cove on Roatán's southwest coast. Holland America, Princess, and Seabourn have also moved there or plan to shift operations. Mahogany Bay gets mixed reviews: most passengers love its sleek, self-contained newness; others have panned the facility as offering no contact with the real Honduras, even to the point of providing a $5 chairlift tram that carries passengers directly to a private beach. Royal Caribbean has stayed put at Roatán's Town Center Port, the original cruise terminal at Coxen Hole, and is investing in the facility's modernization. Celebrity, Norwegian, and Oceania call there. Shore excursions around the island can be arranged from either terminal. Snorkeling, catamaran sailing, dolphin swimming, and zip lining are always crowd pleasers.

A few—very few—Holland America itineraries call at Puerto Cortés on the mainland, with shore excursions along the coast, and even the possibility of a very long day trip to the Mayan ruins at Copán.

**Carnival.** Carnival is known for its large-volume cruises and template approach to its ships—*Legend, Valor, Dream, Triumph, Glory,* and *Conquest* call here—two factors that probably help keep fares accessible. Las Vegas–style shows and passenger participation are the norm. ☎ 888/227–6482 ⊕ *www.carnival.com.*

**Celebrity.** Spacious accommodation and its guest-lectured Enrichment Series are hallmarks of Celebrity cruises. *Solstice, Century, Equinox, Eclipse,* and *Millennium* call here. ☎ 800/647–2251 ⊕ *www. celebritycruises.com.*

**Holland America Line.** Holland America cruises focus on passenger comfort and are classic in design and style. They manage to be refined without being stuffy. The MS *Maasdam* calls at Roatán; MS *Ryndam,* at Puerto Cortés. ☎ 877/932–4259 ⊕ *www.hollandamerica.com.*

**Norwegian Cruise Lines.** Its tagline is "Whatever floats your boat"—*Pearl, Dawn, Star, Epic,* and *Spirit* are Norwegian's boats that come here—and Norwegian *is* known for its relatively freewheeling style and variety of activities and excursions. ☎ 866/234–7350 ⊕ *www.ncl.com.*

**Oceania.** Before arrival at any port—Oceania's *Regatta* is Roatán's newest arrival—you can attend a lecture to acquaint you with its history, culture, and tradition. ☎ 800/531–5619 ⊕ *www. oceaniacruises.com.*

**Princess Cruises.** Not so great for small children but good at keeping tweens, teens, and adults occupied, Princess strives to offer luxury at an affordable price. The line's *Crown Princess* docks in Roatán. ☎ 800/774–6237 ⊕ *www.princess.com.*

**Royal Caribbean.** Striving to appeal to a broad clientele, the line offers lots of activities and service on its Roatán-bound *Voyager of the Seas, Mariner of the Seas,* and *Grandeur of the Seas,* as well as many shore excursions. ☎ 866/562–7625 ⊕ *www.royalcaribbean.com.*

**Seabourn.** Officially, it's The Yachts of Seabourn, known for sophisticated, personalized service on its megasize yachts, of which *Legend* docks here. ☎ 800/929–9391 ⊕ *www.seabourn.com.*

# HONDURAN SOUVENIRS

You won't waltz away with a souvenir ancient Mayan ceremonial headdress—it would be illegal to take such an item out of the country anyway—but Honduras will provide the answer to the "What did you bring me?" questions you're sure to hear upon your return home. (And don't forget to treat yourself to a keepsake, too.)

All of Honduras's best-known souvenirs have made it to many points of sale around the country if you need the efficiency of one-stop shopping. (San Pedro Sula's Guamilito market, the vendors in Valle de Ángeles near Tegucigalpa, and Roatán's amazing shop Yaba Ding Ding are three places that seem to have everything from around the country. The international airports in San Pedro Sula and Tegucigalpa also have a few quality shops.) No matter where you make your purchase, quality is high, variety is good, and price is reasonable. One word of warning though: the indigenous clothing and textiles you see for sale here are frequently Guatemalan-made, especially the closer you get to the border. (Always ask.) If you like it, go ahead and buy it, but it won't be a MADE IN HONDURAS memento of your visit.

## Baskets

Palm, wicker, bamboo, and even pine needles get woven into elaborate basketry in several communities in Western Honduras in an age-old process that has never been industrialized. Many small baskets purchased in souvenir shops give you a twofer and contain bags of coffee or spices.

## Ceramics

Honduras's most distinctive souvenir is its indigenous Lenca clay pottery, crafted in the villages around Gracias. Artisans fashion their works with their hands, cornhusks, and twigs in a process that has changed little through the centuries. Some have likened the brown, white, cream, and red patterns on the plates, bowls, cups, urns, and vases as resembling works of the Navajo in the southwest United States, but, of course, the designs have different meanings. The pottery provides an added benefit in addition to simply looking nice: nearly all the pieces you see are made by women's cooperatives, so your purchase helps provide employment at the local level and keeps an ancient art alive.

## Cigars

Experts rate Honduran cigars right up there with the best Cuban product. The industry here has its roots in Cuba, with cigar manufacturers having set up shop in southern Danlí when Castro came to power. Tobacco has a longer history in western Santa Rosa de Copán, the center of cultivation in colonial times. Either is a good place to purchase fine cigars.

## Coffee

Honduras hasn't extensively promoted its fine coffee to the tourist market the way neighboring Guatemala and Costa Rica have. In general, a mediocre-quality coffee stays behind for the local market, with the good stuff being exported. Your best bet for export-quality product is a souvenir shop or even a last-minute purchase at the airport on your way home. The foil packages will fit perfectly into your carry-on.

## Hammocks

You may have spent a lazy afternoon in a hammock at an out-country Honduran hotel. Some half-dozen local manufacturers make fine-quality Honduran hammocks if you'd like to continue that lazing back home.

## Mahogany

Mahogany is prized as one of the world's most durable woods, and Honduran mahogany will not disappoint. Vendors here do actually sell mahogany doors and trunks, but for ease of transport and to avoid the hassle of shipping your purchase, you may want to stick with a small box or necklace that you can pack for the trip home.

## Shirts

Though not usually lumped in under the "handicrafts" heading, Honduras does produce T-shirts of fine quality, and really does sell more than the LIFE'S A BEACH shirts you'll see in the Bay Islands. T-shirts with decorative Mayan hieroglyphs are sure to please the history-minded traveler or person on your shopping list. For something more elaborate yet, Omoa, on the Caribbean coast, is a center for embroidered, tropical-style guayabera shirts, buttoned up and with a straight hem, worn untucked.

# MARKET SAVVY

Chances are, you fall into one of two marketing types: you're either the type who delights in haggling in a traditional market, or you approach the notion with a bit of distaste, meekly agreeing to the first price quoted you. Regardless of your style, we offer these tips for shopping in a Honduran market.

■ Brush up on your Spanish numbers. Vendors may speak limited English on the mainland, but the Bay Islands, where many more people speak English, are a different story.

■ Market vendors are not set up to take credit cards. Have cash in hand, preferably small bills. Paying in lempiras rather than dollars will frequently fetch you a better price.

■ Bargaining takes place in markets. Prices are generally fixed in standing shops, although the shop person might be open to bargaining if you pay in cash—businesses pay high commissions on credit-card purchases in Honduras—and if you don't go shopping with a guide (who, in turn, will expect the shop to pay him a "finder's fee" commission).

■ If you do bargain in a market, counteroffer a bit more than half the quoted price. From there, you and the seller can compromise, often something in the 75% range.

■ Don't bargain too hard. Items are already reasonably priced, and those extra lempiras mean more to the seller than to you.

■ Once you and the vendor agree on a price, it's understood that you've made a commitment to buy the item. Honor it.

# WHAT'S NEW

## Two Capital Museums

Tegucigalpa has seen the opening of two new world-class museums, and both make phenomenal additions to the list of things to see in the capital. The fun Chiminike, on the south side of the city, is an interactive museum for kids, but we think adults will appreciate its quirky exhibits, too. (The museum takes its name from a character in a Honduran children's story.) The downtown Museo Para La Identidad Nacional, in a restored 19th century building, does an excellent job of conveying what its name (the Museum for National Identity) says it will, and is a must for anybody even marginally interested in Honduran history.

## Smoke-free Honduras

Honduras enacted tough new no-smoking laws in June 2010. Lighting up is prohibited in all indoor areas of businesses, including offices, stores, bars, restaurants, and nightclubs.

## The Mayan Calendar

Who would have thought a millennia-old calendar would become one of the world's hottest pop-culture properties? The intricate Maya long-count calendar comes to an abrupt end on December 21, 2012. (The calendar had a good 5,126-year run, having calculated the beginning of the world to be our August 11, 3114 BC.) Will the gods grant another cycle? Many visitors have already made reservations for that date to be on hand at Copán to see for themselves what might happen. Expect lodging rates to go sky-high for the holiday season in 2012.

## Mahogany Bay

Roatán, in the Bay Islands, opened a new cruise port on the southwest coast of the island in 2010. The venture was financed by Carnival Cruises, which hosts several other cruise companies at the facility. It's the ultimate in "self-contained," and if you prefer, there's no reason to ever leave the facility, although not everyone likes the fact that it provides little contact with the real Honduras.

## Tela Bay

The Caribbean coast near Tela is slated for major resort development in coming years. The project has been on the drawing board for decades, and some have touted this as Honduras's answer to Cancún. A rollercoaster economy—most recently it's been the 2008 collapse of the world's financial markets and the 2009 political crisis—has put the brakes on the project several times through the years. With an upswing in the economy again, you may see things start up in the next couple of years. The project is certain to change the face of the coast near Tela, making this one "What's new" development that not everybody is thrilled about. We'll leave the verdict to you.

## Better Times Post-2009

Honduras experienced an old-fashioned, cart-the-president-off-to-exile, Latin American military coup in June 2009. The commotion of the aftermath went on for months and dried up investment and tourism. Most realize now that the news footage beamed to the outside world presented a lot worse picture than anything that actually took place on the ground, and the tourists who were here during that time reported no disruption to their routines. A new president was elected in November of that year—that's when elections were scheduled to take place as it was—and the situation returned to normal. As things pick up again and visitors return, everyone seems relieved to put the events of 2009 behind them.

# RETIRING IN HONDURAS

Honduras gets high marks as one of the Western Hemisphere's up-and-coming retirement destinations. The magazine *International Living*, which many regard in as the bible in the field, cites several advantages to living in Honduras. The country has a lower cost of living and a moderate climate. The four hub destinations—Tegucigalpa, San Pedro Sula, La Ceiba, and Roatán—boast good private health-care facilities. Real estate is easy to own for foreigners. Honduras has decent in-country transportation and communication, and deep-water ports make it easy to import household effects. Best of all, Honduras is close to the United States and has four international airports. Tegucigalpa and San Pedro Sula are just two hours by air from Miami or Houston.

## Legalities

Honduras has set up three legal categories for foreigners who wish to reside within its boundaries. A *rentista* must demonstrate a guaranteed income of at least $2,500 per month from a source outside Honduras. A *pensionado* is a retiree who can guarantee income from a pension, public or private, of at least $1,500 per month. An *inversionista* is an investor who is making a business investment of at least $50,000 in a Honduran entity. An on-site attorney is advisable and necessary to help navigate the paperwork, no matter which category you're considering.

## Who's Here? Where are they?

Americans and Canadians make up the majority of foreigners who have retired to Honduras. Hands down, Roatán in the Bay Islands has become the destination of choice, with neighboring Utila running a close second. (Guanaja, the third Bay Island, is just starting to take hold for those who see themselves as island pioneers.) The sheer number of foreigners who have moved to the Bay Islands facilitates adventures that were much more taxing a decade or two ago, like building a home or finding an English-speaking real estate agent or lawyer. Contractors and shopkeepers are used to dealing with gringos, and most speak good English. (English is practically the Bay Islands' second language. Some might say it's the first.) Roatán, especially, is rich with opportunities for foreigners to meet up for events or volunteer work.

You'll feel a bit more like you're staking out new territory if you decide to retire to Honduras's mainland—less English is spoken, for one thing. Smaller foreign communities have established themselves in Copán Ruinas, where some have become involved in the tourism industry, and in pleasant, lofty Valle de Ángeles, outside Tegucigalpa. On the Caribbean coast, La Ceiba and Trujillo have also attracted foreign residents, and neighboring Tela is expected to do so in coming years with its expected boom in development.

## Try before you buy

Do not fall prey, though, to the dreaded "Sunshine Syndrome" that afflicts countless visitors to Honduras. Pause and take a deep breath if you find yourself on vacation here and starting to utter the words: "Honey, we met that nice real estate agent in the hotel bar. You know we should buy a house here. Or we could open up a bed and-breakfast." Some succumb without a second thought, go back home and sell the farm, and return, only to find that living in Honduras bears scant resemblance to vacationing here. Experts suggest doing a trial rental for a few months. See if living the day-to-day life in Honduras is for you.

# ADVENTURE VACATIONS

Like its Central American neighbors, Honduras has latched onto the eco/nature/adventure bandwagon that Costa Rican tourism began driving successfully in the 1990s. Offerings are far fewer than those of its southern neighbor: Costa Rica counts an astounding 80-plus zip-line canopy tours, but we can count the number in Honduras on one hand. That said, Honduras gets good grades for what is here—selection is sure to grow in coming years—and for the quality standards of its adventure-tour operators. The world also awards Honduras high marks for preservation of its natural protected areas, although a perpetual dearth of funds plagues the system and often makes that maintenance a labor of love more than anything. Honduras has experimented with turning over administration of some national parks to private foundations—La Tigra, near Tegucigalpa, and Cusuco, just outside of San Pedro Sula, are the best-known examples—and the jury has ruled the approach successful so far. Bottom line: Honduras has plenty of nature to enjoy and plenty of operators to help you enjoy it.

## Diving

For many, Honduras equals diving, and with the Bay Islands encompassing part of the world's second-longest barrier reef, the underwater life to be spotted here is amazing. The industry is less developed in Honduras than in Belize and Mexico, which both share that same long reef. That translates into less expensive diving and certification. (Beware though: A few places are a little *too* cheap, and may scrimp on safety.)

**Anthony's Key Resort** is Honduras's largest dive center, a resort and scuba operation in one, with six 42-foot boats to take you out for a day or half day, and multiday packages that include accommodation and a complete range of courses if you need them. (⌧ *Sandy Bay, Roatán* ☎ *445–1003* ⊕ *www.anthonyskey.com.*)

**Ocean Connections Dive Center** is a well-established dive shop with two branches in Roatán. These folks specialize in smaller groups and offer the complete spectrum of PADI-affiliated courses, from novice to advanced. ⌧ *West End and West Bay, Roatán* ☎ *445–1925* ⊕ *www.ocean-connections.com.*

## Bird-watching

Some 700 bird species—eagles and egrets, tanagers, and toucans—have been logged in this country about the size of Ohio, but with a much greater variety of ecosystems. Experienced birder? Head out on your own at Lago de Yojoa and tackle some of its 400 species. Logistics become more difficult if you're headed to La Mosquitía, Honduras's other top bird-watching destination.

**La Moskitia Eco Aventuras** has eight-day birding tours here; lodging is rustic. La Moskitia can also customize birding tours to your tastes and time constraints. ⌧ *El Toronjal, La Ceiba* ☎ *440–2124* ⊕ *www.lamoskitiaecoaventuras.com.*

## Horseback Riding

Tours on horseback are quite popular around the country. Many operations are nothing more than a guy and his horse, though. We recommend always going with an established company. **Basecamp Tours** has a popular three-hour horse trip that takes in the countryside around Copán Ruinas with a visit to a Chortí indigenous community. The views are stunning. ⌧ *C. de la Plaza, 1½ blocks west of Parque Central, Copán Ruinas* ☎ *651–4695* ⊕ *basecampcopan.wordpress.com.*

**Omega Tours** operates half-day horseback trips along the beach near La Ceiba, as well as a daylong combo ride that takes in beach and jungle. ✉ *El Naranjo, La Ceiba* ☏ *440–0334* ⊕ *www.omegatours.com.*

## Hiking

With plenty of national parks and Lenca villages to take in, sometimes the only way to get somewhere is to walk, and there is no better way to appreciate the backcountry. Trails are mostly well-maintained, but play it safe; an experienced guide or outfitter will help navigate unfamiliar territory.

**Mountain Travel Sobek,** based in California, leads weeklong hiking tours in Pico Bonito National Park that also include boating at the Cuero y Salado Reserve and a visit to the ruins at Copán. ✉ *1266 66th St., Emeryville, CA 94608* ☏ *888/831–7526* ⊕ *www.mtsobek.com.*

**Cosuca-Celaque** is a local association of guides based in the highland town of Gracias. They specialize in nearby Parque Nacional Celaque, one of the largest tracts of cloud forest left in Central America. The rough conditions make hiring a guide worth it. ✉ *Gracias* ☏ *656–0627.*

## Cultural Encounters

Honduras is its people, of course, and the concept of going to communities and interacting with local people on an organized cultural excursion is just catching on. These qualify as adventure tours because sometimes hiking, boating, horseback riding, or motor-vehicle travel over rough roads are the only means of getting to these out-of-the-way places.

**La Ruta Moskitia** has a variety of culture-adventure excursions lasting seven to nine days. As you'd expect from the name, they take you to the Mosquitía for visits to indigenous communities, but also include rafting, trekking, and animal spotting. ☏ *406–6782* ⊕ *www.larutamoskitia.com.*

**Mesoamerican Ecotourism Alliance (MEA)** offers tours that visit Río Esteban, a Garífuna community on the Caribbean coast with a chance to learn about women's cooperative projects and local artisan workshops. There's snorkeling, hiking, and boating on the tour operated by this Colorado-based company, too. ✉ *4076 Crystal Ct., Boulder, CO* ☏ *800/682–0504* ⊕ *www.travelwithmea.com.*

## Rafting

White-water sports in Honduras are mostly about the Río Cangrejal and its Class III to Class V rapids. The river runs near the Caribbean coast, 30 minutes from La Ceiba. Some outfitters bill the Cangrejal as apt for beginners, but we disagree. Some experience is best before tackling this one.

**Garífuna Tours** takes you on a six-hour excursion out of La Ceiba to the Cangrejal; it's a moderately strenuous rafting tour. ✉ *C. 9, Tela* ☏ *448–1069* ⊕ *www.garifunatours.com* **Jungle River** ✉ *Av. La República, La Ceiba* ☏ *440–1268* ⊕ *www.jungleriverlodge.com.*

## Kayaking

Not everyone wants the close group experience and camaraderie that white-water rafting requires. Consider a tour in an individual sea kayak around the Bay Islands as an alternative.

**Uncommon Adventures,** a Michigan company, offers eight-day sea-kayaking trips that originate at their lodge in Roatán. Day trips explore the reef at Pigeon Cay, the island's mangrove tunnels, and other secret channels. ✉ *PO Box 254, Beulah, MI* ☏ *866/882–5525* ⊕ *www.uncommonadv.com.*

# HONDURAS LODGING PRIMER

No matter what your budget, no matter what your comfort needs, you'll find something in Honduras to suit your taste. There's plenty of variety among accommodation here, whether you're looking for a tried-and-tested international chain, a boutique property, local hospitality at a family-run inn, or a cheap, clean hostel. And here's the good news: Lodging in Honduras is affordable, too, and nobody has been priced out of the market in any region of the country. (Many countries can't make that claim these days.) Even five-star luxury in the big cities won't cost you an arm and a leg. The downside is that once you get out of the Copán-Roatán orbit, sheer numbers of lodgings are smaller than what you might expect. (Tegucigalpa has a surprisingly small number of decent hotels for a capital city of one million people.) Volunteer groups frequently book blocks of rooms in mid-priced hotels, too, even in Tegucigalpa and San Pedro Sula. That makes reservations a good idea no matter where you plan to stay, no matter what day of the week, no matter what time of the year.

Hotel isn't the only tag you'll find on accommodation in Honduras: *hospedaje, hostal, pensión, posada, casa de huespedes,* and just *casa de* (something) also denominate somewhere to stay. Unfortunately, there are no hard-and-fast rules as to what each name means, and no entity truly regulates such matters, though hotels and posadas tend to be higher-end places. With that in mind, our own descriptive labels follow:

## Chain and Chainlike Hotels

Messrs. Hilton, Marriott, and Clarion and their friends have all set up shop in Honduras, but only with big-city outlets in Tegucigalpa and San Pedro Sula. Without fail, all provide the same dependable service you've come to expect from their properties back home. And most provide a few Honduran touches, freeing you from that "Wow! This could be a hotel in Chicago" feeling that sometimes envelopes you when you walk into a chain property anywhere in the world. Not to cast aspersions on that approach, for that's exactly what many travelers look for: the reassurance of familiar surroundings. Other properties in the two big cities—the Honduras Maya in Tegucigalpa and the Gran Hotel Sula and Copantl in San Pedro Sula, for example—don't belong to any group of hotels, but provide the same types and level of service you'd find at a Marriott or Hilton. Chain or not, all these hotels discount rates on weekends when their business-travel clientele have left.

## City Hotels

Large- and medium-size cities in Honduras all have midrange hotels that market themselves to *hombres de negocios,* or business*men.* (Honduras really does have a growing number of female business travelers, and all are welcome, of course. These places just need to update the outmoded text in their brochures.) They may lack a concierge and pool, but all are clean and comfortable—admittedly, sometimes a bit institutional—and have the basics that a business traveler is looking for at a fraction of the price the big guys charge. They're perfectly acceptable for leisure travelers, too. Since these properties, like their chain counterparts, focus on business travelers, many discount their rates on the weekend as well.

## Small Inns

Honduras truly shines in its selection of smaller, locally owned inns with 5 to 15 rooms each. In many smaller destinations, large midrange hotels tend to be impersonal, institutional setups aimed at passing business travelers. If you're looking for local flavor, consider a smaller inn or bed-and-breakfast. Especially in the highlands, many are housed in colonial-era buildings, and those that are newly constructed make every effort to echo that same style with rooms arranged around a courtyard or garden. You don't always have to sacrifice hot water or room service for a touch of culture. You'll find plenty of guesthouses and boutique hotels that combine colonial class with modern amenities.

## Resorts

The Bay Islands and the Caribbean are the province of Honduras's only true resorts, with Tela on the mainland slated for major resort development in coming years. Isla del Tigre, the country's Pacific beach destination, has a couple of much smaller versions of such lodgings, but mention of the term *resort* usually brings the north coast and the islands to mind. Even then, Honduras has few such properties, and doesn't begin to count the resort population of Mexico or even Costa Rica. Do your homework: a few of these lodgings cater to specific clientele, in particular the dive resorts in the Bay Islands. All are welcome at any property, of course, but if you're not a diver yourself, you may tire of the dinnertime conversation about the manta rays everybody spotted that day. Diving or not, the resorts that are here provide plenty of attentive service.

## Lodges

Lodges—both eco- and not-quite-so—are what you'll encounter in Lago de Yojoa, the Mosquitía, Pico Bonito National Park, and certain sections of the Caribbean lowlands. Some pamper you with amazing luxury unexpected in such isolated locations. Others are more back-to-nature rustic. Some are off the beaten path and do require a bit of choreography to get to, so plan on staying at least a couple of nights to offset travel time and logistics. All do provide you with the opportunity to get up close and personal with nature, and if you're a guest at one of these places, join in the evening conversation, usually over dinner served family style, about your wildlife sightings that day. If you're seriously interested in sustainable accommodation, it pays to do your research. The *eco* prefix is bandied about very loosely here. Sometimes the term will be used simply to describe a property in a rural or jungle location, rather than somewhere that is truly ecologically friendly.

## Hostels and Budget Hotels

Honduras has a good selection of cheap, shared accommodation. Budget lodging terminology varies: hostel, *hostal,* and *la casa de* are commonplace names, and some places are just listed as a hotel or *pensión.* Staff in most Honduran hostels is young, enthusiastic, and knowledgeable, and can often inform you about Spanish classes and excursions. Hostels proper do tend to cater to party animals, so if you're traveling with kids, a family-run hotel might be quieter. While the country still offers a bed for the night in the $10 range, loosening the purse strings and spending $30 to $40—still a bargain by any standard—buys much more comfort in terms of private room and bath.

# FLAVORS OF HONDURAS

Even Honduras's biggest boosters will admit in a moment of candor that haute cuisine is not the big draw here. One chef we spoke with lamented that even some upscale restaurants will plop a plate of meat, cooked vegetables, and *puré* (the term used for mashed potatoes here) in front of you and call it a fancy meal. (We've become wary of restaurants here that describe their offerings as *cocina internacional* or "international cuisine." The term sounds, oh, so chic, but generally turns out bland and meaningless.) Yet even though Honduras isn't known for its culinary delights, you will encounter some pleasant surprises in this country whose cuisine mixes Spanish, indigenous, and African elements. Although there are definite regional differences—corn is ever-present in the highlands, and seafood and coconut are ubiquitous on the Caribbean coast and Bay Islands—these days, you can find pretty much everything everywhere.

## The Staples
The national dish is the generically named *plato típico*, consisting of some combination of meat, rice, beans, cheese, plantains (called *tajadas*), and perhaps eggs or avocados. This "typical plate" can always be livened up by the hot sauce on the table, often a homemade variety. Local restaurants serve it for lunch, and it makes a filling, reasonably priced meal. (You can then do like most Hondurans and eat a lighter meal in the evening.) A Honduran invention, *baleadas* (corn or wheat tortillas with beans and cheese) are cheap, pleasant snacks and handy for vegetarians, who can ask for one *sin carne* (without meat).

Another tasty choice comes from neighboring El Salvador, but Honduras has adopted it as its own: the *pupusa*, a golden-fried patty of corn, beans, and cheese, usually served with a vinegary blend of cabbage and onion called *repollo*. *Nacatamales* (cornmeal and chicken wrapped in banana leaves) are found all over Central America, but in Honduras they can be very moist and delicate. Hondurans eat a ton of them over the holidays; families prepare large batches of tamales in December and then have an easy dish to steam and serve during the busy week between Christmas and New Year's. *Carne asada* (marinated, grilled flank steak) is reserved for special occasions, and served with *chimol*, a Honduran condiment that mixes diced tomatoes, bell peppers, onion, cilantro, lemon, and vinegar. Ever present in local Honduran restaurants, but generally too elaborate for a home meal, is the *anafre*. The term refers to a clay pot containing heated cheese and mashed beans, and used as a dip, fondue style.

## Start Off the Day
A good breakfast (*desayuno*) is key to kicking off the day right—so insisted our mothers—but Honduran moms must really take that advice to heart. Order the típico breakfast at your hotel, and they'll haul out eggs, plantains, sausage, cheese, refried beans, tortillas, coffee, and juice. Fortify you for the morning it certainly will—and maybe well into the afternoon, too—but many visitors find it to be too much, and opt for the *Americano* breakfast of cereal, toast, and juice, or the Continental, with bread, fruit, and coffee, instead.

## A Bounty of Fruits

You'll find fruit abundant—*mango verde* or *mango tierno* (baby green mango) in the spring is not to be missed—and often dressed up in novel ways, with a sweet hot sauce or with lime and a ubiquitous mixture of cumin, pepper, and salt called *pimienta*. Honduras was the original banana republic, and the fruit is still a major export even if, thankfully, the big corporations no longer run the country. Smaller bananas (*bananos*) stay behind for the local market and end up in salads, soups, and side dishes. Pineapple (*piña*) is another important export, and you can certainly partake here, but pineapple frequently ends up as fermented fruit vinegar (*vinagre de piña*), which adds a tangy zest to any salad. Be sure to try one local variant of pineapple, the *azucarrón*, about half the size of the regular fruit and much sweeter—that is, if your body can stand the extra blast of sugar. Honduran cuisine is said to use more coconut (*coco*) than that of its Central American neighbors. Try rice and beans—the name of this Caribbean dish is always in English—its two namesake ingredients cooked for hours in coconut milk.

## From the Lake and the Sea

Seafood is popular and abundant throughout Honduras, but especially along both coasts. A seafood conch soup (*sopa de caracol*) is flavored and thickened with (what else?) coconut milk and filled with the tuber cassava (yuca), plantains, local vegetables, and spices. Fried fish served whole is a Honduran specialty, as are shrimp and lobster dishes. Spanish distinguishes between seafood (*mariscos*) and freshwater fish (*pescado*). Honduras's best-known example of the latter is the fried fish from the country's largest lake, the Lago de Yojoa, usually freshwater bass served with pickled onions and plantains.

## Should You or Shouldn't You?

Street vendors' fare can look tantalizingly seductive, especially charcoal-grilled *elote*, a version of corn on the cob. One of the country's best-kept secrets is *frita de elote* (a deep-fried, sizzling mash of corn and sugar), sold by competing little girls along the road near Lago de Yojoa. Every town has its seeming army of *baleada señoras* selling their namesake fare on the street. Do you have a cast-iron-enough stomach to partake of street fare? We can't answer that for you, but we do strongly suggest erring on the side of caution. Know that everything you can buy on the street, you can also order in a sit-down, local restaurant, and that might be a better option.

## Times and Tips

Mealtimes are similar to those in the United States, with lunch at noon and dinner at 7 or even earlier. To combat the heat and make the most of the sunlight, Hondureños are early risers, so breakfast is likely to be at 7 or 8, a bit later if you are staying on the beach. Among locals, lunch is the biggest repast of the day, with the evening meal meaning lighter fare. In elegant restaurants (meaning those with tablecloths) a tip of at least 10% is about right, whereas anywhere else, small change will do just fine. Reservations are rarely necessary, except where indicated.

# WHEN TO GO

Honduras has no truly bad time to visit, although if we had to pick one no-go month, it might be October, when the entire country can be deluged with rain. Coming here during the rest of the rainy season need not be a hardship. The countryside is lush and green, the air is fresh, and it is a nice contrast to the parched conditions you see in March and April. But a tropical country plus the North American winter—you do the math. December through April is the big tourist season here as northerners flee those frigid temperatures. Lodgings fill up and reservations are always advisable. They're a must during Christmas and Easter weeks, when Hondurans are apt to be traveling, too, and competing for available hotel space. The country experiences a second, shorter high season during July and August, prime North American and European vacation time.

## Climate

The northern coast is hot and humid year-round. The rainiest time of year on the Caribbean runs from October through January, although wet weather can come at any time of year. June, July, August, and September are usually hotter and drier. The rest of the country experiences much the opposite phenomenon, with a May-to-October rainy season and a dry season the rest of the year. Altitude really matters more than anything in Honduras. Tegucigalpa and the central and western highlands enjoy warm days and cool evenings, that proverbial "eternal spring" that everyone likes to talk about. San Pedro Sula and the Caribbean lowlands, as well as the Pacific coast, are usually sweltering, but you can often count on sea breezes to moderate the heat on the coast and in the Bay Islands.

Here are the average daily maximum and minimum temperatures for the four hub Honduran locales.

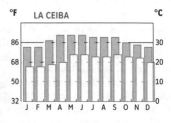

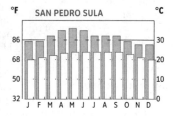

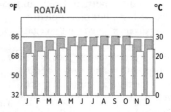

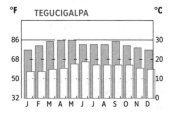

# Tegucigalpa

**WORD OF MOUTH**

"[In Tegucigalpa] we hired our hotel driver to take us to Valle de Ángeles and Santa Lucía, which is a really pleasant trip. We also visited the art gallery and the new museum. The central square is an interesting place to hang out and people-watch. We also saw a Garifuna dance troupe."

—Heather49

"I stayed at the Humuya Inn, which was a small, comfortable place that was larger than a bed-and-breakfast but much smaller than a major hotel. The staff were all extremely friendly, called us by name, arranged a driver to Valle de Ángeles (a pleasant excursion out of the city), helped us change money, etc."

—mmb23

Updated by
Jeffrey Van
Fleet

No one we know mentions Tegucigalpa, Honduras's congested capital, as their favorite place in the country, but on a sunny afternoon when there's a breath of a breeze, you may decide you want to linger a while longer. This city of more than 1 million people sits in a valley surrounded by beautiful pine-covered mountains, and at an altitude of 3,300 feet, you can't beat the moderate springlike climate.

There are plenty of nearby villages to explore, and national parks filled with exotic flora and fauna are a short drive away. But the city streets, sometimes set at a sharp incline, can be just as exhilarating. Plaza Morazán, the lively main square, is a great place to get to know the people. The very heart of the country's largest city is a place to gossip with neighbors, get your shoes shined, and enjoy an ice-cream cone. Take a peek inside the beautifully restored cathedral. Don't miss Iglesia Los Dolores, either; it's several blocks northwest of the square, and has rows of souvenir stalls to explore. A couple of newish blockbuster museums have won rave reviews in world circles and complement the small existing collection of galleries and exhibition halls in the capital. You'll eat well here, too: A trip back to Tegucigalpa will be a chance to chow down on something other than the beans, rice, and chicken you've been eating elsewhere in Honduras.

Was there ever a more fun place name to say? Practice it: tay-goo-see-GAHL-pa. But by about the time you master it, you'll realize that everyone affectionately and pragmatically shorthands it, spoken and written, to Tegus (TAY-goose). Generations of tourist brochures dutifully repeated that the city's name is a contraction of two words from the language of the area's indigenous people: *teguz* (silver) and *galpa* (hill). That's their story, and they're still sticking to it. Sounds like good public relations, but historians now doubt that version because the indigenous people here were not mining silver. The accepted meaning these days, among scholars at least, is not quite as glitzy: Tegucigalpa probably means "the place of colored stones." The first Spanish settlers did see that there was silver, nevertheless, and the mining industry brought wealth to the region. The city spread down from the hills and across the Río Choluteca. Though Tegucigalpa dates from 1578, it did not become the country's capital until 1880.

With its winding streets lined with colorful houses built into the hillsides, the city retains many characteristics of a provincial town. But the surge in population has brought rumbling buses and blaring horns, and economic doldrums, natural disasters, and political turmoil have taken their toll on Honduras's capital through the decades. Most visitors to the capital do focus on the latter—the negatives—unfortunately. They head out-country the minute their plane lands and don't return until it's time to fly home. And make no mistake: you should not sacrifice precious beach/island/ruins/nature time for extra days in the capital.

## TOP REASONS TO GO

**Get lost in Honduras's colonial past.** Scattered among the haphazard downtown architecture are a few well-preserved colonial-era gems. These are no dusty artifacts, though, and serve today as thriving parish churches, government buildings, museums, and galleries.

**Discover small-town Tegus.** Glittering? Cosmopolitan? Debonair? Um, not really. Wander the streets, talk to the people, and discover why the capital is really an overgrown small town at heart.

**Get out of town.** Some of Tegucigalpa's best attractions lie outside the city itself. City residents flock to the charming villages of Santa Lucía and Valle de Ángeles on weekends. Follow their lead.

**Take in a cloud forest.** A misty, otherworldly fairyland of orchids, bromeliads, and ferns awaits just north of the capital at La Tigra, one of Honduras's top (and most accessible) national parks.

2

But since Tegucigalpa does take some time to grow on you, it's all the more reason to spend more time in the city than most people give the place. If you come to the capital on business or with one of the many mission groups that work in urban health care or education—the needs are great here—you will get a chance to focus on the former, that "big old provincial town" side to Tegucigalpa.

# ORIENTATION AND PLANNING

## ORIENTATION

Sprawling Tegucigalpa is made up of dozens of different neighborhoods. Those called *barrios* are usually older and more centrally located than the more upscale *colonias*. As long as you know which neighborhood you're headed to, getting to your destination won't be a problem. In theory, knowing that *avenidas* (avenues) run north–south and *calles* (streets) run east–west should make getting around much easier. In practice, Tegucigalpa's hills and ravines—scenic though they are—play havoc with anything resembling an orderly grid of streets. Several highwaylike boulevards—they're sometimes spelled *bulevar*—let you zip between sectors of the city. Few maps, however, have details like street names. Familiarize yourself instead with the city's landmarks, as locals will refer to these when giving directions.

**Barrio El Centro.** As in urban areas the world over, Tegucigalpa's downtown has seen development march out to the far reaches of the city. Most maps, ours included, place the center city at the very top, since development of economic and touristic note has expanded south. If you want to do sightseeing up big here, nearly everything you want to see—colonial-era churches and 19th-century villas—is concentrated in the city center and within walking distance of the Plaza Morazán, the pleasant central park, and the cathedral. Spanish colonial cities were laid out that way, and Tegucigalpa is no exception. Hatillo (where you'll find the exceptional La Cumbre restaurant) is a short taxi ride north of here.

**Comayagüela.** This sector southwest of the center city—you can see it across the Choluteca River from downtown—was a separate city until 1932 when it was incorporated into the capital. You might pass through here if you arrive or depart on an intercity bus or if you decide to brave the sprawling San Isidro market. ■ TIP→ Comayagüela is one of the capital's poorer areas and we don't recommend lingering here.

**Colonia Palmira.** Several countries, the United States included, base their embassies in this part of town, and embassies usually know the good neighborhoods. Tegucigalpa at its most pleasant lies in this sector just southeast of downtown. Boulevard Morazán is Palmira's main drag, but head just off Morazán and the streets turn leafy and quiet, and you'll find a nice collection of hotels and restaurants.

**Southern Tegucigalpa.** It's a catchall term for a sprawling collection of colonias to be sure. Hemmed in by mountains to the north, east, and west, Tegucigalpa's path of least resistance has been south, and here is where the city's economic development has occurred. At first glance, it seems a nondescript land of shopping malls, fast-food restaurants, and car dealerships. The big international hotel chains are here as are the international airport and a fun new children's museum.

## TAKE IT ALL IN

**If You Have 1 day:** A day is what most visitors give Tegucigalpa, and it's ample time to explore the historic center of the city. Any visit to a Latin American city should start at its heart, its central plaza, the Plaza Morazán in the case of this city. Look inside the sumptuously restored cathedral on the eastern edge of the plaza. Walk a few blocks north to the Iglesia Los Dolores, admire its beautiful facade, and browse the artisan stalls in the plaza fronting the church. Take a taxi up to El Picacho, the mountain that overlooks the city. Head back down in the afternoon and learn everything you could want to know about Honduran history at the Museo para la Identidad Nacional.

**If You Have 2 days:** Two days let you explore the historic center of the city but give you more breathing room to linger over the sights and sample more restaurant and shopping options, especially in leafy Colonia Palmira to the east of downtown. Two of the capital's most impressive sites entail detours from the city center and can each take up a half day: the new Chiminike children's museum is fun for kids and adults of all ages, and the church and basilica in the suburb of Suyapa have been sites of pilgrimage for the faithful for over 250 years.

**If You Have 3 days:** Spend your first day in Tegucigalpa exploring the streets of the capital. The nearby villages of Santa Lucía and Valle de Ángeles, with their cobblestone streets, are a great place to stroll on your second day. Weekdays are pretty quiet in Valle and Santa Lucía; if your schedule permits it, come out here on the weekend when there's more going on. Get up early the next day so you have plenty of time to explore Parque Nacional La Tigra, a beautiful example of a tropical cloud forest.

# PLANNING

### WHEN TO GO
Tegucigalpa, nestled in the mountains at 3,300 feet, has one of those proverbial, pleasant "eternal spring" climates. The city enjoys warm afternoons that fade into cool evenings. Expect rain for a couple of hours most afternoons from May through October; showers become more prolonged as the rainy season progresses. The rains dissipate by November, and you'll encounter brisk weeks until after Christmas. Things begin to warm up by January, and March and April are the hottest months of the year.

### GETTING HERE AND AROUND
#### AIR TRAVEL TO AND FROM TEGUCIGALPA
Three North American airlines fly daily to Tegucigalpa: American from Miami; Continental from Houston; and Delta from Atlanta. The flights arrive and depart in the middle of the day. Taca flies here from other cities in Central America, with easy connections via San Salvador. Taca Regional has flights to San Pedro Sula and the Bay Islands. Sosa flies to San Pedro Sula, the Bay Islands, and Puerto Lempira. CM Airlines flies to San Pedro Sula, Roatán, and Puerto Lempira. Central American Airways flies to San Pedro Sula, La Ceiba, and Roatán.

**Airlines and Contacts American** (✉ *Edificio Palmira, Av. República de Chile, Col. Palmira* ☎ *232–1414* ⊕ *www.aa.com*). **Central American Airways** (✉ *Aeropuerto Internacional Toncontín* ☎ *233–1614*).**CM Airlines** (✉ *Aeropuerto Internacional Toncontín* ☎ *234–1886* ⊕ *www.cmairlines.com*).**Continental** (✉ *Edificio Palic, Av. República de Chile, Col. Palmira* ☎ *220–0999* ⊕ *www.continental.com*). **Taca** (✉ *Centro Comercial Criolla, Blvd. Morazán, Col. Palmira* ☎ *221–1856* ⊕ *www.taca.com*).**Taca Regional** (✉ *Aeropuerto Internacional Toncontín* ☎ *221–1856* ⊕ *www.flyislena.com*).

#### AIRPORTS AND TRANSFERS
About 7 km (4 mi) south of downtown Tegucigalpa, Aeropuerto Internacional Toncontín (TGU) has been nicknamed the "Stop and Drop," referring to the steep descents necessary to reach the short runway. A few international flights land here, although San Pedro Sula hosts many more.

There are special taxis at the airport, usually nicer cars and minivans. They charge more than regular city taxis, but their direct access to the airport often makes it worth the money. Expect to pay L150 to L200 to get to most hotels.

**Airport Information Aeropuerto Internacional Toncontín** (✉ *Blvd. de la Comunidad Económica Europea* ☎ *233-1115*).

#### BUS TRAVEL TO AND FROM TEGUCIGALPA
There is no single bus station connecting the capital with the rest of the country. Many companies have their terminals in Comayagüela, the community across the Río Choluteca from downtown. It's a rough neighborhood, so be on your guard. A few companies have moved their terminals to more spacious digs in the southern part of the city.

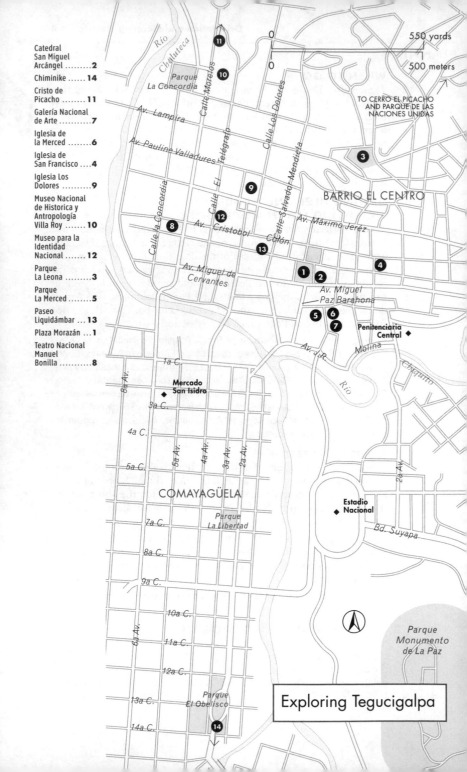

Exploring Tegucigalpa

2

If you're headed north, Viana and Hedman Alas travel to San Pedro Sula and La Ceiba. They offer clean, comfortable coaches with air-conditioning, snacks, and even movies. Sáenz Primera has six departures per day to San Pedro Sula and three to Choluteca. El Rey Express has a decent hourly direct (meaning just a couple of stops) to San Pedro Sula. Cristina offers a slightly less frequent service to La Ceiba, from which you can hop off to Tela. Cotraibal has two morning departures to Trujillo.

The only buses west are the slow ones labeled *servicio a escala* (fre-quently-stopping, or local, service),

> **PREVIEW YOUR LANDING**
>
> The Internet video site YouTube (⊕ www.youtube.com) contains short clips showing an American Airlines plane landing at the capital's Toncontín International Airport. (A search on the site for PLANE LANDING TEGUCIGALPA calls them up.) Although the runway has been lengthened since the footage was shot—984 feet in 2010—these give you an idea of the odd approach pilots must navigate to land here.

but El Rey and Los Norteños will take you to Comayagua, Siguate-peque, and Lago de Yojoa. La Sultana heads to Santa Rosa de Copán four times a day, and El Junqueño can get you to Santa Bárbara.

**Domestic Bus Companies Cotraibal** (⊠ 7 Av. between Cs. 11 and 12, Comay-agüela ☎ 237–1666). **Cristina** (⊠ Blvd. de la Fuerzas Armadas de Honduras, Col. Florencia ☎ 220–0117 or 220–1555). **El Junqueño** (⊠ 8 Av. between Cs. 12 and 13, Comayagüela ☎ 237–2921). **El Rey** (⊠ Av. 6 and C. 9, Comayagüela ☎ 237–6609). **El Rey Express** (⊠ C. 12 and Av. 7, Comayagüela ☎ 237–8561). **Hedman Alas** (⊠ 11 Av., between Cs. 13 and 14, Comayagüela ☎ 237–7143 ⊕ www.hedmanalas.com). **La Sultana** (⊠ 8 Av., between Cs. 11 and 12, Comay-agüela ☎ 237–8101). **Los Norteños** (⊠ C. 12, between Avs. 6 and 7, Comay-agüela ☎ 237–0706). **Sáenz Primera** (⊠ Blvd. de la Comunidad Económica Europea, Col. Prados Universitario ☎ 233–4229). **Viana** (⊠ Blvd. de las Fuerzas Armadas de Honduras ☎ 225–6583 ⊕ www.vianatransportes.com).

**BUS TRAVEL WITHIN TEGUCIGALPA**
Enough pickpocketings and robberies of foreigners on city buses have occurred that we don't recommend them as a mode of transport within the capital. Stick with taxis instead.

**CAR RENTAL**
The vehicle of choice for exploring Honduras—especially if you are heading off the beaten path—is the four-wheel-drive double-cabin pickup. Rental cars are not cheap, however. A number of international companies, including Alamo, Avis, Hertz, and Thrifty, are based at the airport. Advance is a well-regarded Honduran firm. Their prices start at L950, or about $50 per day for the most basic four-door sedans.

**Rental Agencies Advance Rent-a-Car** (⊠ C. República de México ☎ 235–9528 ⊕ www.advancerentacar.com).**Alamo** (⊠ Aeropuerto Internacional Toncon-tín ☎ 233–4962 ⊕ www.alamo.com).**Avis** (⊠ Aeropuerto Internacional Toncontín ☎ 233–1420 ⊠ Blvd. Suyapa, in front of Emisoras Unidas ☎ 239–5712 ⊕ www.avis.com). **Hertz** (⊠ Aeropuerto Internacional Toncontín ☎ 280–9191 ⊕ www.

*hertz.com*).**Thrifty** (✉ *Aeropuerto Internacional Toncontín* ☎ *233–0933* ✉ *Col. Prados Universitario* ☎ *235–6077* ⊕ *www.thrifty.com*).

## CAR TRAVEL

Unless you are taking a day trip outside the city, driving in Tegucigalpa is best avoided. In Barrio El Centro, parking is an ordeal and traffic snarls are frequent. Directional signage is sparse, and thanks to the city's hills, the orderly grid of streets fizzles out once you leave downtown. Many intersections have no stop signs or stoplights. Avoid the hassle and use taxis for getting around town.

## TAXIS

Taxis are your best transportation option around the city, and should be your only transportation after dark, even if going just a few blocks. Have someone from your hotel call you a cab at night rather than you trying to hail one. Same when heading back: have the restaurant or bar get a taxi to take you back to your hotel. Taxis solicit your business by honking. If you take them up on it, discuss the price immediately. All prices should be around L50 to L60. If the driver seems unimpressed by how much you'll pay, ask to be let out at the corner—that usually closes the deal. Certain taxis are *colectivos*, in which several people going in the same general direction share a ride. It's a good compromise between the expense of a regular taxi and the inconvenience and risk of a bus. Look for lines of people in the side streets around Plaza Morazán, or yell out your destination when a half-full taxi honks at you.

If you'd like to call a cab, Pioneros is prompt and efficient, and has 24-hour service.

**Taxi Company Pioneros** (☎ *225–5563, 225–4346, or 225–1555*).

## EMERGENCIES

Clínica Viera, on Avenida Cristobal Colón, accepts walk-ins around the clock. Drugstores are found everywhere in the city. Farmacia Rosna has English-speaking staff on duty daily 9 AM to 7 PM. Pharmacies take turns staying open all night, so check the schedule on the door of any shop to locate the nearest open one. The U.S. Embassy is on the eastern edge of Colonia Palmira.

**Embassy U.S. Embassy** (✉ *Av. La Paz, Colonia Palmira* ☎ *236–9320; after hours: 238-5114* ⊕ *honduras.usembassy.gov*).

**Hospital Clínica Viera** (✉ *Av. Cristobal Colón, Barrio El Centro* ☎ *237–3160*).

**Hot Lines Ambulance** (☎ *195*). **Fire** (☎ *198*). **Police** (☎ *199*).

**Pharmacy Farmacia Rosna** (✉ *Paseo Liquidámbar, Barrio El Centro* ☎ *237–0605*).

## TOUR OPERATORS

Agencies specialize in different destinations, so check around for the best price to where you are headed. Trek de Honduras organizes adventure trips to remote regions. Destinos de Éxito offers a five-hour city tour as well as excursions to Parque Nacional La Tigra, Santa Lucía, and Valle de Ángeles. Explore can take you on a Tegucigalpa city tour, a visit to Santa Lucía and Valle de Ángeles, and Parque Nacional La

Tigra, as well as to farther-flung destinations such as Comayagua, and arranging transfers to San Pedro Sula, La Ceiba, and Copán Ruinas.

**Tour Companies Destinos de Éxito** (✉ *Edificio Europa, Col. San Carlos* ☎ *236-9651* ⊕ *www.destinosdeexito.com*).

**Explore** (☎ *8990-8590* ⊕ *www.explorehonduras.com*).

**Trek de Honduras** (✉ *Edificio Midence 218, Barrio El Centro* ☎ *239-9827*).

**VISITOR INFORMATION**
The friendly Instituto Hondureño de Turismo in Colonia San Carlos is worth a visit for information about the city.

**Tourist Information Instituto Hondureño de Turismo** (✉ *Edificio Europa, 2nd floor, Col. San Carlos* ☎ *222-2124* ⊕ *www.letsgohonduras.com*).

**MONEY MATTERS**
U.S. dollars and traveler's checks are the easiest, and usually the only, currency you can exchange in Honduras. Try Banco Lafise near Plaza Morazán. Most banks and malls have ATMs available as well. Normal banking hours are 9 to 4 weekdays. They are located in a financial center in Multiplaza with branches that are open from 10 to 7 Monday through Saturday, if you miss regular banking hours.

**Banks Bancahsa** (✉ *Av. Cristobal Colón at C. Los Dolores, Barrio El Centro* ☎ *237-1171*). **Banco Lafise** (✉ *Plaza Morazán, Barrio El Centro* ☎ *237-4000* 🖨 *237-1835*). **Credomatic/BAC** (✉ *Edificio BAC, Blvd. Morazán* ☎ *238-7200 or 206-7200*).

**HEALTH AND SAFETY**
Health isn't a concern in the capital; stick with bottled water and you should be fine.

Tegucigalpa is generally safe, provided you dress down, don't wear flashy jewelry or watches, and avoid handling money in public. It's a good idea to keep your money in your front pocket rather than a back one, where it is easier to steal. In markets and other crowded areas, hold purses or handbags close to the body; thieves use knives to slice the bottom of a bag and catch the contents as they fall out. Avoid walking anywhere at night. Taxis should be your only mode of transportation after dark.

| WHAT IT COSTS IN HONDURAN LEMPIRAS | | | | |
|---|---|---|---|---|
| | ¢ | $ | $$ | $$$ | $$$$ |
| Restaurants | under L75 | L75–L150 | L151–L250 | L251–L350 | over L350 |
| Hotels | under L750 | L750–L1,250 | L1,251–L1,750 | L1,751–L2,250 | over L2,500 |

Restaurant prices are per person for a main course at dinner. Hotel prices are for two people in a standard double room in high season.

## A BIT OF HISTORY

Few traces remain today in Tegu-cigalpa of the original indigenous Lenca people who inhabited this region in precolonial times. (The western part of the country provides a better opportunity to acquaint yourself with Lenca culture.) Once Spanish colonists arrived, Teguci-galpa became the city that silver built. Local legend holds that the precious metal was discovered here on September 29, 1578, the feast day of St. Michael the Archangel, the city's patron saint and for whom the cathedral is named. Historians doubt the account, but it makes a good story and was enough to christen the city *La Villa Real de Minas de San Miguel de Tegucigalpa* (the Royal City of the Mines of St. Michael of Tegucigalpa).

Economic growth continued unabated through the 19th century. In 1880, the government moved the capital here from Comayagua in central Honduras, wanting to be closer to the economic action. But by the turn of the last century, Honduras had become known for another product. Its lucrative banana trade—Honduras was the original "banana republic"—meant a shift of the economic center of gravity to the northern coast and lowlands. With the boom days over, the 20th century was a rollercoaster ride for Tegucigalpa. It doubled in size with its 1932 incorporation of next-door Comayagüela. That sector of the city suffered terribly during 1998's Hurri-cane Mitch, which hung over Hondu-ras for five days letting loose floods and mudslides. While no longer Honduras's economic center—that title belongs to San Pedro Sula these days—Tegucigalpa is still the coun-try's political center and remains relevant on a national level.

# EXPLORING TEGUCIGALPA

Nearly all of Tegucigalpa's sights concentrate in Barrio El Centro, its historic downtown. The scarcity of acceptable center-city accommoda-tion means you'll probably stay elsewhere in town and will need to taxi downtown to see the sights. A half day gives you a rushed overview; a full day lets you explore more leisurely. Think about winding up your downtown sightseeing day around 4 PM. Taxis become difficult to find during the evening rush hour, and wandering around downtown on foot at night is risky. (It gets dark here between 6 and 6:30 PM.) Walk-ing the center-city streets during the day entails the same precautions you'd take in any new city: watch your things.

One of the capital's top sights, the new Chiminike children's museum, lies outside downtown in the southern reaches of the city.

## BARRIO EL CENTRO

### TOP ATTRACTIONS

**Catedral San Miguel Arcángel.** The capital's gleaming cathedral presides over the eastern edge of Plaza Morazán and is named for the city's patron saint, the archangel Michael. The domed structure, flanked by towering palms, has stood on this site since 1765. Earth tremors and

## HOLY WEEK IN TEGUCIGALPA

It's an anomaly of anomalies that the holiest week of the Christian calendar sees Latin Americans at their most secular—many of them take advantage of the week off and flock to the beach. Hondurans are no exception. But if you stay behind, it's a chance to see Hondurans at their most devout, too, as many of those who've eschewed the beach participate in a live re-creation of *Semana Santa* (Holy Week), Jesus's last week on earth.

The old colonial capital of Comayagua holds the country's largest Holy Week observances *(see ⇨ Holy Week in Comayagua in Western Honduras, below)*, but Tegucigalpa has begun in recent years to resurrect its old traditions, too.

The end result is that the capital doesn't become quite the ghost town that it used to during Holy Week. Downtown churches—Dolores, San Francisco, El Calvario, and the cathedral—all participate in the processions. Celebrations get underway on Palm Sunday with a reenactment of Jesus's entry into Jerusalem, late Thursday night sees the recreation of his arrest and trial, and Easter observances begin at dawn. But Good Friday is the day to be here if your schedule permits; the most elaborate processions are on this day and are notable for the intricate colored-sawdust carpets constructed along Avenida Miguel de Cervantes. There's plenty of pre-parade opportunity for photos before the parading of the Christ figure tramples the carpets.

rain took their toll on the edifice through the centuries, but after a five-year, $500,000 restoration, completed in 2009, the cathedral is fabulous once again. For decades, the building's exterior was painstakingly whitewashed each year; the restoration project returned the cathedral to its original salmon color. Sunlight streams into the apse, where you'll find the glittering gold-and-silver altar sculpted by Guatemalan artist Vicente Galvéz. Mass is held regularly in the cathedral, as are occasional chamber-music concerts. The Plaza Morazán was recently renovated and rebuilt with attractive open-air seating. ⊠ *Av. Miguel de Cervantes and C. Hipolito Matute, Barrio El Centro* ☎ *Free* ◑ *Daily 9–4.*

**Iglesia Los Dolores.** This towered church dating from 1732 is dedicated to human sorrow, earning it a special place in the hearts of poverty-stricken Hondureños. On the facade—it's the most ornate of any church in the city—you'll see carvings representing the last days of Christ, including the cock that crowed three times to signal that Christ had been betrayed. Although the building keeps official opening hours, unofficially it is frequently closed during the week. If you can get inside, the interior, dominated by a colorful dome, features paintings of the Crucifixion. The church is known to be the nexus of a system of colonial-era tunnels, none of which are open to the public any longer. One leads to the cathedral, six blocks away; others were secret routes to private homes. Local lore holds that the tunnels: a) contain colonial gold worth millions of lempiras; b) served as secret escape routes used by scally-wag government officials; c) are haunted; or d) are any combination of the above. The church faces a lively square filled with stalls selling

## A GUIDE TO GRAFFITI

The June 2009 military coup and ensuing political crisis unleashed a barrage of partisan graffiti on many areas of Tegucigalpa. It is slowly being painted over, but much still remains—and occasionally gets augmented—giving certain neighborhoods of the capital a shopworn look. Some of the terminology you'll see follows below; other graffiti is not printable in a family book such as a Fodor's guide.

ASESINOS: assassins

DICTADOR: dictator

EJÉRCITO: army

GOLPE: coup

LADRONES: thieves

LOBO: Porfirio Lobo, the current president, elected in November 2009

MEL: Manuel Zelaya, the deposed president

MICHELETTI: Roberto Micheletti, the interim president who assumed power

Thankfully, things are calm these days in Tegucigalpa, outside the occasional march that does nothing more than snarl traffic. Most folks here are relieved to have put the 2009 events behind them.

inexpensive goods. ⌂ *C. Los Dolores at Av. Máximo Jérez, Barrio El Centro* ⌂ *Free* ⊙ *Daily 9–4.*

**Fodor's**Choice ★ **Museo para la Identidad Nacional.** The Museum of National Identity is a recent addition to the pantheon of downtown galleries and museums, and has established itself as one of Tegucigalpa's most rewarding attractions. A 19th-century building that served first as a hospital and then as the government's Palace of Ministries has been converted into the country's foremost museum of history—and the results are impressive. The second-floor installations take you through everything that has happened in Honduras from its geological formation up to the present day. (That includes not shying away from the 2009 political crisis.) A film entitled Copán Virtual is presented several times a day and guides you through the Mayan city's construction. It's a good introduction to Copán if you're headed that way, and is included in your admission price. The first floor contains temporary exhibits. Everything is labeled in Spanish here, but for an extra L50 you can rent a portable audio unit that gives you commentary in English about what you're seeing. Although the concept of the museum gift shop hasn't really caught on in Honduras, this facility is an exception. Stop by the small shop on your way out and browse the selection of candles and leather goods made by an area women's cooperative. ■TIP→ **Admission is free on Thursday to school groups, and they come en masse; if your schedule permits, another day of the week is more peaceful.** (⌂ *C. El Telégrafo and Av. Miguel Paz Barahona, Barrio El Centro* ☎ *238–5412* ⊕ *www.min.hn* ⌂ *L60* ⊙ *Museum: Tues.–Sat. 9–5, Sun. 10–4; Copán Virtual: Tues.–Fri. 10, 11:30 AM, 2, 3:30 PM; Sat. 10, 11:30 AM, 1, 2, 3:30 PM; Sun. 11:30 AM, 1, 2, 3:30 PM.*)

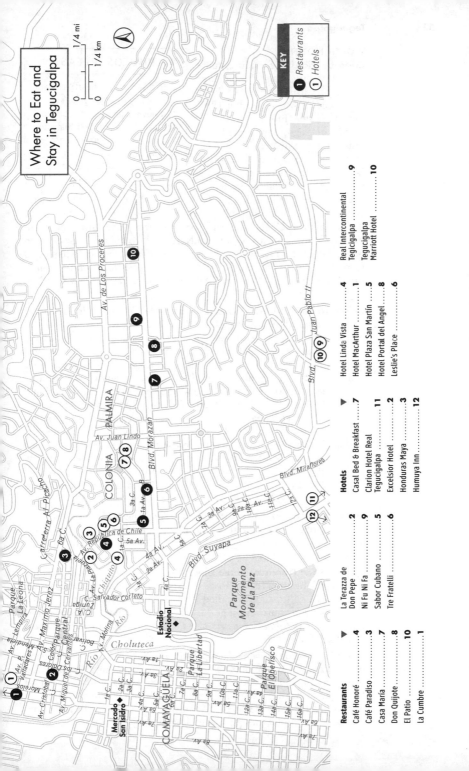

## Where to Eat and Stay in Tegucigalpa

**KEY**

**1** Restaurants
**1** Hotels

**Restaurants** ►

| | |
|---|---|
| Café Honoré | **4** |
| Café Paradiso | **3** |
| Casa María | **7** |
| Don Quijote | **8** |
| El Patio | **10** |
| La Cumbre | **1** |
| La Terazza de Don Pepe | **2** |
| Ni Fu Ni Fa | **9** |
| Sabor Cubano | **5** |
| Tre Fratelli | **6** |

**Hotels** ►

| | |
|---|---|
| Casal Bed & Breakfast | **7** |
| Clarion Hotel Real Tegucigalpa | **11** |
| Excelsior Hotel | **2** |
| Honduras Maya | **3** |
| Humuya Inn | **12** |
| Hotel Linda Vista | **4** |
| Hotel MacArthur | **1** |
| Hotel Plaza San Martín | **5** |
| Hotel Portal del Angel | **8** |
| Leslie's Place | **6** |
| Real Intercontinental Tegicigalpa | **9** |
| Tegucigalpa Marriott Hotel | **10** |

**WORTH NOTING**

**Cristo de Picacho.** Standing guard over the city, this monumental statue of Christ has been a landmark since it was erected in 1997. On the same hill is an ancient Coca-Cola sign, constructed with individual white letters using the same idea as Southern California's famous HOLLYWOOD sign. It is visible from many places throughout the city, and its proximity has led irreverent residents to dub the Cristo statue "the Coca-Cola Christ." From here there's a beautiful view of the valley. It all sits in the Parque de las Naciones Unidas, a great place to have a picnic, although it can be crowded with locals on weekends. A small zoo in the park has seen better days. A taxi is the easiest way to get up here. Expect to pay L100 from downtown. ⊠ *Cerro El Picacho, 6 km (3½ mi) north of downtown, El Picacho* ☎ *No phone* ⌑ *Park entrance: L20* ☉ *Weekdays 8–3, weekends 9–4:30.*

> **NO PHOTOS, PLEASE**
>
> Snap away to your heart's content outside any of Tegucigalpa's downtown churches, the cathedral included, but all request that you refrain from photography once you get inside.

★ **Galería Nacional de Arte.** Housed in the 1694 Convento de San Pedro Nolasco and adjoining the Iglesia de la Merced, the bright and airy National Gallery of Art displays some wonderful artifacts, including finely detailed pre-Columbian ceramics and intricate Mayan sculptures from Copán. The museum has a dozen exhibition halls holding lovely examples of religious and colonial art; these serious works contrast nicely with the more comic modern works on the patio. Upstairs you'll find paintings by Pablo Zelaya Sierra and other 20th-century Honduran artists. The building has had many uses through the centuries, including as an army barracks and a cockfighting arena. To our minds, the building's current incarnation is its best so far; though small, this is one of Latin America's top art museums. As a bonus, this is one of the few such facilities in the country to present information in both Spanish and English. ⊠ *Av. La Merced, Barrio El Centro* ☎ *237–9884* ⌑ *L60* ☉ *Mon.–Sat. 9–4, Sun. 9–1.*

**Iglesia de la Merced.** Two *retablos,* or small religious paintings, flank the attractive altarpiece housed inside this 17th-century church. It's adjacent to the Galería Nacional de Arte. ⊠ *Av. La Merced, Barrio El Centro* ⌑ *Free* ☉ *Weekdays 9–4.*

**Iglesia de San Francisco.** Three blocks east of Plaza Morazán lies the first church built in Tegucigalpa. Construction on the building, which sits on a leafy little square called Parque Valle, began in 1592. Inside this Franciscan church are a guilded altar and colonial religious paintings. ⊠ *Av. Cristobal Colón and C. Salvador Corieto, Barrio El Centro* ⌑ *Free* ☉ *Daily 9–4.*

**Museo Nacional de Historia y Antropología Villa Roy.** This hillside mansion near Plaza La Concordia, once home to President Julio Lozano who was ousted in a 1956 military coup, houses the National Museum of History and Anthropology. (Despite the name, the focus is entirely on history here.) For those who read Spanish, there is some quirky information on the republic's struggles after it gained its independence, but the information gets extremely detailed—likely more than you need unless you are a student of Honduran history. ⊠ *Plaza de la Concordia, Barrio El Centro* ☎ *222–1468* 🔲 *L60* ⏰ *Weekdays 8–4.*

**Parque La Leona.** A 20-minute walk north of Plaza Morazán, up some steep and twisting cobbled streets, will bring you to this charming park that is well worth the effort to get here. Lovely views of Tegucigalpa are even nicer at night, and locals say the winking lights look like a nativity display. Many of the older houses in this beautiful, but somewhat dishevelled, neighborhood once belonged to European settlers. ⊠ *C. Hipolito Matute, Barrio El Centro* 🔲 *Free.*

**Parque La Merced.** A few blocks south of Plaza Morazán, this small park provides weary travelers with some shady places to sit. Older men in wide-brimmed hats tend to perch here, making the most of the relative calm to read their newspapers and gossip. The park is the site of a 19th-century university; today its auditorium houses art exhibits and is a music-performance venue. ⊠ *C. Bolívar, Barrio El Centro* 🔲 *Free.*

**Paseo Liquidámbar.** You might not realize it as a bus chugs by belching a cloud of smoke, but Tegucigalpa really is putting forth an effort toward making itself a more pleasant place to live and visit. One of its little gems—it's a work in progress at this writing—is the five-block-long downtown pedestrian mall between the Teatro Nacional Manuel Bonilla and Plaza Morazán. The unusual moniker "Liquidámbar" comes from the genus name for the American sweetgum tree, grown throughout Honduras; locals, however, simply refer to the promenade as the Calle Peatonal (pedestrian street). Bricked pavement, modern iron street lamps, new benches, and tiled colonial-style street signs make Liquidámbar a pleasant place for a stroll. You'll find a few U.S. fast-food places here as well as the ubiquitous Espresso Americano, Honduras's answer to Starbucks. Stores are geared toward local shopping needs rather than much tourist interest. The Champs-Elysées it is not, but we credit the city for creating a pleasant public space for residents and visitors alike. (⊠ *Paseo Liquidámbar, Barrio El Centro*).

**Plaza Morazán.** Crowded night and day, the city's central park—folks here frequently refer to the public space as the Parque Central—is where everyone comes to chat with friends, purchase lottery tickets, have their shoes polished, and listen to free afternoon concerts. As it was recently refurbished with new benches and outdoor seating, you'll want to sit here for a while to admire the cathedral's facade and watch the pigeons playing peekaboo near the equestrian statue of Francisco Morazán, born in Tegucigalpa and president of the Central American Federation in the 1830s, which included Guatemala, El Salvador, Nicaragua, and Costa Rica. ■**TIP➔ On the topic of those pigeons, they seem to have amazingly accurate aim. Watch where you sit.** ⊠ *C. Bolívar and Av. Miguel de Cervantes, Barrio El Centro.*

**NEED A BREAK?**

The unpretentious but crowded **Espresso Americano** (⊠ *Plaza Morazán, Barrio El Centro* ☎ *238–2508*) serves up some of the best coffee in the country. This is the original location, but you'll find many others across Honduras. **Super Donuts** (⊠ *Paseo Liquidámbar, Barrio El Centro*) has a buffet breakfast and lunch. Specialty baked goods, tamales, and fresh fruit juices are always tasty.

**Teatro Nacional Manuel Bonilla.** The National Theater, built in 1915 and named after the early-20th century president who advocated for its construction, has an ornate interior that was modeled after the Athenée in Paris. Check the schedule for events that range from classical-ballet performances to rock concerts. ⊠ *Av. Miguel Paz Barahona and C. La Concordia, Barrio El Centro* ☎ *222–4366* ⊕ *www.teatronacionalmanuelbonilla.hn.*

### SOUTHERN TEGUCIGALPA

Fodor'sChoice **Chiminike.** This might be the world's only museum that teaches you ★ about the hows and whys of flatulence, complete with sound effects. ☺ Appropriately, it comes at the, um, tail end of your walk through a giant gastrointestinal tract. If that doesn't satisfy your appetite for the offbeat, you can learn about vomiting, sneezing, and body odor, too. It's all part of the immensely popular El Cuerpo Humano (Human Body) section of Tegucigalpa's fun, interactive new children's museum, which plenty of adults enjoy, too. Other exhibits acquaint kids with conservation of the environment and skills of commerce. Displays are all labeled in Spanish, but the friendly museum staff can help you if your abilities in that language are weak or nonexistent. ■ TIP➜ As you'd expect, weekends are mobbed here. A visit during the week lets you take in the activities in relative peace and quiet. Just look for the blue-and-purple building on the hill down the road from Las Cascadas shopping mall. Chiminike, by the way, is the name of a frog in a popular Honduran children's story. (⊠ *Blvd. de las Fuerzas Armadas de Honduras, next to Supreme Court, Southern Teguchigalpa* ☎ *291–0339* ⊕ *www.chiminike. org* ☎ *L50* ☺ *Tues.–Fri. 9–12 and 2–5, weekends 10–1 and 2–5*).

# WHERE TO EAT

Tegucigalpa has a few outstanding restaurants, although not as many as you'd expect in a city of one million people. You'll find a good selection along Boulevard Morazán and in Colonia Palmira, to the east of Barrio El Centro. It's an up-and-coming area for dining and drinking with the smart and trendy crowd. A few other restaurants have sprung up on the outer fringes of the city, and you'll find a couple of old standbys downtown, too. All the U.S. chains are here if you get a hankering for something from back home.

### BARRIO EL CENTRO

$ ✕ **Café Paradiso.** That just might be the ghost of Che Guevara plotting LATIN AMERICAN the next revolution off in the corner of this unpretentious little coffeehouse with a slightly political bent. Paradiso serves local beverage specialties, but is best known for its *carajillo* (coffee with cognac). The food is basic but filling, with locals leaning toward favorites like the *tortilla española* (Spanish omelet). While you wait, peruse the selection of books on Honduran history and politics, or stop by on Thursday evenings when a film is screened. ⊠ *Av. Miguel Paz Barahona at C. Las Damas, Barrio El Centro* ☎ *237–0337* ▭ *No credit cards* ☺ *Closed Sun.*

**$**  ✕ **La Terraza de Don Pepe.** How many restaurants keep a shrine to the
CENTRAL  Virgin Mary on their premises? At the entrance to the restrooms, no
AMERICAN  less? This downtown eatery does. The statue of the Virgin of Suyapa,
Honduras's patron saint, appeared wrapped in newspaper in Don Pepe's
men's room one night in 1986. A miracle or a drop-off by a thief? You
can decide *(see ⇨ Suyapa in Side Trips from Tegucigalpa, below).* Standard Honduran fare—hearty chicken, beef, and pork dishes—are served
here; the lunchtime plato del día, a combination of meat, rice, and
vegetables, includes a beverage and is a good bargain. ⊠ *Av. Cristóbal
Colón, Barrio El Centro* ☎ *237–1084* ▭ *No credit cards* ⊘ *Closed Sun.*

## COLONIA PALMIRA
**$$$**  ✕ **Casa María.** Frequented by the country's upper crust, this genteel res-
CONTEMPORARY  taurant has plenty of rooms that can be closed off for presidential meet-
★  ings. Yet Melba Robelo, the Nicaraguan owner, makes sure everyone
feels welcome. The fish dishes, made with the freshest ingredients, all
have intriguing flavors. Try the onion soup with Swiss cheese, followed
by breaded *camarones* (shrimp) served with butter and tarragon. The
famous *crepes de manzana* (apple crepes) are served with almonds and
liqueur. The service is irreproachable. ⊠ *Blvd. Morazán at Av. Ramón
Ernesto Cruz, Col. Palmira* ☎ *239–4984* ⌂ *Reservations recommended*
▭ *AE, MC, V* ⊘ *Closed Sun.*

**$$**  ✕ **Café Honoré.** Hearty soups, tasty pastas, huge sandwiches, and abun-
FRENCH  dant salads are the draws at this restaurant in Colonia Palmira. The
outdoor terrace is a good spot for a beer, or even a bottle of French
wine. If it's cloudy, head into the wood-paneled dining room. The café
space also includes a European-style deli and a salon. ⊠ *Av. República
de Argentina 1941, Col. Palmira* ☎ *239–7566* ▭ *AE, D, DC, MC, V*
⊘ *Closed Sun.*

**$$**  ✕ **Don Quijote.** One of the oldest still-operating restaurants in Tegucigalpa,
SPANISH  Don Quijote has been in business for more than three decades. Straight-
forward Spanish dishes are the specialty, especially the *paella valenciana,*
made with rice, saffron, vegetables, chicken, and seafood. Another highly
recommended dish is the hearty *fabada asturiana* (a meaty stew). There's
also a fully stocked bar. ⊠ *Blvd. Morazán, next to Centro Comercial
Lomas del Blvd., La Pedrera* ☎ *239–7920* ▭ *AE, MC, V.*

**$$$**  ✕ **El Patio.** Tegucigalpa's best-known Honduran restaurant dishes up
HONDURAN  ample helpings of *típico* (traditional) food. The rustic building with
brick patio evokes an old Honduran country home. You can watch
your food being prepared on the open grill, with *pinchos* (Honduran-
style chicken, beef, or pork kebabs) being special favorites here. It's all
accompanied by anafres, a dip of refried beans and cheese. The waitstaff
wear traditional Honduran clothing (think white dresses and pants with
thin, colorful stripes). ⊠ *Blvd. Morazán at Av. República Dominicana,
Colonia Palmira* ☎ *221–4141* ▭ *AE, D, DC, MC, V.*

**$$$$**  ✕ **Ni Fu Ni Fa.** It's a testament to any Argentine restaurant when you see
ARGENTINE  a city's Argentine community dining there, and that's the case with this
Honduran-owned minichain of restaurants (there are also branches in
San Pedro Sula, Honduras, and Antigua, Guatemala). It's not just the
Argentines, though; the high-quality imported cuts of beef draw diners
of all nationalities to this place off Boulevard Morazán. The best deal

here is the four-person platter with a selection of steak, pork, ribs, and chorizo. Top it off with a trip to the ample salad bar and a bottle of Argentine wine. The restaurant's name translates as "more or less, " but this place is definitely more. ⊠ *Av. República de Perú, Colonia Palmira* ☎ *221–2056* ⊟ *AE, D, DC, MC, V.*

$$$     ✕ **Sabor Cubano.** Just as much a nightspot as Cuban restaurant, this
CUBAN   old standby is immensely popular with the capital's Cuban community. Island recipes such as *ropa vieja*—the translation, "old clothes," may sound unappetizing, but it's really shredded flank steak in tomato sauce—are standard fare here. The full bar's selection of daiquiris, Cuba libres (rum and Coke), and mimosas will transport you back to Old Havana. There's live music and dancing on the back patio weekend nights, and if you'd like to wow your friends back home with a few moves, the place offers salsa lessons on Tuesday evenings. ⊠ *Av. República de Argentina, Colonia Palmira* ☎ *235–9947* ⊟ *AE, MC, V* ⊘ *Closed Sun., no dinner Mon.*

$$$     ✕ **Tre Fratelli.** A lot of Italian eateries around the world go by the name
ITALIAN Tre Fratelli (three brothers), and while this restaurant in the Plaza Criolla on Boulevard Morazán is part of a small Central America-California chain to boot, its atmosphere is warm and unchainlike. There are inside seating and a popular patio dining area. Generous servings of pasta, tasty fish dishes, a good wine selection, and pleasant salads at accessible prices—along with the obligatory checkered tablecloths—have made this place a tremendous hit with travelers and locals alike. ⊠ *Centro Comerical Criolla, Av. República de Argentina 216, Col. Palmira* ☎ *232–1942* ⊕ *www.trefratelli.com* ⊟ *AE, D, DC, MC, V* ⊘ *Closed Sun.*

### HATILLO

$$$     ✕ **La Cumbre.** Long considered the city's most romantic restaurant, La
GERMAN  Cumbre arguably has the best panoramic view of Tegucigalpa going. By day or (especially) by night, it is worth the trip out here to view the world from this privileged vantage point. The elegant dining room serves classic German dishes such as *Jägerschnitzel* (pork or veal cutlets in mushroom gravy), and a few non-German dishes, too. Try the pork medallions with mango sauce. ⊠ *Km 7.5 Carretera a Hatillo* ☎ *211–9000* ⊕ *www.lacumbrerestaurante.com* ⌕ *Reservations recommended* ⊟ *AE, MC, V* ⊘ *No dinner Sun.*

## WHERE TO STAY

Tegucigalpa has only a moderate selection of decent hotels; variety and availability are not as large as you'd expect in a capital city of one million people. That said, you can still manage to choose between elegant high-rises, older favorites that are full of personality, or intimate hostels with personalized service. Business travelers frequent Tegucigalpa on weekdays, and many of the mission groups who often stay in the city through the weekend use smaller places as their base. Reservations are a good idea any day of the week, any time of the year. The good news is that prices are very reasonable here for what you get, even at high-end lodgings, and hotels that cater to business travelers discount their rates on weekends.

## TEGUCIGALPA IN BOOKS AND MUSIC

American author William Sydney Porter (1862–1910)—history knows him better by his pen name, O. Henry, of "The Gift of the Magi" and "The Ransom of Red Chief" short-story fame—hid out in a Tegucigalpa hotel from July 1896 to January 1897, a fugitive from embezzlement charges in Texas. It was here that he penned his book *Cabbages and Kings*, describing late-19th century Honduras at the height of its banana trade with the United States. The book is best known today for popularizing the term *banana republic*, which Porter used to describe a backwater country controlled by the interests of multinational corporations. The ill health of his dying wife, Athol, necessitated the author's return to Texas. Following her death, Porter was arrested, convicted, and imprisoned. He served a three-year sentence but denied the charges to his final days.

The late rock musician Warren Zevon never confirmed it, but the lyrics "Now I'm hiding in Honduras; I'm a desperate man" from his song "Lawyers, Guns, and Money" are assumed by many to be a reference to Porter's self-exile in Tegucigalpa.

Many hostelries in Barrio El Centro, the old downtown, have seen better days. We suggest only a couple of hotels there, but they are solid recommendations and would be worth reviewing regardless of their location. Colonia Palmira, east of downtown, contains the biggest variety of lodgings and is a convenient place to base yourself. The Honduras Maya, Tegucigalpa's original business-class hotel, holds court here as well as a trio of similarly styled medium-size lodgings. Palmira is also home to a few small inns, impressive for their family-style surroundings and service. The big international chains, with all the amenities a business traveler could desire, have set up shop in the southern reaches of the city along with one smaller hotel with more personality. If you arrive in the capital on an intercity bus, your first encounter will be with the Comayagüela district southwest of downtown where all the terminals are. The neighborhood is sketchy, and you should cab it elsewhere rather than trying to stay there.

No matter which neighborhood you use as your base, always come and go by taxi after dark; it's the safest mode of transport at night. Have the front desk call a cab for you rather than you trying to flag one down in the street.

### BARRIO EL CENTRO

$$ 🖼Hotel MacArthur. Even though it's in the center of the city, this budget-price hotel is remarkably quiet. After a day exploring the Tegucigalpa, it's nice to return for a nap in one of the spacious rooms or a dip in the pool. Numbers of windows in rooms vary, making some brighter than others. Ask to see a couple before deciding. The manager is extremely helpful, dispensing information about the region. **Pros:** friendly management; good budget option in city center; unheard-of pool in heart of downtown. **Cons:** rooms have a dated look; some rooms are dark. ⊠ *Av. Lempira 454, Barrio El Centro* ☎ *237–9839* ⊕ *www.hotelmacarthur.*

*com* ⤴ *43 rooms, 2 suites* ⚒ *In-room: a/c (some). In-hotel: restaurant, pool, Internet terminal, Wi-Fi hotspot, parking (free)* ▤ *AE, MC, V.*

## COLONIA PALMIRA

$    🏨 **Casal B&B.** Okay, bed-and-breakfast is a misnomer here—Casal is really a hotel in a rambling converted house—but an ample breakfast is included in the rates. Rooms are plain, although some come with a balcony. Ask to see a selection before deciding. It makes for a good budget option in otherwise more-expensive Colonia Palmira. **Pros:** friendly owner; good location. **Cons:** plain rooms; offsite parking available only at night. ⊠ *Av. República de Perú, Col. Palmira* ☎ *235–8891* ⤴ *12 rooms* ⚒ *In-room: a/c, refrigerator, Wi-Fi. In-hotel: laundry service, Internet terminal, parking (paid)* ▤ *AE, D, DC, MC, V* ¶⃝ *BP.*

$$$–$$$$    🏨 **Excelsior Hotel.** This wonderful hotel is one of the more recent additions to downtown Tegucigalpa's hotel scene, but the Excelsior is located close to the neighborhood's border with Colonia Palmira, and it's got a very strong Palmira vibe. The Excelsior is a business-class hotel, but thanks to exceptionally friendly staff it seems a tad less formal than the other hotels around town in this category. Comfy rooms, orthopedic mattresses, hypoallergenic sheets and plush duvets add to the little touches here. **Pros:** friendly, attentive service; more Honduran flavor than most business-class hotels here; downtown, but Colonia Palmira is just a couple of blocks away. **Cons:** need to exercise care in this neighborhood at night. ⊠ *Av. Miguel Cervantes 1515, Col. Palmira* ☎ *237–2638* ⊕ *www.hotelandcasinoexcelsior.com* ⤴ *85 rooms* ⚒ *In-room: a/c, safe, refrigerator (some), Wi-Fi. In-hotel: restaurant, room service, bar, pool, laundry service, Internet terminal, parking (free)* ▤ *AE, D, DC, MC, V* ¶⃝ *BP.*

$$$$    🏨 **Honduras Maya.** The view of El Picacho Cristo, a 30-foot statue of Jesus perched on a nearby hill, is one of the best reasons to stay at this local landmark, the capital's original business-class hotel and an enduring favorite. This high-rise has undergone an extensive refurbishing and sparkles once again. The lobby is welcoming and the rooms are spacious. There is an updated gym and even a large pool. Dine in the pleasant terrace restaurant or stop by for a drink in the cozy bar with views from its own terrace. **Pros:** more Honduran flavor than the international chains; terrific views; friendly service. **Cons:** some disruption from remodeling going on at this writing. ⊠ *Av. República de Chile, Col. Palmira* ☎ *280–5000* ⊕ *www.hotelhondurasmaya.com* ⤴ *164 rooms, 5 suites* ⚒ *In-room: a/c, safe, Wi-Fi. In-hotel: restaurant, room service, bar, pool, gym, spa, laundry service, Internet terminal, parking (free)* ▤ *AE, D, DC, MC, V.*

$$    🏨 **Hotel Linda Vista.** If you're not careful, you might miss this colonial-**Fodor'sChoice** style hotel on its quiet street in the heart of Colonia Palmira—there's ★ no sign in front. Once you find it and step inside, however, its tiled floors, Honduran artwork, and pastel colors will make you feel that you've left the city behind. A scant six rooms here and a devoted return clientele mean you should make reservations in advance. You enter three of the rooms from inside the house; the other three are accessed from the flowered patio with beautiful views of the city. (*Linda vista* means "beautiful view," and the name is apt.) There's parking for only

two cars, but with all the hassles of driving in Tegucigalpa, we recommend not having a vehicle in the city at all. **Pros:** lovely manager; feels secluded in the heart of the city; terrific views. **Cons:** no sign in front; difficult to find. ⊠ *C. Las Acacias 1438, Col. Palmira* 🕾 *238–2099* ⊕ *www.lindavistahotel.net* 🖗 *6 rooms* ₰ *a/c, safe, Wi-Fi. In-hotel: restaurant, room service, bar, laundry service, Internet terminal, parking (free)* ⊟ *AE, D, DC, MC, V* ¹○¹ *BP.*

**$$$** ⊡**Hotel Portal del Ángel.** Hotel Portal del Ángel combines colonial ele-
★ gance with sleek modern design. Gilt mirrors and baroque religious art bring a hallowed air to the lobby, whereas cool colors and clean lines brighten the courtyard. You can dine here beneath pale-blue-and-lemon-colored arches where plants climb up bits of twirling wrought iron. Panels of hand-carved mahogany are used for headboards in the generously sized rooms. In the heart of Colonia Palmira, the hotel is close to trendy bars and restaurants. **Pros:** lovely rooms. **Cons:** offsite parking available only at night (but we don't recommend a car in the city anyway). ⊠ *Av. República de Perú 2115, Col. Palmira* 🕾 *239–6538* ⊕ *www.portaldelangelhn.com* 🖗 *19 rooms, 5 suites* ₰ *In-room: a/c, Wi-Fi. In-hotel: restaurant, room service, bar, pool, laundry service, Internet terminal, parking (paid)* ⊟ *AE, D, DC, MC, V* ¹○¹ *BP.*

**$$** ⊡**Leslie's Place.** You'll be offered fruit-flavored beverages upon your arrival at this friendly bed-and-breakfast. That won't be the last thoughtful touch provided by the exceptionally caring staff. Count on all-day coffee and an afternoon selection of appetizers. Rooms are spacious and cheerful, and it's a pleasure to get lost in the attractively tiled corridors of the converted house, which has a colonial feel despite only dating from the 1970s. Breakfast is served amid the green fronds that shade the patio garden, which overlooks a children's play area. **Pros:** friendly staff; cozy surroundings in a neighborhood of non-descript hotels. **Cons:** fills up quickly. ⊠ *Calzada San Martín 452, Col. Palmira* 🕾 *220–5325* ⊕ *www.dormir.com* 🖗 *7 rooms* ₰ *In-room: a/c, Wi-Fi. In-hotel: gym, laundry service, Internet terminal* ⊟ *AE, D, DC, MC, V* ¹○¹ *BP.*

## SOUTHERN TEGUCIGALPA

**$$$$** ⊡**Clarion Hotel Real Tegucigalpa.** A truly elegant lobby is your introduc-
**Fodor's Choice** tion to the Clarion Hotel Real Tegucigalpa, the most imposing of the
★ capital's large hotels. Geared to business travelers, it has a floor reserved for executives where you are pampered with a drink in the evening and breakfast the next morning. Some rooms are on the small side, although all are luxuriously appointed and a true bargain for a hotel of this stature. The pool is very attractive, and the gardens are immaculate. **Pros:** terrific value for a hotel of this category. **Cons:** Wi-Fi in standard rooms costs extra. ⊠ *Blvd. Juan Pablo II, Col. Alameda* 🕾 *286–6000* ⊕ *www.realhotelsandresorts.com* 🖗 *167 rooms* ₰ *In-room: a/c, safe, Wi-Fi. In-hotel: restaurant, room service, bar, pool, gym, spa, laundry service, Internet terminal, parking (free)* ⊟ *AE, D, DC, MC, V* ¹○¹ *CP.*

**$$** ⊡**Humuya Inn.** Once a private home, this friendly little inn is set in a
**Fodor's Choice** leafy neighborhood far from the center of the city. Sunlight streams
★ through the windows of the rooms, which have what we are tempted to call the comfiest beds in Honduras. High ceilings, ceramic-tile floors,

and locally made crafts make them feel particularly homey. Breakfast, with fresh banana and coconut breads, is included in the rate. Lunch and dinner are also available. If you want to make your own meals, the apartments have full kitchens. The place can be difficult to find, so before you leave home, ask the staff to e-mail or dictate the directions in Spanish for you to hand to your taxi driver once you get into town. **Pros:** super friendly service; quiet street. **Cons:** difficult to find; fills up quickly. ⊠ *Col. Humuya 1150* ☎ *235–7275* ⊕ *www.humuyainn.com* ⇨ *9 rooms, 3 suites, 5 apartments* ⌂ *In-room: a/c, safe, refrigerator, Wi-Fi. In-hotel: restaurant, laundry service, Internet terminal, parking (free)* ⊟ *AE, MC, V* ⦿ *BP.*

$$$$   ⊞ **Real InterContinental Tegucigalpa.** Built with business travelers in mind, this grand hotel in the heart of the city's financial district offers secretarial and courier services and conference facilities with state-of-the-art equipment. When you finish that meeting, head to the pool or the fully equipped gym. Great shopping is nearby, but you really never need to leave the area, as Multiplaza has plenty of boutiques to keep you occupied. Many of the comfortable rooms have CD players and VCRs, and one is designed for people with disabilities. **Pros:** all the business amenities you could desire, close to entertainment and shopping. **Cons:** need a car to stay here. ⊠ *Av. Roble s/n, across from Multiplaza, Col. Florencia* ☎ *290–2700, 888/424–6835 in North America* ⊕ *tegucigalpa. honduras.intercontinental.com* ⇨ *157 rooms, 7 suites* ⌂ *In-room: a/c, safe, refrigerator, Wi-Fi. In-hotel: 2 restaurants, room service, bar, pool, gym, spa, laundry service, no-smoking rooms, Internet terminal, parking (free)* ⊟ *AE, D, DC, MC, V.*

$$$$   ⊞ **Tegucigalpa Marriott Hotel.** The Marriott here began life as a Crowne Plaza hotel, and many locals still refer to it that way. Whether a Marriott or Crowne Plaza, this hotel could be the outlet of any upscale U.S. chain anywhere; that may be perfectly fine with you, or you may seek something that says "Honduras" more than this place does. (Bahía, the hotel gift shop, is an exception; you'll find a nice selection of Lencan pottery for sale here.) Do expect a solid, quality Marriott experience here in any case. As with the other hotels out in this part of town, you need a car or taxi to get anywhere, but the Marriott does offer free shuttle service to the nearby Multiplaza. **Pros:** comfortable surroundings; nice sports bar; distinctive gift shop. **Cons:** sameness of chain lodging; no room Wi-Fi (noticeable omission in a hotel of this stature). ⊠ *Blvd. Juan Pablo II, Col. Florencia* ☎ *232–0033* ⊕ *www.marriott. com* ⇨ *154 rooms* ⌂ *In-room: a/c, safe, refrigerator, Internet. In-hotel: 2 restaurants, room service, bar, gym, spa, laundry service, Internet terminal, Wi-Fi hotspot, parking (free).* ⊟ *AE, D, DC, MC, V* ⦿ *BP.*

# SHOPPING

Although it may seem more authentic to buy your Honduran souvenirs at their out-country source, the capital really can provide the answer to all your shopping needs if you're pressed for time. Many suggest that Tegucigalpa's best handicraft shopping is really in Valle de Ángeles, a favorite weekend destination about an hour outside the city. If you can't make it out to Valle, there are plenty of choices in the capital, too.

In Barrio El Centro, you will find a number of handicraft shops facing Avenida Miguel de Cervantes, which runs along the southern edge of Plaza Morazán. A block north is Calle Liquidámbar, a refurbished pedestrian street lined with shops frequented by locals (and mostly geared toward local shopping needs).

Don't ignore the gift shops in the large hotels; a couple of them offer outstanding selections of quality keepsakes of your visit. Although it may not occur to you to seek out souvenirs in a large shopping center, mall stores here and there have some terrific offerings, too.

### HANDICRAFTS

Souvenir vendors set up shop every day in the small plaza that fronts the **Iglesia Los Dolores** (✉ *C. Los Dolores at Av. Máximo Jérez, Barrio El Centro*). Much of what's for sale here is standard kitschy tourist fare, but you'll find a few nice pieces of Lencan pottery and other artisan work for lower prices than in a store with four walls.

Spruce up your dining room table with placemats, table runners, and glassware from **In Vitro** (✉ *Av. República de Panamá 2139, Col. Palmira* ☎ *232–3452* ⊕ *www.invitrohonduras.com*).The works here come from cooperatives near Valle de Ángeles and in the Mosquitía.

**Casa de Oro** (✉ *Plaza Miraflores, Blvd. Morazán, Col. Palmira* ☎ *239–7936*) sells a nice selection of silver jewelry with Mayan designs.

The Marriott hotel's gift shop, **Bahía** (✉ *Blvd. Juan Pablo II, Col. Florencia* ☎ *232-0033* ⊕ *www.marriott.com*) keeps a terrific selection of Lencan pottery and leather handbags.

The museum gift shop at the **Museo para la Identidad Nacional** (✉ *C. El Telégrafo and Av. Miguel Paz Barahona, Barrio El Centro* ☎ *238–5412* ⊕ *www.min.hn*) may be small, but it has some distinctive candles and leather purses in stock.

### BOOKS

Stock up on English-language books, magazines, and newspapers at **Metromedia** (✉ *Av. San Carlos, Col. Palmira* ☎ *221–0771* ✉ *Multiplaza, Blvd. San José Bosco, Col. Florencia* ☎ *232–1294*),which has a main store in Colonia Palmira and a branch at Multiplaza.

**Librería Guaymuras** (✉ *Av. Miguel Cervantes and C. Las Damas, Barrio El Centro* ☎ *237–5433* ⊕ *www.guaymuras.hn*) is Tegucigalpa's best Spanish-language bookstore with a good selection of novels and nonfiction works on history and politics.

### SHOPPING MALLS

Tegucigalpa's upper crust does its shopping in malls. One of the glitziest shopping centers in the capital is **Multiplaza** (✉ *Blvd. San José Bosco, Col. Florencia*). Stroll among the upscale shops, see the latest releases at the movie theater, and stop for a bite at the food court.The 130-store **Las Cascadas** (✉ *Blvd. de las Fuerzas Armadas de Honduras, Col. Florencia*) with theaters, food court, and upscale shops, is fast becoming a southside alternative to the long-established Multiplaza.The capital's newest mall is **Los Próceres** (✉ *Blvd. Morazán, Col. Palmira*) ; you could spend quite a while exploring its 91 stores.

## MARKETS

Most Hondurans wouldn't be caught dead at a shopping mall—or perhaps better expressed, couldn't afford the prices there. They buy all of life's necessities at a traditional market, which tosses in the sights and sounds of the real Central America for no extra charge. Only if you're feeling extremely intrepid, you can check out the capital's largest market, the enormous labyrinth of the **Mercado San Isidro** (⊠ *between Avdas. 5 and 7 and Cs. 1 and 2, Comayagüela*) in the Comayagüela district across the river from downtown. The upside is everything—and we mean everything—is for sale here in quantities large and small. (This is the kind of place where you could buy just one safety pin.)

The big downside is that tales of pickpocketings and purse snatchings are legion, although they are less likely to happen in the market building itself than in the surrounding streets. ■ **TIP→ If you go—and consider carefully whether you want to—take a taxi to and from and take nothing of value with you.** If you're hell-bent on seeing a local market and are able to spend a half day outside the city, Valle de Ángeles's **Pabellones Artesanales** *(see ⇨ Side Trips from Tegucigalpa, below)* is a much safer and calmer experience.

## CIGARS

Honduran cigars, which rival those from Cuba, are a popular souvenir. In Multiplaza is **Tabaco Fino** (⊠ *Blvd. San José Bosco, Col. Florencia* ☎ *No phone*). Near the American Embassy, **Casa Havana** (⊠ *Blvd. Morazán, Col. Palmira* ☎ *236–6632*) sells cigars.

**Casa de Puros** (⊠ *Los Próceres, Blvd. Morazán, Col. Palmira* ☎ *243–0213*✉ *Aeropuerto Internacional Toncontín* ☎ *233–0531* ⊕ *www. casadepuroshn.com*), with shops in Colonia Palmira and at the airport, has a fine cigar selection.

# NIGHTLIFE AND THE ARTS

Tegus's weeknights can be a tad drowsy, but Friday and Saturday nights get quite lively. (In fact, many nightspots keep Wednesday-through-Saturday schedules only.) Around Colonia Palmira you'll find good bars and restaurants, and Blvd. Morazán is home to the glitziest clubs. Pick up the current edition of *Honduras Weekly* to find out what's happening around town.

Don't be intimidated by the signs asking customers to leave their guns at the door. Most businesses and offices display such signs. (The numbers are small, but enough people do carry guns that businesses make their preferences known.) Remember to take a taxi after dark, even if you're going just a few blocks away. Management at most nightspots will be happy to help you get a cab when you're ready to head back to your hotel. All indoor venues are no-smoking.

## NIGHTLIFE

### BARS

One of the liveliest bars in town is **Taco Taco** (⊠ *Av. República de Argentina 2102, Col. Palmira* ☎ *232–2024*), where you compete with the itinerant mariachi and salsa musicians to be heard. Just off Boulevard

Morazán near Colonia Palmira, **Salt & Pepper** (✉ *C. Castaño, Col. Minitas* ☎ *235–7738*) comes the closest of any place in the city to replicating the flavor of an English pub.

**Rojo, Verde y Ajo** (✉ *one block from Blvd. Morazán, Col. Palmira*) is a popular restaurant and bar, with a great atmosphere and jazz music. The name translates to Red, Green, and Garlic. Downtown restaurant **La Terraza de Don Pepe** (✉ *Av. Cristóbal Colón, Barrio El Centro* ☎ *237–1084*) serves a good selection of beers at its top-floor terrace and has karaoke on weekends.

Hotel bars are a good place to end the evening or to while it away if you don't feel like going out. Guests and nonguests are always welcome. The name of **Mirador** (✉ *Av. República de Chile, Col. Palmira* ☎ *280–5000* ⊕ *www.hotelhondurasmaya.hn*) in the Honduras Maya Hotel means "lookout," and the name is apt, with its lovely view of the city lights from its terrace.

At the Marriott, the **Winner Sports Bar** (✉ *Blvd. Juan Pablo II, Col. Florencia* ☎ *232–0033* ⊕ *www.marriott.com*) has a big-screen TV— and we mean big—with soccer usually on. There's live entertainment weekend nights. **Nau** (✉ *Avd. Roble s/n, Col. Florencia* ☎ *290–2700* ⊕ *tegucigalpa.honduras.intercontinental.com*) at the Real InterContinental Tegucigalpa overlooks the hotel pool.

### CLUBS

In Colonia Palmira is a cluster of clubs that are popular with foreigners and locals alike. South of Colonia Palmira, Avenida Juan Pablo II is popular with the young-and-trendy crowd. **Confetti's** (✉ *Blvd. Morazán, Col. Palmira*) is one of the city's most popular discos.

**Bamboo** (✉ *Blvd. Morazán, Col. Palmira* ☎ *232–2024*) disco gets good crowds most nights, especially when there are events, such as beer promotions or concerts. Dress to impress here; the place can be a little velvet rope-y.

The music is loud and the drinks flow freely at **Kabbalah** (✉ *Av. República de Panamá, Col. Palmira* ☎ *238–5435* ⊕ *www.kabbalahlounge.com*), one of the capital's hottest new clubs. Dance to live salsa music Friday nights at **La Caramba** (✉ *Off 4ta Avenida, Col. Rubén Darío* ☎ *239–8440*), just south of Colonia Palmira.

The music is more techno than '70s at **Studio 54** (✉ *Complejo Casa Vieja, Col. Palmira* ☎ *9917–3600*), but the dancing is no less fervent than it was at the famed New York club of some three decades ago.

**Tropical Port** (✉ *Av. Juan Pablo II, Col. Alameda*) is best known for its thumping disco music. **El Nilo Ai Kap Bar** (✉ *Av. Juan Pablo II, Col. Alameda*) is an enormous disco with an Egyptian theme, open Wednesday through Saturday; it draws a good crowd especially on the weekend.

### CASINOS

Try your luck at blackjack, roulette, baccarat, and the slot machines at the **Casino Royale** (✉ *Av. República de Chile, Col. Palmira* ☎ *280–5000* ⊕ *www.hotelhondurasmaya.hn*), the capital's only true casino. It adjoins the Honduras Maya Hotel. Dress up and bring your passport to get in.

**FILM**

The downtown **Café Paradiso** (✉ *Av. Miguel Paz Barahona at C. Las Damas, Barrio El Centro* ☎ *237–0337*) screens indie films each Thursday evening and has Tuesday-night poetry readings. If your Spanish is up to it, **Sabor Cubano** (✉ *Av. República de Argentina, Col. Palmira* ☎ *235–9947*) is a good place to both see a movie and people-watch.

The six-theater multiplex **Cinemark** (✉ *Blvd. Juan Pablo II, Col. Florencia* ☎ *231–2044* ⊕ *www.cinemarkca.com* ☺ *noon–about 11 pm*) in the Multiplaza shows Hollywood releases a few weeks after their U.S. premieres. Most films are shown in English with Spanish subtitles. Children's movies are the exception: they're dubbed.

**THE ARTS**

**Teatro Nacional Manuel Bonilla** (✉ *Av. Miguel Paz Barahona and C. La Concordia, Barrio El Centro* ☎ *222–4366* ⊕ *www.teatronacional-manuelbonilla.hn*) hosts frequent performances by music and dance groups, including Honduras's highly regarded National Symphony Orchestra. Ticket prices are about half of what you'd pay for a comparable event back home. Didn't pack your formal eveningwear? No one will look askance at you as long as you don't show up in shorts, jeans, or a T-shirt.

## SPORTS AND THE OUTDOORS

As it is in most countries in Latin America, soccer is akin to religion in Honduras, especially with the national team advancing to the 2010 World Cup competition in South Africa for the first time in decades. (No matter that Honduras did not win single a match there; all eyes and ears were glued to TV and radio respectively when their beloved team played.) In fact, the populace is so passionate about fútbol that a game with El Salvador in 1969 sparked a war—although the underlying conflicts were more serious. The fútbol season runs October to July, when **Estadio Nacional** (✉ *Barrio Morazán, Col. Palmira*) hosts matches weekends and Wednesday. Check the local papers for times. Admission is about L25.

# SIDE TRIPS FROM TEGUCIGALPA

## SUYAPA

*7 km (4½ mi) southeast of Tegucigalpa.*

France has Lourdes. Portugal has Fátima. Mexico has Guadalupe. In the far southern suburbs of Tegucigalpa is Honduras's very own site, Suyapa, where the faithful believe that the Virgin Mary has worked miracles. Tradition holds that a farmer stopped for the night here in 1747. A sharp object poked him in the back as he slept on the ground. He cast it away several times, assuming it to be a stone, only to have it return to the same position. On closer inspection, he noticed it was a 6-cm. (2½-inch) figure of the Virgin Mary with indigenous features. The farmer and his family built a shrine to the Virgin in their home.

Upon hearing of the ill health of a military officer, they prayed for his recovery. The officer recovered, and was so grateful that he ordered a church constructed to house the figure. In the two-and-a-half centuries since, thousands of Hondurans have made similar appeals and attribute betterment of their health and welfare to the Virgin of Suyapa, now the country's patron saint.

This is quite a miraculous Virgin, certainly in terms of appearing to get around on her own accord. In 1986 she went missing, reappearing some time later in the men's room of La Terraza de Don Pepe restaurant in downtown Tegucigalpa. Whether she got to the restaurant on her own or was stolen and abandoned there is debated, but the eatery has a shrine in her honor to this day.

### GETTING HERE AND AROUND

A taxi is the easiest way to reach the basilica in Suyapa. Plan on paying about L150 for a trip from the city center, and about half that if you're staying at one of the big chains on the south side of Tegucigalpa.

### EXPLORING

The statue of the Virgen de Suyapa can be found in the 16th-century **Iglesia de Suyapa,** an intimate church where the flickering of candles lit by the faithful can be quite humbling. The figure, so tiny you'll need to squint to see it, is housed above the altar. Religious items, such as decorative prayer cards featuring the image of the Virgin, are for sale in the stalls down the steps from the church. Each February there is a pilgrimage to celebrate the day of the Virgin of Suyapa, and many vendors and food stalls are set up. ⊠ *Blvd. Suyapa.*

Overshadowing the smaller church is the mammoth white-and-gray gothic **Basílica de Suyapa.** The beautiful sky-blue stained-glass windows are inspirational, but the basilica's haughty air makes it far less intimate than the church. It was built in 1954 to house the Virgen de Suyapa and to accommodate the crowds who pay homage, but she is not fond of it. On many occasions she has left it at night, found back at her original perch the following morning. She consents to be displayed here on her feast day, February 3, when pilgrims descend on the town to honor her. ⊠ *Blvd. Suyapa, across from Universidad Nacional Autónoma de Honduras (UNAH)* ☏ *No phone* ⊕ *www.virgendesuyapa.hn* ☽ *Daily 8–noon and 2–5.*

## SANTA LUCÍA

*14 km (8½ mi) northeast of Tegucigalpa heading out of the city on Av. de Los Próceres.*

Santa Lucía is a pleasant mining town—this is the first locale where colonial-era silver was struck in the 16th century—with plenty of winding cobblestone streets, red-tile roofs, and colorful gardens. Only 14 km (8½ mi) northeast of the capital, it is surrounded by hills thick with pines. While Tegucigalpa is hardly the balmy tropics, the capital will seem positively sweltering by comparison when you arrive here at Santa Lucía's 5,000-feet altitude. Evenings can be brisk. Like Valle de Ángeles farther down the road, Santa Lucía hums with activity on Saturday and

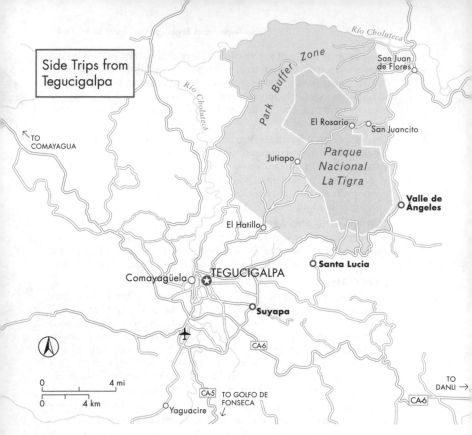

Side Trips from
Tegucigalpa

Río Choluteca

Park Buffer Zone

San Juan
de Flores

Río Choluteca

El Rosario    San Juancito

TO
COMAYAGUA

Jutiapo

*Parque
Nacional
La Tigra*

Valle de
Ángeles

El Hatillo

**Santa Lucía**

Comayagüela     ★ TEGUCIGALPA

**Suyapa**

CA-6

0          4 mi

0          4 km

CA-5   TO GOLFO DE
FONSECA

Yaguacire

TO
DANLI →

CA-6

Sunday; both towns are favorite weekend getaways for capital residents.
The town is quiet other days. No matter what the day of the week, you
might stumble upon a few Americans here: the Peace Corps uses Santa
Lucía as a training base for its volunteers assigned to Honduras.

### GETTING HERE AND AROUND

The drive to Santa Lucía takes about 30 minutes from the capital on
a good but hilly two-lane road. Watch for the turnoff to Santa Lucía
about 12 km (7 mi) after leaving Tegucigalpa. Buses to Santa Lucía
leave the capital every 30 to 45 minutes until about 5 pm from a stop
on Avenida Los Próceres and Avenida República Dominicana across
from the monument to Simón Bolívar. Travel time is about 30 minutes.
Tickets are L20.

The town itself strings along the main road. Strolling the streets of Santa
Lucía is more difficult than in more-compact Valle de Ángeles nearby;
a car is useful for getting around.

### EXPLORING

The pretty whitewashed **Iglesia de Santa Lucía** (⊠ *Parque Central,* ☎ *No
phone* ⊗ *Hours vary*) dates from the town's founding in the mid-16th
century. It is most notable for the wooden crucifix called Christ of
Las Mercedes, a gift from King Felipe of Spain and brought here by
the Spanish in 1574. Church doors are always open on Sunday; other

days of the week, you may need to ask at the parish offices next door if someone can let you inside.

Check out all that is creepy and crawly at the small but informative **Serpentario Santa Lucía** (✉ *Parque Central,* ☎ *No phone* 🖃 *Free, donation requested* ☉ *Daily 9–4*), with a small collection of snakes, both venomous and nonvenomous. They represent a variety of the snakes found around the country, although most are native to the nearby Parque Nacional La Tigra.

## WHERE TO STAY

$$  🏨 **Hotel Santa Lucía Resort.** Signs for the Hotel Santa Lucía Resort appear the moment you leave Tegucigalpa, and by the time you arrive, you'll feel you already know the place. Once you see all the pine trees and feel the brisk air, you'll know you've left the tropics behind. Rooms in the main lodge are bigger than those in the cabins scattered around the property. A few come with a small kitchen. **Pros:** wonderful seclusion; friendly staff. **Cons:** rough last stretch of road to get here; chilly at night; some dated rooms; a few rooms have a musty smell. ✉ *1½ km (1 mi) before entrance to Santa Lucía* ☎ *779–0540* ⊕ *www.hotelsantaluciaresort.com* 🛏 *24 rooms* ♿ *In-room: no a/c, no phone, kitchen (some), Wi-Fi. In-hotel: restaurant, bar, laundry service, Internet terminal, parking (free).* ▭ *AE, MC, V* ◎| *BP.*

$  🏨 **Posada de Doña Estefania.** This pretty bed-and-breakfast offers a spectacular view of the pine-covered mountains. Filled with quaint touches, the inn is the perfect place to watch the sunset from your private patio. Continental breakfast is served in the café, where you can enjoy wine or beer in the evening. ✉ *Just before Catholic church* ☎ *779–0441* 🛏 *5 rooms* ♿ *In-room: no a/c, no phone, no TV. In-hotel: bar, parking (free)* ▭ *No credit cards* ◎| *CP.*

# VALLE DE ÁNGELES

*22 km (14 mi) northeast of Tegucigalpa, 8 km (5 mi) past turnoff to Santa Lucía, heading out of the city on Av. de Los Próceres.*

It bustles with tourists from the capital on weekends, but during the week Valle de Ángeles maintains the atmosphere of a colonial mining town of centuries past. Sunday is the day to arrive, when you can ride around in a horse-drawn cart or browse among the crafts found under five *pabellones* (pavilions). It's worth taking time to look for mahogany bowls, reed baskets, woven hammocks, embroidered blouses, bead necklaces, and bizarre ceramic chickens in bright shades of crimson.

Valle is also one of Honduras's blossoming real estate destinations. It hasn't quite achieved Roatán's boom status yet—and we hope it never does—but it is home to a small but growing expatriate population.

It gets brisk out here. Although at 4,300 feet altitude, Valle is not quite the elevation of nearby Santa Lucía, you'll notice a slight chill in the air when you come out here from Tegucigalpa. The unique climate means it's nursery country; on your way here, you'll pass a string of roadside *viveros* (nurseries) where folks from the city come out on weekends to purchase plants for their houses and gardens.

The old church in the central square lacks the colonial charm of the one in Santa Lucía, but the nearby park has a painted fountain surrounded by lush trees. A comical macaw sometimes plays hide-and-seek on the roof of the bandstand.

> **NOT IN THE TROPICS ANYMORE**
>
> Honduras's decidedly untropical national tree and animal are the pine tree and white-tailed deer, respectively. Both are abundant in the forested hills around the capital.

### GETTING HERE AND AROUND

With weekend traffic, plan on the drive to Valle de Ángeles taking about 30 to 45 minutes on a good but hilly two-lane road. Valle-bound buses leave Tegucigalpa every 30 to 45 minutes until about 5 PM from a stop on Avenida Los Próceres and Avenida República Dominicana across from the monument to Simón Bolívar. Travel time is 45 minutes. Tickets cost L20.

Although Valle has more people than Santa Lucía, it seems more compact with its orderly grid of streets organized like a traditional Spanish colonial town. A few of these have been designated for pedestrians only.

### EXPLORING

Little Valle de Ángeles has a surprisingly decent museum, the **Museo Santa María** (✉ *Barrio Abajo* ☎ 767-2090 ⊕ *www.museosantamaria. com* ☉ *Daily 8–5* ☞ *L20*), with a flashy, musical Web site. The museum houses several displays about the history and culture of Valle and surrounding area, and is especially strong on the region's mining heritage.

The center of Valle de Ángeles can seem like one big artisan market, especially on weekends when visitors come out here from Tegucigalpa. You'll never see so many T-shirts, but there is much more for sale here. Wander inside the **Pabellones Artesanales** (✉ *one block east of Parque Central* ☎ *No phone* ☉ *Daily 9–5*). The name means "artisan pavilions" in Spanish; you'll find Lenca pottery, handcrafted leather, dolls, and straw mats, all at prices lower than you'll find anywhere back in the capital.

### WHERE TO EAT

$    ✕ **Carnes El Español.** You smell the sizzling chorizo and *carnitas* (chunks of beef) cooked by Don Manolo even before you see his popular restaurant. ✉ *Parque Central* ☎ *No phone* ☐ *No credit cards*.

LATIN AMERICAN

$    ✕ **El Anafre.** This restaurant is named for a traditional Honduran mush of refried beans, cream, and cheese served with tortilla chips in a clay container, but don't be misled: other items on the menu, the pastas and pizzas in particular, are good here, too. It's a great place to down a beer, as it is often open until 10 or later. ✉ *Parque Central* ☎ 766–2942 ☉ *Closed Mon. and Tues.* ☐ *MC, V*.

LATIN AMERICAN

$$$    ✕ **La Florida.** A combination pony farm, playground, and miniature zoo, La Florida is a popular place for families and weekend events. There is a restaurant with typical Honduran beef and chicken dishes, as well as anafres of refried beans and cheese. The outdoor area has a small swimming pool, children's playground, and sand volleyball, as well as shaded picnic and dining areas. Don't miss the L10 pony rides, if you belong to the under-10 age bracket. There is a very large stable of ponies

LATIN AMERICAN

and horses, and they offer trail rides for adults as well. In the back is a small zoo with the white-tailed deer of Honduras and a tapir, as well as many birds. ⊠ *Main rd. to Valle de Ángeles* ☎ *766–2121* ◷ *Closed Mon. and Tues.* ⊟ *No credit cards.*

## WHERE TO STAY

$$ 🏨 **La Posada del Ángel.** This colonial-style hotel, complete with a grassy courtyard, is popular with weekend crowds from Tegucigalpa. All rooms have splendid mountain views. There's a pool and plenty of activities for the kids. Reservations should be made a few days in advance for weekends. **Pros:** wonderful seclusion. **Cons:** fills up on weekends; chilly at night. ⊠ *C. Principal* ☎ *766–2233* ⊕ *www.hotelposadadelangel.net* 📞 *25 rooms* ⚲ *In-room: no a/c. In-hotel: restaurant, bar, pool, parking (free)* ⊟ *AE, MC, V* ⏐◎⏐ *EP.*

$ 🏨 **Villas del Valle.** Just over two-dozen cabins scatter around this property on the edge of town heading out to the village of San Juancito. Stay in the brick ones—they're much nicer than the drywall units, although all are a bit on the plain side. An aboveground pool keeps the kids who stay here happy. **Pros:** wonderful seclusion; friendly staff. **Cons:** fills up on weekends; chilly at night; not within walking distance of town. ⊠ *Km 1, highway to San Juancito* ☎ *766–2534* ⊕ *www.villasdelvalle. com* 📞 *27 cabins* ⚲ *In-room: no a/c, no phone, kitchen (some), refrigerator (some), Wi-Fi. In-hotel: restaurant, bar, pool, laundry service, Internet terminal, parking (free).* ⊟ *MC, V* ⏐◎⏐ *EP.*

# PARQUE NACIONAL LA TIGRA

*20 km (12 mi) north of Tegucigalpa on road to Jutiapa.*

One of the most accessible national parks in Honduras, Parque Nacional La Tigra protects a cloud forest considered one of the most beautiful in the world. Just 20 km (12 mi) north of Tegucigalpa, the park feels worlds away. You'll forget the crowds in the capital as you wander among the orchids, bromeliads, and treelike ferns that tower above you. If you start early in the morning, you can see much of the park in a day, but you'll gain even more by spending the night. With patience and a bit of luck you might spot ocelots, peccaries, armadillos, and white-faced monkeys, but don't consider your visit a wash if you don't see them; they are extremely reclusive. You will be able to spot many of the more than 350 species of birds here. La Tigra is second only to Lago de Yojoa as Honduras's top birding destination *(see* ⇨ *Lago de Yojoa in Western Honduras.)* The bird-watcher's Holy Grail, the magnificent resplendent quetzal with its showy plumage, is here, too, but difficult to locate.

Logging and mining had almost entirely stripped the area of its trees until the Honduran government set aside the land for conservation in 1982. (This was the headquarters of the El Rosario Mining Company.) Most of the trees you see are secondary growth, but the park is a reassuring example of what can be accomplished by environmentally-minded officials.

### GETTING HERE AND AROUND

Two entrances take you into the 241-square-km (93-square-mi) park, each with a visitor center where you can talk with rangers and pick up a trail map. The western entrance at Jutiapa is more accessible from Tegucigalpa, but the one at El Rosario has an old mining hospital that has been converted into a hostel with dorm-style accommodations. Overnighting in the park is a great way to appreciate the early-morning-birding hours, before other tourists arrive. Contact the Fundación Amigos de la Tigra (Amitigra).

There are currently eight different trails, including one designed with children in mind. The Sendero Principal leads from one end of the park to the other. The other seven trails branch off this main pathway. More challenging trails include La Cascada, which leads to a waterfall, and La Esperanza, which winds its way to the highest point in the park. The Sendero Bosque Nublado gives you the best sense of being in a cloud forest with its dewy vegetation. The short Sendero Granadillas clocks in at less than 1 km (½ mi) and is a good choice for kids. Bring plenty of water and layers of clothes you can peel off when you work up a sweat. Be prepared to get wet and muddy. (Although being in a cloud forest means subjecting yourself to moisture year-round, you'll get less wet during Honduras's November–April dry season.) Paths are well marked, but a guide will help you spot creatures you would otherwise miss.

### SAFETY

Under no circumstances should you leave the marked trails at any time: soggy, muddy off-path ground is ripe for slips and falls. Nor should you enter any of the abandoned mineshafts you'll see here.

### ESSENTIALS

**Fundación Amigos de la Tigra (Amitigra)** ⊠ *Edificio Italia, Col. Palmira* ☎ *238–6269 in Tegucigalpa* ⊕ *www.amitigra.org* ⊙ *Daily 9–5.*

### WHERE TO STAY

$ ⊡ **Ecoalbergue El Rosario.** This cabin in the clouds is operated by the Amitigra Foundation, a nonprofit organization that supports La Tigra National Park. Reservations should be made in advance through its offices in Tegucigalpa. You can also arrange transportation through Amitigra. Accommodation here is basic, but the caretakers are happy to make you breakfast and dinner. The warm shower is a real treat in the wilderness. **Pros:** secluded; real "get back to nature" feeling. **Cons:** difficult to get here; spartan accommodation; chilly at night. ⊠ *El Rosario* ☎ *238–6269 in Tegucigalpa* ⚐ *In-room: no a/c, no phone, no TV* ⤶ *2 rooms* ⊟ *No credit cards.*

# Southern
# Honduras

**WORD OF MOUTH**

"I recently made my first trip to Honduras's south. (I'd never gone any farther south than Tegucigalpa before.) I was pleasantly surprised. It's quiet and understated and, for the time being, you'll feel like you have the area to yourself. Actually, I doubt it will become overrun with tourists any time soon. The bigger colonial towns in western Honduras get all the press, but I'd rank Yuscarán up there with them any day."

—Jeff

By Jeffrey Van Fleet

Even old Honduran hands scratch their heads when someone mentions the country's southern region. (The remote Mosquitía in the northeast part of the country manages to attract more international visitors than southern Honduras does.) But it's really no effort at all if you're already in Tegucigalpa, and you'll be repaid warmly by what you find in this least-traveled part of Honduras.

*Warm* is the operative word when considering travel in the south. The devil takes his winter vacation here, Hondurans are fond of saying about the southern part of their country. Make no mistake: as the landscape tumbles down from lofty Tegucigalpa to the Pacific Ocean, it swelters here down south, with sunbaked Choluteca, the region's largest metropolis, proudly proclaiming that it is also Honduras's hottest city. (For better or for worse, residents have accepted their climate for what it is and have even tried to put a positive spin on it.) But don't write off the entire south as hellishly hot: slightly higher-elevation, temperate areas around Yuscarán and Danlí do provide pleasant, welcome relief from the stifling heat.

Farming and fishing are the mainstays here in this fertile region— mangoes, sugar, tobacco, pineapple, corn, cattle, and shrimp are all in abundant evidence in the south—but the country over a century ago decided to focus on the agricultural potential of the northern Caribbean lowlands, which are more spacious and, with nearby ports, more easily accessible to North American and European markets. The south has languished ever since and is today economically one of Honduras's least developed regions.

Paradoxically, those visitors most familiar with this part of the country are those who have little interest in Honduras at all. The country's short 137 km (85 mi) of the Pan-American Highway pass through here as a quick link between El Salvador and Nicaragua; these 85 mi are seen by anyone who is driving or busing through Central America. Southern Honduras's treasures are fewer and do require a bit more searching, but if you treat the area as more than a rest stop as you're headed for countries south, you'll be amply rewarded. The south will never be able to compete with the Caribbean coast, one of the world's premier fun-in-the-sun destinations, when it comes to where Honduras directs its tourism-building dollars. Frankly, we hope the region never turns into Tela or Roatán either, and the Pacific coast's amazing sunsets are something the Caribbean side can only dream about.

## TOP REASONS TO GO

**Bask in the colonial past.** The town of Yuscarán might not have a must-see sightseeing list with items for you to check off, but few Honduran towns have preserved their colonial heritage as lovingly as this oasis tucked away in the hills.

**Enjoy a good cigar.** Not that we would ever advocate smoking, but if you're already a connoisseur of fine cigars, the colonial town of Danlí is your place to buy a quality Honduran product and learn how the tobacco is grown, harvested, cured, and rolled. The climate is nearly perfect for the fine art of cigar making.

**Find a secluded beach.** *Beach* and *privacy* long ago became a contradiction in terms on much of Honduras's Caribbean coast, but on Isla del Tigre, just off the Pacific coast, they're practically synonyms.

**Pay homage to "El Sabio."** Arguably Honduras's most revered figure, independence hero José Cecilio del Valle ("the Wise One") was born in Choluteca. A visit to his home gives you insight into the history of this sometimes-complicated country.

# ORIENTATION AND PLANNING

## ORIENTATION

Though this region always gets lumped under one "Southern Honduras" heading because of its small size and proximity to Tegucigalpa—we do it, too—you can really think of it as two distinct areas. (Most visitors who do make it to this part of the country take on only one region or the other.) The colonial towns of Yuscarán and Danlí hide themselves away in the cooler hills east of the capital, but both lie a bit too far outside the Tegucigalpa orbit to be easy day trips from there. South of the capital, lowland Choluteca and Isla del Tigre off the Pacific coast in the Gulf of Fonseca enjoy—*endure* would be a better word—warmer temperatures. Honduras shares sovereignty over the gulf with neighboring El Salvador and Nicaragua; the rest of the islands in that body of water, all visible from Isla del Tigre, belong to El Salvador.

**Yuscarán.** An enchanting town not too far from the capital wins rave reviews for its efforts to preserve its preindependence heritage. Some 200 tidy whitewashed buildings connected with a network of cobblestone streets around a shady central park form its colonial-era core. The town makes a pleasant place to spend the day soaking up the past.

**Danlí.** A visit to the town that tobacco helped prosper is a must for anybody who appreciates a fine cigar. Its natural conditions are ideal for tobacco cultivation, nearly identical to those back in Cuba from where a group of cigar manufacturers fled a half century ago to set up shop here. Oh, and Danlí contains a pretty restored colonial sector, too.

**Choluteca.** Even if the south's hub city (and Honduras's fourth largest) is seen by most as merely a way station, Choluteca offers a couple of interesting historical sites, and is revered by Hondurans as the birthplace of one of its independence heroes. It provides a chance to fuel up your car, wallet, and stomach, too, in a region where such services are few and far between.

**Isla del Tigre.** Honduras's outpost in the Gulf of Fonseca, the inlet of the Pacific Ocean that it shares with El Salvador and Nicaragua, is the Pacific coast's beach central. Except for dry-season weekends and Christmas and Holy Weeks, when residents of the capital flock here, the island is pretty quiet and is almost unknown among international visitors. If you seek a quiet, secluded beach—and that's becoming a scarce commodity on the country's Caribbean coast—Isla del Tigre might just be your kind of place.

### GREAT ITINERARIES

**If You Have 2 days:** Head east from Tegucigalpa to take in the colonial towns of Yuscarán and Danlí. Pick one in which to base yourself and visit the other as a half-day trip. (Yuscarán has one tiny hotel worth choosing for its cozy charm, but reservations are a must. Danlí's main lodging is much larger—space is rarely a problem—but the place is kind of nondescript.) In whichever order you choose, stroll around Yuscarán's colonial center and immerse yourself in its small-town past, peeking in at the exhibits at the Casa Fortín. In Danlí, make a point to visit one of the cigar factories.

**If You Have 3 days:** Three days gives you ample time to take in Isla del Tigre. Get an early start from Tegucigalpa and head south. Negotiate your passage with one of the boatmen at Coyolito on the mainland; 15 minutes later you'll be on Honduras's very own Pacific island. Three days allows you time to sample the island's three beaches most popular with visitors, and factors in time to discover lesser known ones, too. If you can arrange your three days to fall over a weekend, more facilities will be open. If you're there during the week, things will be *very* quiet.

## PLANNING

### WHEN TO GO

Southern Honduras, especially its Pacific coast, sees a slightly shorter wet season than the rest of the country, with the rains arriving in June and becoming gradually stronger until September. By mid-October they begin to taper off, but October and November are still lush and green. December sees slightly cooler temperatures, although no time of year in this warm region could ever be called "chilly." March and April can become unbearably hot and parched on the coast, although residents of Tegucigalpa do flock to the beaches near Choluteca and on Isla del Tigre for Holy Week and on weekends. The island is blessed with ocean breezes that mitigate the intense heat even during the hottest months. Any time of year, the higher elevations of Yuscarán and Danlí provide a respite from the heat of the coast; you will notice a distinct temperature difference in these two towns, even to the point where you'll appreciate long sleeves in either town after the sun goes down.

## GETTING HERE AND AROUND

### AIR TRAVEL

No domestic airports exist in this region. The south lies so close to Tegucigalpa that most visitors traveling by air arrive and depart via the capital's Aeropuerto Internacional Toncontín.

Contacts **Aeropuerto Internacional Toncontín** (☎ 233–1115 in Tegucigalpa).

### BUS TRAVEL

Large coach-style buses travel many times daily between Tegucigalpa and Choluteca. Smaller buses connect the capital with Yuscarán and Danlí.

### CAR TRAVEL

Major roads are good in the south. Secondary roads are passable with occasional potholes. Renting a car is not possible in this region. Pick up a vehicle back in Tegucigalpa.

### HEALTH AND SAFETY

A hat with a brim, plenty of sunscreen, and a filled water bottle are musts in this sunbaked region. Riptides on the Pacific coast always pose a risk for swimmers. Never swim alone—that's sound advice anywhere—but especially on Isla del Tigre's oft-unpopulated beaches.

Hospital del Sur in Choluteca is the region's largest hospital.

Hospitals **Hospital del Sur** (✉ C. Oriente 5, Choluteca ☎ 782–0231).

### MONEY MATTERS

Banks and ATMs are scarce in this region. (They're nonexistent on Isla del Tigre.) Replenish your wallet in Tegucigalpa or as you pass through Choluteca. Danlí also has a bank and an ATM. Yuscarán has a bank without an ATM. Businesses here tend toward the small, mom-and-pop side. Many do not accept credit cards and are not equipped to handle dollars.

### RESTAURANTS AND CUISINE

Fancy, upscale dining does not really exist here. When you come to the south, prepare yourself for small, family-run restaurants serving filling, basic cuisine, much the same as the *típico* (traditional) Honduran fare you've been dining on elsewhere in the country.

Corn is king in the south, with Danlí the self-proclaimed "corn capital of Honduras." It's natural that corn shows up in many dishes in this region. Bread and tortillas here are all made from corn flour. The staple tamales come in many forms and sizes, and if corn can be incorporated, southerners know how to do it. *Tamalitos,* literally "little tamales," are filled with corn and served with sour cream. *Montucas* are tamales filled with grated corn, mixed with sugar, milk, cloves, and the meat of your choice—chicken, beef, or pork. *Atol* is a corn pudding usually served so runny that you can drink it as a beverage. It can also be chilled and solidified, more like a pudding to which we are accustomed. And good, old-fashioned corn on the cob is called simply *elote.*

## A BIT OF HISTORY

The history of southern Honduras could be subtitled *A Chronicle of What Might Have Been*. Yuscarán was once a major center of silver mining. Amapala, on Isla del Tigre, was once the country's largest port. The entire region was once Honduras's breadbasket, a fertile agricultural region that supplied the country with its food. Then came a new-fangled product called the banana. The multinational industrial giants that took control of its cultivation in the late 1800s saw more promise in the flat, expansive Caribbean lowlands than in the isolated south, which had no space to grow, no terrain suitable for construction of a railroad, and more difficult port access to U.S. markets. (Those were pre-Panama Canal days, after all, and an 1849 plan to construct a canal through Honduras between the Pacific and Caribbean coasts never got off the ground.) The entire country made a 180-degree turn and began to look north rather than south. Development in the south has never caught up.

**ABOUT THE HOTELS**

Acceptable accommodation is sparse in this region, with the destinations we list each having, at best, a couple of decent hotels, and many of those having a small number of rooms. That makes reservations a good idea any time of the year. Remember also that many smaller places in this part of the country have no Internet access. You'll need to call to make a reservation. The good news? Lodging is extremely reasonably priced in this part of Honduras. You'll never pay more than $75 a night for two people—and usually it's much, much less. Beach lodgings do raise their rates slightly on weekends during the dry season and during Christmas and Easter weeks.

| WHAT IT COSTS IN HONDURAN LEMPIRAS | | | | |
| --- | --- | --- | --- | --- |
| | ¢ | $ | $$ | $$$ | $$$$ |
| Restaurants | under L75 | L75–L150 | L151–L250 | L251–L350 | over L350 |
| Hotels | under L750 | L750–L1,250 | L1,251–L1,750 | L1,751–L2,250 | over L2,250 |

Restaurant prices are per person for a main course at dinner. Hotel prices are for two people in a standard double room in high season.

# YUSCARÁN

*61 km (37 mi) east of Tegucigalpa.*

The charming colonial town of Yuscarán sits a little too far out from Tegucigalpa to be an easy lunch trip (at least not in the way closer Santa Lucía and Valle de Ángeles are), but it gets high marks for having better-preserved colonial atmosphere. As happened in the capital, silver was struck here in the late 17th century, and Yuscarán boomed through the end of the 1800s. The entire town was declared a national monument in 1979, and some 200 buildings from the pre-independence era remain intact here with strict standards on their maintenance. The town of about 2,000 Yuscaranos sits in the semitropical Pacific Slope, a transitional area between the highland capital and the coastal lowlands. Though it isn't as high as Tegucigalpa, at 850 meters (2,800 ft) of elevation the town still enjoys a pleasant year-round springlike climate that is a welcome refuge from southern Honduras's stifling heat.

Sparkling whitewashed buildings line the winding streets that radiate from a tree-shaded central square. Prisoners constructed and, for years, maintained the town's cobblestone streets (Honduras's national penitentiary being located just outside of town). Hurricane Mitch in 1998 badly damaged the facility and the inmates were transferred elsewhere; the city now has a regular maintenance crew and does itself just as proud.

This is mango country par excellence, with Yuscarán celebrating its most important crop in a Festival de Mangos the first weekend in June. Sample the town's signature fruit—you never knew there were so many ways it could be prepared—and watch the spectacle of residents playing donkey polo, exactly what the name implies.

### GETTING HERE AND AROUND
Highway CA-6 heads east out of Tegucigalpa toward Danlí. The turnoff to Yuscarán is at the crossroads of El Empalme, 47 km (28 mi) east of the capital. Yuscarán lies another 14 km (9 mi) south.

Buses leave eight times daily from Tegucigalpa for Yuscarán. The two-hour trip deposits you at the town's Parque Central.

### MONEY MATTERS
Yuscarán has a branch of Banco Occidente that will exchange dollars and lempiras, but it has no ATM.

### ESSENTIALS
**Banks Banco Occidente** (⊠ *Parque Central*).

## EXPLORING

**Casa de Fortín.** The 1850 home that once belonged to Yuscarán's wealthy, prominent Fortín family has been converted into a small city museum with exhibits of what the area was like in the 19th century. To be honest, the house itself is far more interesting than the rudimentary displays on mining and agriculture. Hours can be irregular. ⊠ *Parque Central* ☎ *793–7160* 🖾 *Free* ⊘ *Weekdays 8–noon and 2–4.*

**Distilería El Buen Gusto.** One of Honduras's most popular alcoholic beverages is distilled right here in Yuscarán. *Aguardiente* literally translates as "burning water," and that might just be the feeling you get in your gullet as it goes down. The liquor is an acquired taste, and it packs a punch. The folks at the El Buen Gusto distillery who make Aguardiente Yuscarán—the label contains an illustration of the town—give informal free tours of their facility and are happy to show you the process of distilling sugarcane into the clear, slightly sweet product everybody refers to in shorthand as *guaro.* Just show up at the distillery during opening hours and someone will show you around. On the off chance that no one is available to give you a tour, you'll be told when you can come back. Tours are in Spanish only. Although El Buen Gusto, in operation since 1939, is the town's largest employer, by informal agreement its product is not for sale in stores in Yuscarán. You can get a small bottle at the end of your tour. ⊠ *Barrio San José* ☎ *No phone* 🖃 *Free* ☉ *Weekdays 7–noon and 1–4, Sat. 7–noon.*

## WHERE TO EAT

Yuscarán's city center has a collection of mom-and-pop restaurants where you can expect a hearty meal served up with a plato típico, *anafres* (bean dip in a clay pot kept warm with coals), and *baleadas* (large wheat flour tortillas).

## WHERE TO STAY

¢ 🏠 **Casa Colibrí.** Yuscarán's best lodging option is tiny, tiny, tiny, with just two rooms—always call ahead—separated by a sitting room. Both guest rooms in this colonial-era home have high ceilings, wood furnishings, and comfy beds, and are decorated with colorful Guatemalan handicrafts. Rooms have no televisions, but you can watch the one in the adjoining sitting room. There's a book exchange, too, and quite frankly, this seems like the kind of place in which to curl up with a good read rather than watch the tube. The location can't be beat: you're right on Yuscarán's central park. **Pros:** friendly owners; cozy rooms; bargain rates; well-appointed furnishings. **Cons:** only two rooms; reservations are absolutely essential. ⊠ *Parque Central* ☎ *793–7611* 🛏*2 rooms* ⚐ *In-room: a/c, no TV, no phone. In-hotel: parking (free).* ▭ *No credit cards* ⦿ *EP.*

## SPORTS AND THE OUTDOORS

**Reserva Biológica Yuscarán.** The cloud-forest reserve just south of town with its three 6,000-ft peaks is worth a visit if you're going to be in the area a few days—and if you have a spirit of adventure. The drive up gets very steep and hair-raising in spots. The confusing layout of the trails means realistically, you should only attempt a visit with a guide. The nonprofit Fundación Yuscarán, dedicated to area conservation, should be your number-one stop in planning a visit to the reserve. *Fundación Yuscarán*⊠ *Parque Central, next to City Hall* ☎ *793–7158.*

# DANLÍ

*92 km (55 mi) east of Tegucigalpa, 30 km (18 mi) north of Nicaraguan border.*

Spanish explorers founded this community in 1667 as San Buena Ventura, but soon after independence the name reverted to Danlí, meaning "water running over sand," the moniker indigenous peoples had once given to the area. (Think "Don Lee" when you pronounce the name of the town.) About 45,000 residents—referred to as Danlidenses—call this workaday community home. At an elevation of 814 meters (2,700 ft), Danlí enjoys the same temperate climate as that of Yuscarán and Tegucigalpa.

## HONDURAN-AMERICANS GO HOLLYWOOD

Two Honduran-Americans have made careers for themselves in showbiz.

Actress America Ferrera is best known for the title role in the hit TV series *Ugly Betty*—the show was itself based on the Latin American soap *Yo soy Betty, la fea* (*I am Betty, the ugly one*)—and also had roles in the films *The Sisterhood of the Traveling Pants* and *How to Train Your Dragon*.

Pop singer David Archuleta was runner-up in the seventh season of *American Idol* and, at just 16 when the 2007 cycle started, was one of its youngest contestants ever. Although both celebrities are U.S. born and raised, Ferrera's mother and father and Archuleta's mother hail from Honduras.

Folks back here in their parents' homeland follow the careers of both stars with interest and pride.

Danlí anchors one of Honduras's two tobacco-growing regions. (The other is Santa Rosa de Copán in the western highlands.) If you appreciate fine cigars, a visit to Danlí will be a must for you. Although the center of town still maintains its colonial charm, there isn't much to draw you here otherwise. Instead, come for the cigar history: Danlí has managed to parlay one of its best-known products into "cigar tourism," with several of the manufacturers here offering short, informal tours of their facilities.

This is also the town that corn built, with *maíz* being a mainstay here since pre-Columbian times. (Johnny-come-lately tobacco arrived here only in the 1960s.) Danlí celebrates its favorite crop each year during the Festival Nacional del Maíz the last week of August.

### GETTING HERE AND AROUND

Danlí sits due east of Tegucigalpa on Highway CA-6. Rapiditos del Oriente operates express minivans that depart from the Mercado Jacaleapa in the capital. Travel time to Danlí is about 90 minutes. The town's bus terminal sits out on the highway at the west entrance to town. A taxi to the center of town costs L15.

### MONEY MATTERS

Danlí has a branch of Banco Atlántida which will exchange dollars and lempiras. It also has an ATM.

### ESSENTIALS

**Banks Banco Atlántida** (✉ *2 block west, ½ block south of Parque Central*).

**Bus Companies Rapiditos del Oriente** (✉ *Carretera CA-6*).

## EXPLORING

**Museo Municipal.** Danlí's only true sight, other than its cigar factories, is a small museum documenting the town's history. Tobacco, mining, corn, and cotton have been the four industries that have propelled Danlí's economy, and their history and their tools are well preserved here. The building itself was the one-time city hall and dates from 1857. It's worth

## A NATURAL CIGAR HUMIDOR

Honduras may have enacted tough new no-smoking legislation in 2010, but that hasn't dampened enthusiasm for one of its best-known exports.

Honduras's cigar industry has its roots in the Cuban Revolution of 1959, when many tobacco entrepreneurs there fled the Castro regime with a few seeds from which to start a new crop and a new life. Like Cuba's neighbor the Dominican Republic, Honduras welcomed the new businesses and new product with open arms, and the quality of Honduran tobacco is likened to that of Cuba's product. Between Honduras and the Dominican Republic, it's been a battle ever since to gain market share in the United States where Cuban cigars have been illegal because of the U.S. trade embargo. Dominican cigars have traditionally slightly edged out their Honduran counterparts. (Those in the know suggest that Honduran cigars are slightly—but only slightly—stronger than Dominican ones.)

The countryside around Danlí is one of Honduras's two tobacco-producing regions; Santa Rosa de Copán in the western highlands is the other (see ⇨ Santa Rosa de Copán in Western Honduras.) Both areas compare favorably to Cuba's Pinar del Río region, the heart of that island nation's industry. Danlí's Jamastrán Valley enjoys average daytime temperatures of 75 degrees and a 75-percent relative humidity, essentially mimicking the conditions inside a cigar humidor.

That said, the industry here has been hit by the double whammy of the world economic downturn—cigars are discretionary spending for consumers, after all—and Honduras's 2009 political crisis. ("Triple whammy" might be a better description: changing attitudes about smoking have undoubtedly played a role, too.) A few of the manufacturers in town have scaled back operations but they hope to gear back up once the economy looks bright again.

Of the plants in Danlí that are still going strong, two welcome visitors to their installations: **Plasencia** and **Tabacaleras Unidas**. (We know: It's smoking, and that entails a whole host of issues. But the process of making cigars is fascinating to observe.) Given the vastly different sizes of the two factories, the tours at each have a much different feel.

Oh, and one final point... a little vocabulary lesson: In Spanish, a cigar is a *puro*. A *cigarro* is a cigarette.

a quick look. Hours can be irregular. ⊠ *½ block west of Parque Central* ☎ *No phone* ⊠ *L10* ⊘ *Weekdays 8–noon and 1–3:30.*

**Plasencia.** This is one of the world's largest cigar factories, employing more than 1,000 people. Its installations are enormous. Arrange tours at least a day in advance by calling. Tours are in Spanish. ⊠ *2 km (1 mi) south of Danlí* ☎ *763–2828.*

**Tabacaleras Unidas.** This is a much smaller cigar-making operation than the area's other visitor-friendly factory Plasencia. In fact, it might very well be the owner who serves as your tour guide. The tour is in Spanish only; call ahead at least a day in advance. ⊠ *2 km (1 mi) south of Danlí* ☎ *763–6072.*

## WHERE TO EAT

$ ✕ **Rincón Danlidense.** Nothing fancy here: you'll be seated at plastic tables
CENTRAL and partake of good Honduran home cooking. *Anafre*, Honduras's ubiq-
AMERICAN uitous bean dip, is a good starter, and *tacos catrachos* (Honduran-style
tacos made with a corn-based filling) make a tasty main course. The
place branches out into hamburgers and enchiladas, too. People come
here from far and wide on weekends for the delicious beef soup. ⊠ ½
*south of Parque Central* ☎ *No phone* ▭ *No credit cards* ⊘ *Closed Mon.*

## WHERE TO STAY

¢–$ ☷ **Hotel La Esperanza.** Danlí's top hotel is really quite basic. Rooms
are arranged around a central courtyard. They are clean and certainly acceptable, but you shouldn't expect any frills. Look at a couple
before you decide. Only about half the rooms have air conditioning,
but depending on the time of year you may be able to get by with just
a fan. **Pros:** decent rates. **Cons:** basic rooms. ⊠ *3 blocks west and 2
blocks south of Parque Central* ☎ *763–2106* ⌁ *52 rooms* ⚭ *In-room:
a/c (some), no phone. In-hotel: parking (free).* ▭ *AE, MC, V* ⎜❂⎜ *EP.*

# CHOLUTECA

*136 km (82 mi) south of Tegucigalpa, 85 km (51 mi) southeast of
Salvadoran border, 47 km (28 mi) northwest of Nicaraguan border.*

Honduras's fourth-largest city—weighing in at 100,000 people—is seen
by most travelers as the country's outpost-slash-way station on the Pan-
American Highway. Indeed, Choluteca hosts many visitors who may
stop only briefly for gas and a bite to eat, but little else. Residents will
tell you that "Cholu" is the hottest spot in the country, and a trip here
during the dry-season months of March and April, when afternoon temperatures regularly soar to 40 degrees Celsius (104 degrees Fahrenheit),
will be all you need to agree.

The city takes its name from the Choluteca River, which, in turn, means
"wide valley." The suspension bridge over the river just outside of town
was built in the 1930s by the U.S. Army Corps of Engineers and is a
city landmark. The 349 km (209 mi) waterway empties into the ocean
just southwest of here. (Upriver, it also passes through Tegucigalpa.)
During years of the El Niño weather phenomenon in the Pacific Ocean,
the river dries up significantly. Osmosis causes salty ocean water to be
sucked into the riverbed, compounding the drought conditions. Yet,
other extremes have occurred, too. This region of Honduras was the
hardest hit during 1998's Hurricane Mitch, which hung over the country for days and battered it without mercy. Choluteca survived some
serious damage, but many of the surrounding hamlets were wiped off
the face of the map. Fortunately, those occasions have been rare.

### GETTING HERE AND AROUND

As the region's hub city and Honduras's fourth largest metropolis,
Choluteca is well served by good roads and public transportation.
Highway CA-5 leads south from Tegucigalpa where it merges into

## SUGAR = ENERGY

Have kids? You've probably determined that sugar gives them extra energy. Honduras has figured out that principle, too, but from a different perspective. The countryside near Choluteca, as well as around San Pedro Sula in the northwest, is sugarcane country, with production in Honduras dominated by seven *ingenios* (sugar-processing mills). During the processing, the liquid cane juice, from which the sugar crystals are extracted, must be separated from the *bagasse*, the wet, fibrous by-product. The burning of the bagasse generates enough electricity to power the mills and also to help supply the nation's power grid, but, alas, only during the November–March harvesting season. Nevertheless, Honduras generates about 10 percent of its annual electricity needs this way, no small accomplishment for a country distressingly dependent on imported oil. That packet of sugar you put in your morning coffee here—that's also a signature "Made in Honduras" product, of course—just might have produced the energy needed to brew your cup.

the Pan-American Highway (CA-1) for the remainder of the drive to Choluteca.

Sáenz Primera travels four times daily from Tegucigalpa to Choluteca on large, comfortable air-conditioned buses. Travel time is 2½ hours. The fare (L150) is twice what the other companies charge, but the extra level of comfort and express service—it shaves an hour off the other guys' travel times—may be worth it. El Rey Express makes the trip three times daily, with stops along the way. Choluteca operator Mi Esperanza makes the Tegucigalpa–Choluteca trip hourly throughout the day in each direction, with stops along the way. Choluteca bus terminals congregate on Avenida Carranza, six blocks south and eight blocks east of the Parque Central.

Many side streets in town degenerate into dirt, making Choluteca dusty in the dry season and muddy in the rainy season.

### SAFETY

Choluteca is nowhere near as "big city" as Tegucigalpa, San Pedro Sula, or La Ceiba, but normal city precautions are in order. Watch your things. Avoid handling large sums of money in public. Take taxis after dark.

### MONEY MATTERS

Choluteca has no shortage of banks and ATMs. A branch of BAC Honduras is downtown with currency exchange and an ATM that accepts Visa, MasterCard, and American Express cards. Realistically, this is the last place to get money if you're heading any farther south to the coast.

### SKIP CEDEÑO

Skip the dark-sand beach at nearby **Cedeño**, plagued with litter and lined with a string of boozy, brawly bars. If you seek a beach outing in this part of the country, you'll do far better with a jaunt over to Isla del Tigre.

**ESSENTIALS**
**Bus Companies El Rey Express** (✉ *C. 12 and Av. 7, Comayagüela* ☎ *237–8561 in Tegucigalpa*). **Mi Esperanza** (✉ *C. 12 and Av. 7, Comayagüela* ☎ *782–0841*). **Sáenz Primera** (✉ *Blvd. de la Comunidad Económica Europea, Col. Prados Universitario* ☎ *233–4229 in Tegucigalpa*).

**Banks BAC Honduras** (✉ *C. Vicente Williams*).

# EXPLORING

**Casa Valle.** Honduras's 100-lempira bill honors everything about Choluteca. On the front of the bill is independence hero José Cecilio del Valle (1777–1833), and in the background of his portrait, the city's landmark suspension bridge over the Río Choluteca. On the reverse you'll see the inscription, CASA DONDE NACIÓ EL SABIO VALLE, the house where Valle was born. To Hondurans, Valle was *El Sabio* ("the Wise One"), a Thomas Jefferson-type figure whose wisdom and foresight guided the country through its early days of independence. His home here on the central park contains a collection of colonial-era exhibits. Valle's statue sits across the street in the central park. ✉ *Southwest corner of Parque Central* ☎ *No phone* 💲 *Free* ⊙ *Weekdays 8–noon and 2–4.*

# WHERE TO EAT

Choluteca has a collection of fast-food places out on the highway at the entrance to town. In town, typical, small Honduran restaurants are the norm. Quite honestly, the best dining option here is the restaurant at the Hotel Gualiqueme. Non-guests are welcome.

# WHERE TO STAY

¢ 🏨 **Hotel Bonsai.** Choluteca's in-town hotels are pretty utilitarian, but pretty inexpensive, too. (You get what you pay for.) Hotel Bonsai, with rooms surrounding a courtyard, is the best of the lot. Look at a couple of the rooms before you decide: in a few of them, the bathroom is only partially walled off from the rest of the unit. Spring for air-conditioning, too—it costs only a few dollars more. Some of the rooms have only fans, and you'll definitely want more than that in the heat. **Pros:** good budget value; near central park. **Cons:** basic rooms; not all bathrooms are fully enclosed. ✉ *½ block south of Parque Central* ☎ *782–2648* 🛏 *12 rooms* ⚐ *In-room: a/c (some), no phone (some). In-hotel: parking (free).* ☰ *MC, V* 🍽 *EP.*

$$ 🏨 **Hotel Gualiqueme.** By far, southern Honduras's snazziest lodging is this hotel—you can't miss it as you're coming into town from Tegucigalpa. The clientele is a mix of business travelers and travelers stopping here on their way through Central America. Although the place doesn't have a business vibe, Choluteca is primarily a business hub for this part of Honduras, so rates are discounted on weekends. Rooms are scattered among several buildings around this tree-shaded property, providing some relief from the heat. A nice pool, much-appreciated air-conditioning and high-ceilinged rooms help on that count, too. All rooms come with two queen-size beds, wood beams, and tile

floors. **Pros:** refreshing oasis in sweltering Choluteca; attentive staff; good value. **Cons:** rooms have a motel feel; removed from center of town; best to have a car to stay here. ⊠ *At bridge at entrance to town* ☎ *782–2750* ⊕ *www.hotelgualiqueme.hn* ⤶ *40 rooms* ♨ *In-room: a/c, kitchen (some), refrigerator (some), Wi-Fi. In-hotel: restaurant, room service, bar, pool, laundry service, Internet terminal, parking (free).* ▭ *AE, D, DC, MC, V* ⋈ *BP.*

---

# ISLA DEL TIGRE

3

*15 min. by boat from Coyolito on the mainland.*

Assuming they ever existed, the *tigres*—jaguars? ocelots? panthers?—believed to have once populated Honduras's very own Pacific island are long gone. Gone also are the pirates, among them Sir Francis Drake, who once haunted these waters. What you have left is a middle-class beach destination for folks from Tegucigalpa, with a couple of decent lodgings and restaurants (and unfortunately, many that are not so decent). The place is offbeat, quirky, and virtually unknown to the outside world.

Isla del Tigre lies in the Golfo de Fonseca, an inlet of the Pacific Ocean. Decades of dispute over control of the gulf among Honduras, El Salvador, and Nicaragua came to an end in 1992 with the help of the International Court of Justice in The Hague. All three nations would maintain sovereignty over the body of water, Honduras would retain its control over Isla del Tigre, and El Salvador would control other nearby islands.

The island—know that Hondurans always refer to Isla del Tigre by the name of its only town, Amapala—is really an inactive volcano that rises out of the water. Honduras established Amapala itself as its first port in 1833. A subsequent move of Pacific operations to mainland San Lorenzo, and development of large port facilities on the Caribbean coast have left Isla del Tigre in a time warp. But the island's fans, who look aghast at the tourism machine that operates in the Bay Islands, say a time warp is exactly what they seek in a beach destination.

## GETTING HERE AND AROUND

Bringing your own vehicle to the island is a hassle. There is no regular car ferry service. Most drivers leave their vehicles at guarded lots in the hamlet of Coyolito on the mainland for a charge of L50 a day. If you have no car, you'll need to disembark from any Tegucigalpa–Choluteca bus just north of the port of San Lorenzo. Minivans or taxis are often waiting to take you on the last hour-long portion of the journey to Coyolito. *Lanchas*, small motorboats, leave the dock

### THE CATRACHOS

Hondurans affectionately refer to themselves as *Catrachos*. There are several versions of the origin of the word. The most commonly accepted one is that it's a corruption of the name of Honduran general Florencio Xatruch, whose soldiers defeated 19th century American invader William Walker. Xatruch's men were hailed as victors when they returned home. Only one problem: nobody knew how to pronounce the general's name.

in Coyolito and charge L20 per person to transport you to Isla del Tigre. They can drop you off at the dock in Amapala or at nearby Playa El Burro, a good option if you're staying at Veleros on that beach.

A community-run tourist office operates at the pier in Amapala weekdays and Saturday mornings and has plenty of useful information about the island.

> **LEAF-CUTTER ANTS**
>
> Stop and watch if you see a procession of tiny green particles on the ground. It's a parade of Central America's famous leaf-cutter ants carrying plant material to their underground nest for nourishment.

The island is essentially circular, with Amapala, its only town, at the 11-o'clock position on a clock. A road, 17 km (10 mi) long, circles the island, mostly hugging its shore. Public buses ply the route but very infrequently. Pickup trucks serve as taxis here. ■**TIP→ Boats can be hired to get you from place to place on the island, an often quicker option than traveling by land.** Expect to pay L20 no matter where you want the boat driver to take you.

### SAFETY
⚠ **Exercise utmost care when swimming at all beaches on Isla del Tigre.** Common wisdom is that waters are calmer at sheltered Playa El Burro near the town of Amalapa. Other beaches are more exposed to the vagaries of the Pacific Ocean and represent more of a threat.

### MONEY MATTERS
Isla del Tigre has neither banks nor ATMs. Bring all the cash you'll need, ideally in lempiras only. The total lack of a banking system on the island means that money circulation has some constraints, and businesses are frequently unable to change large bills. Bring bills in as small a denomination as possible. In a pinch, the Restaurante El Faro de Victoria will change U.S. dollars, but at an unfavorable rate to you.

### ESSENTIALS
**Boat Transportation Lanchas** (✉ *Amapala*).

**Tourist Info Tourist Office in Amapala** (✉ *Amapala* ☎ *795–8407*).

# EXPLORING

Isla del Tigre's sights are natural ones. The volcano summit sits in the center of the island. Some 20 beaches ring the island; visitors congregate at three of them.

**Cerro Vejía.** A glance at the reverse of the L2 bill gives you a preview of the island's most prominent natural feature. Isla del Tigre is really an inactive volcano, the Cerro Vejía, which locals frequently refer to as simply *El Cima* ("the Summit"). If you can get to the top—the volcano measures 783 meters (2,580 ft) in elevation—the views of the gulf, the ocean, and the three countries (Honduras, El Salvador, and Nicaragua) are stupendous. The path up heads inland from the naval post halfway between Amapala and Playa Grande. Plan on three hours each way, and it's no small feat to make the hike in this very warm climate. Until

1990, a U.S. military station on the top of the volcano was used to monitor troop movements in the Contra war in next-door Nicaragua. The Drug Enforcement Administration (DEA) also used the facility to monitor drug trafficking in the region. The site has now been abandoned. ⊠ *Center of Isla del Tigre.*

**Playa El Burro.** The closest beach to town lies just east of Amapala. It is the calmest beach for swimming since its sheltered location directly faces the mainland. El Burro gets muddy at low tide—that's the most common complaint about this beach. A few food stands pop up every weekend, and for finer dining, the seafood restaurant at Veleros is right here. ⊠ *East of Amapala.*

**Playa Grande.** Visualizing the island as a clock, its most popular beach sits at the nine-o'clock position, facing the Salvadoran mainland. Less shelter from the ocean makes for rougher swimming at Playa Grande. But this beach does not have the mud problem evident at Playa El Burro, which does make for a more pleasant stroll along the sand. A slew of makeshift food stands spring up on weekends, seriously cutting into the space here. Local legend holds that pirate treasure is buried somewhere here on the beach. ⊠ *3 km (2 mi) south of Amapala.*

**Playa Negra.** Isla del Tigre's prettiest beach is the black-sand strand on the southwest corner of the island. With almost no shelter from the Pacific Ocean, swimming is rough here. A couple of lodgings on Playa Negra—we don't recommend them as places to stay—have hotel restaurants. A few food stands magically appear on weekends, too. ⊠ *6 km (3 ½ mi) south of Amapala.*

## WHERE TO EAT

$$    ✕ **El Faro de Victoria.** The island's best-known restaurant is this pleasant,
CUISINE TYPE    open-air joint just to the right of the docks in town. (Note that if you're here during the week, this will likely be the only in-town restaurant open.) Seafood reigns here. Choose from such dishes as garlic shrimp or *pescado sudado.* The name, which translates as "sweaty fish," sounds less appetizing than it really is. It's merely fish poached in foil. El Faro serves up a decent burger, and ample french fries accompany every main course. Wash your meal down with one of several cold Honduran beers on the menu. ⊠ *At the pier, Amapala* ☎ *795–8543* ☐ *MC, V.*

## WHERE TO STAY

$    ☷ **Hotel Mirador de Amapala.** What is billed as the island's top hotel is still quite basic. Peach-colored rooms have two beds and a table, but little else for furnishings. Units climb a hillside, but despite the name of the hotel referring to a *mirador* (lookout), only those at the top command any real views. The public areas are the draw, with several terraces built into the complex that are perfect for lounging the day away with a good book and a drink. Rates are discounted 20 percent during the week, Sunday through Thursday night. **Pros:** decent restaurant; good value with rates including both breakfast and dinner. **Cons:** not right on the beach; basic rooms. ⊠ *Amapala* ☎ *795–8407* ⊕ *www.*

## TWO LAST NAMES

The immigration form you're given to fill out on your flight to Honduras has a space asking for your *segundo apellido* (second last name). You won't have one, but Hondurans all do.

Here's how the system works: If a Pedro Castillo marries an Ana Morales, and they have a son, Juan, his full legal name will consist of surnames from both his father and his mother: Juan Castillo Morales (although he'll probably shorthand it to Juan Castillo). When Juan grows up and marries, his children will take his Castillo surname and his future wife's first surname. Juan's Morales name is lost to future generations.

Let's go back to our friends Ana and Pedro. Like most Honduran women, Ana likely decided to keep her own last names when she married, and not take Pedro's, a tradition that existed here long before liberated North American and European women adopted such customs. Of course, Ana might choose to call herself Ana Morales *de Castillo* (of Castillo), a convention usually seen only in aristocratic circles. If Ana outlives Pedro, she could choose to go by Ana Morales *viuda de Castillo* (widow of Castillo), a quaint tradition rarely seen these days.

*miradordeamapala.com* ➥ *30 rooms* ♿ *In-room: a/c, no phone. In-hotel: restaurant, room service, bar, pool* ⊟ *MC, V* ⦿ *MAP.*

¢ 🖼 **Veleros.** As with every lodging option on Isla del Tigre, things are pretty plain and simple, but Veleros is immaculate—that's something you can't say about every hotel on the island—and service is friendly. Rooms contain comfortable beds and tile floors. You can pay a discounted rate off the already low prices if you don't use the air-conditioning, but you'll definitely want to spring for the air. You'll likely find yourself lounging around on the deck, lazing in one of the hammocks, or hanging out at the seafood restaurant ($$). The lobster is a steal at L360. **Pros:** friendly owners; good seafood restaurant; terrific budget value; right on beach. **Cons:** basic rooms. ⊠ *Playa El Burro* ☎ *795–8040* ➥ *3 rooms* ♿ *In-room: a/c, no phone. In-hotel: restaurant, bar, beachfront* ⊟ *MC, V* ⦿ *CP.*

## NIGHTLIFE

The island is *very* quiet at night. Nightlife consists of whiling away the evening over a restaurant meal, and El Faro de Victoria in town or Veleros out at Playa El Burro fit the bill perfectly.

## SPORTS AND THE OUTDOORS

The friendly folks at **Aquatours Marabella** (⊠ *Playa El Burro* ☎ *795–8050*) can take you on a number of boating excursions around the island and around the gulf. Most popular is the half-day trip that encircles Isla del Tigre, stopping at a couple of less-known beaches along the route. The price is L1,000 per person.

# Western Honduras

**WORD OF MOUTH**

"We did enjoy the town of Copán Ruinas . . . especially the chocolate-covered bananas for a quarter. You can also buy coffee and cardamom and cardamom coffee in town."

—ttraveler

"I spent a week in Copán and definitely found a lot to do in the area. In addition to the ruins, which took an afternoon (we picked up a good guide onsite), we also visited Macaw Mountain Bird Park (beautiful natural scenery and cool birds, a bit touristy but nice), went zip lining at Hacienda San Lucas, did the daytrip with Finca El Cisne (horseback riding, springs, meals; I would consider an overnight if I were there again)."

—mmb23

Updated by
Jeffrey Van
Fleet

Western Honduras marries its indigenous and colonial heritages like nowhere else in the country. Small communities tucked into the green mountains of the Highlands maintain their old religious, cultural, artistic, and medicinal traditions. As you explore, you'll find yourself whisked back to another era.

For 2,000 years the Maya resided in the region that Hondurans call El Occidente ("the West"), creating the distinctive art and architecture that can still be seen at the ancient city of Copán. The Lenca, who are believed to have lived alongside the Maya, had an equally vibrant, although less-well-known, culture.

Yet it is the Lenca who are the indigenous group most in evidence in western Honduras today, especially in small villages near the cities of Gracias and Santa Rosa de Copán, where residents live much as their ancestors did.

The city of Copán, one of the world's premier archaeological sites, lies in the jungle near the border of Guatemala. Often dubbed the Paris of Central America, Copán is known for its soaring pyramids, mammoth stelae, and an intricately carved staircase that tells the story of the highly advanced civilization that thrived here for hundreds of years. For good reason, it is Honduras's number one tourist attraction (though residents of Roatán in the Bay Islands might disagree).

But not all is human-made in this region: Lago de Yojoa is the country's largest natural lake and a haven for birders (there are some 400 species of birds to be spotted). Near Gracias sits one of the isthmus's largest reserves, Parque Nacional Celaque, a land of pine trees and cloud forests that contains Honduras's highest peak within its boundaries.

Anchoring the region is San Pedro Sula, Honduras's second largest city and the engine that propels the country's economy. Aeropuerto Internacional Ramón Villeda Morales, located here, is the country's busiest airport and makes an easy gateway to the region. San Pedro Sula will always be the region's pocketbook—and major airport—but never its heart and soul. If you're like most visitors, San Pedro will be your classic first-night, last-night destination, with the rest of your time spent elsewhere.

The people here are more outgoing than in many parts of Honduras, and they are more than happy to converse with newcomers.

## TOP REASONS TO GO

**Ponder the mysteries of the Maya.** Other Mayan ruins in Mesoamerica are bigger and taller, but none can top Copán for intricate artwork and few ruins complexes are as accessible as this one is.

**Bird to your heart's content.** The Lago de Yojoa, in the center of the country, is Honduras's bird-watching venue par excellence, with your choice of almost 400 species to add to your life list.

**Explore Honduras's colonial past.** Spanish conquistadors made history in this region of Honduras, and the small colonial communities of Comayagua, Santa Rosa de Copán, Copán Ruinas, and Gracias evoke a distant past that much of the rest of the country has forgotten.

**Stay at a charming inn.** You'll find the whole gamut of accommodation here in Western Honduras, but it's the colonial inns in Copán Ruinas, Comayagua, and Gracias that provide a distinctive lodging experience and transport you back to pre-independence Honduras.

4

# ORIENTATION AND PLANNING

## ORIENTATION

Think of Western Honduras as a lopsided triangle with a mountainous center. Near the northern apex sits the city of San Pedro Sula, likely your first encounter with the region. At the southwest point of the triangle lie the Mayan ruins of Copán. Along the eastern edge are the colonial city of Comayagua and the Lago de Yojoa, the country's largest natural lake. In the center of the region are the colonial towns of Gracias and Santa Rosa de Copán. The lack of decent roads east of Gracias means that Western Honduras gets thought of as two distinct regions, with Comayagua and Lago de Yojoa frequently visited as a separate trip from one that would include Copán Ruinas, Santa Rosa de Copán, and Gracias. Although everybody uses the term montañas (mountains) to describe the region, there is nothing here much over 9,000 feet, and most of the terrain you'll have to negotiate is in the mile-high range. These are not the Andes.

**San Pedro Sula.** The country's economic boomtown will likely be your first and last encounter with this region because a large airport is here. This is big-city life Honduran style, and there is no better place to take care of those odds and ends like shopping and getting cash.

**Copán and Copán Ruinas.** They're two attractions for the price of one: The ruins of the famed Mayan city sit in the southwest part of the country near the Guatemalan border. Next door is the fun tourist town of Copán Ruinas, with its terrific selection of lodgings, restaurants, and non-archaeological activities.

**Santa Rosa de Copán.** The highlands' largest city is really just a big small town at heart. There aren't really any specific must-see sights here, but visitors still find themselves lingering a couple of days and soaking up the colonial vibe.

**Gracias.** A visit to the lovely colonial town of Gracias would be worthwhile on its own, with its cobblestone streets and restored pre-independence buildings. But the small city anchors an area of natural and cultural wonders in the form of the Parque Nacional Celaque and nearby Lenca villages, respectively.

**Lago de Yojoa.** The name of the country's largest lake defines a small region rather than a specific town. Birders, especially, get a dreamy, far-off look in their eyes when the name is mentioned. It's one of Central America's premier bird-watching destinations.

**Comayagua.** Honduras's first capital sits smack-dab in the center of the country and has preserved its colonial heritage better than any other city here. It's closer to Tegucigalpa than San Pedro Sula and can be accessed easily from either direction.

## GREAT ITINERARIES

**If You Have 3 days:** After arrival in San Pedro Sula, head southwest to the town of Copán Ruinas and get settled into your hotel. Take one day to explore the Mayan ruins. You can walk there from town or take one of Copán's fun *tuk-tuk* (three-wheeled) taxis. If you're like most visitors, you'll pack your second, and only remaining, day here with all the other activities for which the area is known: a bird park, a butterfly garden, zip lining, horseback riding, shopping . . . the list is endless. Treat yourself to a third day, and you won't have to cross any items off your to-do list.

**If You Have 3 to 5 days:** Begin in San Pedro Sula and head southeast to Comayagua. (You can begin in Tegucigalpa, too, in which case head northwest.) A day gives you ample time to take in Comayagua's four main colonial churches and the archaeology museum. If the museum of religious art has reopened by the time you read this—it was badly damaged in a 2009 fire, and still closed at this writing—that's a must-see, too. After spending the night in Comayagua, head north to Lago de Yoja along CA-5, the highway connecting San Pedro and Tegucigalpa. Bird-watching and hiking easily fill several days here. You can probably just show up if you come during the week, but weekends get crowded here at the lake so make reservations. Top off your lake visit with one of D&D Brewery's microbrews.

**If You Have 5 days:** A visit to Copán from San Pedro Sula occupies three days, but tack on an excursion to Santa Rosa de Copán and Gracias, two of Honduras's premier colonial cities. Unfortunately, no road connects Copán Ruinas to Santa Rosa, meaning you must backtrack to the crossroads town of La Entrada. That does add a couple of extra hours. However, once there, you can base yourself in either Gracias or Santa Rosa—both have good lodgings to choose from—and visit the other as a day trip.

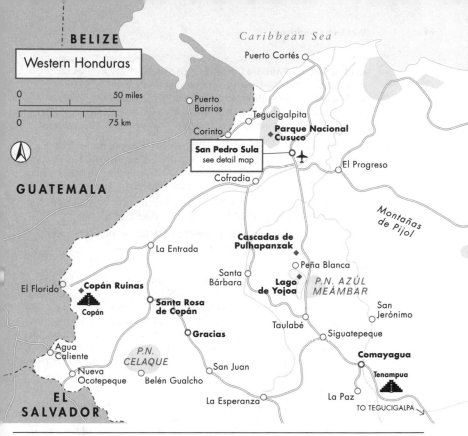

Western Honduras

0 ————— 50 miles
0 ————— 75 km

BELIZE

Caribbean Sea

GUATEMALA

EL SALVADOR

Puerto Cortés
Puerto Barrios
Tegucigalpita
Corinto
**Parque Nacional Cusuco**
**San Pedro Sula** see detail map
Cofradía
El Progreso
**Montañas de Pijol**
La Entrada
**Cascadas de Pulhapanzak**
Peña Blanca
Santa Bárbara
**Lago de Yojoa**
*P.N. AZÚL MEÁMBAR*
El Florido
**Copán Ruinas**
Copán
San Jerónimo
**Santa Rosa de Copán**
Taulabé
Siguatepeque
**Gracias**
Agua Caliente
*P.N. CELAQUE*
San Juan
**Comayagua**
**Tenampua**
Nueva Ocotepeque
Belén Gualcho
La Esperanza
La Paz
TO TEGUCIGALPA

## PLANNING

### WHEN TO GO

San Pedro Sula, sitting in the lowlands, is often sweltering, but temperatures become more bearable as you gain altitude. Copán Ruinas is a bit cooler. The true highlands around Santa Rosa de Copán and Gracias enjoy a pleasant springlike climate year-round, similar to Tegucigalpa's, with warm afternoons and cool evenings. Comayagua and Lago de Yojoa lie at slightly lower altitudes and are a bit warmer, but nothing like the furnace that San Pedro can be. The entire region experiences the same rainy-season/dry-season distinction that most of Honduras does. Rains arrive in May and taper off by the end of October, although the highlands around Gracias see rain well into November.

### GETTING HERE AND AROUND
#### AIR TRAVEL

American flies twice daily from Miami to San Pedro Sula. Continental flies once daily each from Houston and Newark. Delta flies daily from Atlanta. Spirit Airlines flies daily from Fort Lauderdale. Taca flies once daily each from Miami and New York's JFK, as well as from many capitals throughout Central America. Isleña specializes in flights to the Bay Islands. CM Airlines flies daily to Tegucigalpa. Central American Airways flies daily to Tegucigalpa, La Ceiba, and Roatán.

**Airlines and Contacts American** ( ☎ *501–0750 in Honduras* ⊕ *www.aa.com*). **Central American Airlines** (*in Honduras* ☎ *547–3652*). **CM Airlines** (*in Honduras* ☎ *668–0868* ⊕ *www.cmairlines.com*). **Continental** (☎ *557–4141 in Honduras* ⊕ *www.continental.com*). **Isleña** (☎ *552–8322 or 552–8335 in Honduras*). **Sosa** (☎ *550–6545 in Honduras* ⊕ *www.aerolineasosahn.com*). **Taca** (☎ *552–9910 in Honduras* ⊕ *www.taca.com*).

About 15 km (9 mi) outside San Pedro Sula, Aeropuerto Internacional Ramón Villeda Morales is Honduras's busiest airport and has connections to many international destinations. There are also frequent flights to the Bay Islands and other parts of the country.

There are no airport shuttle buses, only private taxis. A taxi to downtown San Pedro Sula should cost no more than L150.

**Airport Information Aeropuerto Internacional Ramón Villeda Morales** (✉ *Carretera La Lima, San Pedro Sula* ☎ *668–3260*).

### BUS TRAVEL

Bus travel is extensive throughout this region, with a mix of large Pullman-style vehicles, converted U.S. school buses, and smaller minivans. Whenever possible, opt for *directo* service. They may still make a few stops, but you'll get to your destination a lot faster than on the slow *servicio a escala* (local service) buses that stop everywhere. Most destinations in this chapter can be reached easily from San Pedro Sula; Comayagua is closer to Tegucigalpa, and in this case bus travel from the capital instead is just as convenient.

### CAR TRAVEL

Traffic can get heavy during rush hour, but driving in San Pedro Sula is a breeze compared to the gridlock in the capital. Since this is the country's most important transportation hub, streets into and out of the city are well maintained, making driving to surrounding areas a pleasure. In the more mountainous parts of the region, you will need a four-wheel-drive vehicle or a sturdy pickup.

There is no shortage of car-rental agencies in San Pedro Sula, and most have offices both in the airport and in town. Two good local companies are Maya and Molinari. There are no rental agencies elsewhere in the region.

**Local Agencies Avis** (✉ *Aeropuerto Internacional Ramón Villeda Morales, San Pedro Sula* ☎ *668–3164* ✉ *C. 1 and Av. 6, San Pedro Sula* ☎ *553–0888 or 552–2872*). **Hertz** (✉ *Aeropuerto Internacional Ramón Villeda Morales, San Pedro Sula* ☎ *668–3157* ✉ *Blvd. Morazán and C. 1, San Pedro Sula* ☎ *550–8080*). **Maya** (✉ *Aeropuerto Internacional Ramón Villeda Morales, San Pedro Sula* ☎ *668–3168* ✉ *Av. 3, between Cs. 7 and 8, San Pedro Sula* ☎ *552–2670 or 552–2671*). **Molinari** (✉ *C. 1 between Avs. 3 and 4, San Pedro Sula* ☎ *552–9999*). **Thrifty** (✉ *Aeropuerto Internacional Ramón Villeda Morales, San Pedro Sula* ☎ *559–2660*).

TAXIS  Negotiate the price before you set off. Although taxis are quite safe by day, at night you should call Radio Taxi or a company recommended by your hotel.

**Taxi Company Radio Taxi** (☎ *557–8801*).

## HEALTH AND SAFETY

San Pedro Sula, Comayagua, and Santa Rosa de Copán have modern hospitals that can assist you with most emergencies. Pharmacies are plentiful in most towns.

A visit to San Pedro Sula entails all the big-city precautions you would take in a large metropolis in a developing country. Lock your car doors while driving here, as there have been robberies. Certain stretches of road between San Pedro Sula and Santa Rosa de Copán are dangerous after sunset, so always travel by day. Other places are reasonably safe with the standard level of care you take when traveling anywhere.

## MONEY MATTERS

Get cash in San Pedro Sula, Copán Ruinas, Santa Rosa de Copán, and Comayagua, all with plenty of banks with ATMs, most open weekdays 9 to 3 and Saturday morning. Elsewhere, you'll find banks but few ATMs. Currency-exchange offices in the airport in San Pedro Sula keep old-fashioned bankers' hours, not useful if you arrive at night, and if you depart on an early-morning flight, not open to change back any leftover lempiras. Most hotels also exchange currency but give less favorable rates. American Express, MasterCard, and Visa are widely accepted in San Pedro Sula and Copán Ruinas, but less so elsewhere.

## RESTAURANTS AND CUISINE

Hearty and filling describes the cuisine of Western Honduras. The region combines the indigenous-influenced food of the highlands—chicken, pork, beans, rice, and lots of corn—with the abundant and varied fruit from the nearby lowlands around San Pedro Sula. The *plato típico* (traditional dish) is everywhere at local restaurants, and the combination of meat, rice, beans, and cheese always makes a filling, inexpensive lunch. The *pupusa,* a golden-fried patty of corn, beans, and cheese, usually served with a vinegary blend of cabbage and onion called *repollo,* has made inroads from nearby El Salvador. Charcoal-grilled corn on the cob makes another tasty treat. One of the country's best-kept secrets is *frita de elote* (a deep-fried, sizzling mash of corn and sugar), sold by competing little girls along the road near Lago de Yojoa. Restaurants have it on their menus, too.

## ABOUT THE HOTELS

All the international chains have set up shop in San Pedro Sula. In the city and elsewhere, you'll find a good network of smaller, less expensive lodgings with plenty of Honduran character. Accommodation in this part of the country is reasonably priced, even in the top-tier lodgings, even in tourist-heavy Copán Ruinas.

| WHAT IT COSTS IN HONDURAN LEMPIRAS | | | | |
|---|---|---|---|---|
| ¢ | $ | $$ | $$$ | $$$$ |
| Restaurants under L75 | L75–L150 | L151–L250 | L251–L350 | over L350 |
| Hotels under L750 | L750–L1,250 | L1,251–L1,750 | L1,751–L2,250 | over L2,250 |

Restaurant prices are per person for a main course at dinner. Hotel prices are for two people in a standard double room in high season.

## A BIT OF HISTORY

By the time Christopher Columbus arrived on the coast of Honduras in 1502, this land had already seen great civilizations rise and fall. Nowhere is this more evident than in Copán, one of the most breathtaking archaeological sites in Central America. For most visitors, the history of this part of the country equals the history of the Maya at Copán. What makes Copán so fascinating to archaeologists is not just its astounding size, but its small details. They have deciphered the hieroglyphics that tell the history of this great city, as well as that of others that existed in the region. If you want to understand the ancient civilizations of Quiriguá in Guatemala or Teotihuacán in Mexico, you'll need to pay Copán a visit.

Dominating the region after the fall of the Maya, the Lenca had no intention of being subjugated when the Spanish arrived in the 16th century.

Lempira, the leader of the Lenca, brought various groups together to battle the conquistadors; his murder at the hands of the Spanish at a "peace conference" provided Honduras with its first national hero. The country's currency is named for this great leader.

But fall the Lenca did, and the Spanish dominated the region for the next 300 years. Gracias was briefly the seat of the Audencia, the ruling council that governed Spain's colony in Central America. Santa Rosa de Copán gained fame and wealth as a center for tobacco cultivation. Comayagua eventually was named the Honduran colony's administrative capital, a role it would continue postindependence, until the seat of government was moved in 1880. All three—especially Comayagua—remain don't-miss repositories of colonial architecture today.

# SAN PEDRO SULA

*265 km (165 mi) northwest of Tegucigalpa.*

"Tegucigalpa thinks," goes the Honduran saying, "San Pedro Sula works." ("La Ceiba celebrates," the maxim continues, but that's a matter to be explored in the Caribbean Coast section of our guide.) Honduras has followed a different path than most developing countries, not concentrating all political, cultural, and economic power in one big capital city. By the beginning of the 20th century, the banana trade with the United States and Europe shifted Honduras's economic power to its northern lowlands and away from Tegucigalpa's mining-based economy. San Pedro Sula, with a railway to the coast that the mountainous capital could only envy, took off and never looked back.

Founded in 1536 by Spanish conquistador Pedro de Alvarado, the country's second-largest city acquired the odd "Sula" at the end of its name from the indigenous word *usula,* which means "valley of birds." (The million or so Sampedranos usually write the name of their city as SPS.) Now a bustling commercial center with little evidence left of its colonial past, San Pedro Sula is the fastest-growing city between Bogotá and Mexico City, thanks to being a hub for the banana, coffee, and sugar

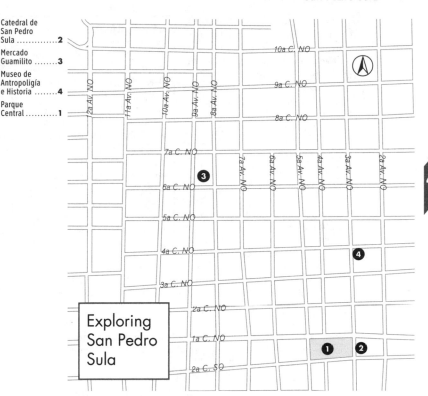

Exploring
San Pedro
Sula

industries. Although San Pedro is slightly smaller than Tegucigalpa, it feels more "big city" than the quaint capital. Despite its single-minded focus on business, San Pedro Sula's convenient location and modern airport make it a convenient gateway if you're planning on exploring the country's western and northern reaches. Its well-maintained roads make it easy to drive east along the coast or south into the mountains.

### GETTING HERE AND AROUND

Built on a traditional grid pattern, San Pedro Sula is an easy city to navigate. Its numbered east-west *calles* (streets) and north-south *avenidas* (avenues) are divided into four quadrants—*noreste* (northeast, abbreviated NE), *sureste* (southeast, SE), *noroeste* (northwest, NO), and *suroeste* (southwest, SO). You'll probably spend most of your time in the southwest quadrant. Many intersections in the center city are not governed by stoplights or stop signs. Avenidas have the right of way at such crossings. Avenida Circunvalación, a ring road, encircles the city. It seems every other vehicle is a taxi, and most rides cost between L40 and L60. Stick with them if you don't have your own vehicle, and always use taxis after dark instead of walking. San Pedro's city buses have seen an increase in crime on a few routes, and we recommend avoiding them entirely.

To get your bearings, start in the center of town at Parque Central, bordered by Calle 1 and Avenida 3. The Hotel Gran Sula across the street is a prominent landmark. The town's few attractions are an easy walk north or south from here. Remember that the area called *abajo de la linea* (literally meaning "below the line"), which means the southeast quadrant below Avenida 1, is a dangerous neighborhood night or day.

All buses arrive and depart from the enormous Gran Central Metropolitana, 4 km (2½ mi) south of San Pedro Sula on the highway to Tegucigalpa. Several companies ply the busy route between San Pedro and Tegucigalpa. Viana Clase Oro, Hedman Alas, Sáenz Primera, and King Quality offer luxury bus services between the two cities.

> ## AZUCARRÓN
>
> If you're like most visitors, you'll fall in love with a Honduran fruit called the azucarrón. It looks like a pineapple, although at about half the size of the typical Hawaiian fruit. Its interior is a brighter yellow than any pineapple you've ever seen, and the fruit is much sweeter. Enjoy it while you're here, because you'll never find it back home. The azucarrón's high sugar content means the fruit ripens quickly and it would never survive the time it takes to ship them to North America.

San Pedro Sula is served by the country's largest airport, the Aeropuerto Internacional Ramón Villeda Morales. There are no airport shuttle buses, only private taxis. A taxi to downtown San Pedro Sula should cost no more than L150. To the chain hotels on Avenida Circunvalación, expect to pay L200.

### HEALTH AND SAFETY
Both Hospital del Valle, San Pedro's largest private hospital, and the slightly smaller Hospital Bendaña have English-speaking staff, many of them foreign trained, accustomed to dealing with expatriate and visitor patients.

The U.S. Embassy in Tegucigalpa operates a branch American Citizen Services Office staffed by a consular agent in San Pedro in the Banco Atlántida building on Parque Central. It is open Monday, Wednesday, and Friday afternoons from 1 to 4.

When you arrive, ask the folks at your hotel front desk for the lay of the land, namely where you should not go. Certain east-side sectors of the city have seen an increase in gang violence, which has captured the attention of the international news media, and are unsafe day or night. (There's nothing of tourist interest in or near these neighborhoods.) Stick to taxis at night. Have your hotel call one if you are going out to dinner, and have the restaurant or nightspot hail one for you when you are ready to call it a night. Beyond that, the standard big-city travel precautions apply: Avoid handling large sums of money in public, keep car doors locked and windows rolled up, and leave the flashy jewelry back home.

**MONEY MATTERS**

As Honduras's center of commerce, San Pedro Sula has no shortage of banks with ATMs. You'll also find ATMs in shopping malls and gas-station convenience stores. Banco Atlántida on Parque Central exchanges dollars and traveler's checks and has a cash machine.

**TOURS**

MC Tours, Explore Honduras, and Mayan VIP Tours are based in San Pedro Sula and lead tours around the region.

**ESSENTIALS**

**Airport Information Aeropuerto Internacional Ramón Villeda Morales** (✉ *Carretera La Lima, San Pedro Sula* ☎ *668–3260*).

**Banks Banco Atlántida** (✉ *North side of Parque Central*).

**Bus Companies Hedman Alas** (✉ *Gran Central Metropolitana* ☎ *553–1361*). **King Quality** (✉ *Gran Central Metropolitana* ☎ *553–4547*). **Sáenz Primera** (✉ *Gran Central Metropolitana* ☎ *553–4969*). **Viana Clase Oro** (✉ *Gran Central Metropolitana* ☎ *556–9261*).

**Consulates American Citizen Services Office** (✉ *Banco Atlántida bldg, Parque Central* ☎ *558–1580* ⊕ *honduras.usembassy.gov/acsoffice_sps.html*).

**Hospitals Hospital Bendaña** (✉ *Av. Circunvalación between Cs. 9 and 10* ☎ *557–4429* ⊕ *www.clinicabendana.com*). **Hospital del Valle** (✉ *Blvd. del Norte, Salida a Puerto Cortés* ☎ *551–8433* ⊕ *www.hospitaldelvalle.com*).

**Pharmacies Farmacia Handa** (✉ *Av. 3 C. at 5, San Pedro Sula* ☎ *550–1068*). **Farmacia María Auxiliadora** (✉ *Av. Circunvalación between Cs. 9 and 10, San Pedro Sula* ☎ *552–7282*).

**Tour Companies Explore Honduras** (✉ *Av. 2 NO at C. 1,* ☎ *552–6242* ⊕ *www.explorehonduras.com*). **Mayan VIP Tours** (✉ *C. 1 at Av. Circunvalación* ☎ *552–7862*). **MC Tours** (✉ *Av. 6 SO at C. 10* ☎ *552–4455* ⊕ *www.mctours-honduras.com*).

# EXPLORING

**Catedral de San Pedro Sula.** On the eastern edge of Parque Central, this massive neoclassical structure was begun in 1949 but not completed for many years. The most important church in town, it is always buzzing with activity. Locals seem to treat it as a community center, and worshippers are surprisingly friendly and talkative. Take a peek inside, but the cathedral lacks the style of Honduras's numerous older churches. ✉ *Av. 3 SO at C. 1* ☉ *Daily 8–6.*

**Mercado Guamilito.** Mornings are the busiest and best time to visit this enclosed market in the northwest section of town. Besides wonderful ebony carvings, artisans also sell colorful baskets and hand-tooled leather goods. ✉ *C. 6 NO between Avs. 8 and 9 NO* ☎ *No phone* ☉ *Mon.–Sat. 7–5, Sun. 8–11:30.*

**Museo de Antropología e Historia.** You will find no better introduction to the country's geography, history, and society than this museum near Parque Central. Spread over two floors, the eye-catching exhibits examine clues about the ancient cultures that once inhabited the region, re-create daily life in the colonial era, and recount the country's more recent history. The sculptures, paintings, ceramics, and other items are labeled in Spanish (and occasionally in English). Budget a good two hours to take it all in. There are also a gift shop and a cafeteria serving a tasty set lunch. A performing-arts space adjoining the museum is the newest venue with offerings for San Pedro's cultural agenda. ⊠ *Av. 3 NO and C. 4 NO* ☎ *557–1874* ⊠*L25* ☯ *Wed.–Mon. 9–4.*

**Parque Central.** Money changers, shoe shiners, watch vendors, and truant schoolchildren mill around San Pedro Sula's central square. Locals lounge beneath the scrawny trees watching the crowds file past. A handful of U.S. restaurant chains have opened in the surrounding blocks, if you need to satisfy your craving for Wendy's, Pizza Hut, Burger King, or McDonald's. There are several small taco shops, cafés, and juice vendors in the area as well. ⊠ *Avs. 3 and 5 SO and Cs. 1 and 2 SO.*

---

# WHERE TO EAT

¢    ✕ **Cafetería Pamplona.** This cheerful eatery on Parque Central serves
SPANISH    up inexpensive Spanish-style dishes that are a welcome change from the beans-and-rice routine. Get here early, as it's only open until 8 PM. Breakfast is a bargain, and the coffee is nice and strong. ⊠ *C. 2 SO at Parque Central* ☎ *550–2639* ▭ *No credit cards.*

$$$    ✕ **Chef Marianos.** San Pedro Sula isn't far from the Caribbean, which
SEAFOOD    means you can easily find delicious seafood. This local favorite is run by a Garífuna family, and everything is as fresh as possible. Recommended are the king crab, jumbo shrimp, and the *negro bello* (a mixed plate of meat, conch, and fish). If it's available, don't pass up the lobster. The service is attentive. ⊠ *Av. 6 SO at C. 10 SO, Barrio Suyapa* ☎ *552–5492* ▭ *AE, MC, V.*

$$    ✕ **Don Udo's.** Originally from Holland, Don Udo Van der Waag fell
CONTEMPORARY    in love with the mountains around San Pedro Sula. Over the years his restaurant here has grown from a casual meeting place where the menu was scribbled on a chalkboard to one of the city's fanciest eateries. Along with excellent beers, you'll find a good selection of wines. Try the stuffed-crab appetizer followed by a tasty jalapeño fillet. Fresh lobster is another treat. If you want to re-create a dish at home, there's a gourmet food store next door. ⊠ *Av. 13 between Cs. 7 and 8 NO* ☎ *557–7991* ▭ *AE, MC, V.*

¢    ✕ **Hasta La Pasta.** Homemade antipasti and hearty pastas, all at reason-
ITALIAN    able prices, make this is one of the most popular Italian restaurants in town. The garden courtyard makes a pleasant place to savor a glass of wine. ⊠ *Av. 22 and C. 2 NO, Col. Moderna* ☎ *550–5494 or 550–3048* ▭ *AE, MC, V* ☯ *Closed Mon.*

$$    ✕ **Tre Fratelli.** This Italian restaurant in the Zona Viva is part of a small
ITALIAN    Central America-California chain, with a branch in Tegucigalpa, too. You'll find inside seating and a popular patio dining area. Enjoy generous servings of pasta, fish dishes, salads, and a good wine selection at affordable prices, along with the requisite checkered tablecloths. ⊠ *Av. Circunvalación at C. 1 SO* ☎ *557–3019* ⊕ *www.trefratelli.com* ▭ *AE, D, DC, MC, V* ☯ *Closed Sun.*

# Where to Eat and Stay in San Pedro Sula

**KEY**

**1** *Restaurants*

**1** *Hotels*

| Restaurants ▼ | Hotels ▼ | |
|---|---|---|
| Cafetría Pamplona .......... **4** | Casa del Árbol .............. **3** | Gran Hotel Sula .............. **6** |
| Chef Mariano's .............. **5** | Casa del Árbol | Hilton Princess |
| Don Udo's .................... **3** | Galerías .................... **1** | San Pedro Sula .............. **8** |
| Hosta La Pasta .............. **1** | Clarion Hotel | Holiday Inn Express ........ **10** |
| Tre Fratelli .................. **2** | San Pedro Sula .............. **4** | Hotel Ejecutivo .............. **7** |
| | Copantl Hotel & Suites .....**11** | Hotel Saint Anthony ........ **12** |
| | Crowne Plaza ................ **5** | Los Jícaros .................... **2** |
| | | Real San Pedro Sula ......... **9** |

## WHERE TO STAY

**$$**  🏨 **Casa del Árbol.** An early 20th-century, wooden, banana plantation
**Fodor's Choice** building has been renovated into a wonderful small inn and is San
**★** Pedro's most distinctive hotel. (You might miss this place if you aren't
looking for it; it's on a downtown street of otherwise boxy, concrete
buildings.) The *árbol* here is a mango tree around which the rambling
house is built. Each immaculate room has a wood desk, Honduran
artwork, and a small balcony, *small* being the operative word here. A
few of the rooms have king-size beds. The back stone patio is perfect
for lingering over a cup of coffee in the morning. To top it off, Hondu-
ran urban hotels don't get greener than this, with much of the power
being generated by solar panels. **Pros:** attentive staff; unique tropical
surroundings in a modern city; central location **Cons:** borders a mar-
ginal neighborhood. ✉ *Av. 6 between Cs. 2 and 3 NO* ☎ *504–1616*
⊕ *www.hotelcasadelarbol.com* 🛏 *13 rooms* ♿ *In-room: a/c, safe, Wi-Fi.
In-hotel: restaurant, laundry service, Internet terminal, parking (free)*
▤ *AE, D, DC, MC, V* ⃝| *BP.*

**$$**  🏨 **Casa del Árbol Galerías.** The folks who brought you the downtown
**Fodor's Choice** Casa del Árbol have branched out, and this suburban property is
**★** another winner. Dashes of color play a key role in this sleek, modern
hotel; rooms are blindingly white except for a painting in each one, created by various female Lenca artists. The painting in a given room might
be red, yellow, green, or blue; smaller versions of the paintings are on
display in the lobby area to give you a preview. Plush beds, marble sinks,
and flat-screen TVs add to the rooms' modernity. Like its sister property downtown, Galerías' green philosophy shines through with solar
panels, low-flow toilets, and light sensors. A restaurant ($$$), serving
fusion cuisine with Lencan and Mayan touches, is off the lobby and has
a rotating selection of main courses. **Pros:** attentive service; beautiful
artwork; excellent restaurant **Cons:** far from city center; can be diffi-
cult to find. ✉ *Col. Jardines del Valle, across from Escuela Bambinos*
☎ *566–4202* ⊕ *www.hotelcasadelarbol.com* 🛏 *27 rooms* ♿ *In-room:
a/c, safe, Wi-Fi. In-hotel: restaurant, room service, bar, pool, laundry
service, Internet terminal, parking (free)* ▤ *AE, D, DC, MC, V* ⃝| *BP.*

**$$$$**  🏨 **Clarion Hotel San Pedro Sula.** Although its sister property in Tegu-
cigalpa gets high marks for being a chain property with Honduran
touches, San Pedro's Clarion is a bit plain in comparison. You will find
all the amenities a business traveler could desire here, and those are
the guests who make up the bulk of the clientele. You're close to shop-
ping and the nightlife of the Zona Viva. **Pros:** many business amenities;
close to shopping and nightlife. **Cons:** fee for Wi-Fi use. ✉ *Av. 17 and
C. 2* ☎ *553–6071* ⊕ *www.clarionhotel.com* 🛏 *37 rooms* ♿ *In-room:
a/c, safe, Wi-Fi. In-hotel: restaurant, room service, bar, pool, laundry
service, Internet terminal, parking (free)* ▤ *AE, D, DC, MC, V* ⃝| *BP.*

**$$$$**  🏨 **Copantl Hotel & Suites.** Long considered one of the city's finest hotels,
this high-rise is a favorite among corporate travelers. There are plenty
of meeting rooms and a wide range of business services available. Many
of the rooms look down on the Olympic-size pool. The panoramic views
of the mountains from La Churrasquería and the steak house on the
seventh floor are unforgettable. There are shops and even an art gallery

where you can browse. The service is uneven, however, and the din that comes from the cocktail lounge at night doesn't promote a good night's sleep. **Pros:** constant activity means it never gets boring here. **Cons:** some rooms are noisy, not a good choice if you crave solitude. ⊠ *Blvd. del Sur across from Multiplaza* ☎ *556–8900* ⊕ *www.copantl. com* ⤷ *192 rooms* ⚿ *In-room: a/c, safe, kitchen (some), refrigerator (some), Wi-Fi. In-hotel: 2 restaurants, room service, bar, gym, spa, tennis courts, pool, parking (free)* ☰ *AE, D, DC, MC, V.*

$$$$ 🏨 **Crowne Plaza San Pedro Sula.** With a great location a few blocks from the central park, this elegant high-rise is among the city's best hotels. All rooms are comfortably furnished and set up for business travelers, so there are connections for your computer and plenty of telephones. For dining there's Antonio's, which serves typical Honduran cuisine, as well as a coffee shop that stays open until midnight. The staff is always ready to help you find your way around the city. **Pros:** centrally located; good restaurant. **Cons:** far from upscale nightlife and shopping. ⊠ *Blvd. Morazán, between Avs.10 and 11* ☎ *550–8080, 877/227–6963 in U.S.* ⊕ *www.ichotelsgroup.com* ⤷ *121 rooms, 3 suites* ⚿ *In-room: a/c, safe, refrigerator (some), Wi-Fi. In-hotel: 2 restaurants, room service, bar, pool, gym, laundry service, Internet terminal, parking (free)* ☰ *AE, MC, V.*

$$ 🏨 **Gran Hotel Sula.** This downtown high-rise is San Pedro's original business-class hotel, and offers a wide range of services at economical prices. Facing Parque Central, it is close to all of San Pedro Sula's major attractions. Business travelers will appreciate the fact that it is near the financial district. Café Skandia, open 24 hours, is a great place for late-night dinners and early breakfasts by the pool. It is also the only coffee shop in Central America with a Viking theme. All rooms have balconies with views of the city. **Pros:** can't get more centrally located; bargain rates for what is offered. **Cons:** far from nightlife and upscale shopping. ⊠ *C. 1 NO between Avs. 3 and 4* ☎ *545–2600* ⊕ *www.hotelsula.hn* ⤷ *125 rooms* ⚿ *In-room: a/c, safe, Wi-Fi. In-hotel: restaurant, room service, bar, pool, gym, Internet terminal, parking (free)* ☰ *AE, D, DC, MC, V.*

$$$$ 🏨 **Hilton Princess San Pedro Sula.** Although it caters predominantly to business executives, this European-style hotel has personalized service that makes it a good option for any traveler. There are plenty of amenities, from the sparkling pool to the gym. The restaurant is decorated in a stark style, whereas the bar more closely resembles an English pub. The concierge is great for tips on restaurants. **Pros:** luxurious surroundings; attentive service; close to shopping and nightlife. **Cons:** not centrally located. ⊠ *C. 10 SO and Av. Circunvalación, Col. Trejo* ☎ *556–9600* ⊕ *www.hilton.com* ⤷ *121 rooms, 3 suites* ⚿ *In-room: a/c, Wi-Fi, safe. In-hotel: restaurant, room service, bar, pool, gym, parking (free)* ☰ *AE, D, DC, MC, V.*

$$$ 🏨 **Holiday Inn Express.** One of San Pedro's newest lodging offerings, this incarnation of the reassuring standby won't disappoint the chain's many fans. Service is friendly, layout and style are familiar, and the do-it-yourself buffet breakfast that the chain is known for greets you every morning. **Pros:** friendly service; close to shopping and nightlife. **Cons:** some reports of noisy air conditioners. ⊠ *Av. Circunvalación between Cs. 12*

*and 13 SO* 📠 *540–3000, 888/465–4329 in U.S.* ⊕ *www.hiexpress.com* 🖥 *110 rooms* ⚫ *In-room: a/c, Wi-Fi. In-hotel: restaurant, pool, gym, Internet terminal, parking (free)* ☰ *AE, D, DC, MC, V* 🍴 *CP.*

**$$** 🖥 **Hotel Ejecutivo.** Business travelers on expense accounts not flush enough for the Clarion or Gran Hotel Sula stay at this dependable, midrange lodging a few blocks from the city center. Rooms contain comfortable beds, a table and chairs, and flat-screen TVs. The hotel also accepts traveler's checks as payment. **Pros:** friendly staff; bargain rates. **Cons:** a few worn furnishings; far from nightlife and upscale shopping. ✉ *C. 2 at 10 Av. SO* 📠 *552–4361* ⊕ *www.hotel-ejecutivo.com* 🖥 *40 rooms* ⚫ *In-room: a/c, Wi-Fi. In-hotel: restaurant, room service, bar, pool, gym, laundry service, Internet terminal, parking (free)* ☰ *AE, D, DC, MC, V* 🍴 *BP.*

**$** 🖥 **Hotel Saint Anthony.** This delightful hotel has splendid views from the pretty rooftop pool. You can feel your tensions fade as you step into the elegant lobby. If you have business needs, there is an executive floor with computer connections. **Pros:** good budget value. **Cons:** several blocks from city center. ✉ *Av. 3 SO at C. 13 SO* 📠 *558–0744* 🖥 *89 rooms* ⚫ *In-room: a/c. In-hotel: restaurant, bar, pool, Internet terminal, parking (free)* ☰ *AE, D, DC,MC, V.*

**$–$$** 🖥 **Los Jícaros.** Orange dominates, outside and in, at this newish lodging several blocks west of Parque Central on a side street right behind the Crowne Plaza. Rooms are decorated with Honduran art and contain comfortable beds, flat-screen TVs, small desks, and tons of closet space. The three fully equipped suites include small patios. **Pros:** personal service; huge amount of closet space. **Cons:** a couple of rooms right off dining area can be noisy; far from nightlife and upscale shopping. ✉ *Av. 11 NO and C. 2* 📠 *550–7003* ⊕ *www.usula.com* 🖥 *7 rooms, 3 suites* ⚫ *In-room: a/c, kitchen (some), refrigerator (some), Wi-Fi. In-hotel: bar, laundry service, Internet terminal, parking (free)* ☰ *AE, D, DC, MC, V* 🍴 *CP.*

**$$$$** 🖥 **Real San Pedro Sula.** A 2007 renovation made this hotel the most
**Fodor's Choice** luxurious lodging in the city. The public areas of the Real are simply
★ grand, with marble and plants everywhere, giving this in-city hotel the vibe of a tropical resort. If you want to opt for true luxury, an executive floor tosses in such amenities as butler service and twice-daily pressings. **Pros:** lavish public areas; close to shopping and nightlife. **Cons:** fee for Wi-Fi use. ✉ *Blvd. del Sur, across from Multiplaza* 📠 *545–2000, 888/424–6835 in U.S.* ⊕ *www.ichotelsgroup.com* 🖥 *149 rooms* ⚫ *In-room: a/c, safe, DVD (some), Wi-Fi. In-hotel: restaurant, room service, bar, pool, gym, spa, laundry service, Internet terminal, parking (free)* ☰ *AE, D, DC, MC, V* 🍴 *EP, CP.*

## SHOPPING

Shopping in the city center is dedicated to the workaday needs of residents and holds little of interest to visitors. The exception is the Mercado Guamilito, dedicated to artisan work and souvenirs. San Pedro's upscale shopping congregates in the outer reaches of the city around the Circunvalación.

**Mercado Guamilito.** This traditional market has managed to accumulate a terrific selection of souvenirs from around Honduras and can be your destination for one-stop shopping if time is limited. ⊠ *C. 6 NO between Avs. 8 and 9 NO* ☎ *No phone.*

**Multiplaza.** San Pedro's original shopping center has undergone improvements and upgrades to keep up with the other malls that have opened through the years, and now logs in at 99 stores. ⊠ *Blvd. del Sur* ☎ *545-2500.*

## NIGHTLIFE AND THE ARTS

The neighborhood where people go to party, the Zona Viva, is west of town near Avenida Circunvalación. People begin to hit the clubs around 10. Places come and go, so pick up a copy of *Honduras Tips* at your hotel to find out which spot is popular at the moment.

BARS An instant hit with the young crowd, **Frogs** (⊠ *Blvd. Los Próceres, near Av. Circunvalación*) is known for its great light system and good music. There are three different bars, including one where you can order food. If you can't stand the karaoke on weekends, you can retreat to the second-story deck overlooking the volleyball court. A local favorite that has been around for years, **Kawama Bay** (⊠ *Av. Circunvalación*) offers a full bar and great music.

In the Hilton Princess Hotel, **Clancy's Bar** (⊠ *C. 10 SO at Av. Circunvalación*) is one of the city's most refined bars. It's a good spot for appetizers before dinner or for a nightcap afterwards. The cheerful **Las Jarras** (⊠ *Av. 16 NO at C. 2*) is a great place to enjoy a few *bocas* (appetizers) in the afternoon.

CLUBS The classiest dance club in town, **Henry's** (⊠ *Av. Circunvalación at Av. 11 NO*) is a favorite with hip and trendy Sampedranos. Locals let loose on the dance floor at popular **Confeti's** (⊠ *Av. Circunvalación, near the exit to Puerto Cortés*). Attracting a slightly older crowd, **El Quijote** (⊠ *C. 11 SO between Avs. 3 and 4*) is the most exclusive of the city's dance clubs.

THE ARTS For cultural events, try the **Centro Cultural Sampedrano** (⊠ *Av. 4 NO at C. 3* ☎ *553–3911*), which often has art exhibitions. It also serves as the public library. **Alianza Francesa** (⊠ *Av. 23 SO between Cs. 3 and 4* ☎ *552–4359*) has a range of cultural events.

**Teatro José Franciscon Saybe.** This new performing-arts space adjoins the Museo de Antropología e Historia and has theater productions and musical performances, all in Spanish. ⊠ *Av. 3 NO and C. 4 NO* ☎ *557-1874.*

## SPORTS AND THE OUTDOORS

**Fundación Ecologista Hector Rodrigo Pastor Fasquelle.** San Pedro Sula's signature outdoor destination is the Parque Nacional Cusuco, a portion of which actually lies within the city limits. (The mountains you see due west of downtown are contained within the park.) Your best bet for a visit to the park is to make arrangements with the Fundación Ecologista Hector Rodrigo Pastor Fasquelle, the private foundation that administers Cusuco on behalf of the Honduran government. The friendly folks at the foundation's downtown San Pedro office can help arrange for a guide and transportation. ⊠ *Av. 7 NO at 1 C in San Pedro Sula* ☎ *552–1014.*

# SIDE TRIPS FROM SAN PEDRO SULA

## PARQUE NACIONAL CUSUCO

*20 km (12 mi) west of San Pedro Sula.*

This swath of premontane (higher elevation) subtropical forest was declared a protected area in 1959, when an ecologist reported that the pine trees here were the tallest in Central America. It's located in the Cordillera del Merendón, a mountain range that runs through Honduras and Guatemala. The park's highest peak is Cerro Jilinco, which towers to 7,355 feet.

Although the park is named for the *cusuco,* or armadillo, you're unlikely to see this shy creature. You're more apt to spot troops of howler monkeys or white-faced monkeys. The park is a birder's paradise, with close to 300 different species, including toucans, parrots, and elusive resplendent quetzals. You can pick up a map of the four trails at the visitor center, but hiring a guide is a good idea because you'll see wildlife you might have missed.

### GETTING HERE AND AROUND

The park is 20 km (12 mi) west of San Pedro, but the trip will take 2½ hours—especially when the rain turns the roads to mush. You'll definitely need a four-wheel-drive vehicle to negotiate the terrain. A portion of the park actually does lie within the city limits of San Pedro, but you'd never know it once you arrive. The private Fundación Ecologista Hector Rodrigo Pastor Fasquelle administers the park on behalf of the Honduran government. The foundation has an office in San Pedro Sula, and the people here can help you with transportation arrangements and hook you up with a guide, a good recommendation rather than trying to negotiate the park on your own.

### ESSENTIALS

 *Fundación Ecologista Hector Rodrigo Pastor Fasquelle*⊠ *Av. 7 NO at 1 C in San Pedro Sula* ☎ *552–1014* 💲 *L225.*

### WHERE TO EAT

Bring your own food if you plan on staying overnight at the cabin in the park.To do so, you'll need to make arrangements with the Fundación Ecologista Hector Rodrigo Pastor Fasquelle, the foundation that administers the park. Check with them for recommendations.

### WHERE TO STAY

Administered by the Fundación Ecologista Hector Rodrigo Pastor Fasquelle, Cusuco has accommodations in two small cabins.

## CASCADAS DE PULHAPANZAK

*70 km (42 mi) southeast of San Pedro Sula.*

The roaring Pulhapanzak Falls are the highest in the country. The thunderous noise draws you down the 128 steps to where you have a good view of the 328-foot waterfall.

Puhlapanzak lies just off Highway CA-5 between San Pedro Sula and Tegucigalpa, near the hamlet of Peña Blanca. The turnoff to the falls is about 60 km (36 mi) southeast of San Pedro. The remainder of the journey takes you to the site over a bumpy road. Public transportation is difficult and convoluted to get to the falls. Your easiest option is a day tour organized by Explore Honduras in San Pedro Sula. The $110-per-person price includes a half-day at Pulhapanzak and a half-day at Lago de Yojoa.

Local children will offer to guide you to the best spots to contemplate nature's glory. Exercise utmost caution if you come here during the rainy season; the steps leading down to the waterfalls can get slippery. A few deaths from falls have occurred through the years.

**Contacts Sendero (Trailhead), Cascadas de Pulhapanzak** (✉ *Near Peña Blanca* ☎ *No phone* ☉ *Daily 6–6* 🎫 *L30*).

# COPÁN RUINAS

*168 km (104 mi) southwest of San Pedro Sula, 10 km (6 mi) east of Guatemalan border.*

Just to the east of the town of Copán Ruinas, the Mayan ruins of Copán are without a doubt one of the most important attractions for tourists in Honduras. The tourism industry in the Bay Islands might dispute the methodology of arriving at the figures, but this is the country's most-visited tourist attraction, and Honduras's outpost on the Gringo Trail. Thousands have visited Copán before you—it is often called "The Paris of the Mayan World," and the site really does live up to the hype—and thousands more will come after.

But there is much more to do while in Copán Ruinas than visit the ruins. While the town retains its colonial charm with cobblestone streets and a pleasant central park, it is also becoming a more modern village with fine dining, lots of services, and a bustling, polished tourism industry unlike anywhere else in the country. Taxis here are most often small three-wheeled vehicles lovingly referred to as tuk-tuks, and a variety of local sites can be reached by horseback. Two days is the typical length of a visit here—one day for the ruins and a second day for other activities—but a third day gives you a chance to take it all in at a more leisurely pace. Many hotels put together multiday Web-only packages that include accommodation and a tour of the ruins.

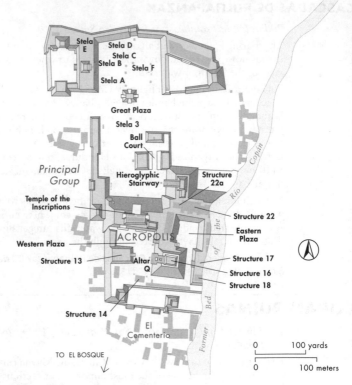

Stela E

Stela D

Stela C

Stela B

Stela F

Stela A

← TO VISITORS CENTER AND MUSEO DE ESCULTURA MAYA

Great Plaza

Stela 3

Ball Court

*Principal Group*

Hieroglyphic Stairway

Structure 22a

Temple of the Inscriptions

Structure 22

Eastern Plaza

Western Plaza

ACROPOLIS

Structure 13

Altar Q

Structure 17

Structure 16

Structure 18

Structure 14

El Cementerio

TO EL BOSQUE

Río Copán

Former Bed of the

0        100 yards

0        100 meters

## GETTING HERE AND AROUND

Copán Ruinas sits due southwest of San Pedro Sula. At the crossroads town of La Entrada, 103 km (65 mi) from San Pedro, the road splits, giving you the choice between travel to Copán Ruinas and Santa Rosa de Copán. The remainder of the journey to Copán Ruinas is over a secondary road that twists and turns in portions and has occasional potholes, but is manageable.

Several bus companies ply the route between San Pedro and Copán Ruinas. Do yourself a favor and spring for one of the three-times-daily Hedman Alas coaches. The extra level of comfort and express service are worth the extra cost (L330 one way). Other bus services can be exhausting—they are crowded and stop everywhere.

Other than on the central plaza, streets in town are narrow and one-way. Driving is a nuisance here. Leave your vehicle in your hotel lot and walk. The town is compact enough, and you can even walk to the ruins. Copán Ruinas's taxis are the motorized three-wheeled Bajaj RE vehicles made in India. Everyone refers to them as tuk-tuks.

New to Copán Ruinas are real street names for the first time with spiffy Maya-style signs. Few local people use or even know the new names, preferring to give addresses in reference to local landmarks, usually the central park. We use both systems—the street signs are useful to help

## HOW DO I GET TO "COPÁN"?

A few places around here incorporate the term *Copán* into their names creating the potential for some confusion. The word alone refers to the archaeological site of Mayan ruins. Copán Ruinas is the nearby town. (You'd think it would be the other way around.) When inquiring about transportation, always specify that you're going to Copán Ruinas. Many Hondurans equate *Copán* with the entire department (province) of Copán and will direct you to its capital, the town of Santa Rosa de Copán. (Make sure you take the right turn or get on the right bus.) To add to the confusion, the drive between San Pedro Sula and Copán Ruinas takes you through a crossroads town called La Entrada, which many call *La Entrada de Copán* (the entrance to Copán), but that refers to the entrance to the Copán Valley). You're not there yet. You still have 65 km (39 mi) to go.

4

you get your bearings—but don't expect anybody to be able to answer "Where is Calle Independencia?"

**Bus Companies Hedman Alas** (✉ *Gran Central Metropolitana, San Pedro Sula* ☎ *553–1361*).

### SAFETY
Things are quite low-key here, but as in any place that attracts a large concentration of tourists, you should keep watch of your possessions.

### MONEY MATTERS
It's no surprise that Honduras's number-one tourist center has plenty of banks with ATMs. Banco Atlántida on Parque Central exchanges dollars and traveler's checks and has a cash machine.

**Banks Banco Atlántida** (✉ *South side of Parque Central*).

### TOURS
The Asociación de Guías de Copán has a lock on guide services at the ruins themselves. You can arrange a guide in advance or when you arrive. They get high marks for their knowledge. Basecamp Outdoor Adventures, with office inside the Café Vía Vía, leads several hikes around the area. An alternative hike shows you how local people live. A nature hike takes you through the hills around town. An all-day expedition hike takes you to visit Maya Chortí villages. Yaragua Tours offers reservations and arrangements for all the major sites in the area, such as caving, hot springs, a canopy tour, and a hacienda tour. Tour prices vary, from about $15 for horseback rides to the waterfalls up to $45 for full-day trips with meals.

**Tour Companies Asociación de Guías de Copán** (✉ *Copán entrance* ☎ *651–4018*).**Basecamp Outdoor Adventures** (✉ *C. de la Plaza, 1½ blocks west of Parque Central* ☎ *651–4695* ⊕ *www.basecampcopan.wordpress.com*). **Yaragua Tours** (✉ *C. de la Plaza, southeast corner of Parque Central* ☎ *651–4147* ⊕ *www.yaragua.com*).

## THE MAYA CALENDAR

The Maya devised an intricate calendar system whose dates you'll see on monuments at Copán, although today's Maya-descended peoples in Honduras have fully adopted the Western Gregorian calendar.

The system is technically a three-in-one interlocking calendar. The Maya did not entirely develop the scheme, but refined during the late pre-Classic period earlier conventions of dating developed by the Olmec civilization of Mexico. Some scholars surmise that the calendar marks the Maya calculation of the beginning of the world at what would correspond to our August 11, 3114 BC.

At the system's base is the Tzolkin calendar made up of 13 cycles of 20 days. Each of the resulting 260 days bears a unique name, combining day and cycle. Why 13 and 20? Theories abound. The human body contains 13 major joints (three for each limb plus the neck.) The domain of the gods also contained 13 levels. The Maya used a base-20 numbering system (as opposed to ours, which is based on 10). Twenty may have been chosen because it's the total number of fingers and toes, suggest some historians. Other experts suggest that 260 days roughly corresponds to the nine months of human pregnancy, and that midwives may have developed the Tzolkin system to aid in prediction of birth dates.

Running in parallel to the Tzolkin system is the Haab calendar, approximately matching the solar year, with 18 months of 20 days each, plus five unnamed days, considered dangerous for many activities. Though Mayan astronomers were able to calculate quite an accurate length of the solar year, those calculations did not form part of the Haab calendar, which remained fixed at 365 days, and had no leap-year fixes to even things out.

Combine Tzolkin and Haab to get a cycle of 18,980 days that lasts 52 solar years, perhaps an average life expectancy back in the Maya heyday. But to describe the entire Maya history, which obviously took place outside the 52-year cycle, it became necessary to create what scholars today refer to as the Long Count calendar. Here's the kicker: the Long Count cycle concludes on December 21, 2012. Whether that will represent the apocalypse or simply a turning over of the odometer, you'll have to decide. (Google MAYA CALENDAR 2012 to see what all the fuss is about.) No predictions have been made, but we do know that lodgings here in Copán Ruinas have already been taking bookings for that date.

## EXPLORING

Although most visitors come here to see the astounding Mayan ruins east of town, you can also learn a bit about that culture at the **Museo Regional de Arqueología Maya.** Though most of this charming little museum's descriptions are in Spanish, the ancient tools and artworks speak for themselves. The exhibit on *el brujo* (the witch) is especially striking, displaying the skeleton and religious artifacts of a Mayan shaman. ⊠ *West side of Parque Central* ☎ *651–4437* ⌨ *L60* ☉ *Daily 9–5.*

## OFF TO AMERICA

American diplomat and explorer John Lloyd Stephens (1805–1852) is credited with "discovering" Copán in 1843. Stephens was actually able to purchase the entire site for $50. He concocted an elaborate plan to disassemble all the structures, float them down the river, load them on ships, and send them to America. We can be grateful that never happened. Despite his harebrained scheme and his paternalistic view of other cultures—Stephens originally surmised that the Maya were too "savage" to have built a city as grand as Copán—historians today regard him as one of the 19th century's important Mayanists.

Stephens' *Incidents of Travel in Central America, Chiapas, and Yucatán* is regarded as an important contribution to the field of knowledge of Mayan culture.

**Casa K'inich.** If your kids have ever wanted to dress as a Copán noble or learn to count to 10 in Chortí, this interactive children's museum is the place. It's a steep walk uphill to get here. Take a tuk-tuk taxi. ✉ *Av. Centroamerica, 6 blocks north of Parque Central* ☎ *651–4105* ⊕ *www.asociacioncopan.org* ✂ *L6; children under 12, free* ☉ *Tues.–Sun. 8–noon and 1–5.*

**Copán.** You'll approach the ruins via a short stone path, about a 20-minute walk, that leads just outside town. Before you reach the ruins you'll reach some carved Mayan statues, and eventually a gate and admissions building. There is a small house in the parking area where the guides gather to lead tours for the day. Their services are well worth the money. They have a wealth of knowledge regarding the life and activities of the ancient Mayan people, and can interpret the hieroglyphs' literal as well as folkloric meaning.

The area open to the public covers only a small part of the city's ceremonial center. Copán once extended for nearly 2 km (1¼ mi) along the river, making it as large as many Mayan archaeological sites in Guatemala. It's also just as old—more than 3,000 years ago there was an Olmec settlement on this site. Because new structures were usually built on top of existing ones, the great temples that are visible today were built during the reigns of the city's last few rulers.

As you stroll past towering cieba trees on your way to the archaeological site, you'll find the **Great Plaza** to your left. The stelae standing about the plaza were monuments erected to glorify rulers. Some stelae on the periphery are dedicated to King Smoke Jaguar, but the most impressive, located in the middle of the plaza, depict King 18 Rabbit. Besides stroking the egos of the kings, these monuments had religious significance as well. Vaults for ritual offerings have been found beneath most of them.

The city's most important **ball court** lies south of the Great Plaza. One of the largest of its kind in Central America, it was used for more than simple entertainment. Players had to keep a hard rubber ball from touching the ground, perhaps symbolizing the sun's battle to stay aloft. Stylized carvings of macaw heads that line either side of the court may have been used as markers for keeping score, although the game was more spiritual than sportslike in nature. Competitions were incredibly physical and players were likely using hallucinogenic substances. The losers—or the winners in some cases—were killed as a sacrifice to Mayan gods.

Near the ball court is one of the highlights of Copán, the **Hieroglyphic Stairway.** This amazing structure, covered with a canopy to protect it from the weather, con-

**STUDYING SPANISH IN COPÁN RUINAS**

Copán Ruinas has great Spanish-language-immersion programs, with plenty of activities for your spare time.

**Guacamaya Spanish School** ⊠ *Av. Copán, 2 blocks north of Parque Central* ☎ *651–4360* ⊕ *www.guacamaya.com).*

**Ixbalanque Spanish School** ⊠ *Av. Los Jaguares, 3 blocks west, ½ block north of Parque Central* ☎ *651–4432* ⊕ *www.ixbalanque.com).*

tains the single largest collection of hieroglyphs in the world. The 63 steps immortalize the battles won by Copán's kings, especially those of the much revered King Smoke Jaguar. Once placed chronologically, the history can no longer be read because an earthquake knocked many steps free, and archaeologists replaced them in a random order. All may not be lost, however, as experts have located an early photograph of the stairway that helps unlock the proper sequence.

The **Western Court** is thought to have represented the underworld. The structures, with doors that lead to blank walls, appear symbolic. On the east side of the plaza is a reproduction of Altar Q, a key to understanding the history of Copán. The squat platform shows a long line of Copán's rulers passing power down to their heirs. It ends with the last great king, Dawning Sun, facing the first king, Yax Kuk Mo.

The **Acropolis** was partly washed away by the Río Copán, which has since been routed away from the ruins. King Dawning Sun was credited with the construction of many of the buildings surrounding this grand plaza. Below the Acropolis are tunnels that lead to what archaeologists agree are some of the most fascinating discoveries at Copán. Underneath Structure 16 are the near-perfect remains of an older building, called the **Rosalila Temple.** This structure, dating from 571, was subsequently buried below taller structures. Uncovered in 1989, the Rosalila was notable in part because of the paint remains on its surface—rose and lilac—for which it was named. Another tunnel called **Los Jaguares** takes you past tombs, a system of aqueducts, and even an ancient bathroom.

Two other parts of Copán that served as residential and administrative areas are open to the public. Although the architecture is not nearly as impressive as that of the larger buildings, they offer a glimpse into the daily lives of ordinary people. **El Bosque** (the Forest) lies in the woods off the trail to the west of the Principal Group. **Las Sepulturas** (the Graves), which lies 2 km (1 mi) down the main road, is a revealing look into Mayan society. Excavations have shown that the Maya had a highly stratified social system, where the elite owned houses with many rooms.

East of the main entrance to Copán, the marvelous **Museo de Escultura Maya** provides a closeup look at the best of Mayan artistry. All the

> ### THE MAYA PORT IN YOUR COMPUTER
>
> The Spanish term for a computer flash drive, the supplemental drive that plugs into the USB port of your PC, is a *llave maya* (Maya key).

sculptures and replicas are accompanied by informative signs in English as well as Spanish. Here you'll find a full-scale replica of the Rosalila Temple. The structure, in eye-popping shades of red and green, offers an educated guess at what the ceremonial and political structures of Copán must have looked like at the time they were in use.

The complex employs a bit of à la carte pricing. The $15 entrance fee covers admission to the ruins, and covers admission to nearby sites like El Bosque and Las Sepulturas. Admission to the tunnels to Rosalila and Los Jaguares is $12 extra. Admission to the Museo de Escultura Maya is $5. You can pay in U.S. dollars or lempiras.

It's a good idea to hire a guide, as they are very knowledgeable about the site. English-speaking ones charge about L400 for a two-hour tour, while Spanish-speaking guides charge about half that. A small cafeteria and gift shop are near the entrance.

A visit to the ruins can last anywhere from one to four hours. If your schedule permits, an early-morning visit is ideal. If you can be here when the gate opens at 8 AM, the weather will be better, both in terms of cooler temperatures and clearer skies during the rainy season. Sunlight is lower, and that makes for better photography. You're also more likely to catch a glimpse of the animal life that calls the park home, especially the white-tailed deer. On your own, you can easily walk through the ruins and admire the structures and carvings. If you have a guide along, you likely will spend more time getting up close to the carvings, and learning about Mayan hieroglyphics and the history that they record. ⊠ *1 km (½ mi) east of Copán Ruinas* ☎ *No phone* ⌨ *Ruins $15 or L300; museum $5 or L100; tunnels $12 or L240* ☉ *Daily 8–4.*

## WHERE TO EAT

There is great emphasis on traditional cooking and foods in Copán Ruinas. In addition to great restaurants, try some of the local *comedores* (diners) and *pupuserías* (pupusa shacks). Many restaurants prepare their version of Mayan cuisine, and other traditional dishes.

$ ✕ **Café San Rafael.** The aroma of freshly ground coffee envelops you
CAFÉ as you walk into this small café set on the patio of a brick house. In addition to the coffee, you'll find a nice selection of Chilean wine and sandwiches made with artisanal cheeses from a farm outside of town. Try the grilled turkey and blue cheese. If you come here for dinner, make it an early one; the place closes at 8. ⊠ *Av. Centroamericana, 1½ blocks south of Parque Central* ☎ *651–4546* ▭ *AE, D, DC, MC, V.*

## ROYAL LINEAGE AT COPÁN

The first king during the Classic period, Yax Kuk Mo (Blue-Green Quetzal Macaw) came to power around AD 435. Very little is known about him or his successors until the rise of the 12th king, Smoke Jaguar (628–695). Under his rule, Copán grew to be one of the largest cities in the region. His successor, King 18 Rabbit (695–738), continued the quest for complete control of the region. The city's political structure was shaken, however, when he was captured by the soldiers of Quiriguá, a city in what is today part of Guatemala. He was brought to that city and beheaded.

During his short reign, Smoke Monkey (738–749) was increasingly challenged by powerful noble families. Smoke Monkey's son, Smoke Shell (749–763), tried to justify his power by playing up the historical importance of great warrior kings. He ordered the construction of the elaborate Hieroglyphic Stairway, the longest Classic Mayan inscription yet to be discovered, which emphasized the supremacy in battle of Copán's rulers. The 16th king, Dawning Sun (763–820), continued to glorify warfare in his architecture, but it was too late. By this time, Copán and its political authority were in decline.

$ **✕ Café Vía Vía.** ECLECTIC Though many backpackers flock here, Vía Vía provides a great meal and atmosphere attractive to nearly any traveler. Food is served from 7 AM to 9 PM every day, and the bar stays open until just before midnight. Great selections of world music, as well as salsa-dancing lessons, bring in lots of people in the evenings. The kitchen specialties include vegetarian dishes, Indian and Thai food, and local favorites, all at great prices. Basecamp Tours, the affiliated tourist information center, is located across the street, making this a great first stop on your visit to Copán. ⊠ *C. de la Plaza, 1½ blocks west of Parque Central* ☎ 651–4652 ☐ *No credit cards.*

$ **✕ Carnitas Nía Lola.** HONDURAN Housed in a charming wooden building, this long-time favorite has sweeping views of the valley from its second-story dining room. Wonderful smells emanate from the meats on the grill, which is crowned with a stone skull reminiscent of those at the nearby ruins. One of the favorite dishes here is the *carne encebollado*, sizzling beef topped with onions and accompanied by a mound of french fries. ⊠ *2 blocks south of Parque Central* ☎ *No phone* ☐ *AE, MC, V.*

¢ **✕ Comedor Mary.** LATIN AMERICAN A long-time local favorite that has morphed into a favorite of visitors offers down-home dining at bargain prices. Pull up a chair to one of the wooden tables and partake of a *pupusa*, the specialty here. The dish originated in neighboring El Salvador and they are that country's answer to the crepe, with a filling of chicken, pork, or beans and tangy cabbage. ⊠ *Av. Mirador, 1 block west and ½ block south of Parque Central* ☎ *No phone* ☐ *No credit cards.*

¢ **✕ Llama del Bosque.** LATIN Named for a colorful flower, this cheerful little place is tucked away on a side street. It feels much larger than it really is because of the sloped wooden ceiling that soars above the dining room. This is the place to come for barbecued meats—try the *pinchos*, which are chunks of beef brought to your table on long skewers. Open for breakfast, lunch, and dinner, this is a longtime favorite in Copán.

✉ *1½ blocks west of Parque Central* ☎ *651–4431* ▭ *AE, MC, V.*

**$** ✗ **Pizza Copán.** The sign in front

ITALIAN may say PIZZA COPÁN, but everybody knows this old standby as Jim's Pizza. You'll find the standard variety of pizza toppings and sizes here at this long-time favorite expat hangout, along with rotisserie chicken and decent burgers.

**TIP**

If you're headed into Guatemala beyond the nearby border crossing at El Florido, we recommend you pick up a copy of *Fodor's Guatemala,* our guidebook to that country.

The place is not open for lunch, per se, but does start serving at 2 PM. ✉ *Av. Centroamericana, ½ block south of Parque Central* ☎ *651–4381* ▭ *No credit cards* ☉ *No lunch.*

**4**

**$$$** ✗ **Twisted Tanya's.** An eclectic open-air dining room on the second floor

LATIN makes Twisted Tanya's great for a romantic dinner or a special occasion.

**Fodor's**Choice There's usually a prix-fixe menu, with several selections for the main

★ course. Even if you already know what you want, the waitstaff enjoy holding up the menu board and describing each item to you with a flair. ✉ *C. Independencia, 1 block south, 1 block west of Parque Central* ☎ *651–4182* ⊕ *www.twistedtanyas.com* ▭ *MC, V.*

# WHERE TO STAY

**$** ⛺ **Casa de Café.** You are several blocks from the center of town here.

**Fodor's**Choice That can be an advantage—peace and quiet—or a disadvantage,

★ depending on your needs, but we lead toward the former. Rooms occupy several buildings behind the owners' house. The original ones are smaller; the newer ones span a portion of the hillside and are larger with exposed-beam ceilings. All have one full or two single beds and white walls. Take breakfast out on the patio, with terrific views of the valley—you can see as far away as neighboring Guatemala—and luxuriate there in the all-day supply of coffee. Not that anything too stressful ever goes on in Copán Ruinas, but an on-site massage pavilion is here to knead your cares away. The owners rent a few houses on the same street, too. **Pros:** very peaceful; removed from hubbub of center of town; owner is encyclopedia of information about Honduras; terrific rates **Cons:** removed from hubbub of center of town. ✉ *1 block south and 4 blocks west of Parque Central* ☎ *651–4620* ⊕ *www.casadecafecopan. com* ➴ *10 rooms* ♿ *In-room: a/c, no phone, Wi-Fi. In-hotel: laundry service, parking (free)* ▭ *AE, D, DC, MC, V* ⦿ *BP.*

**$** ⛺ **Hacienda San Lucas.** In a century-old hacienda, this country inn is

★ one of the most charming lodgings in the area. Flavia Cueva's tender care shows in all the details, from the carefully crafted wooden furniture in the simple but elegant rooms to the hammocks swinging from the porch outside. The restaurant, near the delightful old stove, serves steaming tamales, tasty adobo sauce, and aromatic coffee. Take a walk to Los Sapos, a Mayan archaeological site where huge stones were carved into the shape of frogs, or go horseback riding through the cool Copán Valley. A nonguest day pass to use the facilities is L40. **Pros:** lovely owner; attentive service; atmospheric restaurant. **Cons:** far from center of town. ✉ *1½ km (1 mi) south of Copán Ruinas* ☎ *651–4495*

⊕ *www.haciendasanlucas.com* ⮌ 8 *rooms* ♿ *In-room: no a/c, Wi-Fi. In-hotel: restaurant* ⊟ *AE, D, DC, MC, V* ⦿ *BP.*

**$$$–$$$$**  ⊡ **Hotel Marina Copán.** Partially facing Parque Central, this colonial-era building has been lovingly converted into one of the town's prettiest hotels. The second-story restaurant overlooks the sparkling pool, shaded by clusters of banana trees. Brilliant bougainvillea lines the paths to the rooms, which are filled with hand-hewn wood furniture and cooled by lazily turning ceiling fans. Once the marimba band starts playing, you might never want to leave the hotel. **Pros:** attentive service; nice shops inside; centrally located. **Cons:** lots of activity here, so not a place to stay if you crave isolation. ⊠ *Av. Centroamericana, northwest corner of Parque Central* ☎ 651–4070 ⊕ *www.hotelmarinacopan.com* ⮌ 49 *rooms, 2 suites* ♿ *In-room: a/c, Wi-Fi. In-hotel: restaurant, room service, bar, pool, gym, sauna, spa, horseback riding, bar, shop, laundry service, meeting rooms, travel services, parking (free)* ⊟ *AE, MC, V.*

**$$**  ⊡ **Hotel Posada Real de Copán.** The closest lodging to the ruins, this Spanish-style hotel is in the hills just outside town. The open-air lobby, filled with tropical flowers, adds to the ambience. Inside the tile-roof buildings are generously proportioned rooms with views of the lush gardens. After a day exploring the dusty ruins, swim a few laps in the palm-shaded pool or relax in the nearby hot tub. **Pros:** can't get any closer to the ruins. **Cons:** far from center of town. ⊠ *2 km (1 mi) east of Copán Ruinas* ☎ 651–4480 ⊕ *www.posadarealdecopan.com* ⮌ 80 *rooms* ♿ *In-room: a/c. In-hotel: restaurant, room service, bar, pool, parking (free)* ⊟ *AE, MC, V* ⦿ *EP.*

**$$**  ⊡ **Hotel Don Udo's.** Don Udo, long famous for his San Pedro Sula restaurant, is also in Copán Ruinas. This small colonial hotel has 16 pleasant rooms that circle the lovely patio, restaurant, and bar. A third-floor sundeck has a panoramic view of the stunning Copán valley and town. There are double rooms, Jr. Suites, and Master Suites, for all group sizes and budgets. The attention to detail and amenities make this luxurious hotel a great value. **Pros:** friendly owner; good views. **Cons:** some rooms get street noise. ⊠ *Av. Mirador, 2 blocks south of Parque Central, Av. del Mercado Municipal* ☎ 651–4533 ⊕ *www.donudos.com* ⮌ 16 *rooms* ♿ *In-room: a/c, no TV (some), Wi-Fi. In-hotel: restaurant, bar, Internet terminal, parking (free)* ⊟ *AE, MC, V* ⦿ *BP.*

**$$**  ⊡ **La Casa Rosada.** Look for the pink house—that's what Casa Rosada
**Fodor's Choice**  means—on the hill a few blocks north of Parque Central. This is eas-
★  ily the most romantic lodging in Copán Ruinas and would be a good candidate for a honeymoon. The entire place exudes colonial elegance, with carved-wood furniture, stone floors, handwoven throw rugs, and Honduran art throughout. (The flat-screen TVs are a concession to a hotel guest's modern needs.) Bathrooms contain bidets, the option of a steam shower, and a speaker system in that shower. One room here is wheelchair accessible, a rarity in Honduras. **Pros:** colonial elegance; attentive staff; nice little touches not seen elsewhere. **Cons:** steep climb up street if walking; one room has non-adjoining bath. ⊠ *C. Acropolis at Av. Mirador, 1 block north and 1 block west of Parque Central* ☎ 651–4324 ⊕ *www.lacasarosada.com* ⮌ 9 *rooms* ♿ *In-room:*

a/c, refrigerator, DVD, Wi-Fi. In-hotel: bar, laundry service, Internet terminal, parking (free) ▤ AE, D, DC, MC, V ⦿ BP.

$$  ⊡ **Plaza Copán.** You can see a lot from the terrace at this hotel on Parque Central. If you ask for one of the rooms on the top floor, which have views of the town's red-tile roofs, you might see horses clip-clopping around the cobbled streets of town. Don't forget to relax with a drink by the small pool in the central courtyard, which is shaded by tall palm trees. The restaurant, Los Arcos, is set behind a lovely colonnade and serves traditional fare. **Pros:** centrally located; good rates. **Cons:** lackluster service. ✉ C. de la Plaza, southeast corner of Parque Central ☎ 651–4039 ⊕ www.plazacopanhotel.com ⇲ 20 rooms ♿ In-room: a/c, Wi-Fi. In-hotel: restaurant, bar, pool, free parking ▤ AE, MC, V ⦿ EP.

$$  ⊡ **Terramaya.** This newest in-town lodging in Copán Ruinas opened in 2010, courtesy of the friendly folks at Casa de Café, and it's another winner for them. Decor in the enormous rooms is minimalist with blindingly white walls and granite sinks. All rooms contain queen beds. The two downstairs rooms overlook their own private gardens. The hotel is perched on a hill and commands stupendous views. The balconies overlook the ruins below, although they are hidden by trees. You'll find a small library of travel and archaeology books here, much appreciated if you'd like to delve into the history of the region. As at the parent Casa de Café out on the edge of town, you can have your tired muscles worked on at a massage pavilion out in the garden. **Pros:** beautiful rooms; well-appointed furnishings; plenty of space. **Cons:** steep climb up street if walking. ✉ Av. Centroamericana at C. El Escribano, 3 blocks north of Parque Central ☎ 651–4623 ⊕ www.terramayacopan. com ⇲ 6 rooms ♿ In-room: a/c, no phone, Wi-Fi. In-hotel: laundry service, parking (free) ▤ AE, D, DC, MC, V ⦿ BP.

$  ⊡ **Yat B'alam.** You'd walk right by this place if you didn't know it was

**Fodor's** Choice  a hotel. The entry to this colonial-style building is arranged like a cob-

★  blestone street lined with a café and three upscale souvenir shops. The second floor housed a scant four rooms arranged around a second-floor patio. The comfy rooms contain tiled floors, dark-wood furniture, and wrought-iron accents. Two of the rooms face a busy street, but all windows here are soundproofed, so there's no street noise. **Pros:** soundproofed windows; attentive staff. **Cons:** smallish rooms. ✉ C. La Independencia ☎ 651–4338 ⊕ www.yatbalam.com ⇲ 4 rooms ♿ In-room: a/c, refrigerator, DVD, Wi-Fi. In-hotel: restaurant, laundry service, Internet terminal, parking (free) ▤ AE, D, DC, MC, V ⦿ EP.

## SPORTS AND THE OUTDOORS

There are almost unlimited outdoor activities available in Copán Ruinas these days. Although the main park holds the majority of the pre-Columbian ruins, many tour operators offer off-road visits to some other interesting Mayan sites. There are also hot springs nearby with pools and spa facilities, and a canopy tour in Los Sapos that offers views of the Mayan ruins from above. If you decide to spend more time in the Copán area, the following tours and tour operators can show you more about pre-Columbian Copán, and the lifestyles of current day Copanecos.

☺ **Enchanted Wings Butterfly Garden.** Here's the place to learn everything you've always wanted to know about butterflies. You'll see more activity if you visit in the morning. You can take a guided tour, or use the laminated cards provided that illustrate the species you'll see. The attraction was set up by a former Peace Corps volunteer, and these folks also operate an on-site botanical garden with some 200 species of orchids. Locals refer to the place as the *mariposario* (butterfly garden). ✉ *Outside of Copán Ruinas on road to El Florido* ☎ *651–4133* 🖅 *L115; children under 12, L50* ☉ *Daily 8–4:30.*

☺ **Macaw Mountain Bird Park & Nature Reserve.** has extensive aviaries and birding facilities, as well as 20 species of rescued birds, primarily Central American macaws, toucans and parrots. (There just might be a special place in heaven for these folks for the good work they do.) Particularly interesting is the exhibit explaining the relationship the Maya had to birds. There are handicap-accessible trails and walkways, too. The on-site restaurant is operated by Twisted Tanya's in town and has a similar eclectic menu. Incidentally, everybody around here refers to the complex as simply "the Bird Park." (✉ *2½ km [1½ mi] north of Copán Ruinas* ☎ *651–4245* ⊕ *www.macawmountain.com* 🖅 *$10* ☉ *Daily 9–5*)

**Copán Coffee Tour.** The Copán Coffee Tour is presented by the owners of the Hotel Marina Copán. Transportation to the finca is provided from Copán Ruinas in a traditional *baronesa* (a covered wagon) reminiscent of those used by plantation workers, but which today is pulled by a truck rather than oxen or horses. The four-hour tour includes a steep climb in elevation. Luckily, visitors are carried by a tractor most of the distance. See how coffee is cultivated in the highlands, then return to the finca to see how it is processed in the wet warehouse, the dry warehouse, and the roasters. At the end of the tour, a delicious meal is served (lunch, brunch, or breakfast). If you don't make it for the tour, you can still sample the coffee at Cafe Welchez, open daily 6 AM to 10 PM, right next door to the Hotel Marina Copán on Parque Central. (✉ *Finca Santa Isabel* ☎ *651–4202* ⊕ *www.cafehonduras.com* 🖅 *$30 (includes breakfast or lunch)* ☉ *Tours daily at 9 and 2*).

☺ **Finca El Cisne.** A century-old ranch about 45 minutes north of town makes for a relaxing day of horseback riding, hiking, and soaking in the on-site thermal springs. You can also learn about the coffee, cardamom, and cocoa production that goes on here. Admission price is $59, but for not much more (a total of $77) you can take part in all the activities here and stay at the adobe guesthouse. ✉ *24 km (16 mi) north of Copán Ruinas* ☎ *651–4695* ⊕ *www.fincaelcisne.com* 🖅 *$59; round-trip transportation $5; children under 12, free* ☉ *Daily 8–6.*

**Honduras Canopy Tours.** Zip-line excursions originated in Costa Rica and are cropping up all over Central America. Copán's very own entry into the field at the entrance to Hacienda San Lucas lets you glide through the air, courtesy of a series of cables and a very secure harness. ✉ *1½ km (1 mi) south of Copán Ruinas* ☎ *651–4105* 🖅 *$35.*

**Luna Jaguar Spa Resort.** This is a newly built facility on the hot springs outside of Copán Ruinas. The resort offers spa treatments and bathing in their beautiful pools and gardens. The natural thermal waters run down a mountainside and into a river that runs hot and cold. There are several smaller bathing facilities in the area as well. (⊠ 20 km [12½ mi] outside of Copán Ruinas ☎ 651–4746 ⊕ www.lunajaguar.com ⊠ Prices vary for spa treatments, massage is $35/45 minutes. Park entrance is $10 ⊙ Daily 10–5)

# SANTA ROSA DE COPÁN

*153 km (95 mi) south of San Pedro Sula.*

Set in one of the most beautiful regions of Honduras, Santa Rosa de Copán has a friendliness that makes you long to linger. (The pleasant springlike climate—the town sits at 1,150 meters (3,780 feet) altitude— is a real plus, too.) It is the kind of highland town that still feels like a village—you get the sense you would know everybody in town within a week or so. The hilltop *casco histórico* (historic center) has been declared a national monument and is being renovated with care, with much work being put into preserving the splendid colonial-era buildings with their tiled roofs lining the narrow cobbled streets.

Santa Rosa is the town that tobacco built. The Spanish crown named it the site of the *Real Factoria del Tabaco* (the Royal Tobacco Factory) in 1793, a role that allowed it to set prices for the newly important crop and would propel it to wealth and prominence. Tobacco is still cultivated here, although it has been joined and surpassed these days by coffee, another signature Honduran export. With its 42,000 people, Santa Rosa is today the largest city in the highlands and the capital of the department (province) of Copán. There is not a list of must-see sights here to check off, but you may find yourself staying a couple of days to soak up the town's colonial past.

### GETTING HERE AND AROUND

Highway CA-6 heads south from San Pedro Sula to Santa Rosa de Copán. Be sure to follow the highway at the crossroads town of La Entrada if you're not going to Copán Ruinas. Presently, no decent paved road connects Santa Rosa with Copán Ruinas, meaning that you must backtrack to La Entrada if you wish to travel between the two.

La Sultana provides bus service several times daily between San Pedro Sula and Santa Rosa de Copán. Travel time is about three hours.

The town is sometimes designated on signs as simply SANTA ROSA. The occasional bus might shorthand it even more to SRC.

### HEALTH AND SAFETY

Hospital Regional del Occidente serves Santa Rosa de Copán.

Being out after dark poses no criminal risks in quiet Santa Rosa de Copán. However, if you have any night-vision issues, beware: side- walks are narrow and curbs are steep and you need to watch closely where you walk. Come to think of it, those are good suggestions in the daytime, too.

### MONEY MATTERS

Banco Atlántida on Parque Central exchanges dollars and traveler's checks and has an ATM.

**TOURS**

Santa Rosa is home to one of the most culturally-informed tour operators in the country, Lenca Land Trails. Historian Max Elvir has learned
local traditions by traveling to nearby villages by mule. If you want to
see the more remote communities such as San Manuel de Colohete, you
will get much more out of the adventure if you go with him.

**ESSENTIALS**

**Banks Banco Atlántida** (⊠ *South side of Parque Central*).

**Bus Contact La Sultana** (⊠ *Barrio Miraflores, Santa Rosa de Copán*
☎ *662–0940*).

**Hospitals Hospital Regional del Occidente** (⊠ *Barrio del Calvario*
☎ *662–0107*).

**Pharmacies Farmacia Central** (⊠ *C. Centenario* ☎ *662–0465*).

**Tour Companies Lenca Land Trails** (⊠ *C. Real Centenario SO and Av. 2*
☎ *662–1374*).

# EXPLORING

Santa Rosa is one of Honduras's two tobacco-growing regions—Danlí,
east of Tegucigalpa is the other *(see ⇨ A Natural Cigar Humidor in
Southern Honduras)*. Cigar making still plays a big role in the local
economy, and nearly everyone seems to be hard at work rolling them.
Some prefer the strong Don Melo or the smoother Santa Rosa, but the
pride of the area is the Zino, made by **Flor de Copán** (⊠ *4 blocks east
of bus terminal* ☎ *662–0111*). A seductively sweet odor engulfs you as
you enter the factory. You can watch workers piling tobacco leaves into
*pilones* (bales). The factory offers informal tours in Spanish, weekdays
at 10 and 2. A shop just west of Parque Central at Calle Real Centenario
168 sells Flor de Copán's products.

Coffee lovers should head to **Beneficio Maya** (⊠ *Between Avs. 11 and 12
NO, Col. San Martín* ☎ *662–1665*) where they can watch the roast-
ing and grading process. Fresh export-grade coffee is for sale on the
premises. The factory is open weekdays 7 to noon and 2 to 5. Take a
taxi, as it's difficult to find.

Set in a lovingly restored 1874 building, the **Casa de Cultura** (⊠ *Av.
Alvaro Contreras, Barrio El Centro* ☎ *662–0800*) buzzes with music
lessons, theater, ballet, and modern dance, and may well have one of
the best children's libraries in Central America. The patio is a pleasant
place to relax.

**Parque Central.** Santa Rosa's pleasant one-block-square central park is
slightly elevated above the surrounding streets. The kiosk in the center
of the park dates from 1900 and today serves as a community-operated
tourist office, open weekdays 9 to 5:30 and Saturday 9 to 1. Stop by
and the friendly folks here can tell you all you want to know about the
town and the surrounding area. The 1803 Cathedral of Santa Rosa faces
the east side of the park. ⊠ *block bordered by Calle Real Centenario,
1 Av. NE, 1 Calle NE, and 2 Av. SO.*

# HONDURAN COFFEE: THE MAGIC BEAN

Walk into your favorite local gourmet coffee joint. Honduras's Central American neighbors occupy prominent positions there but not so Honduras itself. It's not for lack of ideal natural conditions. The country has the high altitude, warm days, cool nights, and distinct dry and rainy seasons necessary to provide quality coffee, and the plant is cultivated in 15 of Honduras's 18 departments (provinces). A drive through the highlands lets you see the spectacle of thousands of busy hands picking coffee during the October–March harvest. Directly or indirectly, the coffee industry employs about one million Hondurans, and the sector contributes 10% of the country's GDP. No question that this is one of Honduras's most important products.

It's been all about branding, a task Honduras has historically neglected to do. We know Guatemalan and Costa Rican coffees. But Honduran? It doesn't quite jog our associations. As a result, Honduran coffee has frequently ended up in mass commercial blends. The proximity of the Western Highlands to Guatemala means that some of the harvest here is even smuggled across the border into that country and sold from there as Guatemalan product, which fetches a higher price on the world market. Germany is the largest market for Honduran coffee; the United States runs a distant second, buying some 20% of the country's crop, but with the variety of competing coffees available, the average U.S. coffee drinker barely knows the Honduran product at all.

"You're not just buying a coffee, you're buying an origin," Carlos Lara, regional director for the **Instituto**

Hondureño de Café (IHCAFE ⊕ *www.cafedehonduras.org*) in Santa Rosa de Copán tells us. Some 90% of coffee production here remains in the hands of small producers, and most is shade-grown, an eco-friendly, bird-hospitable method of cultivating coffee; both are factors, Lara says, consumers like to hear about and that are now being bundled into the promotion of Honduran coffee.

IHCAFE delineates five coffee-growing regions. **Agalta Tropical** comes from the mountainous area around Tegucigalpa and the east, and is known for its acidic honey and citrus flavors. The creamy, slightly chocolaty **Azul Meámbar** is cultivated in the region around Comayagua. As the name indicates, the full-bodied, slightly chocolaty **Copán** comes from the area around Copán Ruinas and Santa Rosa de Copán. **Montecillos**, from the higher elevation La Esperanza region, gives you bright acidity with hints of fruity, floral flavor. The soft, aromatic, fruity **Opalaca** hails from the countryside around Gracias.

Here's the rub for you, dear coffee-loving reader: True to the economic realities of developing countries, the good stuff is exported, leaving behind a mediocre bean for the local market. On top of that, Hondurans make coffee with hideous amounts of sugar. Your best bet for a good cup is an upscale hotel or restaurant that will have export-quality coffee on hand and will be attuned to foreign tastes. Souvenir shops also sell foil bags of export-quality product. Their small size fits nicely into your carry-on for the trip home.

# WHERE TO EAT

$   ✕ **Flamingo's.** Considered one of the finest restaurants in town, this is
CONTEMPORARY   the place to come for a quiet meal. A touch of elegance is added by the
white- or melon-colored tablecloths. Dishes include such specialties
as pork with onion sauce. The wine list includes some decent Chilean
options. ⊠ *Av. 1 between C. Real Centenario and C. 1 SE, Barrio El
Centro* ☎ *662–0654* ⊟ *AE, D, DC, MC, V.*

$   ✕ **Weekends Pizza.** A Honduran-German couple operates this friendly
ITALIAN   pizza joint. They make thick-crust pizza with fresh organic ingredients
grown on their farm outside of town and herbs cultivated out on the
restaurant patio. Italian, vegetarian, and Hawaiian pizzas are expected,
but for something different, try the Copaneca, an offering made with
a topping of sausage, avocado, fried beans, and cilantro. Sandwiches,
salads, calzones, and lasagna are on the menu, too, if pizza doesn't
interest you. No alcohol is served. The place opens at 9 AM; although
there is no breakfast per se, you can stop in for the freshly baked bread
these folks make in the morning. ⊠ *C. 2 SO and Av. 4 NO* ☎ *662–4121*
⊟ *AE, D, DC, MC, V* ⊘ *Closed Mon.–Tues.*

# WHERE TO STAY

$   ⛻ **Hotel Casa Real.** A bit out of the way from the city center is this
very modern offering. The public areas and restaurant are glitzy in
a resortlike way and seem a little out of place in Santa Rosa. Rooms
are very plain with beds, tables, and chairs and little else. It's a good,
solid option. **Pros:** modern furnishings; friendly service; good rates.
**Cons:** several blocks from city center. ⊠ *C. 2 between Av. 3 and 4 NE*
☎ *662–0801* ⊕ *www.hotelcasarealsrc.com* ⊅ *52 rooms* ♺ *In-room:* no
*a/c (some), Wi-Fi. In-hotel: restaurant, room service, bar, laundry ser-
vice, Internet terminal, parking (free)* ⊟ *AE, D, DC, MC, V* ⊚| *BP.*

$   ⛻ **Hotel Elvir.** Enjoy a glass of *timoshenko,* a fruity spirit flavored with
cloves, at the rooftop bar of this colonial-style hotel. By far the best
lodging in town, it has a beautiful patio and smart lobby. Comfortable
rooms have cozy beds and modern baths. The restaurant is good but
a little overpriced. **Pros:** friendly staff; most centrally located lodging
in town. **Cons:** a few rooms get noise from the patio. ⊠ *C. Real Centenario at Av. 2 SO* ☎ *662–1374* ⊕ *www.hotelelvir.com* ⊅ *41 rooms,
2 suites* ♺ *In-room: a/c, Wi-Fi. In-hotel: restaurant, room service, bar,
pool, laundry service, Internet terminal, parking (free)* ⊟ *AE, D, DC,
MC, V* ⊚| *BP.*

¢–$   ⛻ **Hotel Santa Rosa.** After entering through an attractive wooden lobby,
you'll be escorted to one of the rooms surrounding a pleasant garden
scattered with rocking chairs. The restaurant serves basic food. **Pros:**
decent budget value; close to bus terminal. **Cons:** basic rooms; far from
center of town. ⊠ *Hwy. CA-4* ☎ *662–2365 or 662–2366* ⊅ *38 rooms*
♺ *In-room: no a/c (some), no phone, Wi-Fi. In-hotel: restaurant, park-
ing (free)* ⊟ *MC, V* ⊚| *EP.*

## SHOPPING

Two blocks east of Parque Central is the covered **mercado** (✉ C. *Real Centenario*), an enticing market that sells everything from shawls to saddles. There's not much to buy of tourist interest—the average resident shops here for day-to-day goods—but it makes for some interesting people-watching. It is also the place to go for a great breakfast; ask for *atol chuco,* a delicious mush of fermented corn served with a few beans, lime, and roasted squash seeds.

# GRACIAS

**4**

*43 km (26 mi) southeast of Santa Rosa de Copán.*

Founded in 1536 by Gonzalo de Alvarado, brother of Spanish conquistador Pedro de Alvarado, Gracias has a fascinating history. Its original name was *Gracias a Dios* (Thanks be to God), after the conquistador's exclamation of gratitude that, after wandering for days in the mountains, he had finally found land flat enough to build a settlement. From 1544–1548, Gracias served as the seat of the Audencia, the royal court that administered Spain's colony in Central America, an area stretching from Guatemala to Costa Rica. Internecine rivalries ended Gracias's glory days and the capital was moved to Antigua, Guatemala. The town's colonial history still resonates in the three churches you'll find along its cobblestone streets. A short walk up to the fort of San Cristóbal provides an inspiring view of the nearby mountains.

Gracias makes a good launching point for visiting nearby Lenca indigenous communities. La Campa and San Manuel Colohete are the most interesting to visit. The tourist industry bills the circuit as La Ruta Lenca (the Lenca Route). Transportation logistics and lack of accommodation in these small towns make organized day trips the best options, and tour operators here are happy to take you. They can also help you get to the nearby Celaque National Park, a large tract of cloud forest that contains the country's highest peak.

### GETTING HERE AND AROUND

Gracias lies southeast of Santa Rosa de Copán. Expect a few potholes along the way, but the drive is reasonable and takes just under an hour. The town is frequently designated on signs and buses as GRACIAS LEMPIRA to denote the name of Lempira department (province) of which it is the capital.

One daily bus operated by Gracianos runs from San Pedro Sula to Gracias, but Congolón has more frequent departures. Crowded minivans leave periodically from

---

### SOME TERMINOLOGY

Stick with the term *indígena* (indigenous) here when describing Honduras's Lenca and other Maya-descended peoples. *Indio* (Indian) is considered pejorative here. (We use the term in this guide only to describe an Indian—as in South Asian—restaurant.) Likewise, if you want to avoid offending anyone, *tribú* (tribe) and *nativo* (native) are words best left to old Tarzan movies.

the bus terminal in Santa Rosa de Copán and make many stops along the way.

Streets in Gracias have no names. Everybody gives addresses in reference to close-by landmarks.

### SAFETY
As in Santa Rosa de Copán, sidewalks are narrow and curbs are steep. Watch closely where you walk, especially at night.

### MONEY MATTERS
Gracias's banks exchange dollars and traveler's checks, but have no ATMs. Stock up on cash in Santa Rosa de Copán or San Pedro Sula. Banco de Occidente has a branch on Parque Central.

### TOURS
Puma Trail Tours can arrange to get you to Parque Nacional Celaque, with basic transportation to the visitor center or a more extensive guided excursion. Cosuca-Celaque is a Gracias-based cooperative of tour guides that can arrange transportation to Parque Nacional Celaque or the Lenca villages south of town.

### ESSENTIALS
**Banks Banco de Occidente** (⊠ *South side of Parque Central*).

**Bus Companies Congolón** (⊠ *Av. 8 between Cs. 9 and 10, San Pedro Sula* ☎ *553–1174*). **Gracianos** (⊠ *Parque Central, Gracias* ☎ *No phone* ⊠ *C. 6 between Avs. 6 and 7, San Pedro Sula* ☎ *No phone*).

**Tour Companies Puma Trail Tours** (⊠ *Av. 2 NO at C. 1, San Pedro Sula* ☎ *656–1223*). **Cosuca-Celaque** (☎ *656–0627*).

---

## EXPLORING

**La Campa,** only 16 km (10 mi) from Gracias on a well-maintained road, is the easiest of the surrounding communities to reach on your own. This lovely Lenca village set in the rugged mountains is well worth visiting just to see the local ceramics—the same red pottery you will see for much higher prices in Tegucigalpa and San Pedro Sula. Of particular note are the *cántaros*—perfectly cylindrical urns—and also bowls, plates, and wind chimes. Just outside town is the home of the Doña Desideria Pérez, a smiling lady who bakes red pottery in the open air. She will happily show you around. Many of the pottery makers around town are happy to let you get your hands dirty and fashion your own work. The complication is that it takes at least 24 hours for your work to dry; you'll have to come back the next day. On top of the hill at the entrance to town is the **Centro de Interpretación de Alfarería Lenca** ( ☎ *No phone* ⊠ *L30* ☻ *Daily 8–4*), where you can see Lenca pottery on display and hear explanations of how it is fashioned.

Also make sure to stop by the 1690 **Iglesia de San Matías.** The whitewashed church is usually closed except for Sunday masses, but if you ask around, you can find somebody to let you in. It's quite plain inside, though. The statue of San Matías was stolen a few years ago, but the uproar was so great that the thieves relented, wrapping it in rags and

## GHASTLY AND GHOSTLY

Legends of spirits (occasionally) benevolent and (mostly) malevolent have permeated Honduran folklore here in the highlands for centuries. *La Siguanaba* appears as a beautiful woman who lures single men wandering the streets at night. Once she has won them over with her feminine charms, she turns into a monster. If you smell sulfur at night, it could be *El Cadejo*, a fierce dog with fiery eyes who is thought to personify the devil himself. (However, certain Cadejos are said to take pity on drunkards and to protect them from harm.) If you are out after dark and hear a slow creaking on the pavement, under no circumstances should you turn around and look, lest you be confronted with the terrible image of the *Carreta Fantasma*, the ghostly oxcart driven by a skeleton.

Many of these legends bear striking resemblance to ghostly figures talked about in other Central American countries. We can't vouch for the authenticity of any of them, but you never know.

leaving it on a bus from Gracias to Santa Rosa de Copán, where it was discovered and returned.

Another 14 km (9 mi) beyond La Campa over a rough road is the remote village of **San Manuel Colohete,** which borders Parque Nacional Celaque and gets the same ethereal cloud-forest mists as you'll find inside the park. The town's stunning 1721 church of the same name is considered to be the most beautiful in the country. Sculpted saints set in niches make the facade quite unusual, while the swirling colors of the frescoed walls and ceilings inside have led people to compare it to the Sistine Chapel. The massive gold-plated altarpiece with a gleaming Cristo Negro (Black Christ) is breathtaking. At his feet (you may have to gently shift some lace decorations) are paintings of the sun and moon that recall the religions that Christianity hasn't managed to completely push aside here. The church is only open for Sunday Masses.

The area around Gracias is considered one of Honduras's best-kept secrets, as it's home to the pristine **Parque Nacional Celaque,** one of the largest tracts of cloud forest left in Central America. At 2,849 meters (9,345 feet), the Cerro de las Minas within its confines is the highest peak in Honduras. The name of the park means "box of water" in the Lenca language, after the 11 rivers flowing from this mountain. The park is home to spider monkeys, as well as birds such as toucans and quetzals. If the Lenca gods are smiling upon you, you might catch a glimpse of jaguars, ocelots, and pumas, but all are painfully shy, so don't count on it.

A 9-km (5½-mi) dirt road leads from Gracias to the park's entrance, more or less a two-hour journey. The visitor center is another half hour beyond that. There is no public transport to the park, but you can hire a car in Gracias. You can stay overnight at the modern visitor center, where you'll find two small cabins with beds, showers, and cooking facilities. The hike to the summit, which takes seven to eight hours, is easier during the dry season, from about February to September. If you want just a taste of the park, you don't need to hike very far from the visitor center to get a sampling, and trails are well maintained here. No matter what the time of year, it gets chilly and wet in the park. Warm, waterproof clothing is a must. ⊠ *9 km (5½ mi) west of Gracias* ☎ *656–1362* ⊠ *L50* ⊙ *Daily 8–4.*

**Termas de Río.** Several hot-springs complexes dot the area around Gracias. The most well run of these is this one on the road to Santa Rosa de Copán. Relax in one of the various pools with water temperatures ranging from 90 to 123 degrees. The complex is managed by the Posada de Don Juan in town, and entrance is free if you're one of their guests. ⊠ *7 km (4 mi) northwest of Gracias on highway to Santa Rosa de Copán* ☎ *656–1480* ⊠ *L100* ⊙ *Daily 7:30 am–9 pm.*

## WHERE TO EAT AND STAY

¢ ⊡ **Hotel Erick.** They are a little spare, but clean rooms at Hotel Erick have a few niceties like cable TV. The friendly owners will let you store your gear here while you explore Parque Nacional Celaque. **Pros:** excellent value for price; friendly owners. **Cons:** spartan rooms. ⊠ *Barrio Mercedes* ☎ *656–1066* ⊲ *24 rooms* ⌂ *In-room: no a/c, no phone, no TV. In-hotel: bar, parking (free)* ⊟ *No credit cards.*

¢ ⊡ **Hotel Guancascos.** A hub of activity, this clean and comfortable hotel is a good in-town option. The restaurant ($) doles out plentiful portions of *platos típicos* (typical dishes), heaping helpings of poultry, and huge bowls of hot vegetable soup. To escape from the midday heat, sip fresh juices made from local berries on the shady balcony overlooking the town. Owner Frony Miedama can set up trips to Parque Nacional Celaque and rents a cabin there called the Cabaña Villa Verde. **Pros:** friendly owner; cozy vibe. **Cons:** higher rooms a steep climb up stairs. ⊠ *Barrio el Rosario* ☎ *656–1219* ⊕ *www.guancascos.com* ⊲ *17 rooms* ⌂ *In-room: no a/c, no phone (some), no TV, Wi-Fi. In-hotel: restaurant, laundry service, Internet terminal, parking (free)* ⊟ *MC, V* ⦿ *BP.*

$–$$ ⊡ **Posada de Don Juan.** One of the highlands' loveliest hotels evokes
Fodor's Choice Gracias's pre-independence heyday as the seat of the Audencia, but
★ the building itself is only about a decade old and lovingly constructed in accurate colonial style. Rooms contain hardwood furniture, high-beamed ceilings, and flat-screen TVs. **Pros:** friendly staff; sumptuous colonial-style accommodation; most centrally located lodging in town **Cons:** a few rooms get street noise. ⊠ *Calle Principal* ☎ *656–1020* ⊕ *www.posadadedonjuanhotel.com* ⊲ *42 rooms* ⌂ *In-room: a/c, refrigerator (some), Wi-Fi. In-hotel: restaurant, room service, bar, laundry service, Internet terminal, parking (free)* ⊟ *AE, MC, V* ⦿ *BP.*

## SHOPPING

An offbeat little shop is **Lorendiana** (⊠ *2 blocks south of market* ☎ *656–1058*). You'll find a selection of Lenca handicrafts, as well as shelves of homemade preserves and hot sauces.

# LAGO DE YOJOA

*100 km (62 mi) south of San Pedro Sula.*

The largest natural lake in the country, shimmering Lago de Yojoa is home to an amazing variety of birds. Upwards of 400 different species are found in the moss-draped trees, from black-bellied whistling ducks and blue-crowned motmots to red-legged honeycreepers and keel-billed toucans. For even more unusual sights, you can grab a pair of binoculars and hire a boat to Isla del Venado.

With a name that means means "eye of water," Lago de Yojoa was once populated by Lenca, Maya, and other peoples. There are many ruins, the most significant being Los Naranjos on the northwest shore. Excavations were stalled for lack of funds but now seem to be back on track. Of course, the main draw of the lake is purely recreational. There are many untouched natural areas around the lake, and it is less well known than other tourist destinations. There are all kinds of trips you can take out onto the lake, the most popular being by catamaran.

### GETTING HERE AND AROUND

El Rey and Norteños offer bus service several times daily to Lago de Yojoa from both San Pedro Sula and Tegucigalpa. All buses stop at Comayagua.

### MONEY MATTERS

The small lake town of Peña Blanca has a branch of Banco de Occidente which exchanges dollars and traveler's checks. Its ATM accepts Visa cards only. The nearest banks with fuller-service ATMs are in Comayagua or San Pedro Sula.

### ESSENTIALS

**Bus Companies El Rey** (⊠ *Av. 7 between Cs. 5 and 6, San Pedro Sula* ☎ *553–4264*). **Norteños** (⊠ *C. 6 between Avs. 6 and 7, San Pedro Sula* ☎ *552–2145*).

**Banks Banco de Occidente** (⊠ *Peña Blanca*).

## EXPLORING

Boating is one of everybody's favorite activities here, and getting out on the lake gives you a better view for spotting birds than staying on land. Boat rental is informal, usually nothing more than a guy-and-his-rowboat operation along the lakeshore. Your best bet is to ask at one of the local hotels for recommendations.

## WHERE TO EAT AND STAY

¢ 🔛 **D&D Brewery.** On the west shore of Lago Yojoa, D&D is a favorite stop for many visitors to the lake; rooms in the main lodge are basic but have private baths and hot water. Private cabins are scattered around the grounds and provide much more seclusion than the rooms. The brewery makes its own beer and sodas—try a Lenca Gold Pale Ale or a vanilla cream soda. Meals are tasty and economical. The folks here also offer tours to various attractions around the lake, such as bird-watching, visiting the waterfalls at Puhlupanzak, and hiking the national park

Cerro Azul Meámbar. By the way, *D&D* stands for "Dale and Dog," denoting guitar-playing owner Robert Dale, who enjoys a good jam session, and his dog, Charlie. **Pros:** good budget value; brewery is a kick to see even if you don't stay here. **Cons:** spartan accommodation. ✉ *Road to Mochito, Lago de Yojoa* ☎ *9994–9719* ⊕ *www.dd-brewery. org* ⤵ *6 rooms, 6 cabins* ⚷ *In-room: no a/c, no phone, no TV. In-hotel: restaurant, bar, pool, parking (free)* ⊟ *MC, V* �️ *CP, EP.*

$–$$   ⊡ **Hotel y Finca Las Glorias.** Set on a coffee and orange plantation, this flower-strewn hotel makes a perfect lakeside retreat. The picturesque bridge leading to an airy pavilion is great for bird-watching, and the catamaran trips on the lake are sublime. From the private balcony of your cabin, you can watch horses and their foals trot around. Cabins have two or three bedrooms and are ideal for families. Weekends tend to fill up, so reserve ahead. **Pros:** tranquil surroundings; lots of activities. **Cons:** difficult to find space on weekends. ✉ *Lago de Yojoa, between La Guama and Peña Blanca* ☎ *566–0461* ⊕ *www.hotellasglorias.com* ⤵ *42 rooms, 6 suites, 4 cabins* ⚷ *In-room: a/c, no phone. In-hotel: restaurant, pool, parking (free)* ⊟ *MC, V.*

$–$$   ⊡ **Posada del Lago.** If you want to relax with a gin and tonic as you gaze at Lago de Yojoa, this is *the* place. Charming expat Richard Joint evokes all things British and is a wealth of information about the area. From your gleaming-white cabin, you can wander down to look at the boats in the marina. Inquire about the *casa de campo* (country house) on the far side of the lake. Sleeping eight, it's great for longer stays. **Pros:** engaging, knowledgeable owner; relaxing vibe **Cons:** difficult to find space on weekends. ✉ *Km 161, Carretera del Norte, Monte Verde, Santa Cruz de Yojoa* ☎ *990–9386 or 990–9387* ⊕ *www. honduyatemarina.net* ⤵ *5 cabins, 1 suite* ⚷ *In-room: DVD. In-hotel: 2 restaurants, bars, tennis courts, laundry service, parking (free), no-smoking rooms, Internet terminal* ⊟ *AE, MC, V.*

# COMAYAGUA

★   *82 km (51 mi) northwest of Tegucigalpa, 183 km (114 mi) southeast of San Pedro Sula.*

Founded in 1537, Santa María de Comayagua was the first capital of Honduras. It was also one of the last bastions of resistance by the Lenca and Nahuatl people, who staged a revolt two years later. President Marco Aurelio Soto moved the seat of power to Tegucigalpa in 1880, allegedly to avenge repeated snubs by the city's haughty upper classes. (Historians today agree the true reason was less colorful: Soto thought it important to move the capital to Tegucigalpa, whose mining industry was then the fulcrum of Honduras's economy.) After a century of decline, Comayagua was declared a national monument in 1972. The focus now is on preserving its colonial-era character as part of a program known as Comayagua Colonial. The impressive project is evidenced in the gleaming-white facade of the Catedral de Comayagua and the immaculately clean Parque Central.

The city of 60,000 doesn't register on most visitors' radars, and that's a shame. With its colonial-era treasures and one of the best museums in the country, Comayagua must not be missed. (A second museum is undergoing reconstruction following a 2009 fire.) Close to Tegucigalpa, you could see its major sights in a long day trip from the capital,

| A CRITICAL E AND L |
|---|
| This is Comayagua, the pleasant colonial-era city near the center of Honduras. Don't confuse it with Comayagüela, the lower-class district of Tegucigalpa. What a difference an E and an L make! |

but staying overnight here lets you take everything in more leisurely. No doubt, some people here lament that their city was stripped of its role as the country's capital over a century ago, but many more say, "Thank goodness. We could have turned into . . . Tegucigalpa!"

**4**

### GETTING HERE AND AROUND

El Rey and Norteños offer bus service several times daily to Comayagua from both San Pedro Sula and Tegucigalpa. All buses stop at Lago de Yojoa.

### HEALTH AND SAFETY

A branch of San Pedro Sula's private Hospital Bendaña operates in Comayagua.

### MONEY MATTERS

Comayagua has several banks. Banco Atlántida, one block north of Parque Central, exchanges dollars and traveler's checks and has an ATM.

### ESSENTIALS

**Banks** Banco Atlántida (⊠ *C. 1 NO*).

**Bus Companies** El Rey (⊠ *Av. 7 between Cs. 5 and 6, San Pedro Sula* ☎ *553–4264*). Norteños (⊠ *C. 6 between Avs. 6 and 7, San Pedro Sula* ☎ *552–2145*).

**Hospitals** Hosptial Bendaña (⊠ *1 block from Parque Central* ☎ *772–0102*).

# EXPLORING

The largest house of worship constructed during the colonial period, **Catedral de Santa María** (⊠ *Parque Central*) dates from 1711. The interior is incredibly ornate, with four hand-carved wooden altars covered in gold. Note the intriguing statue of Santa Ana, the mother of the Virgin Mary, carrying a diminutive Santa María, who in turn is holding a tiny infant Jesús. Phillip II of Spain donated a Moorish clock from the Alhambra in Granada for the tower, and Hondureños claim it is the oldest in the Americas. As the so-called *reloj arabe* (Arab clock) dates from around 1100, it could well be true.

At the north end of town is the 1629 **Iglesia de la Caridad** (⊠ *C. 7 NO at Av. 3 NO*). In the back is the country's only remaining open-air chapel, originally used for the conversion of indigenous peoples, in what was then socially segregated Comayagua. The church's interior is famous for its statue of *El Señor de la Burrita* (*Lord of the Burro*), which is paraded through town on Palm Sunday.

## HOLY WEEK IN COMAYAGUA

No city in Honduras does Semana Santa (Holy Week) as big as Comayagua does, with the city's four anchor churches collaborating in elaborate religious processions that take place much of the week. If you plan to be here then, make hotel reservations months in advance and expect to pay higher rates than you would the rest of the year. Most lodgings impose minimum stays of three or four nights during the week. (You cannot breeze in on Thursday night and out again on Friday.)

Palm Sunday kicks the week off with the reenactment of Jesus' entry into Jerusalem on a donkey. The night of Holy Thursday commemorates the Last Supper and Jesus' arrest.

Good Friday is the biggest day of the week with an elaborate procession marking the way to the Crucifixion. Residents cover the streets with decorative sawdust carpets. Get there early to admire them and take photos before the marchers trample them to dust. The city thoughtfully installs ladders along the route before the parade begins to let you get the best photo angle. (You may have to wait in line.) Saturday night sees the stark Easter Vigil. Easter morning itself begins with the Carreritas de San Juan (Races of St. John), as figures of St. John and Mary Magdalene race through the city looking for Jesus' body. The week concludes with the triumphal Easter Mass at the cathedral.

Three blocks southeast of Iglesia de la Caridad is **Iglesia San Francisco** (⊠ *Av. 2 de Julio at C. 7 NE*), founded in 1560. The bell in the tower was brought from Spain and dates back to 1460, making it the oldest in the Americas. The church houses an elegantly carved baroque altarpiece from the 18th century.

Dating from 1550, **Iglesia La Merced** (⊠ *C. 1 at Av. 2 NE*) was the first church to be built in Honduras. One of the oldest in the Americas, it houses a magnificent altarpiece. It was badly damaged in a 1774 earthquake but was lovingly restored in subsequent decades.

★ The elegant old building that holds the **Museo de Arqueología** served as the country's first presidential palace. The museum today provides arguably the country's best collection of Lenca artifacts. It contains well-preserved items from around Comayagua, from cave art to colorful pottery to *metates* (the stones the Lenca used for grinding grain). It also houses interesting fossils and an important collection of jade. A workshop at the back has been transformed into a school where men and women train as carpenters, stonemasons, blacksmiths, and in the other old trades needed to rebuild the city according to the old traditions. Exhibits are labeled in English and Spanish. A small cafeteria is open for breakfast and lunch. ⊠ *C. 6 NE at Av. 2 de Julio* ☎ *772–0386* 💰 *L80* ⊙ *Tues.–Sat. 8:30–4, Sun. 9–5.*

Sadly, the one-time bishop's palace housing Comayagua's most fabulous museum, the **Museo Colonial de Arte Religioso**, was badly damaged in a 2009 fire and is still closed at this writing. Miraculously, 80 percent of the museum's treasure trove of religious art from the colonial era was saved. The varied collection of 15th- to 18th-century artwork from local

## A U.S. MILITARY PRESENCE

Eight km (5 mi) south of Comayagua sits the massive Soto Cano Air Force Base, home to around 450 U.S. military troops. Although the Honduran constitution prohibits foreign troops from being stationed in the country, a gentlemen's agreement with the United States, in effect for three decades, has permitted the U.S. presence with the stipulation that the facility be under Honduran military command.

The base, which Hondurans refer to as Palmerola, was command central in the 1980s for the Contra War in neighboring Nicaragua. That dispute has, thankfully, ended and the number of U.S. troops has been drawn down significantly, but Soto Cano has taken on new strategic importance these days following the U.S. withdrawal from the Panama Canal in 1999. Today, the base serves as a launching pad for operations in the war on drugs and for relief missions for disasters in Central America and the Caribbean, including the January 2010 earthquake in Haiti.

churches includes paintings, sculptures, and jewels used to adorn the statues of saints. The building is undergoing reconstruction with plans to open to the public at a yet unspecified future date; do check when you're here just in case, though, as to miss it if it is reopened would be a shame. ⊠ *Av. 2 de Julio between Cs. 3 and 4 NO.*

## WHERE TO EAT AND STAY

$$ ✕ **Villa Real.** This is the best restaurant in the city. Tables are set in a
LATIN AMERICAN pretty, overgrown garden beside a trickling fountain. Enjoy the hint of
**Fodor's** Choice a breeze as you sample *pechuga marsala* (chicken breast with vegeta-
★ bles). The plato típico is also quite satisfying. Ask the manager to show you around the historic building. ⊠ *Parque Central behind cathedral* ☎ *772–0101* ▤ *MC, V.*

$ ⊡ **Hotel Colonial Casa Grande.** Though not Comayagua's largest lodging,
**Fodor's** Choice the Casa Grande is its best offering, and the rates are terrific for what
★ you get. This colonial-era house has been converted into a cozy bed-and-breakfast with stone walls, hand-painted tiles, wood floors, and lots of sumptuous carved-wood furniture. **Pros:** colonial elegance; bargain rates for what's offered; central location. **Cons:** a couple of rooms get street noise. ⊠ *C. 7 NO* ☎ *772–0772* ⊕ *www.hotelcolonialcasagrande. com* ⋧ *11 rooms* ⧠ *In-room: a/c, Wi-Fi. In-hotel: restaurant, laundry service, Internet terminal, parking (free)* ▤ *AE, D, DC, MC, V* ⦿ *BP.*

$$ ⊡ **Hotel Santa María de Comayagua.** With a huge pool that's a welcome respite from the heat, this hotel has all the extras that matter most. Rooms are clean and fresh. Although outside the city, the hotel is only a 10-minute walk from the historic center. **Pros:** good value; comfortable surroundings. **Cons:** motel-like rooms; out on highway; outside of city center. ⊠ *Km 82, Carretera Tegucigalpa-San Pedro Sula* ☎ *772–7872* ⊕ *www.hotelsmc.com* ⋧ *28 rooms* ⧠ *In-room: a/c. In-hotel: restaurant, bar, pool* ▤ *AE, MC, V.*

$    📷 **Villa Real.** A charming 18th-century house with a horse-drawn carriage in the entranceway houses a pleasant inn. Rooms here are an odd mix: some ooze colonial luxury, with hand-carved furniture, others are quite plain. (There is a price difference between the two, but the extra splurge is worth it.) Ask to see a couple before you decide. **Pros:** some very atmospheric rooms; best restaurant in town. **Cons:** some plain rooms. ✉ *Parque Central behind cathedral* ☎ *772–0101* ⊕ *www.villarealcolonial.com* 🔑 *10 rooms* 🛏 *In-room: a/c, Wi-Fi. In-hotel: restaurant, room service, bar, pool, Internet terminal, parking (free)* ▭ *MC, V* ⦿ *BP.*

# The Caribbean Coast

**WORD OF MOUTH**

From San Pedro Sula you can either bus or fly to La Ceiba. Check out the Omega [Jungle] Lodge for great hiking, rafting, kayaking, horseback riding, and a great jungle setting.

—hopefulist

Updated
by Maria
Gallucci

The northern coast of Honduras is a world away from the country's interior. Chaotic urban grids give way to mellow coastal towns. Steep green mountains slope sharply into verdant jungle canopies and salty turquoise waters. National parks and reserves ring vibrant beachfront promenades and port cities with sandy streets and brightly painted buildings. The residents are just as diverse, with cultures and languages that offer a unique panorama of Honduran history.

The coast is mostly the domain of the Garífuna people, descendants of African slaves who were shipwrecked in the Caribbean. They first settled on the island of Saint Vincent in the Lesser Antilles, but in the 18th century the British forcibly moved them to Roatán in the Bay Islands. Many eventually migrated to the mainland, and they now inhabit the Caribbean coast from Belize to Nicaragua. Many Garífuna people along the coast live in thatched-roof huts next to the sea, getting by mostly by fishing. Women tote patterned parisols, dress in colorful tunics, and wrap flashy scarves around their heads.

In Garífuna music, dancing, and native language you can note a distinct West African influence. Beats thump from hardwood drums as dancers circle their hips in the traditional *punta* form, perhaps the best-known genre across the Caribbean. Octogenarians can still sing and dance long after younger people collapse from exhaustion. Some of their songs are filled with images of poverty and loss, whereas others are more like oral history put to music. Religious rituals, especially those focusing on death, are very much in evidence here, and respect for the ancestors is central to the culture.

The *mestizo* (people of mixed Spanish and indigenous descent) population, or *ladinos*, mostly reside in urban centers or further inland. Many have lived here since the time of the Spanish conquest, while others arrived in the late 20th century to work at the ports and banana plantations. Small villages tucked into the foothills are emerging to bring their ancestral knowledge of nature and artisanry to travelers passing through. Young adults train to offer mountain hikes and local tours, and artisan cooperatives invite visitors to their workshops to meet the craftsmakers. Descendants of the indigenous Lenca empire line gift-shop shelves with burnished pottery hued black by pine smoke. Native Pech artisans twist tree bark into tinted twine, or *majao*, to weave pouches, bracelets, and accessories.

The regional cuisine along the coast happens to be the country's best, with specialties such as *sopa de caracol* (conch soup) and *tapado de pescado* (steamed fish and coconut-milk stew) served with *machuca* (mashed yuca). *Pan de coco* (coconut bread) is another favorite in the area, as is the bitter Garífuna spirit *gifiti,* a fusion of rum and medicinal herbs. Rice and beans cooked in coconut milk and *tajadas* (fried plantain slices) are ubiquitous side dishes sure to top off every meal. Garífuna favorites include *ereba* (cassava bread), *bundiga* (plantain gravy) and plenty of fried fish and chicken dishes.

# ORIENTATION AND PLANNING

## ORIENTATION

The cities along the east–west-running northern coast string neatly along the oceanfront, wrapping around ports and closely hugging the shoreline. Towns are united by their shared histories of Spanish explorers, pirate attacks, and banana plantations, plus the Garífuna culture. Remnants of limestone fortresses and fruit-hauling railroad tracks still linger in urban centers, while the outskirts are lined with impressive mountain forests. Vacationing Hondurans come here on long weekends to lounge on the beaches and soak in the sun, while many foreign travelers opt for outdoor activities such as ocean kayaking, rafting, boulder climbing, and canopy tours.

**Omoa.** The small waterfront town has lost its once-seductive beaches due to changing currents but is still pleasant; it's a good stopover for travelers heading to or from Belize or Guatemala.

**Puerto Cortés.** Family-friendly municipal beaches here at Honduras's largest port attract many weekenders from San Pedro Sula. This up-and-coming destination is a big hub for business travel and is the preferred stopover for Guatemala-bound tourists who prefer a bit of bustle.

**Tela.** Wooden cottages painted turquoise and peach and a beachfront strip of bars and eateries add color to this former port town. Once the headquarters for the United Fruit Company, Tela is nestled between two outstanding nature preserves and a string of friendly Garífuna beaches.

**La Ceiba.** Hailed as Honduras's "party city" for its tireless number of clubs and bars, La Ceiba is the heart of the Caribbean coast. Ferries to the Bay Islands and international flights come and go from here, but the town has lots more to offer. The nearby Cangrejal River and Pico Bonito National Park have plenty of jungle activities, and Sambo Creek to the east is a relaxing beach escape.

**Trujillo.** Undulating streets and quiet parks lead out to crystal waters in this historic town. Christopher Columbus first stepped foot on the American mainland here, and U.S. mercenary William Walker is buried in the old cemetery. Artisan shops sell Garífuna and Pech handicrafts, and palm-thatched *champas* serve seafood on the beach.

### GREAT ITINERARIES

**If You Have 3 days:** Head straight into La Ceiba. If you're in the mood for a peaceful beachfront getaway, check out one of the cute bed-and-breakfasts just east of Sambo Creek. Canopy tours, lagoon kayak trips, and natural hot springs are easy day trips from here. If you're up for a big adventure, stay in an ecolodge along the Cangrejal River or in the Pico Bonito National Park and sign up for rafting, horseback riding, or a mountain trek. There's time to stay at both the beach and in the

## TOP REASONS TO GO

**Discover Garífuna Culture.** The coastal villages of African descendants are full of cultural surprises. High-energy music and dancing ring out in the evenings, and tropical dishes of seafood, coconut, and cassava fill your table.

**Rafting in the Jungle.** La Ceiba's Cangrejal River is one of Central America's best for white-water rafting. Top-notch tour operators offer exhilarating rides between and over massive boulders, through low-hanging clouds, and past walls of endless green.

**Explore the Wildlife.** Botanical gardens, hot springs, mangroves, and tropical forests across the coast afford one-of-a-kind encounters with howler monkeys, crocodiles, thousands of bird species, and brilliant blossoms and fruit trees. Take a kayak tour or a hike, or glide through it all on a canopy line.

jungle for those who want a mix. For all-night dancing when you're back in La Ceiba, arrange a hotel shuttle and swing by the Zona Viva on Thursday and weekend nights.

**If You Have 5 days:** Start in La Ceiba and opt for a one- or two-day hike through the pristine forests around towering Pico Bonito. If the skies are clear on the following day, arrange an early morning snorkeling trip from Sambo Creek to the Cayos Cochinos, a spectacular archipelago that's actually part of the Bay Islands. Ask ahead of time and Garífuna villagers on Chachahuate Key will prepare you a lunch of fried fish and plantain chips. Tours end around 2 PM, so use the afternoon to relax on the beach or stroll through the Parque Central.

On the next day, drive one hour west to Tela and zip over to the Jardín Botánico Lancetilla, a fascinating sprawl of exotic plant and bird species. Back in town, take a walk past historic buildings recalling the banana republic heydays of the 1900s, and grab dinner along the beachfront promenade. Wake up early the next morning and take a tour through the Parque Nacional Jeanette Kawas, where howler monkeys and dolphins reside in mangrove swamps and turquoise reefs. If you're here on the weekend, you can attend a dance thrown by Garífuna groups.

**If You Have 7 days:** A full week on the northern coast affords a great deal of options. Spend the first few days rafting, hiking, and relaxing in La Ceiba's Cangrejal and Pico Bonito areas. Take an early morning yoga class at the riverfront Casa Verde studio or ride in a basket along a zip line to the Juan Pablo Segundo weaving cooperative. Spend two nights in Tela and visit the town center, botanical garden, and Parque Nacional Jeanette Kawas. On the way back to La Ceiba, skip the Cayos Cochinos and take a short flight or ferry to enjoy the beautiful beaches of Roatán, the largest of the Bay Islands and the best option for travelers with children. Nearby Utila is a diver's and snorkeler's paradise and is a better bet if you prefer an active nightlife.

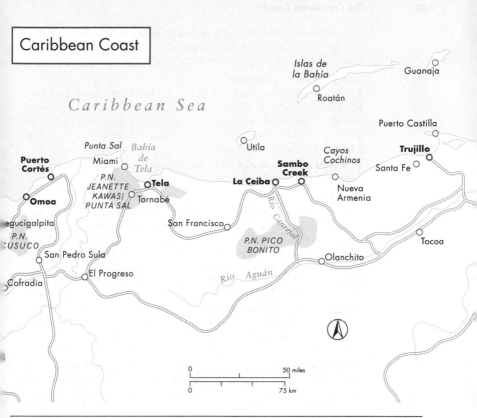

# Caribbean Coast

*Caribbean Sea*

## PLANNING

### WHEN TO GO

The northern coast is hot and humid year-round. The rainy season here runs from October through January (compared to May to November in the interior), although wet weather can come at any time of year. June, July, and August are usually hot and dry. Heavy rains are likely to cause flooding and mudslides along highways, and rafting tours and boat trips will cancel activities in the event of a storm. If you have a trip scheduled during a downpour, stay in touch with your tour operator for updates.

### GETTING HERE AND AROUND
#### AIR TRAVEL

La Ceiba is an important transportation hub for travelers headed to mainland communities such as Tela and Trujillo or to the Bay Islands. Isleña and Sosa have daily flights to Tegucigalpa, San Pedro Sula, and Roatán. Sosa also flies regularly to Guanaja and Utila, plus Puerto Lempira and Brus Laguna in La Mosquitia. Lanhsa has flights Monday to Saturday to Roatán, Guanaja and San Pedro Sula. Aviac also flies to Tegucigalpa, Guanaja, Roatán, Puerto Lempira, and Trujillo.

**Airlines and Contacts Isleña Airlines/TACA** (✉ *Mall Megaplaza, 1st level, La Ceiba* ☎ *441-3354 or 441-3190* ⊕ *www.tacaregional.com*). **Sosa** (✉ *Av. San Isidro,*

*La Ceiba* ☎ *443–1399 or 443–2519).* **Lanhsa** (✉ *Aeropuerto Internacional Golosón, La Ceiba* ☎ *442–1283 or 414–5959* ⊕ *www.lanhsa.com)* **Aviac** (✉ *Col. San Luis Casa 5102, Carretera El Batallon, Tegucigalpa* ☎ *263–3198* ⊕ *www.aviachn.com).*

## AIRPORTS AND TRANSFERS

Aeropuerto Internacional Golosón is 12 km (7 mi) from La Ceiba. Most taxis will charge around L150 to get you to your hotel, although shared *colectivo* taxis will cost between L20 to L50 depending on your destination. Many hotels offer free shuttles from the airport or can call a trusted cab to come pick you up.

**Airport Information Aeropuerto Internacional Golosón** (✉ *Carretera La Ceiba–Tela, La Ceiba* ☎ *441–3025).*

## BUS TRAVEL

Buses run frequently along the country's northern coast. La Ceiba is unusual in that it has a central bus station, although the deluxe bus companies such as Viana and Hedman have their own terminals. *Direct* can be a relative term depending on the bus company. Deluxe operators stop for no one, while most other lines go to only one city, meaning direct trips will still stop for many people along the route, including food vendors and bus-to-bus salesmen.

**Transportes Mirna** and and **Tela Express** run between La Ceiba and Tela. The (supposedly) hourly service by **Catisa-Tupsa** between San Pedro Sula and La Ceiba stops at Tela, as do the **Cotraibal** and **Cotuc** buses that travel from San Pedro to La Ceiba and Trujillo, with stops in Tocoa.

**Expresos del Atlántico** offers speedy direct buses between Puerto Cortés and San Pedro Sula, whereas **Impala** and **Citul** offer achingly slow service. There are no direct buses to Omoa, although buses en route to Puerto Cortés will drop passengers off at the Omoa exit. A public bus swings by the stop every 15 minutes or so.

**Bus Information Catisa-Tupsa** (✉ *Terminal San José, La Ceiba* ☎ *441–2539* ✉ *Terminal Metropolitana, San Pedro Sula* ☎ *509–0442).* **Citul** (✉ *Av. 4 between Cs. 3 and 4, Puerto Cortés* ☎ *665–0466* ✉ *Terminal Metropolitana, San Pedro Sula* ☎ *547–1462).*

**Cotraibal** (✉ *Barrio El Centro, Trujillo* ☎ *434–4932* ✉ *Terminal Metropolitana, San Pedro Sula* ☎ *9763–0513).* **Cotuc** (✉ *C. 18 de Septiembre, Trujillo* ☎ *444–2181* ✉ *C. Principal, La Ceiba* ☎ *441–2181).* **Expresos del Atlántico** (✉ *Parque Central, Puerto Cortés* ☎ *No phone* ✉ *Terminal Metropolitana, San Pedro Sula* ☎ *No phone).* **Hedman Alas** (✉ *Supermercado Ceibeño 4, Hwy to Trujillo, La Ceiba* ☎ *441–5347).* **Impala** (✉ *Barrio San Ramón, Puerto Cortés* ☎ *665–0606* ✉ *Av. 2 between Cs. 4 and 5, San Pedro Sula* ☎ *553–3111).* **Viana Clase Oro** (✉ *Blvd. 15 de Septiembre, La Ceiba* ☎ *441–2330).*

## CAR TRAVEL

If you are looking to rent a car along the coast, head to La Ceiba. Most agencies have offices in town and at the airport, and many include insurance in the rate.

Major highways along the coast are well-paved and efficient, although local roads are subject to potholes and heavy flooding during the rainy season. Drivers here frequently speed, honk, and turn without signal, and livestock is likely to cross the road, so expect adventure and stay alert. Various police checkpoints stop cars to check license and registration, but the process is usually quick.

**Rental Agencies Advance Rent a Car** (✉ *Hotel Posada del Caribe, Col. El Toronjal, La Ceiba* ☎ *442–8087* ⊕ *www.advancerentacar.com*). **Avis** (✉ *Blvd. 15 de Septiembre, La Ceiba* ☎ *441–2802; 9986–0033 at the airport* ⊕ *www. avis.com*). **Econo Rent a Car** (✉ *Col. El Toronjal, by Hotel Emperador, La Ceiba* ☎ *441–6538*). **Molinari** (✉ *Parque Central, La Ceiba* ☎ *443–0055* ✍ *molinarirentacar@yahoo.com*). **Toyota Rent a Car** (✉ *Carreterra a Tela, La Ceiba* ☎ *441–0140 or 441–2532*).

## HEALTH AND SAFETY

Three essentials go a long way when traveling the northern coast: sunscreen, bug repellent, and plenty of purified water. The strong heat and brutal midday sun make it likely that travelers of all skin tones will burn, so always keep a bottle of sunblock on hand. Rest in the shade periodically and hydrate constantly, as travelers might feel light-headed and dizzy after an extended time outdoors. Malaria is no longer a major concern in the coastal cities, but the mosquitoes, or *zancudos*, can still be a nuisance, especially after it rains.

The coast is fairly laid-back, so violent crime is rare. Petty theft, on the other hand, is somewhat common. Keep your wits about you and stow cash, cameras, and valuables in your front pocket. Backpacks are a common target, so don't forget about yours as you walk through crowds.

La Ceiba has some of the best hospitals in the country. There is no shortage of good clinics throughout the northern coast. Pharmacies are everywhere, so ask at your hotel which is the nearest.

**Tourism Police Puerto Cortés** (☎ *9859–2822*). **Tela** (☎ *448–0253, 448–2079*). **La Ceiba** (☎ *441–6288, 441–0871, 9884–3141*).

## MONEY MATTERS

Cash is king on the northern coast. Ironically, ATMs are not. In Omoa, they don't exist at all. It's a good idea to make withdrawals ahead of time in case you find that the nearest cash machine is miles away; gas stations and city centers are a good place to find them. Many machines offer to dispense lempiras or dollars, but they're only stocked with Honduran bills. Finer establishments accept credit cards, but the rest take either currency. Informal money changers that linger in bigger cities tend not to visit the coastal cities. Banks will change currency and cash traveler's checks at reasonable rates. Bank hours are generally 8 to 4 on weekdays and 8 to 11:30 on Saturday.

## RESTAURANTS AND CUISINE

Breakfast on the Caribbean coast is much like that of inland cities—rice, beans, tortilla, egg and cheese, or perhaps a *baleada* (similar to a quesadilla). Dinner is essentially the same, adding a piece of spicy fried chicken or tough beef to the plate. Lunchtime, however, is the delicious exception. Seafood is the natural meal choice, as fishermen haul in fresh fish, shrimp, conch, and lobster just about every day.

The coastal speciality is *pescado frito*, a fried yellowtail fish served—head, bones, and all—with sides of lettuce, tomato, and slices of fried plantains (*tajadas*). At many beachfront restaurants, the catch of the day is cleaned and gutted right outside the kitchen before it hits the fryer. Seafood soup (*sopa marinera*) is flavored and thickened with coconut milk, and filled with yuca, platano, and other local vegetables. Garlicy breaded conch and lobster dishes are equally as popular, although some restaurants decline to serve either of these shellfish as they're locally overharvested. (We recommend not purchasing either for this reason.)

Some kitchens pride themselves on their *ola de mariscos* (literally, "wave of seafood") platters, which pile every sea critter imaginable onto the same plate, sometimes adding steak. Sometimes conch and lobster are included; if so, you can ask if it's possible to have an ola de mariscos without these overharvested items.

The majority of locally owned restaurants have strikingly similar menus of seafood, fried chicken, and pork chops. Expat-run eateries tend to offer alternative fare such as pastas, pizzas, hamburgers, and Tex-Mex dishes. Both types open early for breakfast, around 7 or 8 AM, and close around 10 PM.

Although the northern coast was once the domain of major foreign and local banana companies, coconuts are more prevalent today. Beach vendors slice open the fruit with a machete as loungers gulp the sweet water from the shell. Coconut milk flavors rice dishes, soups, and fish fries. Some local farmers have replaced livestock with exotic orchards full of fruits like the Southeast Asian rambutan; the spiky, fire-red sphere is sold roadside by the bag. Peel back the furry exterior to suck on the chewy, milky-white fruit surrounding a seed (the Chinese lychee is similar but with a smooth exterior). It's not graceful, but it's tasty.

## HOTELS

Tourism infrastructure in northern Honduras has been building up substantially since about 2005. Every city has its share of no-frills, family-run *hospedajes*, but an ever-increasing number of cities have a wider variety of lodging options. The majority accept credit cards and are fitted with Wi-Fi and satellite television, with a few exceptions accepting only cash or not providing Internet. As with elsewhere in Honduras, prices fluctuate depending on the season, but not by much. Hotels are busiest December through February, during Holy Week, and June through August. The low season coincides with the rainy season in October and November.

Along the coast, former houses and beachfront lodges have been converted into bed-and-breakfasts with a small number of rooms, communal lounge areas and excellent personal attention from the owners themselves, many of whom are American or Canadian expatriates. These places cater mostly to foreign travelers, while national tourists largely occupy every place else.

Hotels oriented toward business travelers have conference halls and meeting centers, and the rooms offer quiet, spacious accommodations with work essentials like broad desks, in-room phones, and Wi-Fi service. In hotels overall, the cheapest rooms have tile floors, whitewashed walls and stiff mattresses, but you'll still find them clean and tidy. Air-conditioning can double the price of a night's stay, as electricity bills are astoundingly high in Honduras. Oscillating or ceiling fans—and often both—are at the ready in all rooms, air-conditioning equipped or no. Pricier rooms are the most luxurious, with hardwood furnishings, attractive interior designs and silky soft linens. Bugs, however, are democratic and will find a way into your room regardless. Few are actually bothersome.

Several cities include family-oriented, all inclusive resorts on the beach with restaurants, bars, swimming pools, massage centers, and a variety of recreational activities. Eco- and jungle lodges in La Ceiba offer all the perks of a top-notch hotel, such as private baths with hot water and Internet access, but with stunning panoramic views exclusive to the tropical forest.

| WHAT IT COSTS IN HONDURAN LEMPIRAS | | | | | |
|---|---|---|---|---|---|
| | ¢ | $ | $$ | $$$ | $$$$ |
| Restaurants | under L75 | L75–L150 | L151–L250 | L251–L350 | over L350 |
| Hotels | under L750 | L750–L1,250 | L1,251–L1,750 | L1,751–L2,250 | over L2,250 |

Restaurant prices are per person for a main course at dinner. Hotel prices are for two people in a standard double room in high season.

### VISITOR INFORMATION

The Honduran Institute of Tourism (IHT) has made a big push in recent years to make the Caribbean coast an accessible tourism hub. Hotels are stocked with city maps and guidebooks. Its U.S.-based partner, Let's Go Honduras (no relation to the guidebook series *Let's Go*), is a great place to ask questions and gather tips, maps, and itineraries. The Web site is lacking, but the staff is responsive and thorough via e-mail. Local tourism chambers also have great contacts with tour groups and hotels. Tela, La Ceiba, and Trujillo all have small visitor centers that can provide directions and other helpful information.

**Tourism Institute Instituto Hondureño de Turismo** (☎ 222–2124 ⊕ www.iht. hn). **Let's Go Honduras** (⊕ www.letsgohonduras.com)

**Chambers of Tourism Cámara Nacional de Turismo (CANATURH)** (☎ 239–9379 or 235–8533 ⊕ www.canaturh.org). **Omoa and Puerto Cortés** (⊕ www. camturcostadeoro.com). **Tela** (☎ 448–1793 ⊕ www.telaescaribe.com). **La Ceiba** (☎ 408–5277 or 440–1791 ⊕ www.laceibainfo.com).

# OMOA

*69 km (43 mi) north of San Pedro Sula; 13 km (8 mi) west of Puerto Cortés.*

A sparkling ocean view and spectacular waterfalls where the Sierra de Omoa meets the Caribbean have made this former fishing village an emerging vacation destination for budget travelers. Tourism has lulled here in recent years after shifting currents flooded Omoa's once-seductive beaches. The town is mostly a resting point for travelers headed

## A BIT OF HISTORY

In 1502, the same year Christopher Columbus docked on the island of Guanaja, the explorer took his first step on the American mainland at the eastern city of Trujillo. British, Dutch, and French pirates soon followed Columbus's path in the hopes of looting Spanish gold. As the Spaniards set up limestone fortresses in Trujillo and Omoa to protect their treasures, Europeans in the Caribbean islands sent shipwrecked African slaves to the island of Saint Vincent in the Lesser Antilles, and later to Roatán in the Bay Islands in 1797. Many of their descendants, the Garífuna people, migrated to the American mainland and settled the coast from Belize to Nicaragua. Today, they represent the dominant coastal culture in Honduras.

Trujillo put itself on the map again in 1860, when U.S. mercenary William Walker was executed at the Fortaleza de Santa Barbara by an official Honduran firing squad. Around the same time, Honduras began shipping small amounts of bananas from the Bay Islands to New Orleans. The eastern Puerto Cortés and western Puerto Castillo made a natural boundary for the banana-plantation boom on the mainland. By the early 20th century, local buyers joined the U.S.-based United Fruit Company, which set up its headquarters in Tela and commissioned a coastal railway to transport executives and export the fruit. When the company moved inland to La Lima in 1970, the northern coast struggled to redefine its regional identity beyond bananas. Four decades later, the Caribbean cities are embracing their role as up-and-coming tourist destinations.

west to the Guatemalan border or onto Belize. Still, the quiet waterfront community is worth a night's stay if you've got the time to slow down.

Spanish explorers in Guatemala City established Omoa and its port in 1536 to ship goods back to Europe. The town was officially incorporated in 1752 and later became Honduras's most important bastion in protecting Spanish gold from looters. Following independence in 1821, the town's influence declined as shipping moved east to Puerto Cortés. With loans from the Inter-American Development Bank, the historic fortress has reemerged as the top historical site in the area.

The town is small, and addresses haven't caught on—hotels on the beach just say they are on *la playa*, a zone mostly huddled around the Muelle Artesanal de Omoa. There is just one main road, so either turn left or right.

### GETTING HERE AND AROUND

It's about an hour's drive from San Pedro Sula to Omoa. Take the Puerto Cortés highway north and get off at the junction toward Omoa (the highway is around 37 mi between San Pedro Sula and Puerto Cortés). No flights are available in the area, and there's no direct bus service.

Secure taxis from the San Pedro Sula airport charge around L1,000 for a direct trip to Omoa. Swiss national Roland Gassman, who runs **Roli's Place,** offers shuttles at $50 for two people, and $20 for each additional passenger. Gassman provides useful and detailed maps of the city at his hostel. The **Three Amigos Tours** run out of Henry's Sunset Playa offers shuttles to and from the San Pedro Sula airport, plus refreshments, for $75 for two people and $25 for each additional passenger. Make shuttle reservations at least a few days in advance. Both services offer tours to various local activities such as the San Ignacio Zoo and Pullapanzak Waterfalls, as well as trips to the Copán Ruins, Tela, and La Ceiba.

For those traveling by bus, **Expresos del Atlántico, Impala,** and **Citul** offer service from Puerto Cortés every day from 5:45 AM to 5 PM and charge around L40 for express and less for non-direct buses. Get out at the bus stop near the Omoa exit on the Puerto Cortés highway. A public bus, or the *urbano*, headed into town swings by the stop every 15 minutes or so.

The town is small and nearly everything can be reached on foot. Bicycle taxis are constantly buzzing around and charge L20 for a ride. Public buses and car taxis circulate on the main road, which heads to Puerto Cortés in one direction and the Guatemalan border in the other.

### MONEY MATTERS
Be sure to bring enough cash, as there are no ATMs in Omoa. The **Banco de Occidente** just off the main road exchanges currency and cashes traveler's checks.

### ESSENTIALS
**Airport Shuttle Roli's Place** (☎ 658–9082 ⊕ www.yaxpactours.com). **Three Amigos Tours** (☎ 658–9166 ⊕ www.playapantera.com).

**Banks Banco de Occidente** (✉ *West of the Omoa highway turnoff, Omoa* ☎ 658–9283 ◷ *Weekdays 8–4, Sat. 8–11:30*).

**Bus Info Expresos del Atlántico** (✉ *Parque Central, Puerto Cortés* ☎ *No phone* ✉ *Gran Central Metropolitana de Autobuses, San Pedro Sula* ☎ *No phone*).**Impala** (✉ *barrio San Ramón, Puerto Cortés* ☎ 665–0606 ✉ *Av. 2 between Cs. 4 and 5, San Pedro Sula* ☎ 553–3111). **Citul** (✉ *Av. 4 between Cs. 3 and 4 Calle, Puerto Cortés* ☎ 665–0466 ✉ *Terminal Metropolitana, San Pedro Sula* ☎ *No phone*).

**Pharmacy Farmacia Vi-ana** (✉ *On the highway, across from the bank* ☎ 658–9198 ◷ *8–5:30, Closed Sun.*).

**Visitor Info Omoa Map** (⊕ www.omoa.net).

## EXPLORING

**Fortaleza de San Fernando de Omoa.** The fortress is surprisingly pretty, with coral and limestone walls of pink, gray, and deep russett surrounded on all sides by mangroves. The fort was built between 1759 and 1775 to protect the Spain-bound gold and other valuables from plundering English, Dutch, and French merchants. It didn't take long, however, for a humiliating defeat for the Spanish. In 1779, the English conquered the fort after a two-day siege, escaping with all the booty before the Spaniards could call for reinforcements. The fort was turned into a defensive post for military troops after independence, and it later served as a prison until 1959. The ticket office is adjacent to the fort in the **Museo de Omoa**, which has restrooms and a pleasant shaded courtyard. Exhibition halls detail the history of Columbus's 16th century colonization expeditions to Honduras and subsequent transatlantic trade routes. An artillery hall features swords and canons used at the fort. Tickets include access to the fortress and museum. ⊠ *Omoa* ☎ *658–9167* ➦ *$4* ☉ *Weekdays 8–4, weekends 9–5.*

## WHERE TO EAT

**$–$$**
SEAFOOD

✗ **Aquí Pancha.** If the rows of seafood *champas* (shacks) lining the beach don't manage to entice you, then this casual open-air restaurant should. Just a step away from the water, the eatery offers delicious ceviche, king crab, and lobster dishes. Doña Pancha herself is often around to help with serving heaping portions of diners' favorites, like garlic-soaked shrimp or breaded conch. ⊠ *La Playa* ☎ *658–9172* ➜ *No credit cards.*

**$$**
INTERNATIONAL

✗ **Henry's Sunset Playa Restaurant & Bar.** This tin-roof beach lodge serves up pizzas, pastas, and Omoa's seafood staples. Sit at a wooden picnic table or in a giant armchair and try an enormous plate of spaghetti in a tasty red seafood sauce. Slices of Canadian pizza come loaded with gooey cheese, ham, salami, and mushrooms. Henry's even does delivery (use the delivery-specific phone number). In the back of the restaurant is a double room ($) with a private bath, air-conditioning, and Wi-Fi. They also have a public laundry service, and Three Amigos Tours is based here. ⊠ *La Playa* ☎ *658–9166; for delivery: 3259–0014* ⊕ *www. playapantera.com* ➜ *AE, MC, V.*

## WHERE TO STAY

**$$**

🏨 **Coco Bay Hotel.** Situated between the main road and the beach, this recent addition to Omoa is ideal for big groups. Each room includes two double beds and a private bath equipped with two showers; the conference hall can seat up to 150 people. Mango trees shade the swimming pools across from the large restaurant shelter. The kitchen will open upon guests' request and serves typical Honduran fare. The hotel grounds are peaceful and tidy, but travelers seeking more lively activity should spend the evening at the beach. **Pros:** great for large groups. **Cons:** hotel has very little charisma or ambiance. ⊠ *Omoa* ☎ *658–9001 or 658–9021* ⊕ *www.hotelcocobayomoa.com* ➦ *21 rooms* ♦ *In-room: phone, a/c, Wi-Fi. In-hotel: restaurant, room service, pool, paid parking.* ➜ *AE, MC, V* ⑩ *EP.*

**$$**

🏨 **Flamingo's.** Cool rooms decorated in pine with private terraces overlooking the ocean make this hotel the top choice in Omoa. The sundeck on the beach is a favorite spot for weddings. The friendly Colombian owners really know how to eat, and delicious dishes ($$) such as bluecrab soup and seafood casserole can't be beat. The tamales may be the best you've ever tasted. **Pros:** feels private; stellar views. **Cons:** might feel less private if an event is being held during your stay. ⊠ *La Playa* ☎ *658–9199* 🖶 *658–9288* ⊕ *www.flamingosomoa.com* ➦ *10 rooms* ♦ *In-hotel: restaurant, bar, pool* ➜ *MC, V.* ⑩ *EP, BP.*

**$**

🏨 **Roli's Place.** Eighty meters before the beach, Roli's Place has a wide variety of accommodations, including hammocks on the porch, dormitory hostel rooms, and comfortable private doubles. The private rooms are on a separate and more peaceful side of the grounds and include air-conditioning and private bath with hot water. The hotel offers tours around the area, including into Guatemala, and can arrange shuttle service to La Ceiba. You can also stop in for travel information and local tips. **Pros:** many lodging types under one roof; Roli is an area expert. **Cons:** only two private rooms available; front desk attendance is flaky. ⊠ *Follow the road past the fortress, Omoa* ☎ *658–9082* ⊕ *www. yaxpactours.com* ⚓ *In-room: no phone, a/c (some). In-hotel: kitchen* ▭ *No credit cards.* ♨ *EP.*

$–$$  ⛱ **Sueños de Mar B&B.** Private beach chairs, a refreshing garden court-yard, and a tucked-away location at the end of la playa give this hotel a cozy feel. Doubles with private bathrooms are situated behind a spacious communal lounge with wicker armchairs facing the beach. The Canadian owners pride themselves on the restaurant, and with imported bacon and sausage for breakfast and hearty baguette sandwiches and fresh salads for lunch, the cuisine is a welcome change from the town's ubiquitous fried-fish fare. **Pros:** excellent cuisine; friendly staff. **Cons:** ongoing construction to fix earthquake damage. ⊠ *La Playa* ☎ *658–9047* ⊕ *www.suenosdemar.com* ⚓ *6 rooms* ⚓ *In-hotel: a/c, Wi-Fi. In-hotel: restaurant, bar, laundry service.* ▭ *AE, MC, V* ♨ *EP, BP.*

## NIGHTLIFE AND THE ARTS

The nightlife in Omoa is very tame. Once the sun sets, diners along la playa might linger at a thatched-roof champa or seafood restaurant for a few more drinks. The younger crowd tends to blast reggaeton music from speakers and gather in the sandy streets. The arts scene doesn't extend much beyond a few women peddling pegboards with beaded jewelry and seashell earrings.

## SHOPPING

The town has no grocery stores or apparel or accessories shops. The pharmacy and various *pulperías* sell first-aid items, bottled drinks, and snacks. Aside from that, most residents drive into Puerto Cortés for other necessities.

## SPORTS AND THE OUTDOORS

Omoa has a great number of day trip activities in the surrounding area. The trail to nearby waterfalls called *los chorros* starts at the end of a dirt road off the highway. The trek to the first falls is about a 4-km (2.5-mi) hike and an additional 1.5 km (1 mi) to the second. It's nearly impossible not to get lost, so it's a good idea to hire a local guide to show you the way. The Parque Ecológico Rawacala located west of Omoa in the community of El Paraíso has hiking trails, fresh swimming pools, and beautiful rain-forest flora. An 800-m (1/2-mi) dirt path off the main road leads to the park entrance. The nearby San Ignacio Zoo is a good place to see local animals in their natural surroundings.

**Rawacala Canopy Tours.** The tour operator has 1,200 meters of zip line, a 20-m Tibetan rope bridge, plus swimming and picnic areas at the Rawacala park. ⊠ *El Paraíso, Omoa* ☎ *516–1158* ⊕ *www.bttours.*

*net/rawakala/rawakala.html* ✉ *$5 to enter park, $25 for canopy tour* ⊙ *Closed Mon.*

# PUERTO CORTÉS

*60 km (37 mi) northwest of San Pedro Sula.*

Puerto Cortés is best known as Honduras's largest port, although the city is slowly but steadily rebranding itself as a tourist destination. The town was founded in 1524 as the Villa de Puerto Caballos, and it now handles nearly all of the country's imports and exports. Just an hour's drive from San Pedro Sula, the port city is the top weekend getaway for families and professionals living in the economic capital, and many foreigners stay for the week on business. Puerto Cortés is increasingly attracting travelers who are en route to Belize or Guatemala, or who are stopping by from Omoa in search of ATMs and the Garífuna beaches. Avoid visiting during Holy Week, when the town of 47,000 people receives some 200,000 extra people.

### GETTING HERE AND AROUND

Minibuses from San Pedro Sula's central terminal leave everyday from 5:45 AM–5 PM to Puerto Cortés and drop arriving passengers off at Av. 4, Calle 3. Buses charge L40 for express service and less for buses that make frequent stops. Some also head straight to the Corinto border crossing in Guatemala, a three-hour drive away from Puerto Cortés. (⇨ *See details on Expresos del Atlántico, Impala, and Citul bus lines in Bus Travel in Orientation and Planning, above.*)

For drivers it's a straight shot north from San Pedro Sula on the Puerto Cortés highway. To travel beyond the port town, buses and cars must head back to San Pedro Sula and head northeast to Tela, La Ceiba, and beyond.

The Nesymein Neydy Water Taxi to Dangriga, Belize, leaves from Puerto Cortés at 9 AM on Monday and Tuesday, with stops in Punta Gorda, and arrives at 2 PM in good weather. From Dangriga, boats leave on Thursday and Saturday at 9 AM. The D-Express to Placencia makes one trip from Puerto Cortés on Monday at 11:30 AM, with a stop in Big Creek along the two-hour journey, and departs once from Belize on Friday at 9:30 AM. For both ferries, it's crucial to buy tickets the day before to secure a spot and present your passport. Departures are often subject to long delays or cancellation.

### ESSENTIALS

**Ferry Info Nesymein Neydy Water Taxi** (✉ *La Laguna Bridge, near Delfin Restaurante* ☎ *No phone* ✉ *$55, plus exit fees).* **"D"-Express** (✉ *La Laguna Bridge, near Delfin Restaurante* ☎ *9991–0778 or 510–1142* ⊕ *www.belizeferry. com* ✉ *$55, plus exit fees* ▭ *AE, MC, V).*

**Hospital Hospital Cemeco** (✉ *Calle 8, Av. 5* ☎ *665–0460* ⊙ *Open 24 hours).*

**Garífuna communities.** Nearby Garífuna communities of Travesia and Bajamar to the east and Marejada and Vacacional have drawn attention for their cultural richness and mid-July dance festivals, but they're a bit out of the way and either isolated or industrial. They're also somewhat unsafe for travelers on their own; go with a guide.

**Cieneguita Beach** (Playa Coca Cola). The best beaches for visitors to Puerto Cortés are to the west and closest to Omoa. Cieneguita is wide, clean, and quiet, and the municipal beaches, also deemed Playa Coca Cola for the nearby soft drink-entitled depot, are bustling on weekends with families and juice vendors.

## WHERE TO EAT

$$$ ✗**Anclas on the Bay.** Positioned on a dock above the water, this seafood joint provides a cool breeze and a festive atmosphere for lunch or early dinners. The casual restaurant has earned local praise for its *ola de mariscos* dish, with shrimp, conch, fish, rice, and wine-soaked veggies. Anclas is one of the few shops to serve buckets of oysters. The plantain *tostones* are marinated in white wine for two hours before being double-fried in olive oil. The eatery also has two-story seating on the beach, but the dock is far more relaxing. Ask here about yacht rentals for fishing and diving excursions. ⊠ *Playa Cieneguita* ☎ *665–2311* ☰ *MC, V.*

## WHERE TO STAY

$$ ⌂ **Hotel Playa.** Exclusive beach access and an extensive private property dotted with gazebos are alluring extras for budget travelers and families. Double and single rooms are spread out on either side of two splash pools and a boardwalk, which becomes a noisy hub on weekends with loud music and playful children. A small in-house restaurant serves fish and shrimp dishes. **Pros:** swim-up pool bar. **Cons:** bathroom pipes give off a noticeable odor. ⊠ *Playa Cieneguita* ☎ *665–0453* ⊕ *www. hotelplayahn.com* ⇆ *22 rooms* ⌂ *In-room: a/c, refrigerator, Wi-Fi. In-hotel: restaurant, pools, beachfront* ☰ *MC, V* ⎮⦿⎮ *EP.*

$$ ⌂ **Hotel y Restaurante Costa Azul "County Beach."** This hotel is most suit-
☾ able for young families and has a central splash pool, a game room stocked with table tennis and billiards, and a trampoline. A large, cool lobby is a refreshing retreat from the municipal beach across the street, and double and triple rooms are simple and comfortable. The restaurant has indoor seating and an outdoor terrace. Specialties like fettuccini alfredo and Argentina-style *churrasco* steak accompany the shrimp, lobster, and crab dishes. **Pros:** family-fun activities, Jacuzzi. **Cons:** kids splashing in the pool make it noisy for courtyard rooms. ⊠ *Coca Cola beach* ☎ *665–4938* ⊕ *www.hotelcostazul.net* ⇆ *60 rooms* ⌂ *In-room: a/c, safe, Wi-Fi. In-hotel: restaurant, pool, laundry service, Internet terminal, free parking.* ☰ *AE, MC, V* ⎮⦿⎮ *BP.*

$$$ ⌂ **Villa del Sol Hotel y Restaurante.** Upscale interiors and a secluded court-yard pool make this hotel the best bet for high-end comfort in the port town. Double rooms with queen-size beds are decorated with warm colors and rich wood furniture. First floor rooms open up to the court-yard, and second- and third-floor rooms have balconies overlooking the beach. The hotel has two restaurants: La Ola, an indoor diner with big cushiony booths, and El Sol, an outdoor deck surrounded by palm trees. Both eateries have large bars and serve traditional seafood

dishes. The customer favorite, the *steak hondureño*, comes topped with an egg, beans, plantain, avocado, and tortilla. **Pros:** caters to business travelers, Jacuzzi. **Cons:** busy street and crowded beach outside. ⊠ *Coca Cola beach* ☎ *665–4938* ⊕ *www.villasdelsolhn.com* ⤴ *17 rooms* ♻ *In-room: a/c, Wi-Fi. In-hotel: 2 restaurants, pool, laundry service.* ▭ *AE, MC, V* †◎| *BP.*

## SPORTS AND THE OUTDOORS

Lounging on beaches and fishing are the most obvious activities in Puerto Cortés, but Roberto Alvarez, Jr., who manages Hotel Playa, also offers excursions to nearby waterfalls and professional mountain-bike rides. The mainland's first PADI diving center is based at the hotel and also offers day trips to the Zapodillo Keys. Contact the hotel for more details.

# TELA

*92 km (57 mi) northeast of San Pedro Sula, 100 km (62 mi) west of La Ceiba.*

Garífuna women stride gracefully along the shore with baskets of coconut bread balanced on their heads near the Bahía de Tela, a delightful town on the northern coast. Its sweeping beaches and undisturbed nature reserves have long drawn visitors from around the world to experience an unexpected blend of tranquility and adventure.

In **Tela Viejo**, to the west of Río Lancetilla, Cajun-style houses with lattices and plank walls in pink, yellow, and turquoise recall Tela's heyday as a so-called banana republic. Vendors at steel street carts push crispy chips of fried plantains, the Garífuna staple, as residents seek shade in the palm-lined **Parque Central.** Busy streets lead out to the leisurely pedestrian walkway along the sand, where world-class restaurants and hotels are shaking this town's sleepy image to draw in visitors.

The *calle principal* (main street) heads east over the historic bridge into **Tela Nuevo**'s residential neighborhoods and secluded villas. Natural parks and tropical excursions surround the former port city on either side.

### GETTING HERE AND AROUND

It's a 1.5-hour drive to Tela from San Pedro Sula. On the highway, head toward the airport and follow signs to El Progreso for half an hour, then follow signs to Tela or La Ceiba for the rest of the way. From La Ceiba, follow signs to Tela, El Progreso, or San Pedro Sula for an hour.

Hedman Alas offers direct buses to the Hotel y Villas Telamar in Tela Nuevo. Buses from San Pedro Sula leave four times a day and cost $13.50. From La Ceiba, buses leave three times for the same price. The company also travels to Tegucigalpa, Copán Ruinas, Guatemala City and Antigua, Guatemala, from Tela.

Viana and Catisa Tupsa buses traveling to La Ceiba from San Pedro Sula make stops at the gas station outside the Tela entrance. From there, grab a cab for L20 to your hotel. Viana buses depart from San Pedro Sula and La Ceiba three times a day. Catisa Tupsa has nine departures from San Pedro Sula and La Ceiba from 6 AM to 5 PM for L70. From

La Ceiba, Cristina buses heading to Tegucigalpa also drop off passengers at the Tela entrance. Buses depart five times from 3:30 AM to 4 PM.

Street cabs are everywhere around town and charge a flat rate of L20. Hailing one is safe, or if you prefer you can wait at one of the many taxi stands. Main roads are well lit at night, but smaller streets are dark and therefore less safe. If you're out for a late dinner or drinks, have the restaurant call you a private taxi.

Garífuna Tours is first-rate and one of the most respected tour operators in Honduras. Run by busy Italian Alessandro D'Agostino, the company has made a name for itself since its inception in 1994 for its trips with trained biologists and local guides. The company offers trips in Tela to the Punta Sal and Punta Izopo national parks, to Laguna de Los Micos, crocodile night watches, and three-, five-, and seven-day eco adventures in the area.

Holliday Expeditions and Tours arranges trips to the Lancetilla botanical gardens, the area's national parks, and tours of the city. Holliday can also schedule cultural performances in Garífuna beach communities with prior notice.

Honduras Caribbean Tours' sportfishing and rafting trips complement the standard trips to Tela's parks, gardens, and lagoons.

### ESSENTIALS

**Banks Banco Atlántida** (⊠ *Tela* ☎ *448–2009* ⊕ *www.bancatlan.hn*).

**Hospitals Clínica Médica** (⊠ *2 blocks south of Parque Central, Tela* ☎ *448–0297*).

**Post Office Tela** (⊠ *Av. 4 NE* ☎ *448–2094*).

**Tour Operators Garífuna Tours** (⊠ *Parque Central, Tela* ☎ *448–2904* ⊕ *www. garifunatours.com*). **Holliday Expeditions and Tours** (⊠ *Av. Honduras, behind the Shell station, Tela* ☎ *448–0320 or 9522–8972* ✐ *hollidayexpedition@gmail. com*). **Honduras Caribbean Tours** (⊠ *Block north of Parque Central, in Casa Azul, Tela* ☎ *448–2623* ⊕ *www.honduras-caribbean.com*).

### EXPLORING

The Spanish settled here in 1524—not in Tela, but in the nearby village of Triunfo de la Cruz. Tela itself gained importance centuries later when it served as the main port for the United Fruit Company. In the early 1900s, the banana giant made this town the headquarters of its subsidiary Tela Railroad Company, whose dulled tracks still crisscross the sandy streets. Fruit operations moved south to La Lima in 1976, and agriculture has mostly shifted to African palm plantations in recent decades. Although the company is gone, the interesting history still remains.

### TOP ATTRACTIONS

Fodor's Choice ★ **Jardín Botánico Lancetilla.** This botanical garden, the second largest in the world, holds more than 1,200 varieties of plants marked by name, country of origin, and date of introduction. Around 365 species of birds have made it their home, and birders come to see a variety of colorful parrots. The garden holds the best collection of Asian fruit trees in tropical America, and a large orchid greenhouse shows off myriad varieties of the national flower. There are short trails through the main gardens, and longer trails go back into the hills and plantations, so there is something for all ages and interests. ⊠ *1 km (½ mi) west of Tela* ☎ *408–7806 or 448–1740* 🔳 *L50, includes guided tour* ⊙ *Daily 7–3.*

★ One of the most geographically diverse nature preserves in the country is **Parque Nacional Jeanette Kawas,** named for a slain environmentalist. The park, also known as Parque Nacional Punta Sal, protects mangrove swamps, tropical forests, shady lagoons, and coral reefs. It is likely you will see as many as 60 howler monkeys having their breakfast if you head out early enough in the morning. The males gesticulate from their perches in the treetops, while the females, many with tiny babies, watch from a wary distance. You may also come across white-faced monkeys, some of which have developed a habit of throwing avocado pits at visitors—be ready to duck. Radiantly colored parrot and vine snakes, almost shoelace thin, ripple through the foliage. They are harmless, but be sure to watch your step.

If you take the Los Curumos trail, you can hear the waves as you reach Puerto Caribe, one of the hiding places of the notorious pirate Captain Morgan. Turtles and dolphins swim here in the turquoise waters. If you snorkel, you may see barracudas and nurse sharks, as well as spindly lobsters taking a slow-motion stroll.

You can see Punta Sal jutting out into the ocean from Tela, which might make you think it's quite close. It's actually difficult to reach, so you should considering hiring a guide. It's also a great way to learn about the exotic animal and plant species (there are 14 types of banana here, for example). The park is only accessible by water, and the trip to the park takes about an hour. Laguna de los Micos has the largest bird population in the park. *Prolansate* ⊠ *Barrio El Centro, 4 blocks from TUPSA bus terminal, Tela* ☎ *448–0301* 🔳 *$5* ⊙ *Daily 6–4.*

★ It's essential to hire a guide if you want to visit **Refugio de Vida Silvestre Punta Izopo,** a wildlife refuge east of Tela that's irrigated by the Plátano and Hicaque rivers. It's easy to get lost in this labyrinth where even locals don't go alone. The best way to see the refuge is by kayak, letting you navigate the maze of mangroves along the Río Plátano without disturbing the wildlife. You can spot howler monkeys, crocodiles, and iguanas, as well as toucans and parrots that come around late in the afternoon. Garífuna Tours organizes late-night crocodile watches here. *Prolansate* ⊠ *Barrio El Centro, 4 blocks from TUPSA bus terminal, Tela* ☎ *448–0301* 🔳 *$5* ⊙ *Daily 6–4.*

**WORTH NOTING**

Tela is a great place to learn more about the Garífuna culture. In the south of old town is the **Casa de Cultura,** a community theater and dance project that helps local youth celebrate their history, music, and customs. The workshop puts on shows at the studio and in hotels around Tela. Call ☎ 448–1292 to inquire about upcoming performances, or write to director Jean Charles Martel at ✍ *jeanemartel@yahoo.fr.*

There are several villages near Tela where you can experience Garífuna life firsthand. To the east of Tela are **Triunfo de la Cruz** and **La Ensenada,** where you'll find a line of homely little restaurants along the water.

Friendly **Tornabé** and **San Juan,** both west of Tela, have a string of beach-front Garífuna eateries; if you need to stay the night here, there's a rustic inn in Tornabé.

West of Tela beyond Tornabé is **Miami,** a pleasant community on the Laguna de Los Micos. This is the most traditional of Tela's nearby Garífuna villages, consisting mostly of thatched huts. Many tour operators can arrange cultural excursions to show the *punta* and *yancunu* dances and help you find places to experience the local cuisine.

## WHERE TO EAT

$–$$  ✗ **Bella Italia.** Crispy brick-oven pizzas served in five sizes (try the meter-
ITALIAN  wide pie!) and savory *panzarotti* pastries keep this kitchen, owned by Italian expats, busy all evening. Vito churns out homemade dishes from the back, while Sissi flits busily between diners, who she says enter as clients and leave as friends. Indoor, terrace, and sidewalk seating offer a warm and inviting atmosphere, and the bar is stocked with local beers and Italian wines and liqueurs. They open at 4:30. ⊠ *C. Peatonal Playera* ☎ *440–1055* ▭ *No credit cards* ☼ *No lunch. Closed Mon.*

$  ✗ **Casa Azul.** This cheery little restaurant is a popular evening hangout
ITALIAN  for tourists, especially since it has a bookstore and a small art gallery. Casa Azul is known for Italian dishes such as pizza and spaghetti and meatballs. The staff is justifiably proud of the "big clean salads." Honduras Caribbean Tours has its office in the front of the restaurant. ⊠ *C. 11 at Av. 6 NE, 1 block north of Parque Central* ☎ *448–2623* ▭ *No credit cards.*

$$  ✗ **La Banana.** Nestled in the heart of Tela's Garífuna community, this
SEAFOOD  small beachfront eatery in Triunfo de la Cruz is known for its selective lunch menu of genuinely Caribbean dishes. Artisan tablecloths in bold tropical colors top simple tables, and amazing refreshing breezes pass through the tall roof of the bamboolike *caña brava.* Lunches such as *sopa de caracol* (conch soup), calamari, and freshly caught mackerel join the rotating menu of Garífuna seafood favorites. The restaurant arranges shuttles to and from hotels in Tela and has six rustic rooms in the back for overnights. ⊠ *Triunfo de la Cruz* ☎ *9994–9806 or 9957–8605* ⊕ *www.caribbeancoralinns.com/La_Banana_Restaurant.html* ▭ *No credit cards.*

## WHERE TO STAY

$$  🏨 **Cesar Mariscos Hotel y Restaurante.** Just a stone's throw from the beach,
★  this stylish hotel has rooms with balconies shaded by lush palms. Hand-hewn wood furniture and carefully selected pieces of art add a homey touch. A light and airy reading room on the first floor is popular with adults, and children gravitate to the tiny playground. Truly delicious seafood is served in the romantic restaurant ($$) or at shaded tables on the sand. Try the spicy *camarones en salsa jalapeño* (shrimp in a creamy sauce seasoned with peppers). **Pros:** Great restaurant; homey decor. **Cons:** Noisy a/c units and aging carpet in some rooms. ⊠ *C. Peatonal Playera* ☎ *448–2083 or 448–1934* ⊕ *www.hotelcesarmariscos. com* ⊅ *20 rooms* ⌂ *In-hotel: restaurant, bar, pool, laundry service, Wi-Fi hotspot* ▭ *AE, MC, V* ⧖*CP.*

$   ⊞ **Hotel Playa Bonita.** Peace, quiet, and boldly seasoned seafood at its restaurant ($$) make this beachside hotel a great retreat after a day of activity-packed excursions. The armoires are handcrafted by local artisans, and Garífuna-themed paintings hang from the walls. Conversation is lively in the casual outdoor restaurant, as members of local cultural and ecological groups often stop by for a bite of zesty panfried yellowtail, oily shrimp dunked in garlic and herbs, or coconut-infused rice. Town native and hotel owner Carlos Aragón is a member of the local tourism chamber and an excellent resource on all things Tela. **Pros:** First floor rooms are equipped for wheelchairs. **Cons:** Removed from the action in Tela Viejo. ⊠ *Costado Oeste de Telamar* ☎ *448–3450* ⊕ *www.hotelplayabonitatela.com* ↘ *14 rooms* ⅊ *In-room: a/c, Wi-Fi. In-hotel: restaurant, bar, pool, laundry service, free parking.* ⊟ *AE, MC, V* ⑂◯⑂ *EP, BP.*

$$$   ⊞ **Hotel y Villas Telamar.** Once home to executives of the United Fruit Company, this luxurious complex sits on 30 acres right on the Caribbean. The enormous wooden villas, with two or three bedrooms, are perfect for families. Each is filled with beautiful mahogany furniture. The pool and the adjoining grounds are a delight, especially on weekend evenings when an orchestra plays salsa and merengue. **Pros:** Beautiful historic landscape; outdoor activities, shopping center. **Cons:** The service in the restaurant is depressingly bad. ⊠ *Across the Río Tela* ☎ *448–2196* 🖷 *448–2984* ⊕ *www.hoteltelamar.com* ↘ *187 rooms, 17 apartments, 38 villas* ⅊ *In-room: a/c, refrigerator, kitchen (some), Wi-Fi. In-hotel: restaurant, golf course, tennis courts, pools, beachfront* ⊟ *AE, MC, V* ⑂◯⑂ *AI.*

$$$   ⊞ **La Ensenada Beach Resort.** The latest to join the mainland's handful of
☾   all-inclusive resorts, this expansive campus is hardly the place to hole up for a week. The resort is just five blocks from Tela Viejo's center and is easily accessible to all of the area's natural parks. Spacious rooms and private villas encompass 50 acres of colorful gardens, a huge pool and a private beach area shaded by, curiously enough, pine trees. Family activities like snorkeling, boating, and volleyball keep guests busy during the day, while the two restaurants, sports bar, and outdoor discotheque give an active ambience in the evening. Three daily buffet meals serve underwhelming meat and seafood dishes. **Pros:** the resort is practically new. **Cons:** food isn't spectacular. ⊠ *Five blocks east of Tela Vieja* ☎ *448–0605* ⊕ *www.laensenadatela.com* ↘ *128 rooms, 32 villas* ⅊ *In-room: a/c, refrigerator, Wi-Fi. In-hotel: restaurant, bar, pools, beachfront, water sports* ⊟ *AE, MC, V* ⑂◯⑂ *AI.*

$   ⊞ **Maya Vista.** There's a stunning view of the bay from the Maya Vista, which enjoys a vantage point high above the city. Clean and comfortable rooms have wide terraces where you can lounge in a hammock as you enjoy bay breezes. In the popular restaurant ($), entrées such as Chinese noodles with peppers are tasty and reasonably priced. You can also order wines by the glass—a rarity in this part of the country. The Canadian owners make sure there's a warm, friendly atmosphere. They know what's going on in Tela, so it's good to check with them. **Pros:** Unique accommodations in the trees. **Cons:** It's a steep hike up a long staircase to get here (take a cab instead). ⊠ *8 C. and Av. 10 NE*

☎ *448–1497* ⊕ *www.mayavista.com* ☜ *9 rooms* ⚂ *In-room: a/c, refrigerator (some). In-hotel: restaurant, bar, Wi-Fi.* ☰ *AE, MC, V* ⦿ *EP, BP.*

## NIGHTLIFE AND THE ARTS

On Friday and Saturday night the discos near the market engage in an all-night battle of the sound systems. Follow the noise if you feel like dancing. Salsa and reggae bands (many dreadfully out of tune) often play in the park, and it's fun to join the locals who perch on the concrete ledges to lend a quizzical ear.

The pedestrian walkway along the beach is well-lit at night, and most restaurants and bars stay open until 11 PM. Grab a cocktail at Cesar Marisco's, a limoncello at Bella Italia, or a cold beer at a casual porch bar along the strip. Most residents advise against walking around when it's dark, so have the staff call a cab if you're not staying in the immediate area.

**Arrecife's Bar & Grill.** Cold beers and seafood dinners are served late at this laid-back beachfront favorite, and it's the last to close on Friday and Saturday. ⊠ *C. Peatonal Playera* ☎ *No phone* ⊘ *Closed Mon.* ☰ *No credit cards.*

**Guaramas Disco Bar.** A restaurant at Hotel y Villas Telamar by day, Guaramas becomes an exclusive dance spot and serves draft beers by night. ⊠ *Across the Río Tela* ☎ *448–2196* ⊘ *Closes at 11 pm* ☰ *AE, MC, V.*

## SHOPPING

The Calle del Comercio in Tela Viejo's center is the main street for shopping in town. A string of local eateries, the Garífuna Tours office and several hardware and clothing stores are on this stretch. The two main banks, Bancahsa and Banco Atlantida, are also found here, along with street food stalls and informal handicrafts vendors.

## SPORTS AND THE OUTDOORS

The best beaches are in the nearby Garífuna villages of Tornabé, San Juan, La Ensenada, and Triunfo de la Cruz, all easily accessible from Tela. Farther west and harder to reach are Río Tinto and Miami. Beaches in central Tela are still pleasant, with panoramic views of Punta Sal and Punta Izopo in the distance.

Garífuna Tours, Holliday Expeditions & Tours, and Honduran Caribbean Tours all offer trips to the villages. Caribbean Coral Inns (⊕ *www.caribbeancoralinns.com)*, which houses the restaurant La Banana, provides shuttles to its locale in Triunfo de la Cruz.

# LA CEIBA

*60 km (37 mi) east of Tela, 200 km (125 mi) northeast of San Pedro Sula.*

The third-largest city in Honduras, La Ceiba was once the country's busiest port. It's named after a huge tree near the dock that sheltered the workers, which should give you an idea of how hot La Ceiba can be. Mild relief is occasionally offered by trade winds off the bay.

La Ceiba has several reputations. It's first known as the axis of mainland Honduras. Domestic flights to the Bay Islands and La Mosquitia depart from the Golosón International Airport, and ferries to Roatán and Utila take off from the Muelle de Cabotaje. From here, travelers can drive west to the Copán Ruins or to coastal towns like Omoa, Puerto Cortés, and Tela. To the east is Sambo Creek, Trujillo and the vast, enchanting Río Plátano Biosphere Reserve.

Heralded as the country's party city, La Ceiba draws large crowds on Thursday, Friday, and Saturday nights to its tireless beachfront strip of two-story discos and palm-thatched watering holes. A popular saying explains that "Tegucigalpa piensa, San Pedro trabaja y La Ceiba se divierte" (or, "Tegucigalpa thinks, San Pedro works, and La Ceiba has fun"). The Feria de San Isidro in May pulls in Hondurans from across the country to the weeklong Carnaval celebration.

La Ceiba, however, isn't content to be just a transportation hub or a magnet for late-night partyers. Tourism outfits in town are strongly pushing to turn La Ceiba into one of the top ecoadventure destinations in Central America, and with good reason. The city is surrounded by some of the Caribbean coast's best natural parks and reserves, and its Cangrejal River lures in rafters and kayakers from around the globe to its rapids. Diving and snorkeling around the Cayos Cochinos archipelago is a quick boat ride away, and a short drive takes you to mangrove forests, hot springs, and canopy lines. Area tour companies and ecolodges offer multiple-day and inclusive packages to help travelers turn a short stay into an activity-packed adventure.

## GETTING HERE AND AROUND

La Ceiba's Golosón International Airport is 12 km (7 mi) from La Ceiba. Taxis from the airport to downtown cost around L150 per car, or L20 per person if you go in a *colectivo*. TACA/Isleña Airlines, Sosa, Lanhsa, and Aviac all fly out of La Ceiba to various destinations, including Roatán, Utila and Guanaja, San Pedro Sula and Tegucigalpa, plus Puerto Lempira and Brus Laguna in La Mosquitia.

By car, the drive to Tela takes around an hour on the two-lane highway. It's another 1.5 hours from Tela to San Pedro Sula. Bus lines here include deluxe lines Hedman Alas and Viana, direct lines Catisa Tupsa and Cristina, plus slower buses Cotraibal and Cotuc. All have daily service in and out of the city.

Though often expensive, tour operators can make otherwise impossible journeys feasible. La Ceiba has many fine tour companies, and is a good place to launch a trip to the remote areas of La Mosquitia. La Moskitia Ecoadventures is among the best-regarded in La Ceiba, and

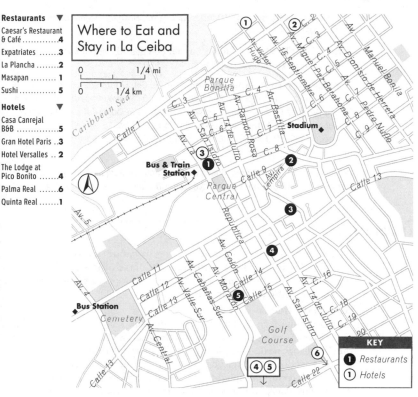

Where to Eat and
Stay in La Ceiba

0 — 1/4 mi
0 — 1/4 km

**KEY**

❶ *Restaurants*
① *Hotels*

head guide Jorge Salaverri is an expert on the region. La Ceiba's three
visitor center branches organize hikes through the Pico Bonito forest
and Cangrejal River watershed. The branch located on the main road
back to the El Naranjo area is open daily.

## ESSENTIALS

**Banks** **Banco Atlántida** (✉ *La Ceiba* ☎ *441–4125* ⊕ *www.bancatlan.hn*).
**Banco Ficohsa** (✉ *La Ceiba* ☎ *443–4447* ⊕ *www.ficohsa.hn*). **BAC/Credomatic̦**
(✉ *Av. San Isidro, La Ceiba* ☎ *443–0668* ⊕ *www.credomatic.com*).

**Bus Contacts** **Catisa-Tupsa** (✉ *Terminal San José, La Ceiba* ☎ *441–2539*).
**Cotuc/Cotraibal** (*Carretera La Ceiba-Tela* ✉ *Barrio Buenos AiresLa Ceiba*
☎ *441–2181*).**Cristina** (✉ *Blv. De la EneeLa Ceiba* ☎ *441–6741*). **Hedman Alas**
(✉ *Supermercado Ceibeño 4, Hwy to Trujillo, La Ceiba* ☎ *441–5347*). **Viana
Clase Oro** (✉ *Blvd. 15 de Septiembre, La Ceiba* ☎ *441–2330*).

**Hospitals** **Hospital Euro Honduras** (✉ *C. 1 and Av. Atlántida, La Ceiba* ☎ *443–
0244 or 440–0930*). **Hospital Suizo Hondureño** (✉ *Prolongación Blvd. 15 de
Septiembre, La Ceiba* ☎ *441–2029 or 441–2518*). **Hospital Vicente D'Antoni**
(✉ *C. de D'Antoni, La Ceiba* ☎ *443–2264*).

**Mail and Shipping** **DHL** (✉ *Av. San Isidro, La Ceiba* ☎ *443–2872*). **Federal
Express** (✉ *Blvd. 15 de Septiembre, La Ceiba* ☎ *443–1244*). **UPS** (✉ *Av. 14 de
Julio, La Ceiba* ☎ *443–4395*).

**Post Offices La Ceiba** (✉ *Av. Morazán and C. del Hospital Vicente D'Antoni* ☎ 442–0024).

**Park Services Fundación Cuero y Salado** (✉ *Calle 15, second floor of Edificio Daytona, Barrio La Merced, La Ceiba* ☎ 443–1990.

**Tour Operators La Moskitia Ecoaventuras** (✉ *Col. El Toronjal, one block north of Pollitos la Cumbre La Ceiba* ☎ 441–2480 ⊕ *www.lamoskitia.hn*). **Garífuna Tours** (✉ *Av. San Isidro and 1ra Calle, La Ceiba* ☎ 440–3252 ⊕ *www.garifunatours.com*). **Honduras Tourist Options** (✉ *Blvd. 15 de Septiembre, near the Central Bank, La Ceiba* ☎ 443–0337 or 440–0265 ⊕ *www.hondurastouristoptions.com*).

**Visitor Centers** (✉ *1st floor, Banco de Occidente on Parque Central, La Ceiba* ☎ 440–1562 ⊙ *Mon. to Fri. 8–4* ✉ *Av. San Isidro and Calle 8* ☎ 440–3044 🎟 *$7 for guided hikes*).

# EXPLORING

La Ceiba is the top spot for adventures in nature and ecotourism in mainland Honduras. Be sure to take advantage of this area's natural treasures, whether it's a short hike through the forest, a two-day rafting tour or a weeklong camping trip in the wild.

## TOP ATTRACTIONS

★ You can't miss Pico Bonito, the majestic peak rising behind La Ceiba that turns a deep blue at dusk. **Parque Nacional Pico Bonito** is named after the 7,989-foot peak. Rugged and little explored, Parque Nacional Pico Bonito harbors some amazing primary tropical wet forest. There are 22 rivers that run through the park, meaning there are numerous cold-water pools where you can stop for a dip. Guides see jaguars and ocelots with impressive regularity, although the enormity of the area means you are lucky if you glimpse these fearsome creatures.

The most popular route through the park leads to a waterfall called La Ruidosa (meaning "The Noisy One"). Trails are fairly well maintained, but it is best to go with a guide. They are found through the **Fundación Parque Nacional Pico Bonito** office in La Ceiba. *Fundación Parque Nacional Pico Bonito* ✉ *Calle 15, Av. 14 de Julio, Barrio La Merced, La Ceiba* ☎ 443–3824 ⊕ *www.honduras.com/parquepicobonito* 🎟 *$7 for adults, $4 for children*.

About 27 km (17 mi) west of La Ceiba, the **Refugio de Vida Silvestre Cuero y Salado** is made up of 132 square km (51 square mi) of tropical forest formed by the confluence of the Río Cuero and Río Salado. This is one of the few places in the world where you can see manatees, aquatic creatures once mistaken for mermaids. In addition to these gentle giants, you may also spot white-faced monkeys, crocodiles, turtles, and several species of herons along the canals. The mangroves are best seen by boat, and the park organizes two-hour guided tours. The Fundación Cuero y Salado visitor center has information about the park.

To get to the park, drive west from La Ceiba, turning right after crossing the Río Bonito. Stop at the railway tracks. From here you can take the small "banana train" run by the Honduran National Railroad or a *burra* (a handcart operated by locals) for the remaining 9 km (6 mi). Trains leave the community of La Union seven times from 7 AM to 2 PM, and return trips are 30 minutes after each La Union departure. ✉ *Edificio Ferrocarril Nacional, La Ceiba* ☎ *3275–4471* 🎫 *$5 round-trip.*

**WORTH NOTING**

**Cacao Lagoon.** The ocean-side lagoon is 24 km (15 mi) east of La Ceiba on the highway to Trujillo. Dugout canoes glide through thick mangrove forests that are home to eight troops of monkeys and many tropical aquatic birds. Cacao and sugar plantations surround the lagoon in the adjacent village. The best way to experience the spot is with a guide from an area tour operator.

**HONDURAS TIPS**

The best on-the-ground source of information on Honduras is *Honduras Tips,* a free magazine based in La Ceiba. You should find a copy in airports, restaurants, and hotels. Published twice a year, it is also available online. It includes a transportation guide featuring current bus and boat schedules.

**Tourist Information Honduras Tips** (⊕ *www.hondurastips. honduras.com*).

**5**

**Glenda's Paradise Hot Springs.** Eight thermal pools simmer at around 40 degrees centigrade (105 Fahrenheit) amidst moss-covered boulders and three gentle waterfalls. The grounds include a cold-water pool, hammock hooks, a picnic area, and a small snack stand. A large sign 500 m after the Sambo Creek detour guides visitors off the highway. ☎ *No phone* 🎫 *$7 for full day, $3.50 for half day* ☉ *Daily 10–6.*

**Butterfly and Insect Museum.** Walls glitter with frames upon frames of tropical butterflies at this quirky showroom. The museum boasts more than 6,000 brilliantly hued butterflies and moths from at least 100 countries. Neat labels, posters, and graphics accompany displays of the splayed-wing beauties in the air-conditioned room, and guided tours are available. ✉ *Casa G-12, Col. El Sauce, Segunda Etapa, La Ceiba* ☎ *442–2874 or 9982–9261* 🎫 *$4 for adults, $2 for children* ☉ *Mon.– Sat. 8–5, Sun. by reservation.*

**Guaruma Nature Trails.** This nonprofit organization is developing ecotourism in the Cangrejal River watershed by improving trails and training the local youth to give guided hikes. The Sendero Guaruma is a two-hour excursion that passes freshwater pools, tropical fruit trees, and medicinal plants. The hike on the Sendero La Muralla lasts four hours and includes a visit to a rural village. Sendero La Vista is also four hours and offers astounding views of the river and valley. ✉ *Las Mangas* ☎ *427–6782* ⊕ *www.guaruma.org.*

## WHERE TO EAT

$$

ITALIAN

✕ **Caesar's Restaurant & Café.** With a couple of tables out on the sidewalk and a cozy dining room within, this Italian eatery has become very popular. The bruschetta *ai pomodori* (toasted bread with tomatoes) makes a tasty starter, especially when followed by the pasta alla puttanesca. Imported beers and wines pair nicely with dinner, and grappa or amaretto will bring things to a fine finish. The restaurant also has small sandwich shops in the nearby La Carniceria meat market and at the Muelle de Cabotaje. ⊠ *Av. San Isidro at C. 13* ☎ *443–1400* ⊟ *MC, V.*

★

$$

AMERICAN

✗**Expatriates.** This rooftop bar and grill, known as Expats, is a welcome respite. Informal and friendly, it is always packed with regulars eager to fill you in on what's happening in the area. A huge menu lists great burgers and grilled food and a wide selection of inexpensive tacos and appetizers; the bar boasts ice-cold imported beers. Aside from great eats, the restaurant is packed with perks. There's a cigar shop, a barside computer, and Wi-Fi throughout the building. Anyone can walk in to make free calls to the United States or Canada, and Thursday nights feature live music. ⊠ *End of C. 12* ☎ *440–1131* ⊟ *AE, MC, V.*

$$–$$$

STEAK

✗**La Plancha.** The town's most popular steak house, La Plancha serves up a 16-ounce *filete especial* that will satisfy the most ravenous diner. There's seafood as well—the shrimp and conch cocktails make a good starter. The service is snappy, whether in the dining room or at the fully stocked bar. ⊠ *Av. Lempira at C. 9* ☎ *443–2304* ⊟ *AE, MC, V.*

$–$$

LATIN AMERICAN

✗**Masapan.** Masapan is a small group of eateries on a downtown corner. The cafeteria has a long, campy, fun buffet that serves many Honduran favorites, including tamales, baleadas, and typical breakfast and lunch plates. It's a great way to sample a variety of local cuisine at one time. Whatever you choose, try a natural fruit juice drink to wash it down. On Saturday, the cafeteria holds a seafood festival; available fish dishes often include a very good *sopa marinera* (fish soup). Two doors down from the cafeteria there is a Masapan Chicken, with fried chicken and fries, and around the corner is the Masapan bakery, for cakes, breads, sandwiches, and more baleadas. ⊠ *1 block north of Parque Central, between Avs. la República and San Isidro* ☎ *443–3458* ⊟ *MC, V.*

$$

JAPANESE

✗**Sushi.** A glowing reputation around town for great fare precedes this aptly named sushi joint. Weathered-tile floors and wire chairs serve as a simple backdrop to the chef's small sushi stand, where he doles out such unique creations as the Tegucigalpa roll, with shrimp, cream cheese, breaded avocado, and eel sauce. The Mimos roll adds local lobster to lettuce, avocado, and soybean leaf. The restaurant is somewhat hidden off the street but faces the Pizza Hut at the UniPlaza mall and is caddy-corner to the Hospital D'Antonio. ⊠ *Av. Morazán between C.14 and C.15, Barrio Independencia* ☎ *442–0312* ⊟ *AE, MC, V* ☯ *Only takeout on Sun.*

## WHERE TO STAY

$$$

🏠 **Casa Cangrejal B&B.** Cool stone cabins with stylish interiors are spread across the garden nestled in the heart of the Cangrejal watershed. The property encompasses natural swimming holes, a weight room, a fire pit for backyard barbeques and a game room. The bed-and-breakfast affords a tranquil forest getaway but with all the frills of an upscale hotel. Rafting and canopy tour operators are right down the street. **Pros:** great common spaces; pristine grounds. **Cons:** cash only; young children not welcome. ⊠ *Km 9, Calle para Yaruca, El Naranjo, south of La Ceiba* ☎ *408–2760* ⊕ *www.casacangrejal.com* ⤳ *4 rooms* ☖ *In-hotel: restaurant, bar, gym, Wi-Fi hotspot* ⊟ *No credit cards* ۞ *BP.*

$–$$   ⊡ **Gran Hotel Paris.** Facing Parque Central, this hotel is a favorite among business travelers. The building's gritty exterior is misleading, as the inside is well kept and comfortable. Rooms are airy, with cool ceramic floors. The pool is a true oasis after a dusty day exploring the coast. The poolside bar is a good spot for an evening drink. **Pros:** downtown location. **Cons:** room fixtures and furniture are a bit dated. ⊠ *Calle 8, facing Parque Central* ☎ *443–2391 or 443–1659* 🖷 *443–1614* ⊕ *www. holaceibita.com/hoteles/hotel_paris.htm* ↪ *84 rooms* ⌂ *In-room: a/c, safe. In-hotel: restaurant, bar, pool, Wi-Fi hotspot, laundry service.* ▤ *AE, MC, V* ⊙l *EP.*

$$–$$$   ⊡ **Hotel Versalles.** Tucked in a quiet corner of the otherwise rowdy Zona Viva, this four-story complex with peach walls and undulating banisters is a cozy place to stay. Regal touches like tapestry-inspired comforters and tassled curtains join wood finishings and marble floors. A fourth-floor bar has just been added and has a game room and wide outdoor deck. The restaurant serves typical cuisine and seafood dishes. **Pros:** social atmosphere; close to nightlife. **Cons:** neighborhood is not lit well at night. ⊠ *av. Paz Barahona and C.2 Zona Viva* ☎ *440–0691 or 440–0715* ⊕ *www.hotel-versalles.com* ↪ *26 rooms* ⌂ *In-room: a/c, Wi-Fi, refrigerator. In-hotel: restaurant, bar, pool.* ▤ *AE, MC, V* ⊙l *EP.*

$$$$   ⊡ **Las Cascadas Lodge.** This impressive resort is set in the most spectacular surroundings, with waterfalls, tropical gardens, and views of the river below. Swim in the rivers, swimming pool, or waterfall pools, or take a hike on one of the marked trails. Private cabins are luxurious and smartly decorated. Airport transfers are included in the price, and homecooked gourmet meals cost $10 at lunch and $15 at dinner. The hosts will be able to arrange tours and activities in the area, such as rafting, hiking, bicycling, and canopy tours. **Pros:** one-of-a-kind views from the lap of luxury. **Cons:** prices are the among the coast's highest; young children not welcome. ⊠ *Km. 6, Rio Cangrejal* ☎ *325/385–7555 (U.S. number)* ⊕ *www.lascascadaslodge.com* ↪ *4 rooms* ⌂ *In-room: a/c. In-hotel: pool, bar, Wi-Fi hotspot* ▤ *AE, DC, MC, V* ⊙l *BP.*

$$$$   ⊡ **The Lodge at Pico Bonito.** Set between two mountain-fed rivers, this
★   breathtaking resort brings you unrivaled luxury amid a verdant tropical forest. Upon arrival you'll be greeted with a frothy cocktail served in a coconut shell, then asked when you would like your massage. All cabins, trimmed in rich mahogany, have private balconies and a handmade hammock. One of the English-speaking biologists can lead you on an early morning tour along the neighboring jungle paths to lookout towers and cascading waterfalls. You probably won't spot the jaguars whose howls punctuate the night, but you might see the semidomesticated ocelot that occasionally visits the lodge. **Pros:** gorgeous facilities. **Cons:** limited on-site activities for adventure-seeking tourists. ⊠ *710, La Ceiba, Atlantida* ☎ *440–0388, 440–0389* 🖷 *440–0468* ⊕ *www. picobonito.com* ↪ *21 rooms, 1 suite* ⌂ *In-room: a/c (some), no TV. In-hotel: restaurant, room service, bar, pool, laundry service, airport shuttle, Wi-Fi hotspot.* ▤ *AE, MC, V* ⊙l *BP.* ⊙ *Closed 2 weeks in Oct.*

$$$$   ⊡ **Palma Real.** The first all-inclusive resort on the mainland, Palma Real
⊙   is set on a pristine stretch of beach. There are cabanas and hotel-style accommodations, a large pool, and even a small water park that is

open to the public Wednesday to Sunday. Splashy colors and intriguing artwork decorate the hotel interiors. There is a tour service on site (TURASER), which can arrange rafting, hiking, and canopy tours. **Pros:** exclusive beach access. **Cons:** rooms could use a second sweeping. ⊠ *Playa Roma, between La Ceiba and Trujillo* ☎ *429–0501 or 429–0508* ⤲ *160 rooms* ⚐ *In-room: a/c, Wi-Fi, safe. In-hotel: 2 restaurants, bars, tennis court, pool, beachfront, laundry service.* ⊟ *AE, MC, V* ⁜ *AI.*

**$$$**  ⊡ **Quinta Real.** The first luxury hotel on the beach in Ceiba, Quinta Real is located in the heart of the Zona Viva. The decor is lavish, with a fine sampling of Honduran and international artwork on the walls. There are thatched tables on the beach or by the charming pool, and Maxim's, the restaurant on the premises, offers fine dining daily from 6:30 AM to 10 PM. **Pros:** accommodating staff; business center. **Cons:** noisy nightlife nearby. ⊠ *On the beach, at Avs. Victor Hugo and 15 de Septiembre* ☎ *440–3311* 🖷 *440–3322* ⊕ *www.quintarealhotel.com* ⤲ *81 rooms* ⚐ *In-room: a/c. In-hotel: restaurant, bar, pool, Wi-Fi, gym, spa, laundry service.* ⊟ *AE, MC, V* ⁜ *CP.*

# NIGHTLIFE

La Ceiba's nightlife is known as the best in Honduras. The clubs are concentrated in an area known as the Zona Viva, located on the Primera Calle, in Barrio La Isla, east of the estuary. This area can be extremely rowdy at night, so don't go alone. There are a few places that allow you to enjoy the atmosphere of the Zona Viva with relative security.

**La Palapa.** A thatched palm roof houses this open-air, two-story bar with great music, drinks, and lively crowds. The kitchen also serves seafood and grilled steaks until late. ⊠ *Zona Viva, next to Quinta Real Hotel* ☉ *Open from 11* AM *for lunch until late.*

**Hibou.** The good sound system and solid Latin beats are the most consistant things at this disco formerly known as Castle Beach; it undergoes a design makeover every six months and is likely to be renamed at least once a year. There is a large beachfront deck outside with no cover charge and lots of seating and room for dancing inside. The outdoor bar serves light food. Big crowds come out on Thursday for Ladies' Night. ⊠ *Calle 1* 🖾 *L100* ☉ *Thur.–Sat.*

**La Casona.** This very popular two-story disco has an outdoor deck, plays popular Latin music, and has a full bar. Ladies' Night on Thursday (men pay a L100 cover) and College Student Night on Friday generally have a full house. If dancing is not your thing, La Casona also has a popular karaoke bar. ⊠ *Av. 4, Barrio La Isla.*

**Le Pachá.** This giant dance hall is a reggaeton-lover's paradise, and big crowds come out for its concerts and sponsored events. There's a beachfront dance floor, a pool deck and an upstairs VIP lounge with faux leather furniture and a great view of the ocean. La Parrilla, the disco's restaurant, stays open all night. Giant white tents covering the building make it hard to miss. ⊠ *Calle 1* 🖾 *L100* ☉ *Thur.–Sat.*

# SHOPPING

La Ceiba isn't quite as bursting with great shops as it is with nightclubs, but the city still has a few key spots for one-stop shopping and authentic handicrafts. Vendors at the central market on Avenida 14 de Julio sell fruit, clothing, and souvenirs.

**Mall Megaplaza.** The two-story shopping plaza houses a supermarket, department store, pharmacies, clothing boutiques, a giant food court, and chain restaurants like Applebee's. The first floor has a row of heavily guarded ATMs. ✉ *Av. Morazán, Col. El Toronjal, La Ceiba.*

**Uniplaza.** This mammoth mall has a classic mall setup, similar to Megaplaza (La Ceiba's other giant shopping complex). Shop for groceries and buy a fancy outfit in one fell swoop. ✉ *Calle 22 at Av. Morazán, Col. El Toronjal, La Ceiba.*

**Buen Amigo.** Intricate weavings, handmade leather goods, knickknacks, gourmet coffee, cigars, and even machetes make this well-stocked souvenir shop the best place for gifts. The large selection of artwork, jewelry, and trinkets is ample but not tacky. ✉ *End of Calle 12, across from Expatriate's, Col. El Iman, La Ceiba* ☎ *414–5504 or 440–1075* ⊗ *Mon.–Sat. 8–6, open Sun. by reservation.*

**Artesanías Sarabi.** Local residents send travelers straight to Don Ángel's workshop for masterfully carved woodwork. He makes custom pieces with advance notice, and he sells bowls, canoes, and centerpieces at the central market. Ask your hotel to put you in touch. ✉ *Km. 6, Rio Cangrejal, El Naranjo, south of La Ceiba.*

**Juan Pablo Segundo Cooperative.** Rosario Lobo started the women's sewing cooperative after Hurricane Mitch devastated her community in 1998. Today, the group sells colorful quilts and crafts all around La Ceiba. Lobo transports visitors to the workshop by pumping a basket down a cable cutting through the forest. ✉ *El Pital, La Ceiba* ☎ *408–7089.*

# SPORTS AND THE OUTDOORS

BEACHES    The closest beach to La Ceiba, **Playa La Barra,** starts beyond Barrio La Isla and continues to the Río Cangrejal. A nicer beach, **Playade Perú,** is about 10 km (6 mi) east of the city. It's extremely popular with out-of-towners on weekends.

WHITE-WATER    The Río Cangrejal is one of the top spots in Central America for white-
RAFTING    water rafting, offering Class II, III, and IV rapids. The river also borders the Pico Bonito National Park, and new resorts and activities are springing up almost daily.

★    One of the original rafting lodges on the Cangrejal River, **Omega Jungle Lodge** (✉ *El Naranjo, south of La Ceiba* ☎ *440–0334 or 9631–0295* ⊕ *www.omegatours.info*) has a top-quality staff of guides for rafting and kayaking trips, as well as horseback riding and jungle hiking. The lodge has operated since 1992, and has dorm-style accommodations or private cabins. The newest accommodations are second-floor suites with screened walls providing incredible views of the verdant hills, and bird-watching from your own room. There is a pool, and meals are served every day in the champa dining room. It's a lot like summer camp for adults, and all the services are the best in town.

**Jungle River Rafting and Adventures** (✉ *Av. La Republica, between Calle 12 and 13, Barrio Solares Nuevo* ☎ *440–1268 or 9802–6648* ⊕ *www.jungleriverlodge.com*) offers half- and full-day rafting trips on the Río Cangrejal, as well as hiking expeditions up Pico Bonito.

DIVING **Pirate Islands Divers.** The only PADI dive shop in the area arranges excursions from Sambo Creek to the Cayos Cochinos, a string of two islands and 13 cays whose reefs attract pros from Roatán and Utila in the Bay Islands. Instructor Tony Marquez offers several package types: two-tank dives with lunch; snorkeling with lunch; and three-day diving packages with courses, lodging, and meals. ✉ *La Ceiba* ☎ *441–9399 or 3323–1280* ⊕ *www.pirateislandsdivers.com.*

YOGA **Casa Verde.** Yoga veteran Wendy Green offers professional yoga classes every morning on an outdoor terrace facing a 60-meter waterfall. The two-acre property holds mango, starfruit, and guava trees and has a private entrance to the Cangrejal River. Weekend and weeklong yoga retreats are available for utter relaxation and meditation. Guests stay in a private cottage and dine on raw-food meals prepared by Green, who also gives Thai massages. ✉ *Km. 6, Rio Cangrejal* ☎ *449–0042* ⊕ *www.wendygreenyoga.com.*

# SAMBO CREEK

Fishing boats and seafood shacks line the shores of this Garífuna community found 15 km (9 mi) east of La Ceiba. For many travelers, the town is a departure point for snorkeling and diving trips to the Cayos Cochinos archipelago. The easternmost side provides a pleasant overnight escape from city life with its string of eateries and hotels; the zone has been fondly nicknamed the "Gringo Gulch" by its growing group of expat residents.

**GETTING THERE AND AROUND**

Colectivo taxis take off from the corner of Avenida San Isidro and Calle 3 in La Ceiba. The price per car is L100, so you can either pay more and zip off, or wait for the car to fill with up to four passengers. Private taxis charge around L120 per car. A large sign on the highway to Trujillo indicates the Sambo Creek exit. A second sign a few meters down directs drivers to the hotel zone.

Day trips to nearby canopy tours, hot springs, hikes, and boulder climbs are a short drive off the highway, and hotels and tour operators can help you arrange excursions. **Kristin and Dante Lombardi** of the Paradise Found Bar & Grille offer all-inclusive getaway vacations for couples. Trips include two nights' stay at Paradise Found, three meals a day, a snorkeling day trip to the Cayos Cochinos archipelago, a canopy zipline excursion and a stop by the natural hot springs ($600 total for two couples). Add-ons such as discovery and scuba diving trips to Cayos Cochinos or airport transportation are available for $40 and $20 per person, respectively.

The **Sambo Creek Canopy Tour** offers a variety of tour options to nearby attractions. A full-day tour ($45) includes a 40-minute horseback ride to the canopy ziplines, followed by a stop at Glenda's Paradise Hot Springs. Excursions that exclude the ziplines, as well as canopy-only tours, are available for half the cost. Canopy platforms here are rustic, though still safe, but are not recommended for children under 12 years old or for overweight adults. Similar tours can also be arranged through TURASER (429-0509) at the Palma Real resort.

**ESSENTIALS**

Tours **Kristin and Dante Lombardi, Paradise Found Bar & Grille.** (✉ *200 m east of Sambo Creek exit* ☎ *9861–1335 or 9552–3258* ⊕ *www. paradisefoundlaceiba.com*) **Sambo Creek Canopy Tour** ( ✉ *Off the highway, near the Sambo Creek exit* ☉ *Daily from 7–6*)

# WHERE TO EAT

**$$** ✕ **Centro Turístico.** The fresh catch of the day is cleaned and prepared
SEAFOOD right outside the kitchen. The menu lists lobster, conch, and yellowtail, plus traditional Garífuna eats like fried cassava and *machuca* (mashed yuca). Tourist Options runs its tours to Cayos Cochinos from the restaurant, so afternoons are usually packed with sun-crisped snorkelers and the boat crew. ✉ *Sambo Creek, beachfront* ☎ *9587–0874 or 8903–7587* 🖃 *No credit cards.*

**$–$$** ✕ **Champa Kabasa.** Sambo Creek's best-known restaurant fills up with
SEAFOOD patrons from La Ceiba on weekends. Once you try the king-crab soup or the shrimp salad, you'll understand why. As a bonus, there's a spectacular view of the Cayos Cochinos. Because the restaurant is so huge, it feels a little deserted on weekdays. ✉ *Sambo Creek, beachfront* ☎ *440–3370* 🖃 *No credit cards.*

**$$–$$$** ✕ **Paradise Found Bar & Grille.** Diners come from out of town to feast
ITALIAN at this second-story champa on the beach. Chef Dante serves hearty portions of Italian family recipes and classic American dishes. His grandmother's lasagna is served once a week with a vinaigrette salad, and brick-oven pizzas come topped with fresh ingredients like roasted shrimp, spinach, and portabella mushrooms. Dante's Best Burger Ever has roasted red peppers, onions, and homemade buns. USDA steaks and barbecue ribs are also on the menu. Two rooms ($$) are available downstairs, and the owners also offer picnics to the nearby natural attractions. ✉ *200 m east of Sambo Creek exit* ☎ *9861–1335 or 9552–3258* ⊕ *www.paradisefoundlaceiba.com* 🖃 *No credit cards.*

# WHERE TO STAY

**$$** 🏨 **Diving Pelican Inn.** The inn offers guests a home away from home, only better. Spacious bedrooms with four-poster beds, warm butternut-hued walls, and unique fixtures and furniture are as cozy as any master bedroom. Ocean views and exclusive beach access sweeten the deal. The owners, Cathryn and Jim, live on the premises and give lots of personal attention or total privacy, depending on the visitor's preference. Jim dishes up hearty breakfasts each morning for $6 each, and the honor bar is stocked with juice, soft drinks, and beer. The inn only accepts cash, but guests can pay 50% ahead of time on PayPal. **Pros:** full concierge service. **Cons:** limited room selection. ⊠ *200 m east of Sambo Creek exit* ☎ *9767–4470 or 3369–2208; U.S. 954/353–3830* ⊕ *www.divingpelicaninn.com* 🖙 *3 rooms* & *In-room: a/c, DVD. In-hotel: laundry facilities.* ☰ *No credit cards* ⫶◯⫶ *EP, BP.*

$–$$    ⊞ **Villa Helen's.** Red zinc roofs and thatched palm huts fill the tropical garden campus that overlooks the ocean. Standard rooms are simple and tidy, and mini-suites have private terraces with patio furniture, hammocks, and panoramic views. A beachfront lounge area has two swimming pools, a turtle pond and plenty of refreshing shade. The restaurant serves coastal classics such as breaded or spicy conch, plus American cuisine like chicken shish kebabs, hamburgers, and club sandwiches. **Pros:** relaxing pool and beach area. **Cons:** room furnishings are aging. ⊠ *200 m east of Sambo Creek exit* ☎ *408–1137 or 408–2494* ⊕ *www.villahelens.com* 🖙 *9 rooms, 6 cabins* & *In-room: a/c. In-hotel: restaurant, bar, 2 pools, spa, Wi-Fi hotspot* ☰ *No credit cards* ⫶◯⫶ *EP.*

# TRUJILLO

*160 km (99 mi) east of La Ceiba.*

Explorer Christopher Columbus first set foot on the American mainland here, and it's said that he thanked God for delivering him from the *honduras* (loosely translated, it means "deep waters"). That footprint paved the way for the establishment of Trujillo, the country's first capital. Others soon followed. British pirates staked out the Bahía de Trujillo and occasionally raided coastal towns to snag gold bound for Spain.

## GETTING THERE AND AROUND

Aviac airlines has regular flights from La Ceiba to Trujillo. The airport is a small gravel lot behind the Hotel Christopher Columbus, just east of the town center. By car, it's about a two-hour drive or less. Take the road from La Ceiba to Tocoa and exit at the Trujillo turn off. Budget bus lines Cotraibal and Cotuc have multiple departures between La Ceiba and Trujillo everyday. The ride is around three hours, with a stop in Tocoa. Buses drop passengers off at the Texaco gas station about 400 m from the town center. A colectivo cab into town should cost between L20 and L50.

## ESSENTIALS

**Airlines Aviac** (⊠ *Col. San Luis Casa 5102, Carretera El Batallon, Tegucigalpa* ☎ *263–3198* ⊕ *www.aviachn.com*).

**Banks Banco Atlántida** (⊠ *Trujillo* ☎ *434–4830* ⊕ *www.bancatlan.hn*).

**Bus Contacts Cotraibal/Cotuc** (⊠ *Texaco gas station, Trujillo* ☎ *434–4932*).

**Hospitals Hospital Salvador Paredes** (⊠ *Calle Principal, Trujillo* ☎ *434–4093*).

# EXPLORING

The fine **Fortaleza de Santa Bárbara,** near the central square, will give you the flavor of those days of conflict with its Spanish canons and European goods. The lines marking U.S. mercenary William Walker's spot of execution in 1860 are still visible. An adjacent museum offers pamphlets and pre-Hispanic artifacts like stone carvings and beaded necklaces. ⊠ *East of Parque Central* 🕾 *434–4535* 🎫 *L57* ☉ *Daily 8:30–5.*

Crumbling tombstones and overgrown weeds add an extra eery touch to the 300-year-old **Cementerio Viejo** (Old Cemetery), where Walker's weathered grave is surrounded by a rusty gate. ⊠ *West of Parque Central* ☉ *Closed Mon.*

# WHERE TO EAT

$–$$

INTERNATIONAL

✗ **Café Vino Tinto.** A grassy lawn with shaded tables and patio seating offers tasty tapas, imported wines, and gourmet lunches. Fish, chicken, and pasta dishes drizzled with bold sauces are served with salad during the day. At night, the menu includes mango and strawberry canapés and well-seasoned beef brochettes. Signs next to the bank at the Parque Central point diners up the road toward this pleasant hilltop eatery. ⊠ *1 block north of Parque Central* 🕾 *9825–2854* ▭ *No credit cards* ☉ *Closed Mon.*

$$–$$$

SEAFOOD

✗ **Restaurante El Delfin** Trujillo families pile around the long wood tables right on the sand as unobtrusive tropical music plays throughout the restaurant. The kitchen serves traditional seafood dishes like shrimp, lobster, and conch, as well as a variety of fried chicken options. The liquor list is the longest in town. A shower is available for diners coming in off the beach. ⊠ *Barrio La Playa* 🕾 *434–4528* ▭ *MC, V.*

# WHERE TO STAY

$–$$

🔛 **Casa Alemania.** An enormous red chalet roof houses this friendly hotel, restaurant, and spa complex. Clean rooms with colorful artwork overlook the water from the reclusive property just outside town. The owner is licensed in acupuncture and skin-care treatments and offers on-site services. True to its name (*Alemania* is Spanish for "Germany"), the restaurant serves hearty breakfasts, German sausage lunches, and hamloaf dinners ($$), and the bar is stocked with German and national beers. The hotel picks up guests from La Ceiba or the Trujillo airport. **Pros:** on-site spa; variety of room accommodations. **Cons:** no Wi-Fi. ⊠ *Barrio Río Negro, east of the airport* 🕾 *434–4466* 🛏 *12 rooms, 12 apartments* 🕭 *In-room: a/c, refrigerator. In-hotel: restaurant, bar, spa.* ▭ *MC, V* ᓫ⊙I *EP, FAP.*

$$

🔛 **Christopher Columbus Beach Resort.** The only resort on the unspoiled beaches of Trujillo, this modern hotel gives you views of the sea or the mountains from your private balcony. Activities including swimming, windsurfing, and fishing from the small private pier. **Pros:** great for families. **Cons:** air strip is literally at the front door. ⊠ *Opposite the airport* 🕾 *434–4966* 🖷 *434–4971* 🛏 *52 rooms, 3 suites* 🕭 *In-room: a/c, Wi-Fi. In-hotel: restaurant, bar, watersports, tennis courts.* ▭ *AE, MC, V* ᓫ⊙I *EP, FAP.*

$ ▦ **La Quinta Bay.** This budget hotel is a five-minute walk from the beach and has neat and basic rooms for groups of two, three, or four. From the balcony, you can see impressive views of smoky-blue mountains to the left and sparkling waters to the right. **Pros:** suitable for big groups; close to the beach. **Cons:** awkward location on a concrete lot; no Wi-Fi. ✉ *Barrio Jerico, airport entrance* ☎ *434–4398* 📞 *25 rooms* ⚲ *In-room: a/c.* ▭ *AE, MC, V* ⵙ *EP.*

$ ▦ **O'Glynn Hotel.** Just three blocks uphill from the park, this bright-white hotel has simple, comfortable rooms with private baths and a very welcoming reception and lounge area. **Pros:** great price for basic lodging. **Cons:** no Wi-Fi. ✉ *3 blocks south of Parque Central, near Cementario Viejo* ☎ *434–4592* 📞 *25 rooms* ⚲ *In-room: a/c, refrigerator (some). In-hotel: bar.* ▭ *No credit cards.* ⵙ *EP.*

$$ ▦ **Tranquility Bay Beach Resort.** A lovely rustic resort just outside of Trujillo, Tranquility Bay is on the beach. Rooms are large and comfortable, and the surrounding garden and beach areas are beautiful. Meals are available in the dining room upon request for $10. The hotel offers snorkeling tours, horseback riding, and hiking treks in nearby villages. Credit cards are accepted only through PayPal in advance. **Pros:** extensive peaceful property. **Cons:** a long drive outside of town. ✉ *Road to Santa Fe* ☎ *928–2095* 📞 *5 cabins* ⊕ *www.tranquilitybayhonduras.com* ⚲ *In-room: no a/c, no phones, safe. In-hotel: Wi-Fi, beachfront.* ▭ *No credit cards* ⵙ *EP.*

## SHOPPING

Aside from the bustling street market near the Parque Central, just a handful of locales offer handicrafts and souvenirs.

**Artesanos WafaGuagle.** The name means "our strength" in Garífuna. A hodgepodge of the coastal culture's woodcarvings, seashell and cocao earrings, maracas, drums, and oil paintings fill the small shop next to the Fortaleza de Santa Barbara visitor's office. ✉ *East of Parque Central* ☎ *434–4535* ⊙ *Daily 8:30–5.*

**Asociación de Artesanos de Colón.** A group of local artisans sell their wares in the pink-and-purple building next to the Cocopando Hotel y Restaurante. The shop offers Lenca pottery, woven-bark purses, and bowls from the Pech, plus Garífuna instruments. Plastic bottles stuffed with plants and herbs are for sale; add rum or cold water, and you've got the Garífuna drink *gifiti.* ✉ *Bo. de Cristales* ☎ *434–3573.*

# Roatán and the Bay Islands

**WORD OF MOUTH**

"We go to Roatán a couple of times a year. As to activities, Sandy Bay area has great reefs within snorkeling distance off shore and in the marine preserve, along with wonderfully secluded beaches. There are several quaint places to stay."

—quest42n8

Updated
by Maria
Gallucci

Surrounded by one of the world's largest barrier reefs, the Bay Islands are a dream come true for snorkelers who can come face-to-face with shy sea turtles and divers who can glide along the bottom with graceful eagle rays. It's also irresistible for those who simply want to relax on a palm-fringed beach far from the crowds found in the rest of the Caribbean.

Located roughly 60 km (37 mi) off the northern coast of Honduras, the Bay Islands are primarily made up of three larger islands: Roatán, Utila, and Guanaja. There are also more than 60 islets and keys, many of them uninhabited, plus the Cayos Cochinos archipelago closer to the mainland. Truly a tropical paradise, these emerald specks in the azure sea have long attracted an eclectic mix of settlers who make up the spicy cultural soup that flavors life on the islands.

The islands were populated by the robust Pech people when explorer Christopher Columbus first set foot on the easternmost island, Guanaja, during his fourth voyage to the region in 1502. He claimed the islands for Spain, and that country soon forced the indigenous people to move to Mexico to work in the gold and silver mines. All the while the Spanish had to fend off pirates like Henry Morgan, who used the islands as a base for raiding Spanish ships in the early 1600s. Today, islanders celebrate the famed privateer by lending his name and daunting image to resort chains, dive shops, and beachfront bars.

The islands were largely uninhabited until the late 18th century, when the British quelled a rebellion by the Garífuna people living on the Caribbean island of Saint Vincent. Some 5,000 survivors were moved to Roatán, the largest of the Bay Islands. The Garífuna didn't much care for the island and emigrated to the mainland town of Trujillo, leaving behind one surviving settlement in the community of Punta Gorda. The sleepy seaside town still remains more than two centuries later.

Residents of the Bay Islands today live much as they have for hundreds of years—fishing, dancing, and holding on to traditions. The Garífuna people and descendents of British settlers today speak a very distinct style of Caribbean-accented English. In Utila, the *Cayons* (natives to the Utila Cays) even refer to mainland Hondurans as "the Spanish." Recently, though, the burgeoning tourism industry has infused the island with a growing population, including many Spanish-speaking mainlanders and a large number of foreign expats. As a result the Bay Islands are now more "Honduran" and more modern at the same time.

Each island maintains a very distinct personality. Roatán is by far the most popular of the Bay Islands, and its endless offering of all-inclusive resorts, bed-and-breakfasts, eateries, and family activities make it the busiest as well. Utila attracts the backpacker crowd with its famously inexpensive dive packages and nonstop nightlife; however,

## TOP REASONS TO GO

**Scuba Diving and Snorkeling.** The colorful coral surrounding the Bay Islands has been attracting divers for decades. There's no need to take a boat out to see the spectacular underwater world—in many places the reef begins only a few yards from shore. Farther out you'll find shipwrecks waiting to be explored. There are plenty of packages for novices and seasoned divers alike.

**Pristine Beaches.** A rainbow of deep blue, turquoise, and translucent waters lap against the wide white beaches that ring the islands and cays. At night, the ocean glitters with the bright light of phosphorescence.

**Vibrant Nightlife.** Beachfront pubs, laid-back cigar shops, upscale lounges and open-air bars with live music define the nightlife in Roatán's West End and Utila Town. Everything's within walking distance, and an evening spent here makes for a lively yet safe place to socialize with islanders, expats, and fellow travelers alike. The party starts on Thursday and carries on all weekend long.

this westernmost island is suitable for all travelers, and the fact that nearly all hotels and restaurants are within walking distance gives it a warm community spirit. Guanaja is mellow and stunningly gorgeous. With most locales only accessible by boat, the island has a pleasant sense of isolation. Some of Honduras's best deep-sea fishing is here, and empty white-sand beaches are therapeutic.

Though closer to mainland Honduras than its island cousins, the Cayos Cochinos, or Hog Islands, are still considered part of the Roatán municipality. The Cayos Cochinos consist of two islands and 13 coral cays; you'll find top-notch diving and welcoming Garífuna communities along the shorelines of these lesser-known gems.

# ORIENTATION AND PLANNING

## ORIENTATION

The Bay Islands form a chain that runs more or less parallel to mainland Honduras's northern coast. The westernmost Bay Island of note is Utila, the smallest of the main three islands and just 29 km (18 mi) from the mainland port of La Ceiba. In the middle is Roatán, found 48 km (30 mi) from the coast, and to the northeast is Guanaja, also roughly 48 km (30 mi) from the nearest mainland point. The world's second-largest coral reef envelops the islands and makes for top-notch diving and snorkeling. On shore, deep green tropical forests and waterfalls offer great hiking and panoramic views of the Caribbean. The Cayos Cochinos are closest to the coast and due south of Roatán; the archipelago is a protected reserve with restricted tourism and welcoming Garífuna villages.

**Roatán.** Diverse neighborhoods give this increasingly popular island a lot of variety beyond its infinite dive sites. There's the sleepy Garífuna village of Punta Gorda up north and the fascinating Venice-like boat town of Oak Ridge. West End and West Bay have pristine beaches;

canopy tours; and the island's best restaurants, resorts, and nightlife options. Sandy Bay has dolphin dives and breezy pine forests, and the best shopping is in Coxen Hole.

**Utila.** Low-key dive resorts, casual eateries, and waterfront bars in the town center are all accessible on foot or by golf cart. Backpackers are drawn to the town's affordable diving and youthful vibe, while travelers with bigger budgets rent beachfront properties tucked into private coves on the north end. Diving is king here, although there's plenty of snorkeling, fishing, and lounging to be had.

**Guanaja.** Undisturbed crystal waters surround lush mountains and dozens of tiny cays on this least frequently visited of the main Bay Islands. Guanaja Town, or Bonacca, is a concrete labyrinth crammed with thousands of residents, but the rest of the island is hardly inhabited at all. This island is hardest to get to, so fewer tourists make the journey, leaving Guanaja with a sense of luxurious tranquility.

**Cayos Cochinos.** The archipelago is part of a protected marine reserve, which divers say makes it one of the top scuba and snorkel spots on the entire reef. Turtles lumber along the shores and snorkelers abound on the Cayo Mayor and Cayo Menor islands. Garífuna communities on the Chachahuate Key offer lodging and fried fish lunches.

## GREAT ITINERARIES

**If You Have 3 days:** If you only have three days, stick to a single island. Which one you pick depends on what you feel like doing. In Utila, sign up for a dive package and spend your mornings in the water. On the first afternoon, take a boat out to the Upper and Lower Cays and walk through the narrow alleys of the floating town. On the next day, take a hike up to Pumpkin Hill for an astounding view of the ocean and Roatán. Spend your last day unwinding at a beachfront bar or on the beaches.

In Roatán, stay at a West Bay resort or a West End cabin. If you're there on the weekend, catch a 10:30 AM dolphin show at Anthony's Key Resort in Sandy Bay. Spend a full day in the tropical animal reserve and canopy tours of West Bay's Gumbalimba Park. For the more adventurous, rent a motor scooter for an afternoon and experience the coastline first-hand. In Guanaja, pick up all necessities in Bonacca Town the first day, and spend the rest of your trip sunbathing, fishing, diving, and relaxing from your hotel.

**If You Have 5 days:** Start in Roatán's West End or West Bay, spending the first day relaxing on the beach and exploring the town. On your second day, visit Gumbalimba Park or take a kayak trip through glassy waters and mangroves around the island. Take a day to rent a scooter or take the bus north to Oak Ridge and glide through town on a water taxi. Venture south to Coxen Hole if you're in the mood for shopping. Spend a day or two diving around the reefs or snorkeling past exotic coral and sea life. If you're diving in Utila for a five-day stay, use the afternoons to hike up Pumpkin Hill, take a mangrove kayak tour, visit the cays, and nap in a beachfront hammock.

**If You Have 7 days:** If you're spending a full week on the Bay Islands, the best way to start is by unwinding. Head to Roatán's gorgeous beaches and take a few days to slow down and soak in the sun. Explore the canopy lines, kayak tours, and snorkeling excursions available around the island. Rise early on the fourth day and take the ferry back to La Ceiba. From there, take a ferry up to Utila. Use your remaining time to dive or snorkel and meet the vibrant community of expats and islanders.

# PLANNING

## WHEN TO GO

The Bay Islands average an annual temperature of 29°C (85°F). The hottest months are May to September, when temperatures tick up into the 90s (though the air is bone dry). The rainy season is generally between early October and January and dive boats run regardless, except during heavy storms. Temperatures might drop to 25°C (77°F) at this time. Hurricane season is mid-September to early November, although the islands are considered below the tropical hurricane belt.

## GETTING AROUND

### AIR TRAVEL TO AND FROM THE BAY ISLANDS

From North America, Taca flies nonstop from Houston and Miami to Roatán, and Delta flies direct from Atlanta. Isleña and Sosa offer daily flights from San Pedro Sula, Tegucigalpa, and La Cieba to Roatán. Sosa also flies six days a week to Guanaja and Utila. Aviac and Lanhsa have charter flights to Roatán and Guanaja from La Ceiba as well.

**Airlines and Contacts** **Aviac** (☎ 263-3198 in Tegucigalpa ⊕ www.aviachn. com). **Delta** (☎ 445-1088 on Roatán). **Lanhsa** (☎ 442-1283 or 414-5959 in La Ceiba ⊕ www.lanhsa.com). **Sosa** (☎ 445-1154 on Roatán; 453-4359 on Guanaja; 443-1399 or 442-1512 in La Ceiba). **TACA/Isleña** (☎ 445-1088 on Roatán).

### AIRPORTS AND TRANSFERS

About 1½ km (1 mi) from Coxen Hole, Roatán International Airport is the destination for all international flights and most domestic flights headed to the Bay Islands. You can also fly into the smaller airports on Guanaja and Utila.

**Airport Information** **Aeropuerto Internacional Golosón** (✉ Carretera La Ceiba-Tela, La Ceiba ☎ 441-3025). **Aeropuerto de Guanaja** (✉ Main Island, Guanaja). **Aeropuerto Internacional Roatán** (✉ Coxen Hole, Roatán ☎ 445-1874). **Utila Airport** (✉ East End, Utila).

### FERRIES

The most popular (and affordable) way to get to Roatán and Utila is by ferry. Boats head out twice daily from the Muelle de Cabotaje in La Ceiba, with two return trips from the islands.

The MV Galaxy Wave makes the trip to Roatán in 90 minutes and has comfortable seats, a snack bar, and a first-class level upstairs. The Utila Princess II takes an hour to make the voyage and is a smaller boat with wood benches and powerful air-conditioning. Ferry rides are subject to cancellation if the weather is bad or the waters are choppy. Stewards walk around with plastic bags for the faint of stomach.

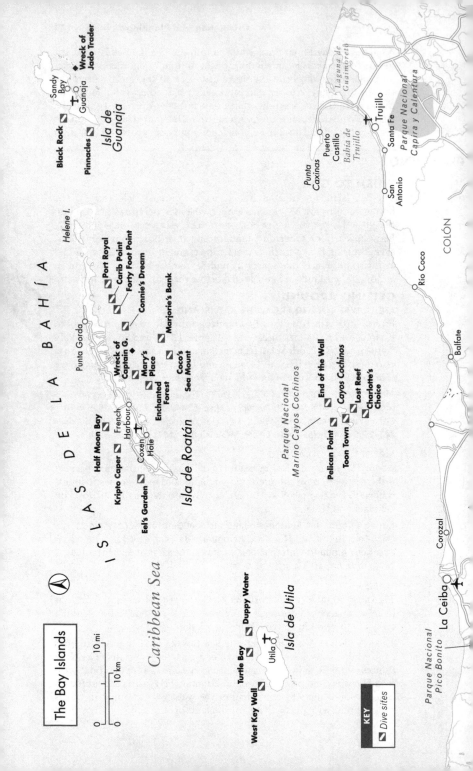

# The Bay Islands

KEY
◩ Dive sites

10 mi
10 km

Caribbean Sea

I S L A S   D E   L A   B A H Í A

Helene I.

Isla de Guanaja

Sandy Bay
Guanaja

◆ Wreck of Jado Trader

◩ Black Rock
◩ Pinnacles

◩ Port Royal
◩ Carib Point
◩ Forty Foot Point
◩ Connie's Dream

Punta Gorda

◩ Wreck of Captain G.
◆
◩ Mary's Place
◩ Marjorie's Bank

◩ Half Moon Bay

French Harbour
◩ Kripto Caper
◩ Enchanted Forest
◩ Coco's Sea Mount

Coxen Hole

◩ Eel's Garden

Isla de Roatán

◩ Turtle Bay   ◩ Duppy Water

Utila

Isla de Utila

◩ West Key Wall

Parque Nacional Marino Cayos Cochinos

◩ Pelican Point
◩ End of the Wall
◩ Cayos Cochinos
◩ Toon Town
◩ Lost Reef
◩ Charlotte's Choice

Parque Nacional Pico Bonito

La Ceiba

Corozal

Balfate

Río Coco

San Antonio

Punta Caxinas

Puerto Castillo
Bahía de Trujillo

Santa Fe
Trujillo

Laguna de Guaimoreto

Parque Nacional Capira y Calentura

COLÓN

Ferries to Guanaja no longer operate, although the Bolea Express, a private speedboat, can be chartered to and from Trujillo. Call ahead to make a reservation and set a price.

**Ferries and Contacts MV Galaxy Wave** (✉ *Muelle de Cabotaje, La Ceiba* ☎ *443–4633* ✉ *Ferry Terminal, Roatán* ☎ *445–1795* ⊕ *www.safewaymaritime. com)* 💳 *$28 one way, $54 round-trip* ☰ *AE, MC, V* ☉ *Daily 9:30 am and 4:30 pm from La Ceiba, and 7 am and pm from Roatán.* **Utila Princess II** (✉ *Muelle de Cabotaje, La Ceiba* ☎ *408–5163* ✉ *Utila municipal dock, Utila* ☎ *425–3390* 💳 *$22 one way* ☰ *No credit cards* ☉ *Daily 9:30 am and 4:00 pm from La Ceiba, and 6:20 am and 2 pm from Utila).* **Bolea Express** (✉ *Zapata dock, Bonnaca Town, Guanaja* ☎ *9944–8571)* ☰ *No credit cards* ☉ *From Guanaja, Mon. and Fri. at 9 am.*

## BUS TRAVEL
On Roatán, minibuses run an hourly service from Coxen Hole east to Oak Ridge and west to West End. All trips cost L20 to L30, depending on the route.

## CAR RENTAL
Renting a car is a popular, if pricey, option on Roatán. The average cost is $35 to $40 per day for sedans and $60 and up for pickups and SUVs. Well-regarded local companies include Arrendadora de Vehiculos and Caribbean Rent a Car.

**Local Agencies Arena Rent a Car** (✉ *Opposite Roatán International Airport, Roatán* ☎ *445–1822).* **Arrendadora de Vehiculos** (✉ *Opposite Roatán International Airport, Roatán* ☎ *445–0122).* **Avis** (✉ *Roatán International Airport, Roatán* ☎ *445–1568).* **Best Car Rental** (✉ *Roatán International Airport, Roatán* ☎ *445–2268* ⊕ *www.roatanbestcarrental.com).* **Budget** (✉ *Roatán International Airport, Roatán* ☎ *445–2290).* **Caribbean Rent a Car** (✉ *Roatán International Airport, Roatán* ☎ *455–6950 or 455–6951* ⊕ *www.caribbeanroatan.com).* **Captain Van's Rentals** (Scooter and motorcycle rentals ✉ *West End, Roatán* ☎ *445–4076* ✉ *West Bay Mall, Roatán* ☎ *445–5040* ⊕ *www.captainvans.com).*

## CAR TRAVEL
The only paved road on Roatán runs the length of the island as far east as Oak Ridge and as far west as Sandy Bay. There are a number of unpaved, unmarked roads leading to various settlements on the southern and northern shores. These are graded from time to time but can be difficult to navigate, particularly if it has been raining. Outside Coxen Hole, most of the roads have no street lights and are hard to navigate at night.

## TAXIS
Roatán is crawling with taxis. *Colectivo* taxis, in which the driver picks up other passengers along the way, are far less expensive than private taxis. A collective taxi ride from Coxen Hole to French Harbour or to West End should not cost more than L70. Private taxis from Coxen Hole should cost around $10 per person to West End and $15 to West Bay. In Utila, three-wheel tuk-tuk taxis roam the streets and charge L20 per person, and shared taxis from the airport cost L50 per person.

## TOUR OPERATORS

You can organize a tour of the islands through a travel company like Bay Island Tours, or hire a taxi driver to bring you around.

**Tour Company Bay Island Tours** (✉ *Coxen Hole, Roatán* ☎ *3376–9574*). **Roatán Island Tours** (✉ *Coxen Hole, Roatán* ☎ *445–1944* ⊕ *www.roatanislandtours. com*). **Pirates of the Caribbean Canopy** (✉ *east of French Harbour, Roatán* ☎ *455–7576* ⊕ *www.roatanpiratescanopy.com*). **Island Life Tours** (✉ *Utila Cays, Utila* ☎ *9937–5457* ⊕ *www.islandlifetours.com*).

## HEALTH AND SAFETY

Sand flies are to the Bay Islands what mosquitoes are to the jungle—inescapable. These no-see-um nuisances can cover exposed skin like freckles, leaving itchy bumps and scratchy rashes behind. Many resorts and developments fumigate the sand, and locals tend to develop a resistance to bites over time. Cactus juice and baby oil help trap the bugs before they bite, while a strong insect repellent can help fend them off. Your best protection, however, is to cover up with lightweight pants and long-sleeve shirts.

As with any tropical destination, wear sunblock and stay hydrated throughout the day. Violent crime on Roatán is reportedly rising, although travelers' biggest concern should be driving on unlit streets at night—fallen branches and potholes abound after a storm.

## EMERGENCIES

There is only one private hospital on the Bay Islands. Wood's Medical Centre, open 24 hours, can handle most emergencies. It can also organize transfers to hospitals on the mainland. There are two hyperbaric chambers on the island to treat divers with the bends, one at Fantasy Island and the other at Anthony's Key Resort. These facilities also have medics on call for emergencies.

The Utila Community Clinic caters mostly to tourists and has a well-stocked pharmacy. The attending physician also runs the Utila Hyperbaric Chamber. The island is now equipped with a helicopter to airlift patients in critical condition to La Ceiba.

**Hospital and Clinic Wood's Medical Centre** (✉ *Coxen Hole, Roatán* ☎ *445–1080*). **Utila Community Clinic** (✉ *Utila Town, Utila* ☎ *425–3154*).

## MONEY MATTERS

Many establishments on the islands accept both dollars and lempiras, so there's not much need to change currencies. There are a number of banks on Roatán, and most offer cash advance on Visa cards. All have branches in Coxen Hole and French Harbour, and some have ATMs in West End and West Bay. Utila has just two cash machines, both of which are near the municipal dock in the town center. Some grocery stores will provide cash advances on credit cards with no additional charge for the transaction. There's a Banco Atlántida in Guanaja Town, but no ATMs.

Banking hours on Roatán are generally 8 to 11:30 AM and 1 to 4 PM during the week, and from 8 to 11:30 AM on Saturday. In Utila and Guanaja, hours are 9 to 4 during the week. While tour operators, resorts, hotels, and nicer eateries accept credit cards, most other places do not.

Banks **Banco BAC Credomatic** (✉ *Coxen Hole, Roatán* ☎ *445–1196*). **Banco Atlántida** (✉ *Coxen Hole, Roatán* ☎ *445–1225* ✉ *½ block from municipal dock, Utila* ☎ *425–3374 or 3375* ✉ *Bonacca, Guanaja* ☎ *453–4262*). **Banco del País** (✉ *MegaPlaza Mall, Roatán* ☎ *480–5332*). **HSBC** (✉ *Coxen Hole, Roatán* ☎ *425–1203 or 1232* ✉ *French Harbour, Roatán* ☎ *455–6695 or 6767* ✉ *across from municipal dock, Utila* ☎ *425–3117 or 3257*).

## RESTAURANTS AND CUISINE

Traditional Bay Island cuisine centers around the obvious ingredient: seafood. The undisturbed reefs and endless waters provide the islands with a bounty of fish such as grouper, wahoo, snapper, and yellowtail, all cooked up in a variety of options. Fried chicken is equally as popular for lunch and dinner. The crispy dish is served along with Honduran staples like rice and beans, plus fried plantain chips. Mainland cuisine such as *baleadas* (tortillas with beans and cheese) is typically served at beachfront stands or in local dives, although they're not nearly as ubiquitous as on the coast. The Garífuna culture is strongest in Roatán, where residents munch on *pan de coco* (coconut bread) and dine on *sopa marinera* (breaded conch and seafood soup).

The most fascinating part of the islands' gastronomy, however, is the eclectic offering of international fare. As more foreign expats grow to call the Bay Islands home, more restaurants offering European, Asian, and Latin American delights are popping up. In Guanaja, there are velvety German sausages and roasted pork at a two-story bar-restaurant. Utila boasts eateries serving authentic Italian dinners, American-style brunches, spicy Indian curries, zesty Caribbean barbeque, and cheesy Mexican treats. In Roatán, there's incredible Thai food, Argentine steak joints, brick-oven pizzerias, and Memphis inspired smokhouses. The wide variety of cuisines here is a tasty alternative to the ubiquitous seafood or heavier Honduran dishes of the mainland. Most international dishes will set you back around L200 to L300.

Travelers opting to stay in dive hotels (as in "diving") or all-inclusive resorts will have most meals provided as part of the package. In-house meals and buffets tend to serve underwhelming beef, chicken, fish, and pasta dishes, but with the generous portions you'll never be hungry. Fast-food restaurant chains such as Wendy's, Bojangles Chicken, and Pizza Hut have recently opened franchises in Roatán, and more are expected to go up as tourism expands. Shopping centers on the biggest island also feature supermarkets and sit-down restaurants.

## HOTELS

The Bay Islands offer visitors lodging options from nearly every point on the pricing scale and can accommodate guests for stays as short as one night or as long as a year. Rooms range from neat and rustic dive hotels to astoundingly luxurious beachfront villas, satisfying budgets of all levels. Prices elevate slightly during the high season, typically from January to June, with rates peaking around Christmas and Holy Week. September is considered the best month to visit, as it narrowly misses both the high season and rainy season.

Roatán is bursting with all-inclusive resorts, many of which feature dive schools, spas, condos, and family-oriented activities. The HM Resorts brand manages seven hotels and resorts. West Bay is home to most of these properties, although Parrot Tree Plantation, Fantasy Island, and Turquoise Bay are located toward the island's center. Dive hotels and bed-and-breakfasts are concentrated in West End, whose unpaved road of restaurants, bars, and nightlife attracts Roatán's younger crowd. Sandy Bay has a boutique hotel, cabins, and Anthony's Key Resort. Outside of the western end of the island and select resort spots, however, you'll only find hospedajes or local motels.

Utila Town, on the island's southeast end, is home to a slew of dive resorts and charming beachfront hotels. Lodging at most dive schools is open to everyone, but divers are given priority if space becomes tight. If you're a light sleeper, opt for a place just outside the town center; a 15-minute walk from the heart of the action can buffer nearly all of the sound of barhoppers at night. Further south are the gorgeous campuses of Laguna Beach Resort and Utopia Dive Village. Larger-than-life mansions on the northeast end are secluded and face the open turquoise waters. Some houses are private, but others are rentals ideal for groups of five or more.

Lodging is limited in Guanaja. Several all-inclusive dive resorts remain after competitors shuttered up following damage inflicted by Hurricane Mitch. Bonacca has a couple of budget motels with basic accommodations. Graham's Place, on a private key just off the main island, is hands down the most well suited place for tourists in Guanaja.

| WHAT IT COSTS IN HONDURAN LEMPIRAS | | | | |
|---|---|---|---|---|
| | ¢ | $ | $$ | $$$ | $$$$ |
| Restaurants | under L75 | L75–L150 | L151–L250 | L251–L350 | over L350 |
| Hotels | under L750 | L750–L1,250 | L1,251–L1,750 | L1,751–L2,250 | over L2,250 |

Restaurant prices are per person for a main course at dinner. Hotel prices are for two people in a standard double room in high season.

## VISITOR INFORMATION

Most resorts and dive hotels in Roatán have plenty of information on localized and island-wide activities and tours. The tourism office sells tickets and arranges tours for fishing, diving, sailing, snorkeling, and park excursions. In Utila, there is no official tourist center, but shops around the dock and realty offices in town are stocked with maps and *Honduras Tips* guidebooks. UtilaGuide.com is a Web site run by local real estate agents and is part directory, part tour guide. GuanajaGuide.com gives a good overview of the island but is a bit outdated.

**Tourism Office Roatán Tourist Information Center** (⊠ *West Bay Beach, in front of Fostor's Resort, Roatán* ☎ *3336–5597* ⊕ *www.roatantouristinfo.com*).

**Chambers of Tourism Canaturh Bay Islands** (⊠ *Casa Romeo building, French Harbour, Roatán* ☎ 455–5854 ⊕ *www.canaturh-bayislands.org*).

**Conservation Bay Islands Conservation Association (BICA) Utila** (⊠ *Utila Town, Utila* ☎ 425–3260 ⊕ *www.bicautila.org*).

## A BIT OF HISTORY

While Mayans ruled much of mainland Honduras in the pre-Hispanic era, the Paya Indians populated the Bay Islands. (Their pottery and jade jewelry are still being found in island burial sites.) The demographic quickly changed, however, after explorer Christopher Columbus arrived on the island of Guanaja in 1502. The Bay Islands soon became a safe harbor and slave depot for the Spanish conquistadors and invading British pirates.

In 1638, the English Providence Company authorized William Claibourne to establish a colony on Roatán, where Spanish settlers had cordoned off their own properties. Bloody land wars ensued, and the British eventually abandoned the Bay Islands until 1742, when settlers returned to rebuild the fort on Roatán. The Spanish took over the territory in 1782. Fifteen years later, the British forcibly removed 5,000 Afro-Caribbean people from the Windward Island of Saint Vincent and left them in Roatán's Punta Gorda, where the slaves' Garífuna descendants still live.

When Honduras gained independence from Spain in 1821, the European settlers again occupied British Honduras, a territory including the Bay Islands and La Mosquitia. The British Empire formally ceded the islands to Honduras in 1859, although with U.S. filibusterer William Walker looking to possess the islands to battle the mainland, the transaction was delayed until July 9, 1860.

The result of a centuries-long tug-of-war is a vibrant mix of Garífuna, British, and Spanish cultures.

6

# ROATÁN

Only about 65 km (40 mi) from end to end, ribbonlike Roatán is the most populous of the Bay Islands. Most villages are along the water's edge, with rows of modest homes looking directly out to the ocean. The west side of the island has recently seen much development, whereas the east side is still largely untouched by tourism. A drive into the mountains will reward you with a panoramic view of the entire island.

The island is divided into seven principal neighborhoods, with dozens more bights and coves dotting the shoreline. Many visitors to Roatán opt to stay at a luxury or family-oriented resort in West Bay, or at a simpler hotel in the vibrant West End. Restaurants and bars are opening in both neighborhoods as the Bay Islands emerge as must-see Caribbean destinations. The airport and principal dock are in Coxen Hole, where cruise ships have converted this western borough into a retail district.

On the opposite side of the island is Sandy Bay, which offers a quiet atmosphere for lodging and an array of marine and ecological activities. French Harbour is Roatán's gritty economic center and houses many of the island's banks and fishing fleets. Further north are Punta Gorda, a traditional Garífuna community, and Oak Ridge, a town built on the water and connected by canals and mangrove forests. Additional resorts and dive shops are scattered along the coast and are easily accessed by the island's only paved road.

## COXEN HOLE

*56 km (35 mi) north of La Ceiba, 1.5 hours by ferry.*

Although it would be a stretch to call this cluster of clapboard houses attractive, the town's rich heritage lends it a unique atmosphere. More cruise ships are docking at the port here each day, which has led to a retail boom and mega shopping plazas aimed at ship passengers. Besides shopping and absorbing the general vibe, there are no attractions here to speak of.

Coxen Hole was named after John Coxen, a buccaneer who lived on Roatán at the end of the 17th century. The town itself, however, wasn't settled until more than a century later. The largest town on the island, it serves as the gateway to Roatán. Here you'll find the airport and most bank branches, as well as ATMs.

### GETTING HERE AND AROUND

Getting here is easy: when you arrive on the island, you'll essentially arrive in Coxen Hole. The airport is just 3 km (1.8 mi) to the east, and the cruise ship dock is on the western end of town. The ferry terminal is nearby, about halfway between Coxen Hole and French Harbour. Colectivo taxis hover around the airport and ferry terminal and charge $5 per person to the West Bay or West End (about a 20-minute drive). Major resorts will arrange for a minibus to pick up guests, and hotels can call a trusted cab to meet you upon arrival. Public transportation runs every hour around the island from sunrise to sunset. Bus No. 1 heads east from Coxen Hole up to Oak Ridge, and Bus No. 2 heads west to Sandy Bay. The fare is L20 to L40, depending on the destination.

### SAFETY

Coxen Hole is for most travelers just a point of arrival or departure, and we recommend you follow suit. There's no roaming tourist police or a social scene to keep the streets feeling secure after dark. If you are here after dark, don't walk around without a guide, as theft and muggings are on the rise.

### MONEY MATTERS

Coxen Hole is one of two banking hubs on the island. Banco BAC/Credomatic, HSBC, and Banco Atlántida have offices and ATMs around town and at the transportation hubs.

### ESSENTIALS

**Police Policia Preventiva** (✉ *Coxen Hole* ☎ *445–3438 or 3449.* **Roatán Tourist Police** ✉ *Roatán* ☎ *9982–8542).*

### WHERE TO EAT

Coxen Hole is home to more fast-food chains and local lunch stalls than fine-dining establishments. However, there are a few nice sit-down restaurants in the area's latest retail developments. The Town Center mall has an Espresso Americano Coffee Shop, Los Ranchos Steakhouse, and Mamasitas Taquería-Bar *(see ⇨ Shopping).*

$   ✕**Bojangles Chicken/Pizza Inn.** Although you didn't come to Central
FAST FOOD   America to eat chicken and biscuits, even locals supplement their diet
with a little fast food now and then. Sweet tea, your basic fried chicken,
and a large variety of cheap pizza will satisfy most weary travelers. A
second franchise is open in French Harbour as well. ⊠ *At the Petro-
sun Gas Station, main highway outside of Coxen Hole* ☎ *445–1208*
🖛 *MC, V.*

$   ✕**H. B. Warren.** The most centrally located supermarket on the island,
FAST FOOD   H. B. Warren has a lunch counter where you can sample some delicious
fried chicken. It's also a great place for a quick breakfast. Colectivo
taxis and public buses depart from the store. ⊠ *Main St.* ☎ *445–1208*
🖛 *AE, MC, V* ⊘ *Closed Sun.*

## WHERE TO STAY

The main street in Coxen Hole has a couple of budget hotels with basic
accomodations and no air-conditioning, but you're better off taking a
cab to the nearby town of West End, where it's safer to walk around at
night and there are infinitely more places to eat. Grab a cab from the
airport, ferry terminal, or H.B. Warren supermarket and head west.
Taxi drivers are prone to overcharging, so settle on a rate around $10.

## SHOPPING

What Coxen Hole lacks in lodging and nightlife, it makes up for in
shopping. Just outside the cruise ship pier is a budding flea and crafts
market with local artisanry, tourist T-shirts, and beach accessories.
Most shopkeepers accept U.S. dollars and can be bargained with.

**Town Center at Port of Roatán.** The upscale mall has two levels of designer
accessories and jewelry boutiques, bookstores, crafts and gift shops,
souvenirs, clothing and footwear stores, plus duty-free shopping.
⊠ *Coxen Hole* ☎ *No phone* ⊕ *www.portofroatan.com* 🖛 *AE, MC, V*
⊘ *Closed Sun.*

**Yaba Ding Ding.** A local arts and crafts gallery, the shop offers an array
of Lenca pottery, Garífuna folk art, silk paintings, handmade candles,
and woodcarvings. The singsong name comes from the Bay Islands
phrase for pre-Columbian artifacts or recovered objects. ⊠ *Coxen Hole*
☎ *445–1683* ⊕ *www.yabadingding.com* 🖛 *AE, MC, V* ⊘ *Closed Sun.*

# PUNTA GORDA

*26 km (16 mi) northeast of Coxen Hole.*

Punta Gorda is a tranquil town on the northeast end of Roatán, where
travelers can catch a glimpse of the enduring Garífuna culture that hails
back to the 18th century. On April 12, residents celebrate their ancestors' arrival to the island with a daylong carnival of dancing, drinking, and rhythmic percussion. Uninterrupted views of azure reefs once
attracted dive hotels to the beachfront community, but the resorts have
since closed up shop, and only a few local eateries serving traditional
seafood remain. A wood sign along the main highway directs drivers
down a steep hill into town.

6

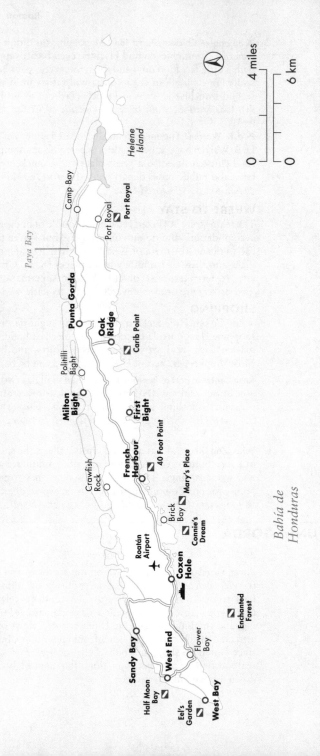

# Roatán Island

Caribbean Sea

4 miles

6 km

Helene Island

Camp Bay

Port Royal

Paya Bay

Punta Gorda

Oak Ridge

Carib Point

Politilli Bight

Milton Bight

First Bight

French Harbour

40 Foot Point

Crawfish Rock

Mary's Place

Brick Bay

Roatán Airport

Connie's Dream

Coxen Hole

Enchanted Forest

Sandy Bay

West End

Flower Bay

Half Moon Bay

Eel's Garden

West Bay

Bahía de Honduras

## OAK RIDGE

*29 km (18 mi) northeast of Coxen Hole*

Boathouses on stilts fringe this fascinating town built on mangrove coves. Motorized canoes putter from dock to dock in Roatán's rendition of the Venetian canals. The area has only recently begun attracting tourists, who come for the excellent fishing, diving, and bird-watching.

### GETTING HERE AND AROUND

Driving north up the main highway, take a right at the Oak Ridge turnoff, and drive downhill to an open parking lot. From there, hire a water taxi to take you around (L30) or arrange a ride in advance with a restaurant or hotel.

Driving north up the main highway, take a right at the Oak Ridge turnoff, and drive downhill to an open parking lot. Public minibuses (L25) depart every half hour on the No. 1 line from Coxen Hole to the banks of Oak Ridge. From there, hire a water taxi to take you around (L30) or arrange a ride in advance with a restaurant or hotel. The last bus out of Oak Ridge leaves around 6 PM, so give yourself plenty of time to catch a ride west. If you're taking a cab, arrange for pickup beforehand, or pay the taxi driver to wait while you tour the area (though this could get costly).

### WHERE TO EAT AND STAY

**$–$$**
SEAFOOD
✕**Hole in the Wall Restaurant.** As you would expect from a restaurant with this name, Hole in the Wall is a local favorite—so much so that the community helped rebuild it after a 2005 fire burned the place to the ground. Come here for the lobster, shrimp, and sirloin steaks; it's a quick boat ride from Oak Ridge, and any water taxi will know exactly where to take you. ⊠ *Jonesville* 🕿 *No phone.*

**$**
SEAFOOD
✕**Windsong Bar & Café.** Windsong serves the catch of the day along with homemade bread and a stunning view of the island's northern shore. The restaurant is a mile past the Oak Ridge exit at the end of the paved highway, so if you're taking the bus, ask the driver if he can stop a little further ahead. ⊠ *Oak Ridge* 🕿 *No phone* ☺ *Closed Tues.*

**$$$$**
🏨 **Reef House Resort.** This isolated plantation is a dedicated diver's paradise. A long drive from the island's western tourist hubs, plus the additional aquatic transit, make for a self-selective group of divers who get to enjoy some of Roatán's healthiest reefs. Rooms equipped with two queen-size beds are linked together in a beachfront lodge with pale-blue walls and a red zinc roof. The resort's most popular package is the seven-night stay, which includes three daily meals, airport shuttles, three daily boat dives, one night dive, and unlimited shore diving. One, five, nine, and 10-night packages are also available as are snorkel-only deals. **Pros:** pristine dive sites.**Cons:** isolated location; a long journey from the rest of Roatán. ⊠ *Sandy Bay* 🕿 *435–1482 or 678/359–1400 from the U.S.* ⊕ *www.reefhouseresort.com* ➪ *12 rooms* 🛏 *In-room: a/c. In-hotel: restaurant, bar, diving.* ▭ *AE, MC, V* ❙◎❙ *AI.*

# SANDY BAY

*7 km (4 mi) west of Coxen Hole.*

On the north coast of Roatán Island, Sandy Bay is a laid-back community that stretches many miles along the sandy beach. It is home to many unique sites and attractions that will bring you closer to the Caribbean lifestyle.

### GETTING HERE AND AROUND

Most places in Sandy Bay are right off the road that runs from West End to Coxen Hole, so minibuses and cabs pass by frequently. Shared taxis from the ferry terminal should cost around L70, while private cabs might charge around $10. Fares should be less from the airport and cruise ship dock. A collectivo cab to West End is about L20.

### SAFETY

Sandy Bay isn't particularly unsafe, but it's not an ideal place to walk around after dark. Most places are buried in the trees with dirt paths leading up to the unlit highway. Bring a flashlight at night and mind the traffic, or stick to the shoreline in the evening.

### MONEY MATTERS

The closest ATMs to Sandy Bay are in the West End. There's one at the gas station and another by the Coconut Tree dive shop on the promenade. However, many establishments in Sandy Bay accept credit cards.

### ESSENTIALS

**Police Roatán Tourist Police** (✉ *Roatán* ☎ *9982–8542*).

### EXPLORING

One of the attractions at Anthony's Key Resort, the **Roatán Institute for Marine Sciences** is an educational center that researches bottlenose dolphins and other marine animals. There are free-to-the-public dolphin shows on Friday, Saturday, and Sunday at 10:30 AM. For a fee you can participate in a "dolphin encounter" ($62 for nonguests), which allows you to either swim, dive, or snorkel with the dolphins. There are also programs for children ages 5 to 14, including snorkeling experiences and the Dolphin Trainer for a Day program ($202 for nonguests). ✉ *Anthony's Key Resort* ☎ *445–3009 or 445–3049* ⊕ *www.anthonyskey.com* ☉ *Mon.–Fri. 7–5, weekends 8–5.*

Well worth a visit is the tiny **Roatán Museum**, named one of the best small museums in Central America. The facility, at Anthony's Key Resort, displays archaeological discoveries from Roatán and the rest of the Bay Islands. ✉ *Anthony's Key Resort* ☎ *445–3009 or 445–3049* ⊕ *www.anthonyskey.com* 💲 *L20* ☉ *Mon.–Fri. 7–5, weekends 8–5.*

With one of the country's most extensive orchid collections, the **Carambola Botanical Gardens** is home to many different varieties of tropical plants. It is also a breeding area for iguanas. There are several trails to follow, and many of the trees and plants are identified by small signs. The longest trail leads up to the top of the hill, where you find an amazing view of the West End of the island and Anthony's Key Resort. Guides can be hired at the visitor center. ✉ *Sandy Bay, across* *from Anthony's Key Resort* ☎ *445-3117* ⊕ *www.carambolagardens. com* ✉ *$5* ⊙ *Daily 8-5.*

## WHERE TO EAT

$$–$$$

JAMAICAN

✕ **Blue Parrot Bar & Restaurant.** Once a popular beer and burger joint, the new owners now serve boldly seasoned Jamaican jerk chicken and Caribbean-inspired seafood favorites. Located next to Seadancer Condominiums, it draws a nice mix of vacationers for lunch and dinner. Tropical music plays around the clock, giving a festive atmosphere to this casual outdoor eatery. ✉ *Seadancer Resort, Sandy Bay* ☎ *9958– 4245* ▭ *No credit cards* ⊙ *Closed Mon.*

$$–$$$

AMERICAN

✕ **The Hungry Kiwi Café.** Formerly called the Que Tal Café, this long time island favorite still serves excellent breakfasts and lunches, plus daily dinner specials like roast lamb or prime rib. The dining area has free Wi-Fi and a full coffee bar. ✉ *Lawson Rock, Sandy Bay* ☎ *445–3295* ⊕ *www.hungrykiwi.com* ▭ *No credit cards* ⊙ *Closed Sun., no dinner Mon.–Wed. during low season.*

$$

AMERICAN

✕ **Oasis Lounge.** American favorites like Black Angus hamburgers, buffalo wings, Philly cheesesteaks, and quesadillas come in generous portions at this lounge and swim-up bar at Guava Grove Villas. The eatery also puts on local art shows, wine and beer tastings, and Tuesday quiz nights. Closing time, 10 PM, might feel early for some. ✉ *Guava Grove, between Km 8 and 9, Sandy Bay* ☎ *9602–2400* ▭ *MC, V* ⊙ *Closed Wed.*

## WHERE TO STAY

$$$$

☾

🏨 **Anthony's Key Resort.** Nestled on a private key, the low-slung cabanas at this luxury resort put the Caribbean at your doorstep. Ocean breezes waft in through the slatted windows, keeping the simple rooms cool and comfortable. If you prefer, a few come with air-conditioning. Either way, you can enjoy blazing sunsets from your private terrace. Water taxis ferry you to the rest of the resort. Renowned for its diving operation, Anthony's Key takes you out on six 42-foot boats. The resort also offers kids' programs (ages 5 to 14), beach picnics, horseback riding, and a wide range of water sports. Diving and snorkeling packages are also available. **Pros:** plenty of family fun; the area's best dolphin show. **Cons:** Internet is Ethernet, not Wi-Fi, and ethernet cords for laptops must be purchased from the front desk. ✉ *Sandy Bay* ☎ *445–1003 or 1-800-227–3483 from the U.S.* 🖷 *445–1140* ⊕ *www.anthonyskey.com* ⬎ *56 rooms* ☖ *In-hotel: restaurant, bar, pool, diving, water sports, children's program (ages 5–14), Wi-Fi hotspot* ▭ *AE, MC, V* ❙⓿❙ *FAP.*

$$–$$$

🏨 **Blue Bahia Resort.** Behind the property's dock (from which you can embark on different types of aquatic adventures), charming two-story cabins with Spanish tile showers and woven seagrass furniture are spread along the shoreline against a backdrop of green forest. A walk-in aviary with rescued toucans adds a splash of life to the tranquil compound. The savory smokehouse lunch and dinner menu is a pleasant surprise of southern U.S. classics. Settle into a seat on the waterfront gazebo and sample the Memphis-style pulled pork, the flavorful Nawlin's gumbo, or the hickory-smoked wahoo served with blue cheese and bacon. The wine rack is always stocked with fine South American bottles. **Pros:** outstanding on-site restaurant; beautiful grounds.

Cons: restaurant closed Tuesday. ⊠ *Sandy Bay* ☎ *445–1003* ⊕ *www. bluebahiaresort.com* ⌦ *9 rooms, 1 penthouse* ⌂ *In-room: Wi-Fi. In-hotel: restaurant, room service, bar, pool, diving* ⊟ *AE, MC, V* ⌶⌾⌶ *BP.*

**$$$$** ⊡ **The Sanctuary.** Four luxurious cottages are spread across this exclusive campus that winds through botanical gardens and out to a secluded cove. Vaulted ceilings and screened-in patios with ocean views help give the rentals a rustic yet high-end feel. The Bamboo, Mango, and Dolphin houses have two bedrooms and two baths, and the Cabana has a single queen-size bed for couples.The property has a private dock and gazebo that overlook the dolphin pen at Anthony's Key Resort. At night, you can hear the dolphins splash around as phosphorescence glitters in the water. Rentals are by the week. **Pros:** tropical seclusion; close to West End nightlife; private dock. **Cons:** like any true cottage, these are home to bugs and critters. ⊠ *Sandy Bay* ☎ *978–9147* ⊕ *www. roatanbeachrentals.com* ⌦ *4 cabins* ⌂ *In-room: no a/c, kitchen, Wi-Fi. In-hotel: beachfront* ⊟ *AE, MC, V* ⌶⌾⌶ *EP.*

### SPORTS AND THE OUTDOORS

Anthony's Key and Blue Bahia resorts host dive centers on their respective properties. Sandy Bay also has some of the best conditions on the island for novice and seasoned windsurfers.

**AKR Instructor Development Center.** The official name for the dive facilities at Anthony's Key Resort, this place facilitates every level of diver and can also facilitate dolphin dives with the Roatán Institute for Marine Sciences. ⊠ *Sandy Bay* ☎ *445–1003 or 800/227–3483* ⊕ *www. anthonyskey.com.*

**Baan Suerte Spa.** This island retreat has spa treatments, yoga, activities like kayaking, a la carte meals and package discounts. ⊠ *Sandy Bay* ☎ *445–3059 wwww.spabaansuerte.com.*

**Octopus Dive Shop.** Offers single dives and 10-tank packages. ⊠ *Sandy Bay* ☎ *445–3385* ⊕ *www.roatan-octopusdiveschool.com.*

**Wind & Fun Windsurfing School.** This is one of the best places on the island to rent windsurfing equipment or take lessons; their instructors are a dedicated bunch. Paddle tennis facilities here are also popular. ⊠ *Sandy Bay* ☎ *445–3292 or 3378–8878* ⊕ *www.windsurfhonduras. com* ⊗ *Closed Mon.*

## WEST END

*5 km (3 mi) southwest of Sandy Bay.*

One of the most popular destinations for budget travelers, West End offers idyllic beaches stretching as far as the eye can see. One of the loveliest spots is Half Moon Bay, a crescent of brilliant white sand. A huge number of dive shops offer incredibly low-priced courses, and a half-mile stretch of restaurants, bars, and gift shops make this Roatán's evening hot spot.

## GETTING HERE AND AROUND

Shared taxis from the Ferry Terminal should cost around $5 per person and $3 from Coxen Hole. Be sure to negotiate the price before getting in the car. Bus 2 and minibuses to West End leave from Coxen Hole every hour and cost L30 a ride.

From Sandy Bay, a collective cab costs $2 or less. Water taxis to West Bay cost $3 or L50 and leave from the West End Marine Park, just a couple minutes' walk left of the town entrance. Taxis arrive in front of Foster's dock.

## SAFETY

Bright street lamps and a steady stream of restaurant goers and bar hoppers keep this tightly knit town relatively safe at night. Don't wander too far off the beaten path, however, as night lighting is lacking everywhere else.

## MONEY MATTERS

West End has two ATMs, one at the gas station and another by the Coconut Tree dive shop. Most hotels and hotel restaurants accept credit cards, although a few eateries still only accept cash.

## ESSENTIALS

**Police Roatán Municipal Police** (✉ *West End to French Harbor* ☎ *445–0416*). **Roatán Tourist Police** (✉ *Roatán* ☎ *9982–8542*).

## EXPLORING

**Roatán Butterfly Garden.** Thousands of butterflies flutter past tropical trees of banana, papaya, and breadfruit in the 3,000 square-feet enclosure. Shaded benches along gravel paths overlook more than 25 varieties of hibiscus, ginger, jasmine, and orchid plants. The park is also home to brilliant red macaws, chatty green parrots, and an array of flitting hummingbirds. Visitors can wander the garden alone or hire a guide for an hour-long tour. To get to the park, walk about five minutes east of the West End entrance along the road to Coxen Hole. ✉ *East of West End entrance* ☎ *445–4481* ⊕ *www.roatanbutterfly.com)* ⛁ *$7* ☉ *Sun.–Fri. 9–5.*

**Underwater Paradise.** Glass-bottom boat and submarine tours are an excellent way to enjoy the West End's coral reefs from a non-dive perspective. Underwater Paradise drops passengers 2 m (7 ft) below the water in an air-conditioned semi-submarine with a crystal-clear bottom view. ✉ *Across the street from Coconut Tree Cabins in Half Moon Bay* ☎ *No phone* ⛁ *$20* ☉ *Daily at 10, 11, and 2.*

**Stanley Submarine.** For a pricey but one-of-a-kind experience, contact Stanley Submarine for the ultimate deep-sea wildlife-viewing excursion. Their two-passenger submarine, named *Idabel*, is piloted by Captain Karl and drops as low as 915 m (3,000 ft) below sea level. The journey promises the chance to spot sharks and mysterious creatures you've likely never imagined. Trips are by reservation only. ✉ *Half Moon Bay* ☎ *3359–2887* ⊕ *www.stanleysubmarines.com* ⛁ *$400 for 1.5 hrs.*

## WHERE TO EAT

$$$–$$$$   ✕ **Argentinian Grill.** Grilled meats served fresh off the *parilla* (charcoal
ARGENTINE   grill) are this steak house's specialty. Juicy fillets of beef tenderloin
accompany local fare like wahoo steaks and lobster tail. Italian pasta
and vegetarian dishes are also available. The service is friendly but slow.
⊠ *In front of Posada Arco Iris, West End* ☎ *445–4264* 🖃 *AE, MC, V*
🕐 *Daily 10:30–10. Closed Mon.*

$$–$$$   ✕ **Coconut Tree International Lounge.** Mediterranean seasonings add zest
SEAFOOD   to deep-water grouper fillets and hearty shrimp burgers at this second-
story eatery near the West End entrance. The lunch menu lists chicken
quesadillas and cheesy fish sandwiches, while dinner is a choice of five
steak and seafood entrees selected by the chef. Try the natural wine, a
homemade blend made by a Swiss expatriate in Tegucigalpa. Chinese
silk curtains and Far East–inspired lanterns add a touch of elegance
to the informal palapa. ⊠ *West End* ☎ *445–4081* 🖃 *MC, V* 🕐 *Daily
10–10.*

$$   ✕ **Go Deep.** The menu changes once a week here to reflect the fresh-
SEAFOOD   est options around. The small yet select number of seafood dishes are
drizzled with olive oil, garlic, and Italian herbs and served at wooden
patio tables and orange cushioned booths. A small tapas menu includes
*jamón serrano* (Serrano ham) and *queso manchego* (Manchego cheese).
⊠ *West End* ☎ *9854–3639* 🖃 *No credit cards* 🕐 *Daily 3–12.*

$$$   ✕ **Tong's Thai Island Cuisine.** Chef Tong says he aims to bring his native
THAI   cuisine far across the globe; thankfully, he's landed for now in the West
End. Spicy noodle dishes are served on the beachfront gazebo, and at
night, the candlelit dock makes for a romantic dinner on the water.
Tong adds a Honduran twist to traditional favorites by adding lobster
to pad thai or squid to vegetable curry dishes. Try the classic *phat bai
ka prao* (a plate of chicken, bamboo shoots, basil leaves, and mush-
rooms). ⊠ *West End* ☎ *445–4110* 🖃 *No credit cards* 🕐 *Daily 12–3
and 5:30–9:30.*

## WHERE TO STAY

$$   🏠 **Casa Calico.** Located on the "quiet" end of West End, Casa Calico
feels as if it's off the beaten path but is still just a short walk to sand
beaches, restaurants, and nightlife. There are nine rooms and five one-
bedroom apartments for monthly rentals. A very popular breakfast is
served daily from 7 AM to 10 AM. Breakfast is included in room prices,
but also open to the public. The grounds lead out to Mangrove Bight,
where guests can rent kayaks and paddle along the gorgeous shoreline.
**Pros:** recently renovated rooms. **Cons:** no beachfront view. ⊠ *North on
the main road in West End* ☎ *9616–0066* ⊕ *www.casacalico.com* ⤳ *9
rooms, 5 apartments* △ *In-room: no phone, kitchen (some), refrigerator,
Wi-Fi.* △ *In-hotel: bar, water sports, Wi-Fi hotspot* 🖃 *MC, V* ｜◎｜ *BP.*

$   🏠 **Chillies.** Run by a friendly British woman, this clean and comfortable
lodging is the destination of most backpackers. In an idyllic setting on
Half Moon Bay, it consists of a cluster of cabins with shared baths.
If you want more privacy, there is a pair of larger cabins with private
baths. Native Sons Dive Center is located here as well; it's very professional and a popular choice among divers. **Pros:** on-site dive school is
one of the best in the area. **Cons:** no hot water in main house or garden

cabins. ⊠ *Half Moon Bay* ☎ *445–4003* ⊕ *www.nativesonsroatan.com/ chillies.htm* ⇆ *5 rooms, 6 cabins* ⚥ *In-room: no a/c (some), no TV. In-hotel: diving, Wi-Fi hotspot* ☰ *AE, MC, V* ⦿ *EP.*

$$$    ⊡ **Cocolobo.** This new hotel on the point in West End has large, airy rooms, with a view of the passing dive boats out front and a small infinity pool in which to relax. Sand beaches are not directly accessible, but intrepid snorkelers will put on a pair of sturdy shoes and pick their way across the rocky coral seashore to one of the ocean entry points. You can see the coral reef just a few feet from shore, and there are buoys that mark some of Roatán's most popular dive sites a bit farther out. Dive packages are available at the hotel, and air-conditioning costs $10 more. **Pros:** A well-balanced blend of luxurious lodging and natural landscapes; top-notch sunset views. **Cons:** Even boutique hotels can't outsmart frequent power outages on Roatán. ⊠ *North on the main road in West End, beyond Seagrape Plantation* ☎ *No phone* ⊕ *www. cocolobo.com* ⇆ *10 rooms* ⚥ *In-room: no phones, refrigerator. In-hotel: bar* ☰ *MC, V* ⦿ *BP.*

$$$    ⊡ **Luna Beach Resort.** If you've ever daydreamed about your own beach house, this may be the place for you. Here you can have a stunningly designed cabin perched high above the silvery sands of West End. All have two or three bedrooms, making them perfect for families. Louvered windows let tropical breezes blow through your sitting room. If you want to mingle with the other guests, stroll down to the pier jutting out into the ocean. Eleven beachfront rooms afford an equally cozy stay on a smaller scale. The upscale bar and restaurant ($$$) have a romantic atmosphere. Enjoy Mediterranean fare as you watch the sun dip below the horizon. **Pros:** rooms for groups of all sizes; quiet beaches; the dive package includes breakfast and lunch. **Cons:** ⊠ *West End* ☎ *445–0009* ⊕ *www.lunabeachresort.com* ⇆ *11 rooms, 11 houses* ⚥ *In-room: no phone, a/c, safe, kitchen (some), refrigerator (some), no TV, Wi-Fi. In-hotel: restaurant, bar, pool, beachfront, diving, water sports, Wi-Fi hotspot* ☰ *AE, MC, V* ⦿ *EP, AI.*

$–$$    ⊡ **Posada Arco Iris.** Turn right as you enter West End and you'll find this friendly lodge run by an Argentinian couple. If you want a little privacy, try one of the rooms, studios, or self-contained apartments with whitewashed walls and colorful tapestries. All have hammocks on the private verandas. Air-conditioned rooms cost $15 extra. **Pros:** convenient location between the "quiet" end and the nightlife strip. **Cons:** Internet access only in the hotel office. ⊠ *Half Moon Bay* ☎ *445–4264* ⇆ *19 rooms* ⚥ *In-room: a/c (some), refrigerator (some). In-hotel: restaurant, room service* ☰ *AE, MC, V* ⦿ *EP.*

$$    ⊡ **Posada Las Orquideas.** Run by the Argentinean family that heads Posada Arco Iris, this three-story waterfront lodge is a cozy and modern option for the non-resort crowd. Roomy doubles are furnished with butternut and forest green fabrics and handmade wooden wardrobes. Studios come with kitchenettes, and every room has a private balcony facing the refreshingly breezy Mangrove Bight. Pull up a lounge chair, kayak around the wharf, or take a short walk to West End's main street. **Pros:** excellent ocean views for a great price. **Cons:** Internet access only in the hotel office. ⊠ *Half Moon Bay* ☎ *445–4387 or 4386* ⊕ *www.*

**6**

*posadalasorquideas.com* ↩ *18 rooms* ঙ *In-room: a/c, kitchen (some). In-hotel: Wi-Fi hotspot, parking* ☰ *AE, MC, V* ⑩⎮ *EP.*

$$ **Pura Vida Resort Hotel.** Popular with divers, this two-story hotel is steps away from the surf. It only takes a few minutes to reach any of 40 different dive sites. Rooms, all of which face the ocean, are clean and comfortable. Judging from the food, you might think that the hotel's popular eatery ($$$) was perched next to the Mediterranean. The family that runs it serves up delicious seafood that calls on their Italian heritage. The atmosphere is convivial—great for people-watching. **Pros:** social atmosphere in the heart of West End; all-inclusive packages available. **Cons:** rooms can get noisy at night. ✉ *West End* ☎ *445–1141* ⊕ *www.puravidaresort.com* ↩ *26 rooms* ঙ *In-room: Wi-Fi. In-hotel: restaurant, bar, room service, beachfront, diving, water sports, laundry service* ☰ *AE, MC, V* ⑩⎮ *FAP.*

## NIGHTLIFE

The perfect place to end the day, **Sundowners** (✉ *West End*) is where tourists and locals all hang out for a cold beer right on the beach. They open around noon. If you come here after taking a dip in the ocean or lying on the sand, you can take advantage of their freshwater shower before ordering a cocktail or a snack. They have a small menu with great appetizers, sandwiches, and burgers.

On the left-hand side of the West End entrance is **Jamming** (✉ *West End*), an informal bar on the beach that cranks up the reggae music when it's not hosting live bands.

**Cigar Bar** (✉ *West End*) feels more like lounging in a friend's living room than a bar. This relaxing, low-key place carries cigars from Honduras, Cuba, Nicaragua, the Dominican Republic, Brazil, and various Africa countries. Guests can sip the bar's specialities—whisky and scotch—on the outdoor deck facing the main street.

## SPORTS AND THE OUTDOORS

Competition among the dive shops is fierce in West End, so check out a few. When shopping around, ask about class size (eight is the maximum), the condition of the diving equipment, and the safety equipment on the dive boat. **Native Sons** (✉ *West End* ☎ *445–4003* ⊕ *www.nativesonsroatan.com*) is one of the most popular dive shops in town. It's run by a native of Roatán who really knows the area. In business for more than a decade, **West End Divers** (✉ *West End* ☎ *445–4289* ⊕ *www.westendivers.com* ) has a pair of dive boats. The company is committed to protecting the fragile marine ecology.

The popular **Ocean Connections** (✉ *West End* ☎ *403–8221* ⊕ *www.ocean-connections.com*) is a well-established dive shop. Just at the entrance to West End, **Coconut Tree Divers** (✉ *West End* ☎ *445–4081* ⊕ *www.coconuttreedivers.com*) is a PADI Gold Palm resort, offering a wide range of dives and dive courses. They also have cabins with air-conditioning and fridges, with a discount for their divers. **Pura Vida** (✉ *West End* ☎ *445–4081* ⊕ *www.coconuttreedivers.com*) is a great option and offers daily dives and certification courses.

# WEST BAY

Down the beach from West End is West Bay, where you'll find some of the area's more luxurious resorts and the best beaches on the island. The reef comes quite close to the shore, so you don't even need a boat to see some of the island's most astounding sea life. ∎ **TIP➔ This neighborhood is great for young families.**

### GETTING HERE AND AROUND
Resorts in West Bay can arrange for shuttle buses to pick up guests at the airport and ferry terminal. A shared taxi from Coxen Hole should run around $5 per person. A 4 km (2.5 mi) road connects West Bay to Roatán's highway, while another road heads in from Coxen Hole via Flowers Bay. Water taxis from Foster's dock to West End cost $3 (about L50).

### SAFETY
West Bay is an endless chain of private hotels and all-inclusive resorts, so the area is generally very safe and brimming with 24-hour security guards. Be mindful of your belongings on the beach, as the sand is open to everyone.

### MONEY MATTERS
West Bay's only ATM is in the lobby of the Mayan Princess Beach Resort. All other nearby cash machines are found in West End and Coxen Hole.

### ESSENTIALS
**Tourism Office** **Roatán Tourist Information Center** (✉ *West Bay Beach, in front of Fostor's Resort Roatán* ☎ *3336–5597* ⊕).

**Police** **Roatán Tourist Police** (✉ *Roatán* ☎ *9982–8542*).

**Gumbalima Nature Park.** This park is part nature reserve, part tacky tourism fun. Macaws, parrots, and monkeys will land on your shoulders as iguanas scuttle around more than 200 tropical tree and plant species. Paved paths lined with boulders lead to sandy beaches and a 91-m (300-ft) high hanging bridge that crosses a lagoon. The park's Canopy Tour is its main attraction, with 13 zip lines traversing the jungle, and there is also snorkeling, shallow water diving, horseback riding, and kayaking. Coxen's Cave is reminiscent of a theme park ride: recreated cave drawings line the walls, and dotting the interior are life-size pirate statues and replicas of maps, weapons, and treasure. Grab a bite at the poolside grill and take a refreshing shower in the outdoor stalls. The park is especially busy on cruise ship days, so head in early to avoid large crowds. ✉ *West Bay* ☎ *9914–9196* ⊕ *www.gumbalimbapark.com* ▭ *$20* ◷ *Daily 7–5.*

$$$
CONTEMPORARY
✕**Beach Club San Simon.** Set in the intimate garden of a very posh, very private beach club, the eatery serves up high-end surf and turf fare. Grilled lobster, shrimp, and grouper are listed alongside vodka-infused baby back ribs and buttery rotisserie chicken—San Simon's specialty. Sun beds and beach cabanas can be rented for half or full days. The club also has free Wi-Fi and private showers for guests. ✉ *West Bay* ☎ *445–5140 or 9642–6336* ⊕ *www.thebeachclubroatan.com* ▭ *AE, MC, V* ◷ *Daily 10–10.*

$$–$$$    ✕ **Bite on the Beach.** On a beautiful deck overlooking the beach, the res-
SEAFOOD    taurant serves up a wide selection of seafood, including conch, crab,
and lobster. The menu changes often, but you'll almost always find
favorites like Thai shrimp with peanut sauce and yellow coconut curry
dishes. It's easily accessible by water taxi from West End, and the restaurant has Wi-Fi for guests. ⊠ *West Bay* ☎ *403–8054* ▤ *AE, MC, V*
⊘ *Closed Sun. and Mon.*

$$$$    ✕ **Vintage Pearl Restaurant & Wine Cellar.** Gourmet dinners and an exten-
CONTEMPORARY    sive wine collection give this eatery an elegant advantage in an area
dominated by resort buffets. Wild ahi tuna is seared in sesame oil and
served with wasabi, and the New Zealand rack of lamb is seasoned
with rosemary and local mint jelly. The cellar boasts more than 50
international wines, including featured favorites from California. Cool
off inside the mahogany wood cabin, surrounded by sea-grape trees, or
enjoy the breeze outside on the waterfront deck. ⊠ *West Bay* ☎ *3311–
4455* ⊕ *www.roatanpearl.com* ▤ *AE, MC, V* ⊘ *no lunch.*

## WHERE TO STAY

In addition to the standard hotels, an alternative lodging option when
visiting Roatán is a short-term home or apartment rental. Recent development and retiring baby boomers have created an abundance of vacation homes on Roatán, which offer privacy and more amenities for your
group or family vacation. **Roatán Life Vacation Rentals** (⊠ *West Bay* ☎ *445–
5036, 970/300–4078 from U.S.* ⊕ *www.roatanlifevacationrentals.com*),
located in the West Bay Mall, has a great selection of homes and condos
all over the island. The rental agency also has an office in the Coral
Stone Plaza in Sandy Bay.

$$$$    ▦ **Henry Morgan Resort.** Bright colors pop out from every corner of this
☾    family-oriented, all-inclusive resort. Rustic wood buildings give off a
cottage-like feel, and the ample game rooms, bar, and lounge areas are
a great place to kick back after a long day in the sun. Hotel rooms surround the giant swimming pool that heads out to the beach, where the
resort staff puts on an array of games and activities for guests of all ages.
An indoor theater hosts live music shows, skits, and movie nights, and
the campus is pleasantly quiet after dark. **Pros:** family-oriented; plenty
of space for beach activities or quiet lounging; game room; free airport
shuttle. **Cons:** Some cottages show their wear. ⊠ *West Bay* ☎ *445–5010*
⊕ *www.henrymorganroatan.com* ⤴ *116 rooms* ♿ *In-hotel: restaurant,
bars, pool, gym* ▤ *AE, MC, V* Ⓑ *AI.*

$$$$    ▦ **Infinity Bay Spa & Beach Resort.** This breathtaking resort has its own
nook at the end of West Bay. Three-story complexes painted peach and
mango bookend the narrow lap pool and tropical garden landscap-
ing. One- and two-bedroom suites come in dimensions labeled deluxe,
premium, junior, and master, and a three-bedroom penthouse is great
for large groups. The upscale apartments have spacious interiors and
kitchens, plus balconies overlooking the sparkling ocean. The resort
can also arrange scuba, snorkeling, fishing and sailing trips, and the on-
site spa offers the ultimate indulgence. **Pros:** impressive natural scenery
and private beach access. **Cons:** towering apartment-like complexes
are an eyesore if you're looking for a tropical getaway. ⊠ *West Bay*
☎ *445–5016 or 866/369–1977 from the U.S.* ⊕ *www.infinitybay.com*

🛏 *60 rooms ♿ In-room: kitchen, Wi-Fi. In-hotel: restaurant, bar, pool, spa, laundry service* ☰ *AE, MC, V* ❘◎❘ *AI.*

$$$ 🏨 **Las Rocas Resort & Diving Center.** Between West End and West Bay, this resort has one- and two-story bungalows with private porches overlooking the ocean. Grab a book and relax in one of the hammocks swaying in the breeze. Run by a friendly duo, the dive shop is very popular. **Pros:** personable staff and first-rate diving, in-room breakfast. **Cons:** on-site restaurant opens late and closes early; fee for in-room Wi-Fi. ✉ *West Bay Beach* ☎ *445–1841* ⊕ *www.lasrocasresort.com* 🛏 *16 rooms ♿ In-room: no phone, no TV, Wi-Fi. In-hotel: restaurant, room service, bar, pool, diving, water sports, laundry service, parking (free), no kids under 8* ☰ *AE, DC, MC, V* ❘◎❘ *BP.*

$$$$ 🏨 **Mayan Princess Beach Resort & Spa.** Set among gardens filled with scarlet hibiscus, these Spanish-style condominiums are along the shore at
� West Bay. A beautiful meandering swimming pool with waterfalls is the centerpiece of the resort. The palm-sheltered beach is just outside your door. If you want to snorkel, the reef is a few yards offshore. This resort is a favorite location for weddings and honeymoons and might just be *the* most popular spot on Roatán for all-inclusive travelers with young families. **Pros:** kid-friendly; the grounds stay lively at night with music on the beach; free airport shuttle. **Cons:** liveliness and child-friendliness might not seem so wonderful if you're here for peace and quiet; the thrice-daily buffets serve underwhelming fare. ✉ *West Bay* ☎ *445–5050* ⊕ *www.mayanprincess.com* 🛏 *60 rooms ♿ In-room: kitchen, refrigerator, Wi-Fi. In-hotel: restaurant, bar, pool* ☰ *AE, MC, V* ❘◎❘ *AI.*

### SPORTS AND THE OUTDOORS

West Bay has great dive sites, but few actual centers. **Mayan Divers** (✉ *West End* ☎ *445–5050, ext. 326 or 786/299–5929 from the U.S.* ⊕ *www.mayandivers.com*) is run inside the Mayan Princess resort. The five-star PADI dive center has a Bubblemaker program for children eight and up, plus discovery and open-water courses for all fanatics.

# FRENCH HARBOUR

*11 km (7 mi) east of Coxen Hole.*

The most bustling community on the island, French Harbour is home to one of the largest fishing fleets in the western Caribbean. The best supermarket on the island, Eldon's, is located at the entrance to the town. It stocks everything you could need for a picnic on the beach or an overnight stay on one of the deserted islets. Like Coxen Hole, however, the town is a gritty industrial town and is a better stop for visiting banks and shopping than as a final destination.

### GETTING HERE AND AROUND

A shared taxi from Coxen Hole costs around $2 per person. The Coxen Hole–Oak Ridge buses make regular stops in French Harbour, and the fare is L20. A second bus going west swings by West End and Sandy Bay. It's easy to catch a cab off the street, and a shared taxi should cost no more than $10 into West End.

## SAFETY

You likely won't be walking around French Harbour or wandering the streets alone at night, so there's little chance you'll encounter any safety issues here. If you are out here after dark, leave any valuables or extra cash at home.

## MONEY MATTERS

French Harbour is one of Roatán's banking centers. Banco Atlántida (☎455–5592), Banco Futuro (☎455–5641), Banco Lafise (☎455–5643), Fianciero Insular (☎455–5258) and HSBC (☎455–7313) all have offices here. The town has two ATMs, one at the HSBC bank and another at Elden's supermarket.

## ESSENTIALS

**Police** French Harbour Police (✉ Main St., French Harbour, Roatán ☎ 3354–6052). **Roatán Tourist Police** (✉ Roatán ☎ 9982–8542).

## EXPLORING

West of French Harbour you'll find **Arch's Iguana Farm,** a strange attraction that has been around for 30 years. Drop in around noon to see the stern-faced lizards have lunch on Arch's driveway. An estimated 3,500 sleepy creatures roam around the reserve, which also has turtles, monkeys, and a fish hatchery. Arch's is open all day, every day. ✉ French Harbour ☎445–1498 ⊒$4.

## WHERE TO EAT

$$–$$$ ✗ **Gio's.** Famous for its king crabs, Gio's is something of an institution
SEAFOOD on Roatán. Served with lemon butter, the seafood comes in heaping portions. There's a slew of other satisfying seafood specialties, as well as great steaks. Sit in the air-conditioned dining room or on the terrace overlooking the Caribbean. ✉ Main St., French Harbour ☎ 455–5214 ⊟AE, MC, V ☾ Closed Sun.

## WHERE TO STAY

$$$$ ▦ **Barefoot Cay.** Guests at this boutique resort arrive to the private cay by boat. Secluded one-bedroom bungalows and two-bedroom villas feature spacious living areas with sophisticated furniture in tropical tones. Louvered wooden doors pull back to reveal the turquoise waters and salty breeze outside. Studio lofts on the mainland have private waterfront balconies and gourmet kitchens. The resort's Barefoot Divers is a PADI five-star Instructor Development Center with a dive shop, retail center, and courses for all levels. The resort also offers packages with meals, lodging, and diving included. **Pros:** friendly personal service and world-class dive center. **Cons:** resort entrance resembles an empty parking lot; beaches are small. ✉ Brick Bay, 1.2 mi west of French Harbour ☎ 455–6235 or 9669–0809 ⊕ www.barefootcay.com ➵ 9 rooms ♺ In-room: a/c, Wi-Fi. In-hotel: restaurant, bar, spa, beachfront, diving, water sports ⊟AE, MC, V ⦿ AI.

$$$$ ▦ **CoCo View.** This hugely popular dive resort is famous for having more repeat business than any other dive hotel in the Caribbean. That's understandable, as the friendly staff ensures that everyone from newcomers to old pros have dives that are fun and challenging. A quintet of boats carries up to 30 people each to a variety of sites. A few dozen wooden cabins are set out over the ocean, so the sound of the waves

will lull you to sleep. CoCo View mostly arranges seven-night dive and non-dive packages, which include all meals, airport transfers, and two daily dive trips. Accessible only by boat, the resort is about 5 km (3 mi) east of French Harbour. **Pros:**highly professional staff leads guests to some of Roatán's finest dive sites. **Cons:** unexceptional meals; snorkeling experiences pale in comparison to the dives. ☒ *French Harbour* ☎ *445–7461 or 445–7500* 📠 *588–4158* ⊕ *www.cocoviewresort.com* ⇨ *26 rooms* 🖎 *In-hotel: restaurant, bar, Wi-Fi, beachfront, diving, water sports, spa, fitness center* ═ *AE, MC, V* ⦿ *AI.*

$$$$ 🏨 **Fantasy Island.** One of the oldest and largest resorts on Roatán, this sprawling hotel offers accommodations similar to those of American hotels. At the efficiently run dive shop you can hop aboard any of the six large wooden boats that take you out to the reef. The restaurant is open for lunch and dinner. **Pros:** stunning Caribbean views. **Cons:** creaky air-conditioning units and mattresses. ☒ *French Harbour* ☎ *455–7499 or 455–7510* ⊕ *www.fantasyislandresort.com* ⇨ *109 rooms* 🖎 *In-hotel: restaurant, bar, tennis court, beachfront, diving, water sports, minibar, Wi-Fi hotspot* ═ *AE, MC, V* ⦿ *AI.*

$$$$ 🏨 **Palmetto Bay Plantation.** West of French Harbour, Palmetto Bay is a cluster of beautifully designed two- and three-bedroom villas. Rooms feature vaulted ceilings, hardwoods floors, and tiled baths. Set in lovely landscaped gardens, this resort beckons with its glittering pool and private beach. The restaurant offers deliciously prepared seafood. On Saturday night you can grab a beer and dance to the live music. **Pros:** dedicated marina. **Cons:** a 30-minute drive off the main road makes this isolated resort even further from the action. ☒ *Crawfish Rock* ☎ *991– 0811* ⊕ *www.palmettobayplantation.com* ⇨ *16 rooms* 🖎 *In-room: Wi-Fi. In-hotel: restaurant, bar, pool, water sports* ═ *AE, MC, V* ⦿ *EP.*

### SHOPPING

**MegaPlaza Mall.** The latest shopping center on the highway has a large pharmacy, a supermarket, plus chain restaurants like Wendy's, Applebees, and Caribbean Pizza Kitchen. ☒ *French Harbour, Roatán* ☎ *No phone.*

# FIRST BIGHT

*19 km (12 mi) east of Coxen Hole.*

Once a family estate, the Parrot Tree Plantation is now virtually a community all itself. The sprawling resort rests between the shores of First and Second Bight—and you don't have to stay the night or buy a villa to enjoy its amenities. Visitors can grab breakfast or a café lunch at the Coffee House, or swing by for dinner and drinks at sunset at the Palapa Bar & Grill along a 3-mile stretch of white beaches. The plantation's **Santé Wellness Center** (☎ *408-5156* ⊕ *www.santewellnesscenter. com* ⊙ *9AM to 4 PM, or by appointment*) offers speciality spa treatments, massages, facials and yoga classes, plus all-inclusive packages for overnight guests.

From Coxen Hole, head east on the main highway past the airport and French Harbour until you reach a grandiose entrance on the right-hand side of the road. Public minibuses (L25) run every half hour to Oak Ridge from Coxen Hole and can drop you off along the way.

## WHERE TO STAY

$$$$ ⬚ **Parrot Tree Plantation Beach Resort.** Far away from the noise and hub-bub of Roatán's more popular locales, Parrot Tree is an expansive property with residential homes, a marina, a retail center, and a spa. The beach resort is at the bottom of a steep hill off the highway. Here you'll find prestigious villas with private patios encircling white-sand beaches and sapphire waters that overlook a secluded sandbar, which guests can access by bridge or kayak. The compound is delightfully peaceful and all but commands relaxation upon entering. **Pros:** A high-end, luxurious getaway in a natural paradise; laundry right in the room; marina-**Cons:** Among Roatán's priciest options. ✉ *First Bight* ☎ 9706–9240 or 713/234–1477 from the U.S. ⊕ *www.parrottree.com* ⤳ *44 villas* ⚙ *In-room: a/c, Wi-Fi, kitchen. In-hotel: restaurant, bar, spa, pool, beach-front, water sports* ▭ *AE, DC, MC, V* ⏀ *EP, AI.*

# MILTON BIGHT

27 km (16 mi) east of Coxen Hole. A sweeping lookout point aptly titled "The View" encourages travelers to steer off the highway and park the car for an amazing vista of the more tranquil side of Roatán.

### GETTING HERE AND AROUND
To get here, drive east along the main road toward Oak Ridge; the turn off will be on the left-hand side.

### WHERE TO STAY

$$$$ ⬚ **Turquoise Bay Resort.** This intimate all-inclusive resort is in its own world on the northeast side of the island. Clusters of whitewashed cabins dot the grassy hill overlooking the—you guessed it—turquoise bay. Palapa umbrellas shade rows of lounge chairs along the 500-foot stretch of private beach where the dock houses kayaks, paddleboats, and jet skis for rent. The resort is popular among couples who wish to indulge in utter peace and quiet, although weekend discounts aim to draw in younger families as well. There's an award-winning dive center on the grounds, and the restaurant has a decent a la carte menu. **Pros:** cozy rooms offer idyllic views of the breathtaking bay; tour operator on premises. **Cons:** escaping the peace and quiet requires a 45-minute drive west. ✉ *Milton Bight* ☎ *413–2229 or 413–2230* ⊕ *www. turquoisebayresort.com* ⤳ *26 rooms* ⚙ *In-room: a/c, Wi-Fi. In-hotel: restaurant, bar, beachfront, diving, water sports, laundry service* ▭ *AE, MC, V* ⏀ *EP, AI.*

### SPORTS AND THE OUTDOORS
The area's only other landmark, the Turquoise Bay Resort, has a very professional **Subway Watersports** office based there with waterskiing and wakeboarding, plus jetski, kayak and paddle boat rentals open to the public. ✉ *Turquoise Bay Resort, Milton Bight, Roatán* ☎ *413-2229* ⊕ *www.subwaywatersports.com.*

# UTILA

*18 km (11 mi) north of La Ceiba.*

The smallest of the Bay Islands, Utila has managed to evade full-scale development. It is small, especially compared to Roatán, and some visitors complain that there isn't much to do. On the other hand, more than a few travelers have planned to drop in for a weekend and ended up staying for a month or more, seduced by the island's easy-going atmosphere and carefree living. Locals, with their penchant for storytelling, make visitors feel right at home.

Known for its affordable diving classes, Utila is very popular with backpackers. This does not mean, however, that you'll be roughing it. The resorts here are small but inviting, like the island itself. Life on the island centers mostly around Utila Town, and dive hotels, restaurants, and bars spread out from either side of the municipal dock. A number of mansions that are available for short-term rentals have gone up on the northern coast of Utila, adding a more luxurious option for big groups or high-end travelers. Hundreds of Utila natives live on the Utila Cays, a quick boat ride from the mainland but culturally a world away.

**6**

### GETTING HERE AND AROUND

Aerolíneas Sosa flies Monday-Saturday from La Ceiba to the Utila Airport on the East End. Taxis into town linger around the airport and cost L50 each for a shared cab and L100 for solo passengers. If you booked your flight through a travel agency, those companies can also arrange for taxis to pick you up.

The easiest way to get to Utila, however, is on the Utila Princess II. The ferry makes the hour-long trip daily from La Ceiba's Muelle de Cabotaje at 9:30 AM and 4 PM, with return trips at 6:20 AM and 2 PM from Utila's municipal dock. Choppy waters or heavy rains can cause cancellations.

There are no direct flights or ferries from Roatán to Utila. From Roatán, travelers can take the MV Galaxy Wave at 9:30 AM back to La Ceiba and hang around the docks until the Utila Princess II's 2 PM departure. Captain Vern Fine also runs a catamaran service between Roatán and Utila. The trip lasts three to four hours and is not advisable for those who are easily seasick. Call ahead of time to reserve a spot on the boat. The captain takes one day off a week, usually Tuesday.

Once you're on Utila, it's quite easy to walk to everything. Three-wheel tuk-tuk taxis zip around Utila Town for L20 to L25 a ride, and golf carts, scooters, and bicycles are available for rent.

### SAFETY

Travelers have little to worry about in convivial Utila. Petty theft, however, can be a problem if you leave bikes, purses, or belongings unattended.

### TIMING

Utila's Carnival celebrations usually run for seven days in mid-July and culminate with a Saturday parade and the Sunday coronation of the Carnival queen. One of Central America's largest electronic music festivals, Sun Jam, takes place the first weekend of August on Water Key, a

3-acre island located 10 km (6 mi) from the mainland. Local fishermen shuttle partygoers from Utila to the daylong fiesta.

**MONEY MATTERS**

Utila has two ATMs around the municipal dock. One is at the HSBC bank and the other at Banco Atlántida. Most dive hotels accept credit cards, but many bars and restaurants do not.

**ESSENTIALS**

**Banks HSBC** (✉ across from municipal dock, Utila ☎ 425–3117 or 3257). **Banco Atlántida** (✉ ½ block from municipal dock, Utila ☎ 425–3374 or 3375).

**Bike Rentals Utila Bike Rental** (✉ East Main St., Utila Town ☎ 425–3940 ☯ Closed Sun.). **Rental Roney** (✉ West Main St., Utila Town ☎ 425–3991 or 3228–1024).

**Cart and Scooter Rental Rita's Club Car Rental** (✉ East Main St., Utila Town ☎ 425–3692 ☯ Closed Sun). **Lance Bodden Rentals** (✉ East Main St., Utila Town ☎ 425–3245 ☯ Closed Sun.).

**Ferries Utila Princess II** (✉ Muelle de Cabotaje, La Ceiba ☎ 408–5163 ✉ Utila municipal dock, Utila ☎ 425–3390 💲 $22 one way ▭ No credit cards ☯ Daily 9:30 am and 4:00 pm from La Ceiba, and 6:20 am and 2 pm from Utila). **Captain Vern's Catamaran** (✉ Coconut Tree docks, West End, Roatán ☎ 9910–8040 ✉ Bush's Grocery, Utila ✐ vfine@hotmail.com 💲 $55 one way ▭ No credit cards ☯ Roatán to Utila, 1 pm, and Utila to Roatán, 6:30 am).

**Groceries** Most supermarkets will give cash advances on credit cards without charging an extra fee. **Bush's Supermarket** (✉ east of Banco Atlántida, Utila ☎ 425–3147). **Henderson's Supermarket** (✉ West Main St., Utila ☎ 425–3148 ☯ Closed Sun.).

**Taxis Truck Taxi Rolando** (☎ 9840–2874). **Van Taxi Driver Paisano** (☎ 435–3311 or 3236–3969). **Van Taxi Hank** (☎ 425–3180 or 3397–1678).

# EXPLORING

**Pumpkin Hill.** From Utila Town, a 4.8 km (3 mi) trail cuts through the muggy tropical forest up to Pumpkin Hill. Standing at 91 m (300 feet) above sea level, the dormant volcano cone is the highest point on the island. Sweeping views of Utila and nearby Roatán can be viewed from the top.

**Brandon Hill Cave.** This cave is the largest among the dozens of caverns that puncture the mountainside. Legend has it that pirates hid their treasure here in the 16th and 17th centuries. To get there from Utila Town, head toward the airport on the paved road and turn left at the first dirt path after the horse stables.

**Pumpkin Hill Beach.** On the paved road out of Utila Town, bear right at the airport runway and onto Pumpkin Hill Beach, a mosaic of fossilized coral and sand patches. From here you can walk about 45 minutes along the beach until connecting with the trail that leads up Pumpkin Hill.

**Utila Cays.** The Utila Cays make for an interesting afternoon excursion. Jewel and Pigeon Cay (also the Upper and Lower Cay, respectively) are home to around 400 people, including local fishermen and the descendants of settlers who came from the Cayman Islands in 1836. The two cays are joined together by a short concrete bridge, and houses, churches, schools, restaurants, and docks are crammed together on these urban islands. Residents, or Cayons, learn Spanish in school but speak Caribbean English at home, and they distinguish themselves from the 2,500 people living on the mainland. A few tasty seafood joints make for a relaxing escape from the Utila Town crowd.

**Whale Shark Oceanic Research Center (WSORC).** Utila is widely known in the diving world as the Caribbean's whale shark capital. These massive creatures can measure as much as 12 m (40 feet) long and weigh up to 20 tons, and they feast mostly on plankton, not humans. The sharks swim close to Utila's shores and can be spotted year-round, an exciting possibility that lures many divers to the reefs here. The Deep Blue Resort has an EcoOcean identification database used to track whale sharks around the globe. WSORC also has monitoring and research programs in Utila. Visitors can join a four-hour encounter trip on Monday, Wednesday, or Friday. ⊠ *West Main St., Utila* ☎ *425–3760* ⊕ *www. wsorc.org.*

**Chepes beach.** Utila's tropical paradise is mostly found in the water. Still, there are a couple of good places on land to take in the island's beauty. String up a hammock or soak in the sun at Chepes beach. The public space is a five-minute walk left of the municipal dock. A few small restaurants and bar shacks ring the sand.

**Bando beach.** The private beach Bando is a 10 to 15 minute walk east of the municipal dock. Entrance is $3 and affords access to lounge chairs, shade, and a more secure setting. A palapa bar serves inexpensive cold drinks. As with any beach in the Bay Islands, be wary of the relentless sand flies.

## WHERE TO EAT

$–$$ **✕ Bundu Café.** Hearty breakfasts and generous dinners please many a
AMERICAN hungry diver at this popular hangout. Start the day with banana pancakes, baleadas, or a taste of the full espresso bar. The lunch menu lists hot submarine sandwiches and chicken nachos, and evening dishes include seasoned fish burgers and veggie enchiladas. The open-air lodge has seating at comfy booths or out on the street-front patio. ⊠ *East Main St.* ☎ *425–3557* ⊟ *AE, MC, V* ☽ *Closed Wed.*

$ **✕ Cayview Restaurant.** Simple dock seating facing the mainland gives
SEAFOOD this Pigeon Cay mainstay a lovely evening view. Fried fish and steaks are listed along with a wide array of burgers, fish, lobster, chicken, and veggies. ⊠ *Utila Cays* ☎ *408–9954* ⊟ *No credit cards.*

$$ **✕ Harbor House.** This third-story eatery is Jewel Cay's tallest building.
SEAFOOD Panoramic windows open to sparkling ocean views, and the second-floor bar and coffee shop is whimsically furnished with a pirate theme (and has a retro soft-serve ice-cream machine). The light dinner menu includes chicken and grilled-cheese sandwiches, plus hamburgers, shrimp fajitas, and juicy grilled fish fillets. All dishes are served with chips and a tasty homemade salsa. The restaurant is closed for lunch but the dinner hours skew early (4 to 8 PM) so a late lunch is possible.

⊠ *Utila Cays* ☎ 9937–5457 ⊕ *www.harborhouseutila.com* ⊟ *AE, MC, V* ⊘ *Closed Mon.*

**$$** ✕**Indian Wok.** Red curtains and tablecloths make this eatery pop out
ASIAN from its subtle setting tucked behind Tranquila Bar. The Wok is known
for its mouthwatering Indian curries and Tandoori chicken, plus sushi
and Southeast Asian classics like Indonesian *satays* (grilled and skew-
ered meats) and Vietnamese spring rolls. ⊠ *West Main St.* ☎ 3320–6909
⊟ *No credit cards* ⊘ *Closed Fri. and Sat.*

**$$–$$$** ✕**The Jade Seahorse.** Looking a bit like a psychedelic museum, this long-
SEAFOOD time favorite is decorated with island paraphernalia and tunnels, sculp-
★ tures and gazebos built from mosaics of colored glass. The best place to
enjoy the big platters of seafood is in the pleasant garden. Stop by for
one of the best fresh fruit shakes you'll find on the islands, and top off
the evening with a drink in the Treetanic tree house bar. The Nightland
cabins have two double beds, spacious bathrooms, and stunning interior
decor. ⊠ *Cola de Mico Rd.* ☎ 425–3270 ⊕ *www.jadeseahorse.com* ⤺ 6
*cabins* ⚐ *In-hotel: Wi-Fi, restaurant, bar, refrigerator, laundry service*
⊟ *MC, V* ⊘ *No dinner Sat.*

**$$** ✕**La Piccola.** Also called Kate's after its owner, this Italian restaurant is
ITALIAN hailed across the island for its authentic, and delicious, cuisine. Home-
made gnocchi, ravioli, and pasta, plus vegetarian dishes and breaded
chicken picatta, are served with a glass of Spanish, French, or Portu-
guese wine at the Main Street dinner spot. The small delicatessen sells
homemade pesto, tomato sauces, marmalades, and imported English
teas. ⊠ *West Main St.* ☎ 425–3746 ⊟ *AE, MC, V* ⊘ *Wed.–Sun. open
5–10 pm. Closed Mon. and Tues.*

**$** ✕**La Pirata Bar & Grill.** The main drag's most popular sports bar offers
AMERICAN breezy harbor views from the open-air, third-floor restaurant. Bacon
cheeseburgers, nachos, chicken fingers, and buffalo wings are the house
specialties, and La Pirata boasts the island's largest liquor selection. The
place gets packed around 10 PM or during   any major sporting event,
and live bands play during the week. ⊠ *Broussard Plaza, 3rd fl., ferry
dock* ☎ 425–3988 ⊕ *www.lapiratabargrill.com* ⊟ *AE, MC, V* ⊘ *Tues.
is Ladies Night.*

**$** ✕**Thompson's Bakery.** Without question the most popular place for
CAFÉ breakfast, this little establishment sells baked goods hot out of the
oven. If you want more substantial fare, try one of the omelets and some
fresh orange juice. ⊠ *Cola de Mico Rd.* ☎ *No phone* ⊟ *No credit cards.*

## WHERE TO STAY

Short-term rentals are expanding their presence on Utila, particularly
along the secluded coral coves of the north side. Converted mansions
and beach houses are ideal for large groups and families who need lots
of room to roam.

**Destination Utila** (⊠ *East Main St.* ☎ 3334–1395 or 678/999–6016 from
U.S. ⊕ *www.destinationutila.com*), located just a few blocks to the right
of the municipal dock, has a variety of two-, three-, and four-bedroom
units around the island.

**Utila Reality** (✉ *Mango Tree Building* ☎ *425–3993 or 888/744–3045 from U.S.* ⊕ *www.utilareality.net*) has a very helpful staff who knows nearly everything about Utila.

$$$$ ⊞ **Laguna Beach Resort.** Perched on the edge of the Caribbean, this resort has bungalows with private decks overlooking the water. The accommodations have a rustic feel, but have amenities such as air-conditioning and private baths. Along with a dive center offering trips to more than 100 underwater wonders, the resort also lets you try your hand at kayaking and other water sports. **Pros:**The resort offers a quiet retreat from the bustling Utila Town. **Cons:**Dining and nightlife are a boat ride away. ✉ *Southeast coast of Utila* ☎ *425–3239 or 800/668–8452* ⊕ *www.utila.com* ↪ *13 bungalows, 1 familiy cabin* ⚐ *In-hotel: Wi-Fi hotspot, restaurant, bar, pool, beachfront, diving, water sports, laundry service* ▤ *AE, MC, V* ⦿ *EP.*

$$–$$$ ⊞ **Lighthouse Hotel.** This peaceful two-story hotel has wraparound balconies and sits just over the water. Simple, breezy rooms have oceanfront views, kitchenettes and splashy turquoise walls. Lounge chairs out on the porch are an ideal spot to unwind with a book or a refreshing evening cocktail. **Pros:**central location with quiet atmosphere.**Cons:** squeaky floorboards in second-story rooms. ✉ *Eastern Harbor* ☎ *425–3164* ✎ *info@utilalighthouse.com* ↪ *12 rooms, 3 suites* ⚐ *In-room: a/c, kitchen, Wi-Fi.* ▤ *AE, MC, V* ⦿ *EP.*

$$–$$$ ⊞ **Mango Inn.** Set amid breadfruit and banana trees, this wooden lodge has generously proportioned rooms with porches where you can relax in a hammock. The pool is a favorite place for divers and families to gather in the afternoon. The restaurant serves up light fare, including a tasty grilled-chicken sandwich and brick oven pizzas. There's a pretty garden where you'll find barbecues on weekends, and Utila Dive Center has its classroom on the campus. **Pros:** the inn houses one of the island's best dive centers. **Cons:** non-cabin rooms feel like dormitories. ✉ *Cola Mico Rd.* ☎ *425–3335* 🖷 *425–3327* ⊕ *mango-inn.com* ↪ *10 rooms, 6 cabins* ⚐ *In-hotel: Wi-Fi hotspot, pool, restaurant, diving, water sports* ▤ *MC, V* ⦿ *EP.*

$ ⊞ **Margaritaville Beach Hotel.** Cabins painted pale blue with peach terrace railings add pleasant touches to this waterfront lodging on stilts. The budget hotel is a comfortable substitute for the dive resorts and hostels that occupy the main town's shoreline. The sandy campus is nestled between popular beachfront bars. **Pros:** location is highly convenient. **Cons:** can get noisy at night; rooms with air-conditioning cost twice as much as those with fans. ✉ *near Chepes beach.* ☎ *425–3366* ↪ *15 rooms* ⚐ *In-room: a/c (some)* ▤ *No credit cards* ⦿ *EP.*

$ ⊞ **Rubi's Inn.** A good budget option is Rubi's Inn. The simple, no-frills wood lodge has a coral beach facing the harbor that is perfect for sunning. The hotel is a close enough walk to the bars and restaurants without being subjected to the late night noise. **Pros:** convenient location but far enough from town to escape late-night noise. **Cons:** rooms with air-conditioning cost double. ✉ *East Main St.* ☎ *425–3240 or 504/208–5154 from the U.S.* ↪ *12 rooms* ⚐ *In-room: a/c (some), Wi-Fi, kitchen. In-hotel: laundry service* ▤ *No credit cards* ⦿ *EP.*

6

$$$$  ☷ **Utopia Dive Village.** Chic bungalows are spread across a shaded gar-
★    den of coral-lined paths and mango trees. Luxurious rooms have four-
poster beds and handcrafted furniture, and the Balinese silk tapestries
and bamboo shutters give off a Far Eastern flair. The dive resort was
developed by seven American friends, one of whom is a gourmet chef
and prepares three outstanding meals a day for guests. Don't turn down
her sumptuous desserts. The staff is very friendly and can help you
arrange trips around the Bay Islands. Utopia has one- to seven-night
packages for vacationers, divers, and honeymooners. **Pros:**a gorgeous
campus and convivial environment. **Cons:** sand flies are particularly
vicious over here. ⊠ *Southeast coast of Utila* ☎ *3344-9387* ⊕ *www.
utopiadivevillage.com* ⇆ *16 rooms* ⚹ *In-hotel: Wi-Fi, restaurant, bar,
spa, beachfront, diving, water sports, laundry service* ☰ *AE, MC, V*
† ⊙ | *EP.*

## NIGHTLIFE

Nightlife in Utila doesn't wait for the sun to set. **Skid Row** (⊠ *West Main
St.*) is an all-day watering hole that is busiest during the late afternoon.
Crispy tacos and personal pizzas make for outstanding bar food. **Drift-
wood Café** (⊠ *near Chepes beach*) serves cold beers and grilled dinners
from the simple gazebo over the water. After dark, you'll find **Bar in the
Bush** (⊠ *Past the Mango Inn*) in the middle of a tropical forest. It's the
noisiest spot on the island and is only open Wednesday and Friday from
10 PM to 4 AM. **La Pirata Bar & Grill** (⊠ *Broussard Plaza, 3rd fl., Ferry
Dock*) is quite lively for dancing most evenings. **Colibri Pool Bar** (⊠ *across
from Hotel Colibri*) serves expertly blended martinis under a single
palapa in the hotel garden. **Tranquila Bar** (⊠ *West Main St.*) is a popular
evening hangout for all age groups. Rock music plays from speakers out
on the dock. After dark, the evening crowds from Tranquila Bar tend
to gravitate to **CocoLoco** (⊠ *West Main St.*), where candlelit tables are
pushed back for an all-night dance party to electronic music.

## SPORTS AND THE OUTDOORS

Warm water, great visibility, and thousands of colorful fish make Utila a
popular destination. Add to this a good chance of seeing a whale shark
and you'll realize why so many people head here each year. The **Bay
Islands College of Diving** (⊠ *Utila Lodge* ☎ *425-3291* ⊕ *www.dive-utila.
com*) is one of Utila's top dive facilities. Classes are small, meaning
you'll get more one-on-one attention than some other schools in the
Bay Islands. If you're looking for a one-stop dive center, look no further
than **Cross Creek Dive Center** (⊠ *Cross Creek Hotel* ☎ *425-3334* ⊕ *www.
crosscreekutila.com*). The bar has great music, and the restaurant is
open for breakfast, lunch, and dinner.

**Coral View Dive Center** (⊠ *near Chepes beach* ☎ *425-3781* ⊕ *www.coral
viewbeachresortanddivecenter.com*) has a relaxed family-friendly atmosphere. The beach hotel is cozy, and the kitchen dishes out seafood
classics and traditional Honduran fare.

**Utila Dive Center** (✉ *Mango Inn* ☎ *425–3326* ⊕ *www.utiladivecenter. com*) is perhaps the largest and most professional school in Utila. In 2004, it was ranked the top dive facility worldwide for entry-level training. For comfortable lodging and courses taught by locals, check out **Underwater Vision** (✉ *toward The Point* ☎ *425–3103* ⊕ *www. underwatervision.net*). The center has been around for 30 years and comes highly recommended by islanders. **Parrot's Dive Center** (✉ *West Main St.* ☎ *425–3159*) is best suited for the backpacker crowd with its inexpensive dives and festive location (it's right beside Tranquila Bar and CocoLoco). Popular with the youthful crowd is **Alton's Dive Shop** (✉ *toward The Point* ☎ *425–3704* ⊕ *www.altondiveshop.com*).

Believe it or not, there is more to Utila than diving. **Kayak Utila** (✉ *Mango Tree Building* ☎ *9857–7355* ⊕ *www.kayakutila.com*) offers two options for four-hour day trips. The first takes kayakers north through the Mangrove Channel and to Rock Harbor bay. The second trip explores the Harbor and South Shore.

The same ladies who do the kayak tours also offer private guided snorkeling trips with **Snorkel Utila** (✉ *Mango Tree Building* ☎ *9628–6363* ⊕ *www.snorkelutila.com*).

**Red Ridge Horse Stables.** Guides lead up to eight riders at a time and offer private lessons around Pumpkin Hill. Reservations are recommended. (✉ *Left of the highway en route to the airport, Utila* ☎ *425–3143 or 3390–4812* 💳 *$35 for 2 hours, $50 for a half day* ☉ *Daily 9–4:30*).

# GUANAJA

*60 km (37 mi) north of Trujillo.*

Guanaja, once populated by the Paya people, has rolling hills covered with evergreens. The easternmost island measures around 18 km (11 mi) long and 5 km (3 mi) wide. Christopher Columbus named it Pine Island when he came across it in his fourth and final voyage to the Americas in 1502. Guanaja Town, also known as Bonacca, is on a small key off the mainland. In earlier years, boats negotiated shallow canals, earning Bonacca the title of the "Venice of Honduras." Today, many waterways have been replaced by narrow concrete alleys, making the entire key accessible by foot. Although the winding roads and bridges make Guanaja Town seem like a maze, the town is so small you can't get lost. There are no cars here, making the island seem as removed from civilization as you can get.

In the 1990s, Guanaja was primed to become the next hot tourism spot in Honduras. But after Hurricane Mitch spent a few days ravaging the island in 1998, much of what had been built was lost. Today, just a few dive hotels remain, and most local eateries open and close with shrimping season. The seclusion, however, is one of Guanaja's biggest selling points.

### GETTING THERE AND AROUND

Guanaja is the least accessible of the Bay Islands. Ferries no longer run between Trujillo and Guanaja, although the private Bolea Express does make trips to the mainland twice a week. The easiest way to arrive is by plane. Aerolíneas Sosa flies twice daily to and from La Ceiba, and charter airlines Aviac and Lanhsa have regular flights as well.

A 3.2-km (2 mi) paved road runs east to west between Savannah Bight and Mangrove Bight on the north end, but the primary way to move here is by boat. With prior notice, most hotels and restaurants will pick you up from the airport and shuttle you around.

### SAFETY
The fact that Bonacca is tiny makes it impossible for crime to go unpunished, so the town stays secure. Around Guanaja, private keys and dive resorts go without incident.

### MONEY MATTERS
Banco Atlántida has a branch on Bonacca, but no ATM. Bring plenty of cash just in case.

### ESSENTIALS
**Airlines and Contacts Aviac** (☎ 263–3198 in Tegucigalpa ⊕ www.aviachn. com).**Lanhsa** (☎ 442–1283 or 414–5959 in La Ceiba, ⊕ www.lanhsa.com). **Sosa** (☎ 453–4359 on Guanaja, 443–1399 or 442–1512 in La Ceiba).

**Banks Banco Atlántida** (✉ Bonacca, Guanaja ☎ 453–4262)

**Ferries Bolea Express** (✉ Zapata dock, Bonacca Town, Guanaja ☎ 9944–8571 ⊙ From Guanaja, Mon and Fri at 9 AM).

**Groceries Commercial Wood** (✉ Bonnaca, Guanaja ☎ 453–4122).**Casa Sikaffy** (✉ Bonnaca, Guanaja ☎ 453–4270).

## EXPLORING

**Fruit Harbour Farm.** If you've come to Guanaja, you're likely planning to either dive or fish with an outfitter, or do nothing at all but unwind. When you're ready for a break, we recommend an afternoon trip to the only slightly incongruous Fruit Harbour Farm, an organic operation run by Hans, a German expatriate. Take a guided tour or horseback ride through the fruit tree orchard and dairy farm. Sip slowly on the powerful wine of fermented fruits and nibble on juicy dried mangoes. If you feel like staying longer, Hans has bungalows for overnights. (✉ Guanaja ✍ fruitharbourfarm@gmx.de).

## WHERE TO EAT

**$$**  ✕**Manati Bar & Restaurant.** Run by German expats, this waterfront eatery is wildly popular with both locals and visitors. Billiards, darts, a breezy terrace and picnic table seating give a casual vibe to this island hangout, which livens up in the evening with the occasional German jam session. The menu constantly evolves and often includes homemade spätzle, roasted pork, and chicken schnitzel. The bar has a big selection of German beers and imported wines. Come out on a Saturday night, and you just might meet the entire island. ✉ Guanaja ☎ 408–9830 or 9914–1224 ▭ No credit cards ⊙ Closed Mon.

GERMAN

**$**  ✕**Mexi Treats.** Cheesy, creamy Tex-Mex classics like refried bean burritos and beefy nachos are served in a pink-and-purple room along

MEXICAN

Bonacca's main drag. Chill out with a frothy *licuado* (smoothie) or a freshly squeezed juice. ✉ *Bonacca* ☎ *453–4170* ⊟ *No credit cards* ☾ *Closed Sat. and Sun.*

$$ ✗ **Pirate's Den.** Locally caught seafood is the draw here, along with excel-
SEAFOOD lent chicken and beef dishes. Stop by on Friday for the weekly barbecue. ✉ *Bonacca* ☎ *453–4308* ⊟ *No credit cards* ☾ *Closed Tues.*

# WHERE TO STAY

$$$$ ⌂ **Bo Bush's Island House Resort.** Tropical forests and mystic waterfalls envelop this dive hotel on Guanaja's solitary northern coast. Mahogany cabins with Spanish tile floors and louvered windows hug the shore-line, where boats gather around the two-storied pier. On the top level, the Green Flash Bar & Restaurant serves the catch of the day and cold beer. The best dive sites in the Guanaja Marine Preserve are right around the corner from the resort. The owner, Bo Bush, leads the inti-mate excursions himself. He can also point you up two paths that lead to the waterfalls. **Pros:** friendly family-run operation; great div-ing and nature treks. **Cons:** rooms are usually prepared only when guests are expected; drop-ins not recommended. ✉ *Guanaja* ☎ *9963–8551* ⊕ *www.bosislandhouse.com* ⤴ *4 rooms* ☄ *In-room: no a/c, no phone, no TV. In-hotel: restaurant, bar, beachfront, diving* ⊟ *AE, MC, V* ⦿ *FAP.*

$$$$ ⌂ **Graham's Place.** Built across a seven-acre cay, this resort is one of the
★ most charming places in the Bay Islands. Delightful pastel accents turn up everywhere—on tree trunks, picnic tables, spacious cottages, and even the birdcages. Coral-lined paths cut across the well-manicured campus, and a walkway ringing the cay leads out to a private lean-to with hammocks. The island's best bar 'n' grill offers an appetizing menu of fresh seafood and fried chicken. For the ultimate in decadence, sip an afternoon cocktail from the swim-up tables facing the hazy-blue mountains on the mainland. The yacht club has a few boats for deep-sea fishing, plus dive and snorkel equipment at the ready. The owner, Gra-ham Thompson, is always around to help out. **Pros:** with all amenities included, you'll never have to leave. **Cons:** although Graham fumigates regularly, sand flies are hungry out here. ✉ *Guanaja* ☎ *3368–5495or 305/407–1568 from the U.S.* ⊕ *www.grahamsplacehonduras.com* ⤴ *4 rooms, 2 suites, 4 cabins* ☄ *In-hotel: Wi-Fi, restaurant, bar, beachfront, diving, fishing, water sports* ⊟ *AE, MC, V* ⦿ *FAP.*

$$ ⌂ **Hotel Alexander.** This budget motel is a solid option for low-key trav-elers. The rooms are simple and clean, and some have private patios facing the sea. Air-conditioning will cost you an extra $13. The hotel's restaurant-bar offers traditional seafood and Honduran dishes. **Pros:** close to the airport; reasonably priced. **Cons:** air-conditioning costs extra. ✉ *Bonacca* ☎ *408–2956* ⤴ *15 rooms* ☄ *In-room: a/c (some). In-hotel: restaurant, bar, beachfront* ⊟ *No credit cards* ⦿ *EP.*

**6**

# CAYOS COCHINOS

*30 km (19 mi) north of La Ceiba.*

Hazy blue-green mountains speckling the horizon beckon from the mainland with pristine coral reefs and a thriving Garífuna culture. The Cayos Cochinos (Hog Islands) archipelago is emerging as a must-see day trip for travelers on Honduras's northern coast. But visitors aren't the only ones who come out. Dive instructors on the larger Bay Islands, it turns out, come here to dive themselves.

The Cayos Cochinos consist of two larger cays, Cayo Mayor and Cayo Menor, plus 13 smaller coral cays. The islands have been a designated Marine Protected Area since 1993. In 2003, the Honduras Coral Reef Fund (HCRF) declared the enclave a Marine Natural Monument. The titles mean that tourism and development are strictly regulated around the archipelago, maintaining the impressive natural beauty of the waters, reefs, and shores.

All visitors pass through the HCRF office to watch a short video on guest guidelines and marine life. Foreigners must pay a $5 tariff toward the conservation and maintenance of the cays. A fine of L5,000 is imposed for anyone caught lifting bits of coral or seashells off the island, a steep procedure meant to keep the Cayos Cochinos intact.

### GETTING HERE AND AROUND

Boats to Cayos Cochinos depart from La Ceiba's Muelle de Cabotaje, the coastal Garífuna towns Sambo Creek and Nueva Armenia, and from Roatán. From the mainland, it's about 45 minutes to Cayo Menor, depending on surf conditions.

Guests at the Plantation Beach Resort on Cayo Mayor can arrange for a yacht to shuttle them from La Ceiba. Tour operator TURASER makes daily trips from its office at the Palma Real Resort outside of La Ceiba. Honduras Tourist Options and Pirate Islands Divers depart from Sambo Creek with prior reservations. Local fishermen can transport tourists out to the islands, although it's better to go with a guide. From Roatán, private charters will sail for three days and two nights to Cayos Cochinos.

Once you're there, it's unlikely you'll need to arrange individual transportation. In the event that you do, locals steering motorized canoes, called *cayukos*, can give you a ride for a negotiable rate.

Guided trips from the mainland or Roatán offer dive and snorkel packages for day trips or overnights and might include lodging and meals. Contact Honduras Turist Options in La Ceiba. If you're traveling from Roatán with Roatán Shore Tours, ask for Captain Hank.

### SAFETY

Venturing out to the Cayos Cochinos without a tour group can be risky; individual water taxis have been said to abandon passengers at the islands upon arrival, and they might not take you to where you really want to go. The ride to the archipelago can be bouncy and choppy, so travelers sensitive to motion should take the proper precautions to avoid getting sick. Slather on the sunscreen, especially if riding in a roofless boat.

**MONEY MATTERS**

No banks or ATMs are permitted in the Cayos Cochinos, so it's cash only here.

**ESSENTIALS**

Conservation **Honduras Coral Reef Fund** (✉ *Av. Victor Hugo, Calle 13, La Ceiba* ☎ *443–4075* ⊕ *www.cayoscochinos.org*).

Tour Operators **Honduras Tourist Options** (✉ *Blvd. 15 de Septiembre, near the Central Bank, La Ceiba* ☎ *443–0337 or 440–0265* ⊕ *www. hondurastouristoptions.com*). **Pirate Islands Divers** (✉ *La Ceiba* ☎ *441–9399 or 3323–1280* ⊕ *www.pirateislandsdivers.com*). **TURASER** (✉ *Playa Roma, between La Ceiba and Trujillo* ☎ *429–0500*).

Roatán Charters **Captain Vern's Catamaran** (✉ *Coconut Tree docks, West End, Roatán* ☎ *9910–8040 lvfine@hotmail.com*). **Roatán Shore Tours** (✉ *Dixon Cove, Roatán* ☎ *3355–8705* ⊕ *www.roatanshoretours.com*). **Subway Watersports** (✉ *Turquoise Bay Resort and Palmetto Bay Plantation, Roatán* ☎ *413–2229 at Turquoise, or 445–5707 at Palmetto* ⊕ *www.subwaywatersports.com*).

# EXPLORING

**Cayo Menor.** The second biggest cay, Cayo Menor, is more than just a mandatory stop. The Honduras Coral Reef Fund arranges scientific expeditions to involve visitors in data collection on endemic species, such as the *hamo negro* iguana and *boa Rosado* serpent. The fund also coordinates programs during turtle migrations to the Cayos Cochinos in July and August.

**Cayo Mayor.** There is great snorkeling on the western end of Cayo Mayor, the largest cay in the archipelago.

**La Ensenada.** Fishing and passenger boats pull up to the white beaches at La Ensenada bay as fins and snorkels poke out of soft blue waters. Behind the shoreline are several recreational trails that cut through the rising rainforest.

**East End.** On the east end of the cay (referred to, suitably, as the East End), trails leading up to the lighthouse offer stunning panoramic views of the islands. This side of the cay is home to around 50 Garífuna villagers and the only school in Cayos Cochinos. The community has recently constructed beachfront cabins to offer visitors a more cultural experience.

**Chachahuate.** This traditional Garífuna cay has lunch, lodging, and snorkeling. Village chief Roman Norales heads the town of 44 fishing families and often oversees tourism in the tiny community, a budding industry that supplies most of the island's income. The communal restaurant prepares fried fish, shrimp, and lobsters for tourists (have your guide put in an order at least an hour in advance). A rustic motel with 16 rooms and shared latrines costs L300 a night per couple.

# WHERE TO STAY

Protective ecological measures have kept this island free of large resorts and hotels. Rustic homestays can be arranged in Chachahuate; Plantation Beach Resort is the only full-service lodging in Cayos Cochinos. The Laru Beya cabins in the East End are the middle ground between minimalist and more traditionally comfortable accomodations.

$    🏠 **Laru Beya.** The name of this East End community project means "the beach's edge" in Garífuna. Two cabins in the middle of town face glittering waters and neighboring cays. Each cabin is equipped with a shared bathroom, three bunk beds, one double, and a single. Fans and electrical outlets are charged by solar panels. The restaurant out front serves traditional fare like fried fish and rice and beans. Stays can be arranged through Honduras Tourist Options or with the hotel directly. **Pros:** great culturally immersive experience; 5% of hotel rates support the local school. **Cons:** no air-conditioning. ⊠ *East End, Cayo Mayor* ☎ *9918–8931 or 9876–7052* ⌑ *2 cabins* ৬ *In-hotel: no a/c, restaurant, beachfront* ▤ *No credit cards* ❑ *EP.*

$$$$    🏠 **Plantation Beach Resort.** This all-inclusive dive resort has been in the Cayos Cochinos for decades. Large lodges with vaulted ceilings and wide balconies are spread across the hillside facing the secluded Ensenada Cove. Wooden docks and walkways wrap around the lush tropical garden, and a wide gravel patio has red deck chairs for sunning. Dive packages include three dives, equipment rental, and three daily meals of fish and international cuisine served buffet style. The resort is also a pleasant option for non-divers looking to escape the booming tourism of some of the other Bay Islands. **Pros:** not restricted to an all-inclusive plan; pickup from La Ceiba is included. **Cons:** the resort itself is cash only (though credit cards are a viable option ahead of time via PayPal). ⊠ *La Ensenada, Cayo Mayor* ☎ *9827–3800 or 3371–7556* ⊕ *www.plantationbeachresort.com* ⌑ *12 rooms* ৬ *In-hotel: no a/c, Wi-Fi hotspot, restaurant, beachfront* ▤ *AE, DC, MC, V (via PayPal only)* ❑ *EP, AI.*

# La Mosquitía

**WORD OF MOUTH**

"For a nature and cultural option look into Río Plátano Biosphere Reserve on the east coast of Honduras. Check out larutamoskitia.com and the World Heritage site for world biosphere reserves to find some awesome off-the-path places."

—Travelnat

By Maria
Gallucci

Step onto a narrow canoe and glide down the river past the infinite verdant jungle, and you'll slowly feel yourself slip into another era. Civilization fades away as the hoots and howls of wildlife intensify and swampy mangroves thicken. Seductive solitude and the mysterious virgin landscape are exactly what make La Mosquitía in northeast Honduras an eco-adventurer's paradise.

Hikers, campers, and nature fanatics are quietly expanding tourism in Honduras's portion of the Mosquito Coast, an expanse of rain forest peppered with indigenous villages and shared with neighboring Nicaragua. Crocodiles and manatees float below water here while ocelots, jaguars, and howler monkeys roam the land and toucans and falcons peek out from the canopies in the "Little Amazon." A handful of small-scale tour companies have put Central America's greatest stretch of complex ecosystems on the map, and yet the focus remains on protecting the wildlife, not pampering the tourist at the expense of the environment.

The region offers demanding jungle trails and wildlife excursions to travelers looking to turn off the cell phone, close the computer, and indulge in a far more rustic experience than even other parts of Honduras have to offer. Adventurers have the run of five distinct protected areas. The Río Plátano Biosphere Reserve is the most celebrated zone in the region and a UNESCO World Heritage site. Tawahka Anthropological Reserve, the second largest zone, offers cultural immersion trips with the indigenous Tawahka tribe. Patuca National Park is a remote tropical rain-forest zone near the Nicaraguan border with some of Honduras's greatest biodiversity, and Cruta Caratasca Wildlife Refuge and Rus Rus Biological Reserve are known for their stunning vistas.

The Mosquito Coast's ominous-sounding name comes not from the pesky insects (although there are more than a few here), but from the Miskitos, the indigenous people native to the land. The native Pech, Rama, Susa and Tawahka groups still account for a small part of the 60,000 inhabitants in the sparsely populated region, and the Garífuna people, or descendents of African slaves, and mixed race *mestizos*, or *Ladinos*, dominate the Caribbean part. While the Ladino population tends to be Roman Catholic, like most of Honduras, the indigenous widely belong to the Protestant faith. More than a third belong to the Moravian Church, an evangelical Christian sect that has played an active role in the region's development since the early 20th century. The Honduran government had largely neglected the coast when the Protestant church first stepped in to build schools, health clinics, and congregations, many of which are active today in the Ahuas municipality, one of six in the department.

La Mosquitía's inhabitants live on the coast or in small jungle villages and subsist mostly on hunting, fishing, and small-scale farming of rice,

## TOP REASONS TO GO

**Explore the ecosystems.** Caribbean beaches, coral reefs, glassy lagoons, mangrove swamps, secluded islands, and pine savanna make for countless excursions in this mystical region. After all, it is Central America's largest contiguous stretch of undeveloped land—not to mention the greatest belt of virgin tropical rain forest north of the Amazon.

**Go trekking and rafting in the jungle.** Mountain trails snake past dangling vines and thick jungle growth, and many offer challenging multiday hikes with rewarding views or leisurely wildlife discoveries. Two-week river rafting adventures down the Río Plátano combine ancient archeology and cultural exchanges with complete immersion in the wild.

**Step back in time.** It's nothing but nature out here in the rain forest. Modern-day distractions are few and far between; you'll be forced to slow down, unplug, and soak in the unbeatable scenery.

**Visit ancient petroglyphs.** Steeped in mystery, these ancient rock engravings in Las Marías are the only remaining clues to an unknown, centuries-old civilization. Man-powered *pipante* canoes push upstream for day trips to the first set, Walpaulbansirpe, or continue on for a second day at Walpaulbantara.

beans, and yuca. Lobster diving and cattle ranching are profitable industries here, but they're threatening lobster populations and leading to damaging deforestation, respectively. Sustainable tourism efforts, on the other hand, are boosting the region's economy by incorporating local guides and family-run accommodations into most travel itineraries.

# ORIENTATION AND PLANNING

## ORIENTATION

La Mosquitía, also spelled Moskitia or the Mosquito/Miskito Coast, covers around 22,000 square km (8,500 square mi)—or 20 percent of Honduras—in the northeastern department of Gracias a Dios. On the western edge of the territory, the Garífuna port towns of Palacios and Batalla are a gateway onto a bounty of crystalline lagoons and pristine rain forest. Raista/Belén and Plaplaya, all tiny Miskito villages, lie slightly to the east on the shores of Laguna de Ibans, which bleeds into the Río Plátano. South down the river are scattered indigenous villages like Las Marías that populate the impressive Río Plátano Biosphere Reserve. East of the river on the Caribbean coast is Brus Laguna, a popular access point into the region for its airport. Still further east is Puerto Lempira and Laguna de Caratasca, the largest lagoon in La Mosquitía.

Jungle trekking, cultural exchanges, and Caribbean beach escapes are among the biggest draws to this autonomous region—which includes reserves of the anthropological, wildlife, and biological persuasions, plus a national park.

**Batalla.** Garífuna dancing and drumming liven up this small waterfront town at the region's western entrance. Traditional home stays offer a glimpse into the African-influenced culture, and mangrove forests in the nearby Bacalar Laguna house Caribbean manatees and myriad species of endangered birds.

**Laguna de Ibans.** Hazy mountains and velvet canopies reflect off the glittering lagoon as dugout canoes zip across the water to surrounding villages. The locally run Sea Turtle Conservation Project takes place each summer in Plaplaya, a Garífuna village on Iban's western fringe.

**Raista/Belén.** A quiet nook of the jungle skirted by sandy beaches is the home of these Miskito hamlets on Laguna de Ibans. Cozy ecolodges and a friendly local community make it easy to immerse yourself in both nature and culture.

**Brus Laguna.** Scrubby pine savannas and breezy Caribbean waters envelop this commercial center on either end. Fishing from Cannon Island and excellent bird-watching are the main draw to this remote waterfront retreat.

**Río Plátano Biosphere Reserve.** This ecological paradise is one of the largest natural reserves on the planet. The diverse array of ecosystems and a burgeoning ecotourism industry make for a broad selection of unique outdoor adventures.

**Las Marías.** Rugged hikes and jungle treks head out from this tiny indigenous village, a must-see in the Río Plátano reserve. Tourism here is a community effort: locally trained guides lead excursions to the Walpaulbansirpe and Walpaulbantara petroglyphs up the river, and artisans proudly share their crafts.

**Puerto Lempira.** An airport, basic hotels, and La Mosquitía's only bank make this capital city on Laguna de Caratasca a preferred place to start before heading into the wilderness. Fishing and beach escapes await in the nearby Miskito villages of Mistruk and Kaukira.

## GREAT ITINERARIES

**If You Have 3 days:** Traveling by land here from other parts of Honduras or from Nicaragua can take days, so make the most of your time and take a one-hour flight to Brus Laguna. From there, hire a motorized canoe to take you across the lagoon to Belén. Spend the afternoon horseback riding down the empty coastline, and meet around the campfire later to hear generations' old stories from Miskito locals. Sleep in the next day in the beachfront cabanas, and take a local water taxi east to Raista. Enjoy a hearty breakfast at the Bodden family ecolodge, then set off on a two-hour jungle hike. Paru Creek offers a refreshing spot for inner tubing at the end of the trek. Rise early on the third day and grab a water taxi back to the Brus Laguna airport for the early afternoon return flight.

**If You Have 5 days:** Fly into Brus Laguna and head straight to Belén. Enjoy the beaches, take a stroll through the jungle, and join a Miskito dance ceremony at night. Arrange in advance for a canoe to pick you up the next morning, and devote the second day to a six-hour journey up the Río Plátano to Las Marías, a Miskito and Pech community in the heart of the reserve. Dine and rest at a locally run ecolodge along the riverbank that night. On the third day, hire a local guide to take you two hours up the river to see the Walpaubansirpe petroglyphs. Stretch your legs on a rugged jungle trek, and relax with a picnic lunch on the beaches near the carvings. If you're up for more adventure, skip the petroglyphs and take a moderate trek to the Cerro de Zapote. Head back down the Río Plátano the next day and spend the evening lounging in Raista, then boat back to Brus Laguna in the morning.

**If You Have 7 days:** From Brus Laguna, take a 45-minute water taxi to the Yamari Cabanas in the Caribbean pine savanna. Cool off in the swimming holes and take an excursion for bird-watching or crocodile spotting. Spend the second day in Belén, and head down the Río Plátano to Las Marías on the third. Pico Baltimore and Cerro Mico, with steep trails and wonderful wildlife-spotting opportunities, are great places for an intense two-day hike. For less rugged travels, take a two-day camping trip to the petroglyphs. On the sixth day, travel the river back to Raista for one last quiet night.

## PLANNING

### WHEN TO GO

True to its name, the rain forest in La Mosquitía gets significantly wet during the rainy season. The best, and driest, months to travel are from February through May and August through November, when the rivers are more navigable and jungle treks less likely to end up as mud baths. Heavy rainfall complicates land travel here from June through September, but it is still possible to make the journey. The weather is typically warm and muggy year-round and cools off significantly at night.

### GETTING HERE AND AROUND

Traveling to and from La Mosquitía will take up several days of your itinerary because of when flights are scheduled. Be ready to spend, at the very least, three days traveling to, through, and from the region.

### AIR TRAVEL

From La Ceiba, Sosa flies three times a week to Brus Laguna and has regular service to Puerto Lempira. SAMI/Aerocaribe Honduras also flies a nine-seat charter from La Ceiba to Brus Laguna, Puerto Lempira, and occasionaly to Raista/Belén and Ahuas.

Flights no longer land in Palacios, once the gateway to the region, and the airport is likely to remain closed indefinitely.

Airlines **Aerolíneas Sosa** (☎ 443–1399 in La Ceiba). **SAMI/Aerocaribe Honduras** (☎ 442–2565 or 433–6016 in La Ceiba).

### BUS TRAVEL

Collective pickup trucks, or *pailas*, make stops in Batalla, but no buses or taxis make their way into La Mosquitía (save for local trucks that run along a dirt road in Laguna de Ibans to Raista and Belén). The six-hour ride is long and grueling, especially when the highway ends and trucks hit the beach, but at a negotiable rate of L500, the fare is far less costly than a plane ticket. Passengers can pay fewer lempiras to sit

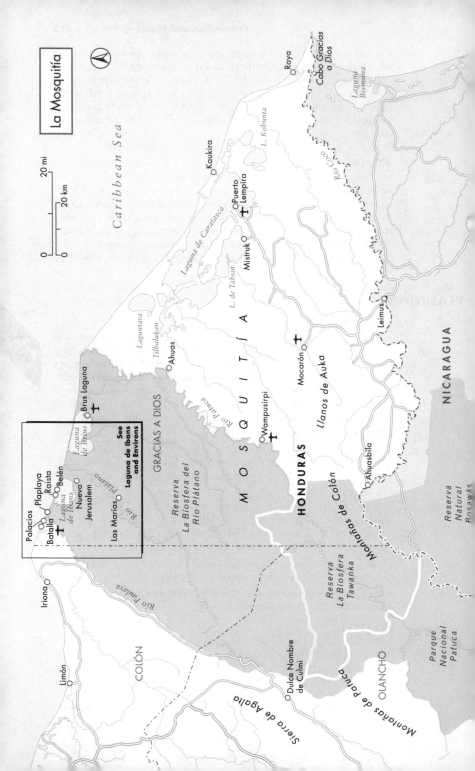

in the truck bed, although low-lying tree branches and erratic driving make this a riskier option.

Trucks head out at 7 AM from the central market in Tocoa, a town two hours southeast of La Ceiba. Cotraipbal and Cotuc bus lines leave La Ceiba for Trujillo at 3 AM and make stops along the way in Tocoa. Pickups return from Batalla the next day at 6 AM. During the rainy season, trips may be cancelled or severely delayed due to flooding on the beach route.

**Bus Information Cotraipbal** (⊠ *Carretera La Ceiba–Tela, Bo. Buenos Aires, La Ceiba* ☎ *441–2182).* **Cotuc** (⊠ *Carretera La Ceiba–Tela, Bo. Buenos Aires, La Ceiba* ☎ *441–2182 in La Ceiba, 434–3777 in Tocoa).*

### BOAT TRAVEL

Lagoons and canals are the streets and the Río Plátano is the highway in La Mosquitía. Residents push narrow pipante canoes with wooden poles for short trips, while sturdier motorized canoes travel longer distances. Direct, or *expreso,* boat services can be arranged, and collective boats offer a slower ride for a fraction of the cost. Prices have risen in the last year with the cost of petroleum, although some captains will still negotiate the fare.

Direct boats run round-trip from Palacios to Raista/Belén, and from Raista/Belén to Las Marías. Boats from Brus Laguna also head to Raista/Belén or Las Marías. One-way colectivo water taxis offer service between Palacios and Raista/Belén, and Brus Laguna to Río Plátano.

### TOUR OPERATORS

■TIP→ Guided tours are hands down the best way to experience La Mosquitía.

Under the guidance of a tour group, travelers can take in the exceptional landscapes and infinite wildlife without having to fret about where to stay, how to get there, or if they have enough cash on hand for dinner. La Moskitia Ecoaventuras and La Ruta Moskitia are particularly reputable tour companies and work with the local community to protect the region's pristine ecosytems.

The culturally focused Garífuna Tours' operator offers a four-day, three-night trek to Las Marías and Brus Laguna. Honduras Tourist Options is a family-run enterprise that offers a five-day rugged adventure in the Río Plátano reserve. **La Moskitia Ecoaventuras'** head guide Jorge Salaverri is an expert on the region. His highly regarded tour company offers 8- and 12-day rafting trips, plus jungle treks and wildlife excursions. La Ruta Moskitia consists of six indigenous communities coordinating to offer four- to nine-day land- or air-based cultural and ecotourism packages. The Web site is also an invaluable resource for the intrepid few who want to map their own excursions. The international Meso-american Ecotourism Alliance teams up with area experts and guides to promote sustainable tourism and local development. In La Mosquitía, the alliance has 14-day rafting trips down the Río Plátano and 9-day hikes geared at bird-watching.

La Ceiba's most popular rafting outfitter, Omega Tours, has beginner-level rain-forest treks, plus challenging river expeditions for experienced outdoor travelers. Anthropologist Dr. Christopher Begley heads rainforest rafting trips with The Exploration Foundation, a U.S.-based tour operator. Excursions focus on archeological ruins and cultural encounters. German-run Turtle Tours has guided trips to the Río Plátano reserve and La Mosquitía's Caribbean end.

**Tour Operators Garífuna Tours** (✉ Ave. San Isidro, 1ra CalleLa Ceiba ☎ 440–3252 ⊕ www.garifunatours.com). **Honduras Tourist Options** (✉ Blvd. 15 de Septiembre, near the Central Bank, La Ceiba ☎ 443–0337 or 440–0265 ⊕ www. hondurastouristoptions.com).

★ **La Moskitia Ecoaventuras** (✉ Col. El Toronjal, one block north of Pollitos la Cumbre, La Ceiba ☎ 441–2480 ⊕ www.lamoskitia.hn).

★ **La Ruta Moskitia** (☎ 406–6782 or 3391–3388 ⊕ www.larutamoskitia.com). **Mesoamerican Ecotourism Alliance** (☎ 800/682–0582 from the U.S. ⊕ www. travelwithmea.org). **Omega Tours** (✉ El Naranjo, south of La Ceiba ☎ 440–0334 or 9631–0295 ⊕ www.omegatours.info). **The Exploration Foundation** (☎ 859/608–2478 from the U.S. ⊕ www.explorationfoundation.org). **Turtle Tours** (✉ La Ceiba ☎ 429–2284 ⊕ www.turtle-tours.com).

## HEALTH AND SAFETY

Strong repellent with DEET and bed netting are two essential companions in La Mosquitía, where mosquitoes carrying malaria and dengue fever still strike with occasional frequency. The easiest way to lower your risk is by covering up with lightweight clothing and steering clear of stagnant water. Travelers spending more than a week in the region might also want to consider taking antimalarial medications before, during, and after an excursion. Coastal towns like Puerto Lempira and Palacios are also ripe with less harmless, and yet incredibly annoying, sand flies. Oil-based lotions and cactus juice help trap the bugs before they can bite, but the easiest way to save your skin is to keep it unexposed.

Puerto Lempira is prone to petty crimes. Drug traffickers from South America increasingly use Palacios to smuggle contraband into the northern hemisphere, and they bring that activity's associated problems with them. Travelers need not discount Palacios altogether, but traveling with an organized tour group is strongly suggested.

**Hospital Hospital Puerto Lempira** is open 24 hours. (✉ 1.5 km (0.9 mi) southwest of town, Puerto Lempira ☎ 433–6012 or 433–6078). **Clínica Evangélica Morava,** (✉ Between Brus Laguna and Puerto Lempira, Ahuas ⊕ www. ahuasclinic.com).

## MONEY MATTERS

La Mosquitía has no ATMs, but the bank in Puerto Lempira, the only one in the region, can issue cash advances on Visa cards. Outside the capital city, every place else takes cash lempiras only. Be sure to have plenty of small bills on hand, as most family-run operations can't break big notes. A five-day trip via land might cost over $400 including transportation, lodging, meals, and tour guides, for example. Keep your cash in a money belt around your waist, not as much to prevent theft, but to ensure that none of your precious bills get left behind.

**Bank Banco Atlántida** (✉ *Puerto Lempira* ☎ *898–7580* ⊕ *www.bancatlan.hn*) ⊙ *Mon.–Fri. 8:30–4:30, Sat. 8:30–11:30.*

## RESTAURANTS AND CUISINE

In a country known for its simple cuisine, the fare in La Mosquitía is inescapably traditional. Complicated transportation in and out of the region essentially guarantees that most of the food is grown right at home, although a few basic staples such as coffee, sugar, and cured meats are regularly brought in on water taxis.

Indigenous villagers subsist principally on rice, beans, and the daily catch of fish, with handmade cheeses and homegrown eggs adding some bulk to the plate. Stopover towns like Puerto Lempira, Batalla, and Palacios have a few minimalist sit-down restaurants that serve chicken, beef, conch, and lobster with *tajadas* (fried plantain chips). Puerto Lempira's general store is a good place to stock up on snacks and fruit to appease grumbling stomachs during a hike.

Further into the rain forest, the only restaurants in Raista/Belén and Las Marías are the tiny dining areas, or *comedores*, found at the locally run ecolodges. Families prepare home-cooked meals for a flat fee of L70 each. Cold soft drinks and beer are usually on hand. Grub at the Bodden family cabins in Raista is exceptionally delicious, with scrambled eggs and toast for breakfast and a rotating lineup of spaghetti and beans or chicken and rice for dinner.

Travelers are largely expected to haul their own lunches along on excursions or treks. If you're on a package tour, most guides will be in charge of handling the middle meal. For adventurers exploring at their own pace, it's a good idea to buy nonperishable foods like canned tuna and granola to stow in a backpack.

## HOTELS

Simplistic cabins and lodges are a suprisingly comfortable option out in the wild. Family-run quarters, or *hospedajes*, have inexpensive rooms and limited space, and they're the only choice for sleeping indoors outside the bigger towns. Las Marías has six hospedajes and Raista has just one, while Brus Laguna and Belén have singular beach cabanas. The nightly rate in most places runs from L130 to L200 per person.

In the rain forest, lodging built from wood planks stands high off the ground with wraparound terraces and thatched palm roofs. Large mosquito nets cascade onto the firm beds below, and candlesticks and matches wait on the ready from the windowsill. Some lodging has shared bathrooms with sinks, showers, and flushing toilets. Others have communal latrines with adjacent showers and a nearby bucket of rainwater for flushing and bathing. The choice is strictly up to the location.

Puerto Lempira has a few decent hotels with simple rooms, private bathrooms, and cable. Smaller motels are small and stuffy but suitable for a night. In Batalla and Palacios, several hospedajes have rustic accommodations for travelers in transit, although decor does not include the ever-important mosquito netting.

## A BIT OF HISTORY

Civilization in La Mosquitía began at least 3,000 years ago with the Cibcha-speaking indigenous tribe from South America. Hundreds of archeological sites and stone ruins here date back from AD 500 to AD 1500, indicating a population boom that coincides with the decline in the Mayan empire to the west. Local indigenous lore hints at the existence of La Ciudad Blanca, or White City, a mysterious lost city whose legend was first recorded by Hernan Cortés in 1526. Although expeditions since then have turned up empty-handed, initiatives headed by the Honduran Institute of Anthropology and History are steadily making new discoveries about the region's ancient past.

Explorer Christopher Columbus preceded Cortés here when he landed on the coast in 1502 and dubbed the region *Gracias a Dios*, or Thanks to God, following a rough voyage from the island of Guanaja. Spanish missionaries struggled for a century to colonize the coast, and they are thought to have coined the name "Miskito" for the native inhabitants. All the while, French and British privateers found cover in the coast's hidden cays and lagoons. History here is in the place names: heavy artillery once buttressed modern-day Cannon Cay, and Brus Laguna, formerly Brewer's Lagoon, is a tribute to a pirate named "Bloody Brewer" who frequented these parts. In the 17th century, the British expanded their trading presence by building alliances with indigenous leaders, whom the Europeans crowned as royalty in the area they dubbed the Miskito Kingdom. The Spanish ultimately took control of the coast in 1787, although the British continually stepped in to preserve the Miskito's sovereignty.

### WHAT IT COSTS IN HONDURAN LEMPIRAS

|  | ¢ | $ | $$ | $$$ | $$$$ |
|---|---|---|---|---|---|
| Restaurants | under L60 | L61–L80 | L81–L100 | L101–L120 | over L120 |
| Hotels | under L100 | L100–L200 | L201–L300 | L301–L400 | over L400 |

Restaurant prices are per person for a main course at dinner. Hotel prices are for two people in a standard double room in high season.

# BATALLA

*36 km (22 mi) northwest of Brus Laguna; 2 hours by boat.*

Bright-green palms and coconut trees shelter small huts and homes hugging the sandy northern shores of the Bacalar Laguna. This mellow Garífuna community has steadily emerged from the shadows of nearby Palacios as local ecotourism efforts, excellent fishing, and a land transit hub draw travelers in for a stopover.

Nights in Batalla ring out with the vibrant drumming and dancing inspired by West African rhythms. The Garífuna culture has livened up Honduras's northern coast since these descendants of slaves arrived from the Caribbean islands in the late 18th century. By day, local guides set out on canoes through the sweeping mangrove forests to spot Caribbean manatees, rare tropical birds, and swinging howler monkeys. This coastal lagoon lies west of the Río Negro and falls within the blanket of the Río Plátano Biosphere Reserve. Its swampy beauty is also protected under the Ramsar Convention on Wetlands, an international treaty signed in Ramsar, Iran, in 1971 to oblige countries to uphold the integrity of their wetlands.

Batalla is still blossoming, however, and its accessibility by land means the grunts and fumes of inland-bound pickup trucks fill the shores every morning. Many travelers only stay here for as long as it takes to hop out of a car and into a canoe. Others, however, opt to stay for the day and take part in Garífuna cultural exchanges or wildlife-seeking boat tours.

### GETTING HERE AND AROUND
Pailas head to Batalla from the municipal market in Tocoa every morning. The trucks take off around 7 AM and usually stop for lunch at a cafeteria along the four-to-six-hour journey. Return trips leave Batalla at 6 AM. Trip fare costs L500, although couples and groups can negotiate discounts or ride in the turbulent truck bed for L250.

Shared boats hover around the shoreline waiting to whisk truck travelers deeper into La Mosquitía. Colectivos charge L150 for the one-to-two-hour trip to Raista/Belén, with a stop in Palacios, while private expreso boats cost L800 per group round-trip.

### SAFETY
So far, Batalla has not been plagued with the safety concerns of neighboring Palacios. The town is quiet with few places to go, but it is still a good idea to take cash and valuables with you if you're stowing your luggage for a day trip or overnight.

### MONEY MATTERS
Bring enough cash with you to last the entire trip, as La Mosquitía's only bank in Puerto Lempira is at least 160 km (99 mi) away.

## EXPLORING

Batalla has two community tours available for visitors, which are essentially the extent of all activities in town. Trips can be arranged upon arrival or ahead of time with tour operator La Ruta Moskitia. Activity costs run from L200 to L300 per person, depending on the size of the group.

**Laguna Bacalar Boat Tours.** A two- to three-hour guided excursion maneuvers passengers through the coastal wetlands and mangrove swamps. Trip goers stay on the lookout for tropical monkeys dangling from high-above perches as parrots and storks peek out from the forest. It's possible to spot an endangered Caribbean manatee gliding slowly below.

**Garífuna Cultural Exchanges.** The audience becomes the performer in this hour-long experience. Visitors to Batalla can experience and participate first-hand in the lively folkloric dances and spiritual Garífuna singing, a cultural richness that is often invisible to travelers passing through.

Evenings end with a buffet of traditional foods like seafood soup with conch and shrimp and *pan de coco*, or coconut bread.

## WHERE TO EAT AND STAY

Batalla has a few family kitchens that serve seafood, rice, and beans ($), but they're still a long stretch from a sit-down restaurant. A handful of rustic accommodations have concrete rooms for around L150 with a stiff mattress, no mosquito netting (which you'll want here), and a shared latrine. This setup is only ideal for travelers taking an early morning *paila*, one of the the rugged pickup trucks that run back to Tocoa.

# PALACIOS

*30 km (19 mi) west of Brus Laguna; 4 hours by boat.*

Palacios has undergone a major transformation in the last few years. The mixed Ladino and Miskito town—the second largest town in La Mosquitía, after Puerto Lempira—was for decades the main entryway into the region. Planes brought passengers to the local landing strip in this former British settlement (whose historic cemetery still remains), and motorized canoes raced travelers across the Bacalar Laguna and deep into the Río Plátano rain forest.

Travel to the town has dropped significantly since the runway shut down indefinitely a couple of years back. Boats across the lagoon in Batalla now make the same trips to Raista/Belén and the Río Plátano, effectively limiting the need to transit through Palacios. On top of that, South American drug smugglers are discretely operating their trade routes in the area.

But the town shouldn't be wiped off the map just yet. For travelers in organized groups, Palacios is still a gateway to fascinating wildlife excursions and rugged jungle hikes. Caimans, sloths, howler monkeys, and spotted margay cats hang around the lagoon, and indigenous Miskito residents can arrange cultural exchanges with guests eager for immersion.

### GETTING HERE AND AROUND

Without the airport, transit to and from Palacios is exclusively via boat. Colectivo water taxis from Batalla frequently make the half-hour trip to Palacios, and rates are negotiable. Shared boats also swing by on the way to Raista/Belén and charge L150 per individual for the two-hour leg. Express boats from Palacios head to Raista/Belén for L800 per group round-trip.

A handful of boats leave Palacios daily at 2 PM for the two-to-three-hour trek to Brus Laguna, and water taxis leave Brus Laguna for Palacios at 3 AM. Fares should run around L400.

### SAFETY

La Ruta Moskitia warns its clients not to spend the night in Palacios, as the town stays noisy at night and can get sketchy after dark. Guests at the secure Hotel Moskitia have little to worry about, and the town is generally safe during the day. Healthwise, sand flies here are especially pesky. Cover up with lightweight clothing and keep a bottle of bug repellent handy to fend off mosquitoes and no-see-ums.

**MONEY MATTERS**

Cash lempiras are the only accepted currency here, so bring plenty of them before you start your trip.

## EXPLORING

Spending the day surrounded by wilderness and staring out into the peaceful Bacalar Laguna account for most of the activities around Palacios. Local ecotourism efforts center across the lagoon on Batalla, and at this writing, the Río Plátano Biosphere Museum is not in operation. Palacios is best thought of as a connection point between the outside world and the outstanding eco adventures waiting deeper in the jungle.

## WHERE TO EAT AND STAY

Basic hospedajes and informal eateries on the water's edge greet the weary budget traveler in need of a place to crash. The best of these is Hotel Río Tinto. The most highly recommended place to stay in Palacios, however, is Hotel Moskitia, which is also where you'll have your best meal.

$ 🏨 **Hotel Moskitia.** This wooden fishing lodge offers the most complete service in Palacios. Twelve rooms can convert to singles or doubles and have private bathrooms, TVs, and fans. The hotel has a small restaurant that serves traditional and international cuisine, plus a bar and meeting center. Guests can also arrange three-to six-day trips into La Mosquitía, or opt for an all-inclusive package at $395/person that covers transportation from La Ceiba, two nights, three meals a day, bilingual tour guides, and activity fees. Pros: running water and generator in-room; serene and secure; organized tours. Cons: town is hard to reach; few nearby activities. ✉ *Palacios* ☎ *442–8059 and 9691–8171 in La Ceiba, or 9996–5648 in Palacios* ⊕ *www.hotelmoskitia.com* ⤢ *12 rooms* ⚐ *In-room: no a/c. In-hotel: restaurant, bar* ⊟ No credit cards ⏱️ MAP, AI.

$ 🏨 **Hotel Río Tinto.** Doña Ana Marmol runs the 15-room Hotel Río Tinto, one of the better bargain options in Palacios, which has a tiny cafeteria and rooms with private bathrooms that cost L150 per night. ✉ *Palacios* ☎ No phone. ⊟ No credit cards.

# LAGUNA DE IBANS

The intricate latticework of crisscrossing mangrove trees along the shore is reflected on the glassy surface of Laguna de Ibans, the smallest yet arguably most picturesque of La Mosquitía's three major lagoons. The open-water portion of the Laguna is about 5 mi across; clouds turn the water's surface into a portrait of the sky as narrow canoes paint ripples in their wake. On the sand bar that separates Ibans from the Caribbean, the jungle views are dotted with the stilted houses and creaky docks that populate a string of Garífuna and Miskito villages.

Tourism to three of this region's communities—Plaplaya, Raista, and Belén—is on the rise. Local initiatives have inspired comfortable guest lodges and community-run ecotours, giving the lagoon the edge over Palacios as a favored point of entry into Las Marías in the heart of the Río Plátano reserve.

Laguna de Ibans, named after a British buccaneer called Evans, enjoys a curious mix of rustic and modern. Families here sleep in hammocks in one-room homes and scrub clothing clean on rocks in the lagoon. They eat homegrown crops from small subsistence plots and bathe with tubs of gathered rainwater. Yet the electric buzz of a diesel generator brings *fútbol* games and music videos to the occasional flat-screen TV, and motorbikes dodge meandering livestock as they zip down bumpy dirt roads.

A stay in one of these villages merits more than just a pit stop. Be prepared for the comparative lack of amenities as compared to some of the other more-developed regions of Honduras, but the chance to unwind, explore, and experience a new culture make them worth the effort.

# RAISTA

★ *13 km (8 mi) east of Palacios; 2 hours by boat.*

A smattering of wooden houses with crops, cows, and chickens hugs the shoreline in this secluded Miskito community. Lush surroundings and surprisingly cozy rooms at the Raista Ecolodge (the region's relative exception to the bare-bones rule), plus a boat service to Las Marías, are attracting an increasing number of visitors whose ultimate destination is the Río Plátano reserve. The town also has a few easy-to-intermediate jungle excursions that add some adventure to the otherwise tranquil village of fishermen and lobster divers.

### GETTING HERE AND AROUND

Boats from Batalla travel one to two hours to Raista/Belén and cost L150 per person. Return trips to Batalla must be arranged ahead of time, so have the staff at your hospedaje radio a water taxi to pick you up.

Direct expreso boats must also be radioed in advance for the six-hour expedition to Las Marías and cost between L500 and L700 per person, depending on the group size. If you forget to line up a boat for the next day, you might be lucky enough to join in another group's ride, but you might also end up stranded in Raista.

### SAFETY

This village is tiny; personal safety tends not to be an issue.

### MONEY MATTERS

There are no ATMs here, and credit cards are generally not accepted; arrive with whatever cash you may need.

### EXPLORING

Excursions can be arranged on-site or in advance with La Ruta Moskitia, a tour group that seeks out local guides and determines costs per person by the number of participants.

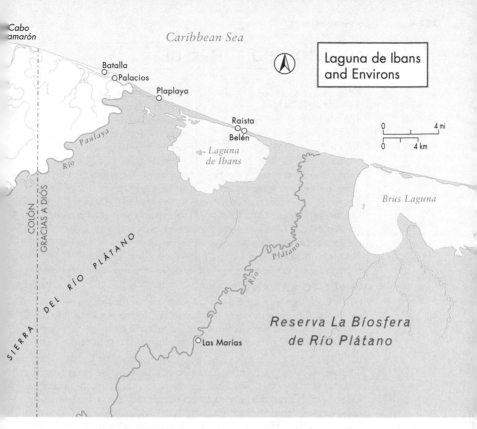

Caribbean Sea

Cabo
amarón

Batalla
Palacios
Plaplaya

Raista
Belén

Laguna
de Ibans

Laguna de Ibans
and Environs

0        4 mi
0      4 km

Brus Laguna

Paulaya

Río

COLÓN
GRACIAS A DIÓS

SIERRA    DEL    RÍO    PLÁTANO

Plátano

Río

Las Marías

Reserva La Bíosfera
de Río Plátano

**Paru Creek.** This four- to five-hour day trip starts across the lagoon in the nearby lowland rain forest, where spotting troops of howler monkeys is possible, albeit unguaranteed. Hikers set off through the jungle on a moderately difficult hike and plunge into the refreshing Paru Creek with inner tubes in hand. From there, it's a tranquil float downstream with bird-watching and wildlife spotting above in the rain-forest canopy. ✉ *Raista, Laguna de Ibans* ⊕ *www.larutamoskitia.com.*

**Jungle Survival Course.** Not that you'll need it here (unless you really plan poorly), but local guides in Raista offer a five-hour training session in jungle survival skills. The course teaches how to find sources of food and drinkable water, how to spot medicinal plants and natural mosquito repellents, plus orientation in the jungle. ✉ *Raista, Laguna de Ibans* ⊕ *www.larutamoskitia.com.*

**Miskito Dancing.** Spend a cultural hour with the local women's group around an evening bonfire. The women perform traditional Miskito dances and songs, along with ancient stories that have been shared from generation to generation. ✉ *Raista, Laguna de Ibans* ⊕ *www. larutamoskitia.com.*

## BLUE MORPHO BUTTERFLIES

At this writing, Raista's most her-alded attraction—its butterfly farm—is closed indefinitely. Local farmers built the Raista sanctuary in the mid-1990s as part of a conservation effort by MOPAWI (Moskitia Powisa Apiska), a Miskito development organization based in Puerto Lempira. Butterflies in the enclosed garden fed on fermenting fruit and laid their eggs there, which helpers later collected and raised into cocoons before exporting the pupae to faraway museums.

But tropical butterflies like the magnificent blue morpho can still be spotted around the Río Plátano Biosphere Reserve. Blue morphos (or Morpho menelaus) remain a prized sight around the lagoon for their shimmering azure wings and iridescent sheen. These natives of Central America spend much of their time in the shade of the tropical forests but can also be spotted in sunny clearings.

### WHERE TO EAT AND STAY

Raista Ecolodge is far and away the best option for lodging in Raista, but in the rare and unlikely event that the lodge is full, a few local women run hospedajes with basic accommodations from their homes. Ask for Doña Exy, whose place has a small *comedor* (kitchen), or Doña Mendilia or Doña Cecilia.

$ 🏠 **Raista Ecolodge.** Eight newly remodeled cabins sit on stilts near the banks of the lagoon. Doña Elma, matriarch of the tourism-pioneering Bodden family, runs the lodge with her daughter Melissa. Upon request, they can cook up tasty and bountiful breakfasts and dinners served in the downstairs dining area, or call to arrange transportation and tours. Spacious rooms, built from wood planks and thatched palm roofs, each have a double and single bed (mosquito netting included), plus access to a wraparound porch facing the water. Candles and purified water are also provided. Communal bathrooms adjoining the lodge have cold-water showers, flushing toilets, and sinks with mirrors; these are perhaps the most modern accommodations in the area. A generator provides electricity only to the kitchen and family house, so bring a flashlight for after sunset. **Pros:** hearty meals; contemporary bathrooms; cozy rooms. **Cons:** no electricity. ⊠ *Raista, Laguna de Ibans* 🕾 *433–8216* ⊕ *www.larutamoskitia.com* 🛏 *8 rooms* ⚒ *In-hotel: restaurant* ⊟ *No credit cards* ⦿ *EP.*

## BELÉN

★ *13 km (8 mi) east of Palacios; 2 hours by boat.*

Belén is sandwiched between two other villages. It starts where Raista meets the airport and ends where Nueva Jerusalén begins, with little indication of any line between the towns. This languid Miskito village is mere steps away from the Caribbean Sea and is an equally short walk to Laguna de Ibans. Whereas Raista is nestled within the jungle's cover,

Belén is sprawled along an empty coastline with endless vistas of the Pico Baltimore mountain range.

### GETTING HERE AND AROUND

From Batalla, boat rides to Belén cost L150 per individual for the one-to-two-hour journey. As in Raista, water taxis must be radioed ahead of time for return trips to Batalla. Direct boats to Las Marías cost between L500 and L700 (the same as from Raista) and require prior reservations.

### SAFETY

This village is tiny; personal safety tends not to be an issue.

### MONEY MATTERS

There are no ATMs here, and credit cards are generally not accepted; arrive with whatever cash you may need.

## EXPLORING

As it does in neighboring Raista, La Ruta Moskitia has a number of adventurous and cultural tours out of Belén, including three-hour horseback-riding trips on the beach and musical presentations put on by the local women's group.

**Brans Jungle Hike.** A boat ride from Belén across Laguna de Ibans takes you to Banaka Creek. A strenuous full-day hike in the rain forest leads to a waterfall, virgin jungle, and a grouping of ancient petroglyphs in the village of Banaka. The carvings here might be a convenient alternative if you don't have the three days it takes to make the trip to the more famous Walpaulbansirpe petroglyphs, near Las Marías. ⊠ *Belén, Laguna de Ibans* ⊕ *www.larutamoskitia.com.*

**Crocodile Night Watch.** Well, more like dusk than full-on night: canoes slither through shaded canals in the early evening as passengers stay on the lookout for crocodiles and caimans. Flashlight beams find the red reflection in reptilian eyes, and the remaining daylight affords decent bird-watching and wildlife observation. ⊠ *Belén, Laguna de Ibans* ⊕ *www.larutamoskitia.com.*

## WHERE TO STAY

$  ⊞ **Pawanka Beach Cabanas.** A short walk out of central Belén and over a worn plank bridge leads to owner Mario Miller's three palm-thatched cabins. The small restaurant here dishes out traditional meals by request and serves Caribbean favorites like lobster and shrimp. Somewhat cramped cabins have beds for a total of 12 guests and large screened walls with views of the grounds. In the rooms, gauzy mosquito nets hang above the beds, and the communal bathroom features the same contemporary fixtures as in Raista Ecolodge. La Ruta Moskitia's guided tours out of Belén all take off from the cabins. **Pros:** on-site restaurant; modern bathrooms; purified water and candles in the room. **Cons:** bathroom is separate from cabins; no electricity. ⊠ *Belén, Laguna de Ibans* ☎ *433–8220* ⊕ *www.larutamoskitia.com* ⌖ *3 cabins* ⌂ *In-room: no a/c. In-hotel: restaurant.* ⊟ *No credit cards* ⧉ *EP.*

## PLAPLAYA

*9 km (5.6 mi) east of Palacios; 1 hour by boat.*

Honduras's easternmost Garífuna village (east of here, it's primarily Moskito villages) has just one tourist attraction, but it's a pretty fantastic one: turtle conservation. For eight months each year, volunteers can join a homegrown conservation initiative to protect the eggs of endangered turtles on the western beaches of the lagoon. Although no formal accommodations exist, families will rent out extra beds in their homes and offer visitors a spot at the dinner table. Garífuna cultural groups also put on drumming and dance shows for groups who make a prior request.

### GETTING HERE AND AROUND

Boats in transit from Palacios to Raista/Belén make stops in Plaplaya with advance warning. The entire ride costs L150, so negotiate a lower price. Local guides or hospedaje staff can also arrange pickup trucks to head out from Raista/Belén.

### SAFETY

This village is tiny; personal safety tends not to be an issue.

### MONEY MATTERS

There are no ATMs here, and credit cards are generally not accepted; arrive with whatever cash you may need.

### EXPLORING

**Sea Turtle Conservation Project.** From February to September each year, Doña Patrocinia heads the grassroots group that organizes volunteer trips during the nesting period of green, leatherback, and loggerhead turtles. Participants head out at night to comb the beaches for turtle nests, collect the freshly laid eggs, and rebury them in a protected sanctuary intended to fend off poachers and predators. The eggs hatch three months later, and the young turtles are released back into the lagoon. Plaplaya villagers also take part in the project during the height of the turtle season, from April to July. ⊠ *Plaplaya, Laguna de Ibans* ⊕ *www.larutamoskitia.com.*

### WHERE TO STAY

A couple of rustic guesthouses with tin roofs and thin mattresses are available to overnight visitors in Plaplaya, and traditional Honduran meals can be prepared upon request for L70. Call or email **La Ruta Moskitia** (☎ *406–6782 or 3391–3388* ⊕ *www.larutamoskitia.com*) to arrange a homestay in advance.

# RESERVA LA BÍOSFERA DEL RÍO PLÁTANO

La Mosquitía has become synonymous with the Río Plátano Biosphere Reserve, and it's not hard to see why. The massive preserve houses more than 525,000 hectares (1.3 million acres) of tropical forests, wetlands, mangrove swamps, pine savannas, and beaches, accounting for the vast majority of this underdeveloped region. Río Paulaya lies to the west and Río Patuca to the east, with the mighty, winding Río Plátano smack in the middle of the protected area. Laguna de Ibans and Brus Laguna also fall within the otherwise mountainous territory.

The biosphere reserve became the first of its kind in Central America in 1980, the same year it was declared a UNESCO World Heritage site. Nearly 400 species of birds have been identified here, including the harpy eagle, king vulture, jabirus, and macaws of the green, scarlet, and military varieties. Close to 40 mammal species like brown-throated sloths, pumas, jaguars, kinkajous, and spider and mantled howler monkeys inhabit the lush tropical landscape, while more than 120 species of reptiles and amphibians live in the distinctive ecosystems.

Guided tours are the easiest way to take advantage of all the reserve has to offer. Rugged camping excursions take hikers up steep mountain trails with sweeping views of the ecosystems below. Rafting trips in the dry season paddle through Class III and IV rapids in Río Sico, along the reserve's western border, or down the Río Plátano. Cultural tours include trips to centuries-old petroglyphs and exchanges with the native Pech and Miskito people, who total around just 2,000 residents. While logging, cattle ranching, and destructive agriculture techniques like slash-and-burn threaten the integrity of the Río Plátano reserve, ecotourism efforts focused on conserving this pristine biosphere offer a promising alternative for economic growth in the underdeveloped region.

# LAS MARÍAS

★ *25 km (16 mi) southeast of Laguna de Ibans; 6 hours by boat.*

The short distance from Las Marías to the coast is deceiving. It's a long haul—nearly 40 km (25 mi) as the river fish swims—to the village, the deepest in the reserve, but the reward is worth the day of travel. Around 100 Miskito and Pech families have carved their homes into this endless expanse of rain forest found 10 km (6 mi) up the Río Plátano. Churches from five denominations, a 24-hour health clinic, and a visitors' center mingle with simple wood-plank homes spread around town. Women carry baskets of jewelry, pouches, and embroideries woven from naturally dyed bark fiber, while children play a muddy game of *fútbol* near the river's edge. With the help of international nonprofit groups, more than 150 community members have been trained to lead hikes and outings with travelers. The *sacaguía*, or head guide, is elected every six months to help arrange trips and coordinate the guides, and he'll usually greet visitors upon arrival to get everything squared off right away. The town itself is extremely placid (read: nothing to do but lie in a hammock), but most visitors use Las Marías as a starting point for rigorous hiking explorations and less intense excursions like wildlife-watching boat trips.

**GETTING HERE AND AROUND**

It takes most of the day to arrive here on a *cayuko*, or motorized canoe. Direct boats, available by previous arrangement only, can take you there from Brus Laguna for L3,500 per group, or from Raista/Belén for L3,000. Passengers are exposed to the elements for most of the six-to-seven-hour haul, so bring plenty of sunblock and bottled water, and keep a raincoat and waterproof pack cover handy just in case. Boats

## RAFTING THE RÍO PLÁTANO

A 10- to 14-day whitewater rafting excursion down the Río Plátano doesn't just take travelers from point A to point B; it offers a unique glance at a remote world otherwise unexplored, combining rare archeological finds and wildlife with cultural encounters and the chance to experience the Río Plátano reserve in its majestic entirety.

Jorge Salaverri, an expert on La Mosquitía and a U.S.-trained forester, leads trips with his La Moskitia Ecoaventuras, as does The Exploration Foundation's Dr. Christopher Begley, an anthropologist with 20 years of experience in the region. Together with naturalist Robert Gallardo, both men offer rain-forest rafting trips through the Mesoamérican Ecotourism Alliance (MEA).

Most 14-day trips begin in Tegucigalpa or La Ceiba and arrive by flight, though it is possible to get there by land. Groups then head to Bonanza, a town bordering the Río Plátano reserve, on the second day. Travelers hike for six hours across rugged terrain as mules haul the gear to arrive in Warsaka, a campsite at the headwaters of the Río Plátano and home to the ancient ruins of El Higerito. On the fourth day, hikers trek to the Lancetillal archeological site replete with stone plazas, monuments, and petroglyphs. Rafting begins on the fifth day in Class II

and III rapids and ends with a visit to the cobblestone walls of the Río Malo archeological site.

On the sixth day, head to concealed caves and an underground creek at Río Camalotal, then go to Los Metates, a village filled with thousands of small stone artifacts. The seventh day takes rafters over smooth waters to El Subterráneo, a narrow gorge full of enormous boulders and rocky Class II rapids. On day eight, difficult waters give way to a calm, three-hour ride to camp and an easy five-hour paddle the next day. Travelers pass the Walpaulbantara petroglyphs on the tenth day and the Walpaulbansirpe carvings on the eleventh, ending the rafting excursion with an overnight and cultural evening in the Miskito and Pech village of Las Marías. The last three days include a six-hour cayuko (motorized canoe) ride north to the Miskito and Garífuna villages around Laguna de Ibans, with a flight back to Tegucigalpa on the final day.

La Moskitia Ecoaventuras, MEA, and The Exploration Foundation offer variations of this itinerary and can focus more on wildlife and adventure than on archeology. Packages with any operator are pricy—from $1,500 to $2,800 depending on the duration and group size—but all camping and rafting equipment, meals, lodging, and guide fees are included.

will stop for lunch breaks along the riverbed, but you'll have to provide your own food.

From Las Marías, local guides can taxi travelers around the river, although this usually takes some time to arrange.

### SAFETY

Violence and crime are rare occurences in this isolated town. However, it's a good idea to keep an eye on any clothing or shoes hanging out to dry, as personal items have a tendency to disappear.

**MONEY MATTERS**

There are no ATMs in town, and credit cards aren't accepted; bring along any cash you'll need.

**EXPLORING**

The dry season is by and large the optimal time to go, as heavy rains in the wetter months make for slippery trails and soggy pipante rides. Local men propel the narrow dugout canoes with thin wooden poles pushed down into the riverbed. This rustic craft is the area's only mode of transportation and is a slow, topsy-turvy ride.

**Walpaulbansirpe.** *Easy, one day, three guides.* A favorite tour among visitors here, this mild day trip starts with a two-hour pipante ride up the Río Plátano. Pull off at the head of the Kuyuzqui trail and take an intermediate one-to-two-hour hike through lush jungle landscape. Moss-covered benches and a creaky, off-limits observation tower are remnants of previous tourism efforts that, at this writing, guides hope will soon be restored. Continue upriver to the petroglyphs and disembark for a picnic lunch. In the dry season, water around the rock carvings dries up and makes for a pleasant rest on the beach. Return downriver to Las Marías in the late afternoon. ⊠ *Las Marías, Río Plátano Biosphere Reserve.*

**Walpaulbantara.** *Easy, two days, three guides.* The extended petroglyphs tour starts off the same as the trip to Walpaulbansirpe. Rather than return to Las Marías, however, you'll spend the night camping or at a nearby hospedaje. On the second day, the pipante continues upriver to the second set of carvings, stopping occasionally for quick hikes along the banks of Río Plátano. Coast back to Las Marías that afternoon. ⊠ *Las Marías, Río Plátano Biosphere Reserve.*

**Village Trail.** *Easy, one day, one guide (optional).* For a true feel of life in Las Marías, follow the flat dirt trail around the village for a couple of hours. A local guide can point out medicinal plants and trees used for crafts, although the walk is easy enough to go it alone. Start at the boat landing and pass the humble one-room homes, a schoolhouse, and local clinic, then cross a narrow bridge to the second river access. The footpath loops around and brings you back to the central part of town. ⊠ *Las Marías, Río Plátano Biosphere Reserve.*

**WHERE TO EAT AND STAY**

Family-run hospedajes scattered around town are rustic but comfortable places to stay. The majority are wood-plank cabins on stilts with thatched-palm roofs and shared outhouses with bucket showers and no toilet seat. Wraparound porches have hooks for hanging hammocks, and sturdy beds with mattresses or foam pads are all draped in mosquito netting. Few places have screened windows, so keep repellent handy when you leave the netted fortress. Lodging costs between L100 and L120 per person, depending on the room and particular hospedaje.

Each guesthouse offers traditional Honduran meals and purified water upon request. Breakfast, lunch, and dinner usually costs L70 per plate, and coffee and soft drinks are extra. Two *pulperías*, or small bodegas, near the center of town sell basic medicines and general food items. Prices tend to be high due to the lengthy importation process.

## HIKING IN RÍO PLÁTANO

Rugged trailblazers and novice adventurers come seeking jungle hikes as far off the beaten path as they can possibly get. Tropical landscape engulfs trekkers as they search for exotic wildlife and climb up steep peaks to majestic panoramic views. Las Marías is the base for a selection of beginner to expert-level hikes.

**Cerro de Zapote.** *Moderate, one day, one guide.* This day hike also can be extended into a camping trip up to Pico Baltimore. From Las Marías, hike through flat terrain up to a steep hill and stop for a picnic lunch. An early start improves your chance for great bird-watching and wildlife spotting. After the break, head back to the village. ⊠ *Las Marías, Río Plátano Biosphere Reserve.*

**Cerro Mico.** *Moderate, two days, three guides.* Take the two-hour pipante ride to Walpaulbansirpe and overnight in tents or at a hospedaje. The next morning, hike along the mixed terrain of rolling trails and steep climbs to Cerro Mico, also called Monkey Hill for its abundance of, well, monkeys. Hike down a different path to a creek that bleeds into Río Plátano and return to Las Marías in the afternoon. Or, head back upriver to check out the second set of petroglyphs. ⊠ *Las Marías, Río Plátano Biosphere Reserve.*

**Pico Baltimore.** *Moderate to difficult, two days, two guides.* A slightly easier option than the Pico Dama hike, this trip starts in Las Marías with a five-to-seven-hour trek through primary and secondary forest, affording a long window of time to spot rare birds and endangered wildlife. Spend the night at a rustic cabin near the mountain's base, and rise early the second day to make the steep two-hour climb to the summit. Enjoy the stunning views of Laguna de Ibans and the Caribbean, then head back down to Las Marías. ⊠ *Las Marías, Río Plátano Biosphere Reserve.*

**Pico Dama.** *Difficult, three days, three guides.* Steep climbs and thick vegetation make this hike, in our opinion, the most challenging adventure out of Las Marías. The trip begins with a two-hour pipante ride upriver to Quebrada Sulawa. Disembark and trek for four hours through flat farmland and primary and secondary forest. The going is slippery; watch your step. Sleep in the simple cabin or pitch a tent at the campsite, then spend the second day on a steep four-hour hike to the mountain's peak, which offers a panoramic vista of the entire biosphere reserve. Hike back to the camp house, and return to Las Marías on the third day. ⊠ *Las Marías, Río Plátano Biosphere Reserve.*

**Doña Rutilia** has the largest lodging in Las Marías, with 20 beds in private rooms situated near the boat landing. She also has the town's only generator and telephone, although rooms are lit only by candlelight after dark. ⊠ *Las Marías, Río Plátano Biosphere Reserve.* **Doña Justa**'s place, near the central health clinic, has cozy accommodations and a pleasant flower garden. ⊠ *Las Marías, Río Plátano Biosphere Reserve.* **Hospedaje Diana** consists of four rooms in two cabins near Doña Rutilia's place. ⊠ *Las Marías, Río Plátano Biosphere Reserve.* **Don Ovidio**'s private rooms are found near the town center. ⊠ *Las Marías, Río Plátano Biosphere Reserve.*

Many travelers on overnight expeditions opt to stay in the basic rooms at **Hospedaje Wehnatara**, near the river. ⊠ *Las Marías, Río Plátano Biosphere Reserve.* **Hospedaje Luis Eden** is very basic yet popular and located on the shores of the Río Plátano en route to Cerro Mico, Pico Dama or the Walpaulbantara petroglyphs. ⊠ *Las Marías, Río Plátano Biosphere Reserve.*

# BRUS LAGUNA

*30 km (19 mi) east of Palacios; 4 hours by boat.*

Adventurous tales of pirates and bloodshed belie the ho-hum nature of this Miskito community along the northeastern edge of the Río Plátano reserve. Waters heavy with alligators might be the only sense of thrill left to a 4,100-person town once called Brewer's Lagoon, a tribute to the British privateer "Bloody Brewer," who sought refuge in the narrow canals. Today, life centers on fishing and cattle ranching in the one-road settlement. For many travelers, Brus Laguna is a godsend for (relatively) speedy access into La Mosquitía.

Three weekly Sosa flights can eliminate days of grueling land travel. Motorized cayuko canoes wait at the boat landing to transport newcomers immediately to Raista/Belén, Palacios, and Las Marías—although newly built cabanas in the adjacent Great Pine Savanna are a good reason to stick around for a bit and enjoy the breezy beaches. The town itself is a one-road municipality with a basic medical center, a police office, community telephones, and a few pulpería general stores. The most notable asset, however, is its top-notch fishing. Snapper, grouper, jack, tarpon, and bonito fish fill the lagoon, which stays salty in the dry period and floods with fresh river water in the rainy months.

### GETTING HERE AND AROUND

Sosa has three flights a week (Monday, Wednesday, and Friday) from La Ceiba to Brus Laguna. SAMI/Aerocaribe Honduras also flies on a semiregular basis to the town.

From Brus Laguna, direct expreso boats can be hired for the two-hour journey to Raista/Belén (L1,500 per group) or the slightly longer trip to Plaplaya and Palacios. Boat rides from Brus Laguna to Las Marías last seven hours and cost L3,500 per group. Colectivo water taxis also travel between the same communities for a fraction of the cost. Any local can point you in the right direction to a water taxi, but the best way to secure a ride is to call

### GUIDED HIKES: WHAT TO BRING

Tour operators, particularly La Moskitia Ecoaventuras, offer a convenient option for longer trails. They'll haul all the necessary camping gear from La Ceiba, so all you need to bring are sturdy hiking boots and a backpack of waterproof and weatherproof clothing. If you go at it alone, the visitor's center in Las Marías rents mosquito netting and linens for a couple of dollars. Water-purification tablets, heavy-duty bug repellent, flashlights, and dry sacks are good to have in either case.

a hotel office or tour company to set you up with their most trusted captains. It's best to plan return trips in advance so that boats can make sure to be there when you need them.

**HEALTH AND SAFETY**

On the off chance that you're staying in Brus Laguna town for the night, stick to your hotel after dark, as streets are unlit and less secure. CESAMO is a small medical center in town that offers basic health services during the week.

**MONEY MATTERS**

There are no ATMs; bring any cash you'd need.

**Medical Contacts CESAMO.** (⊠ *Next to the police station in the town center* ⊙ *Closed weekends.*)

# EXPLORING

Brus Laguna, like its counterparts to the west, has a few community trips arranged by tour operator La Ruta Moskitia, including two-to-three-hour horseback rides across the pine savanna. Trips to the vast forest region require a 40-minute boat ride out of the main town, where the Yamari Savannah Cabañas reside. Prices will vary by activity and group size.

**Cannon Island Excursion.** A quick boat ride from the savanna forest takes you to Cannon Island. The British used the minifortress in the 18th century to protect the entrance to Brus Laguna and ward off attacks by Spanish naval forces, who competed with England for control of the Mosquito Coast, and European pirates. Cannons and other heavy artillery still line the island's beaches. ⊠ *Brus Laguna* ⊕ *www.larutamoskitia.com.*

**Traditional Miskito Fishing.** Local Miskito guides lead a two-hour tour out on the lagoon to showcase their centuries-old fishing techniques with wooden poles and handmade nets. The trip is also a good opportunity to learn more about the indigenous culture and language. ⊠ *Brus Laguna* ⊕ *www.larutamoskitia.com.*

**Savanna Kayaking.** This moderately difficult trip starts in a translucent creek near the pine savanna. Kayakers paddle around the canals and lagoon for an hour or so while spotting a diverse number of birds up above. ⊠ *Brus Laguna* ⊕ *www.larutamoskitia.com.*

**Yamari Savannah Tubing.** A local guide will point out wildlife during an hour-long hike across the shrubby forest. At the end of the trail, hop into the clear creek and float on an inner tube back to the cabañas. ⊠ *Brus Laguna* ⊕ *www.larutamoskitia.com.*

# WHERE TO STAY

Brus Laguna's inland town center has a few standard hotels if you're here to catch an early flight the next morning; the best of these is Hotel La Estancia. If you have extra time to spend, the most pleasant accommodations are a 40-minute boat ride away in the Great Pine Savanna.

$$    ☶ **Hotel La Estancia.** While it's not as nice as other places farther from town in the surrounding countryside, this is the best in-town option and is comfortable enough. It's the perfect place to stay for an early flight out of the airport the next day. Owner Jose Osvaldo Cruz can help with travel tips on the area. **Pros:** while Wi-Fi is spotty, it'll likely come as a welcome novelty if this isn't your first stop in La Mosquitía; next to dock and La Ruta Moskitia office. **Cons:** ceiling fans only; rooms with private bathrooms cost extra. ✉ *Main St., Brus Laguna* ☎ *433–8043* 💬 *12 rooms* ◊ *In-room: no a/c, Wi-Fi. In-hotel: Wi-Fi hotspot.* ⊟ *AE, D, DC, MC, V* ¶◎¶ *EP.*

$    ☶ **Yamari Savannah Cabañas.** If Brus Laguna is secluded, then these three waterfront cabins are as far away as it gets. Stilted houses with large breezy patios overlook a placid river with swimming holes and the grassy horizon of surrounding pine savanna. Each room has four single beds, screened walls, candles, purified water, and mosquito netting; and shared bathrooms feature modern fixtures. A separate comedor dishes up breakfast, lunch, and dinner upon request. Macoy and Dorcas Wood operate the cabins and can arrange for transportation from the boat landing in Brus Laguna. **Pros:** pleasant seclusion; excellent bird-watching. **Cons:** no electricity; it's a 40-minute ride from town to get here. ✉ *Great Pine Savanna, Brus Laguna* ☎ *443–8009* ⊕ *www. larutamoskitia.com* 💬 *3 cabins* ◊ *In-hotel: restaurant, water sports* ⊟ *No credit cards* ¶◎¶ *EP.*

# LAGUNA DE CARATASCA AND EASTERN LA MOSQUITÍA

A covey of small ponds, large lakes, tiny islands, and grassy savanna stretch for 50 km (31 mi) in Laguna de Caratasca, the largest lagoon in La Mosquitía. Dense tropical rain forest and low-lying shoreline brim the murky waters near the Nicaraguan border. The shallow lagoon, which measures less than 3-m (10-feet) deep on average, draws artisanal fishermen and leisurely anglers out each morning to calmer parts of the cove. Caribbean manatee-spotting and abundant bird-watching opportunities also attract wildlife enthusiasts to Eastern Mosquitía, a natural boundary shared with Nicaragua.

## PUERTO LEMPIRA

*100 km (62 mi) southeast of Brus Laguna; 1 hour from La Ceiba by plane.*

Puerto Lempira, the capital of the Gracias a Dios department, is the closest semblance of city life in all of La Mosquitía. The town of nearly 6,000 people sits on the southeastern edge of Laguna de Caratasca on an inland islet, and residents are mostly Ladinos or indigenous Miskitos. Shrimping and small-scale fishing comprise most of the industry in the region's economic center, along with government administration jobs. MOPAWI, a Miskito development organization, also has its office here.

The airport makes Puerto Lempira a popular transit hub for connecting flights into Nicaragua and mainland Honduras, and many charter planes head deep into La Mosquitía from here. A crop of decent hotels, convenience stores, a bank, and Internet access lend the town a touch of modernity, although travelers rarely come to visit the city itself. Those who do stay often arrive to volunteer with the various development and environmental projects taking place in the region. Nearby Miskito villages Mistruk and Kaukira, however, do afford pleasant freshwater fishing trips and relaxing beach escapes, and it's easy to bike there from the city center on dirt roads (as paved ones haven't quite caught on).

### GETTING HERE AND AROUND

Reaching Puerto Lempira over land poses quite the challenge, so most travelers opt to arrive (or leave) by plane. Aerolíneas Sosa and SAMI/ Aerocaribe Honduras both have offices in town and at the airport. Sosa flies from La Ceiba at 6 AM Monday to Saturday, and return flights leave at 8 AM. SAMI leaves La Ceiba at 6:30 AM Monday to Saturday and returns from Puerto Lempira around 9 AM.

### SAFETY

Organized crime does exist in connection to La Mosquitía's budding role in the hemispheric drug trade, but the town is still sufficiently safe for visitors. Heavy flooding on unpaved roads during the rainy season can be dangerous terrain for drivers.

### MONEY MATTERS

One of Puerto Lempira's biggest attractions is the bank. Though it doesn't have an ATM, Banco Atlántida will exchange traveler's checks for lempiras and issue cash advances on Visa cards. As with the rest of the region, most establishments do not accept credit or debit cards.

### EXPLORING

Canoes traverse back and forth across intricate waterways in Laguna de Caratasca, shuttling fishermen to their daily catch and adventurers along the vast savanna landscape. Visitors can hire private water taxis from the town's edge for sightseeing excursions or to stop by a Miskito community for a day of total seclusion.

**Mistruk.** This tiny village of 400 people makes for a tranquil day trip to the Laguna de Tansing, just 18 km (11 mi) south of Puerto Lempira. Shady beaches ring the lagoon, whose freshwater attracts lots of waterfowl; head here for great bird-watching. Taxis from the city charge around $40 round-trip, although the journey is also enjoyable on two wheels (weather permitting). Informal bike shops in Puerto Lempira should charge under $10 for daily rentals. If your afternoon escape turns into an overnight, a string of family-run bungalows in town ($) provide basic accommodations with private baths.

**Kaukira.** Sport fishing and bird watching draw a handful of travelers out to this isolated town on the northeast side of Laguna de Caratasca. Snapper, snook, and tarpon fish flood the lagoon surrounding this beachfront community. Colectivo boats leave for Kaukira from Puerto Lempira's main dock every day (except Sunday) around 10 AM. Boats charge L120 for the hour-long trip, and colectivo taxis in Kaukira should cost L20 a ride. Return trips, however, are less guaranteed.

Before taking off, check at the docks if an afternoon service from Kaukira to Puerto Lempira is expected to run. If not, private expreso boats charge around L2,000 one way. Puerto Lempira native Ralston Haylock is a respected tour guide who can arrange trips to Kaukira and runs a basic lodge there for overnight visitors. His contact number (☎ 504/433-6081) is for a community telephone and is often hard to reach. Your best bet to find him is to ask around town.

## WHERE TO EAT

$ ✕ **Kabu Payaska Restaurant.** Puerto Lempirans call this quaint seafood
HONDURAN restaurant the best around the lagoon. At times it's also the busiest, particularly in the evenings, so be ready for the possibility of a slight wait for the delicious food. ⊠ *Calle Principal, a block north of the municipal dock, Barrio El Centro, Puerto Lempira* ☎ *433–6341 or 433–6615* ▤ *no credit cards.*

$ ✕ **Lakou Payaska.** The Lakou Payaska restaurant opposite Hotel Yu Bai-
HONDURAN wan has been a culinary staple in Puerto Lempira for years. The kitchen offers standard fried chicken dishes as well as lobster, conch, and shrimp served with the ubiquitous rice and beans. ⊠ *Calle Principal, Barrio El CentroPuerto Lempira* ☎ *9568–2142* ▤ *no credit cards.*

## WHERE TO STAY

$ ▦ **Hotel Kabu Payaska.** Comfortable single, double, and triple rooms have private baths, and for the best seafood in town you need only stumble downstairs, but the rooms have no air-conditioning and noise from the restaurant can travel at night. **Pros:** tasty on-site seafood joint; waterfront. **Cons:** evening crowds can get loud. ⊠ *Calle Principal, a block north of the municipal dock, Bo. Punta Fría* ☎ *433-6341 or 433-6615* ◛ *17 rooms* ◊ *In-room: no a/c. In-hotel: restaurant.* ▤ *No credit cards.*

$ ▦ **Hotel Lino.** Unlike the other hotels in Puerto Lempira, this hotel is found further in town and away from the lagoon, giving it a quieter and safer atmosphere. Simple accommodations include single, double, and triple rooms with air-conditioning and private baths. Guests can charge the hotel bill to Visa cards at the gift shop downstairs. **Pros:** rooms are quiet and have a/c. **Cons:** no waterfront vistas here. ⊠ *behind the Mercado Municipal, Bo. El Centro* ☎ *433-6675* ✎ *arlandlino@yahoo.com* ◛ *12 rooms* ◊ *In-room: a/c.* ▤ *V.*

$$–$$$ ▦ **Hotel Pinares.** Air-conditioned rooms with WiFi, plus a front desk that takes Visa cards, make this lagoon-front hotel the most modern lodging option in town. Single, double, and triple rooms with private baths are available, and guests can opt for 24-hour a/c or save a few hundred lempiras and use it only at night (or, save even more cash and stick with just the fan). Rooms are fairly quiet at night, as the hotel is a short walk from town center. A small restaurant serves seafood and traditional Honduran dishes. **Pros:** rooms have a/c and Wi-Fi; the hotel accepts Visa cards; waterfront. **Cons:** most expensive hotel in town. ⊠ *Calle Principal, Barrio San Francisco* ☎ *433-6679 or 433-6682* ⊕ *www.hotelpinareshn.com* ◛ *19 rooms* ◊ *In-room: a/c, Wi-Fi. In-hotel: restaurant, 2 pools.* ▤ *V.*

7

$    ⊡ **Hotel Yu Baiwan.** Situated on the lagoon, the hotel has single and double rooms with either air-conditioning units or fans. Its convenient central location and nearby Laku Payaska restaurant can make for noisy nights during busy weekends, however. **Pros:** good restaurant and downtown location; waterfront. **Cons:** noisy at night. ⊠ *Calle Principal, right off the municipal dock, Barrio El Centro* ☎ *9568–2142* ⊄ *16 rooms* ⟡ *In-room: a/c (some). In-hotel: restaurant* ▤ *No credit cards.*

# Side Trips to Nicaragua

**WORD OF MOUTH**

"Nobody ever mentions Nicaragua, the true vacation destination. Nicaragua, known as the land of lakes and volcanoes, can offer everything from beaches, active and nonactive volcanoes, markets, colonial cities and much more."

—Rudynica

Updated by
Jeffrey Van
Fleet

Nicaragua's fractured past and historic lack of visitors have left it in a bit of a time warp. But that's exactly a strong selling point according to Nicaragua's growing number of fans. Ever-increasing visitor numbers mean the facilities they seek (snazzy hotels, yummy restaurants, wireless Internet) are ever-increasing, too, but for the moment, you'll experience an exhilarating feeling of standing on the edge, of being in on a secret the rest of the world has not yet uncovered.

*"Si pequeña es la patria, uno grande la sueña,"* read the words on Nicaragua's 100-córdoba bill. Poet laureate Rubén Darío knew his country well when he made this statement: "If your homeland is small, you imagine it large." This New York State–sized nation of 5 million people has played a role in history completely out of proportion to its size. A turbulent past, cold war politics, and natural disasters grabbed late-20th-century headlines.

But the past is mostly the past here, much to everyone's relief, and a new generation of travelers is discovering a new Nicaragua. You can, too; the northern part of the country is easily reached from Honduras. Nicaragua now has a genuine interest in showing itself off to the world. The country has simplified entry requirements, streamlined banking procedures, opened new lodgings of all stripes, and taken a Madison Avenue–approach to marketing itself. And more than two decades of peace haven't hurt either.

That said, what goes around always comes around in Nicaragua, and separating the country and its history and politics into their component parts is rarely possible. That's especially true now that Daniel Ortega and the Sandinistas, who led the overthrow of the hated Somoza dictatorship in 1979 and ruled during the disordered 1980s, came back to power in 2007. (Democratic elections, rather than revolution, ushered Ortega and Company into office this time around.) Reaction has been mixed, but everyone expects this tenure to be different, especially now that the genie of capitalism is out of the bottle and has no intention of going back inside.

Nicaragua remains one of those glass-half-empty or glass-half-full places. Though conditions are improving all the time, it's not always smooth sailing for travelers if you venture too far off the beaten path. But that Nicaragua functions as well as it does, given its unusual history, is a tribute to the determination of its citizens. Today you'll find an economically struggling but remarkably friendly country, where travelers are still rare enough to incite curiosity in many places.

## TOP REASONS TO GO

**Arts and Markets.** Great buys can be had all over Nicaragua, but the best shopping town is Masaya, Nicaragua's artisan and folklore center, halfway between Managua and Granada. A lively, scruffy market competes with a more sterile but easier-to-navigate shopping complex, one of the country's most popular day excursions. In both places, look for shoes, leather goods, hammocks, pottery, and paintings—the country is full of artists making lively, colorful, primitivist-style paintings.

**Colonial Towns.** Liberal León, founded in 1524, has kept its architectural heritage largely intact and is one of Latin America's lesser-known but better-preserved colonial cities. León did suffer some damage during the revolution and the Contra war, but it is lovingly restoring its architectural treasures and is making a valiant effort to make up for lost time.

**National Parks and Volcanoes.** Some 18% of Nicaragua's territory is set aside in 76 protected areas with designations such as "national park" or "wildlife reserve," but few have any facilities for visitors. The most visited is Volcán Masaya National Park, which includes the volcano's multiple craters and Lake Masaya. Several other areas have unofficial park or reserve status, and will probably be "upgraded" at some point; these include the volcanoes on Ometepe Island—Madera and Concepción—and Volcán Mombacho, outside Granada.

# ORIENTATION AND PLANNING

8

## ORIENTATION

Most of the country's population inhabits the largely deforested western Pacific lowlands. Highways and public transportation are excellent in the corridor that runs from the Honduran border to León and south. Secondary roads are sometimes potholed but passable. Nicaragua's north Pacific coast is virtually unknown in international circles. You'll see Nicaraguans from León at the beaches in this part of the country. Matagalpa anchors north-central Nicaragua's highlands, a cool respite from the year-round sweltering lowland heat.

**León.** One of Nicaragua's premier colonial cities and the country's second largest urban area proudly wears its left-wing politics on its sleeve. You can't throw a stone without hitting a colonial-era church here—not that we'd suggest trying that—and León is diligently working to restore its colonial treasures to their former glory.

**Poneloya.** Almost unknown in international circles are Nicaragua's north Pacific beaches. Poneloya is a favorite weekend destination for León residents. Come here during the week and you'll have the place to yourself.

**Volcán Momotombo.** It may seem foolhardy, but every major city in Nicaragua lies in the shadow of a volcano. The perfect cone of Momotombo is León's very own, and its ash has fertilized the soil here for centuries.

**Matagalpa.** Nicaragua's sunbaked western plains give way to the cool hills in the north-central part of the country. Matagalpa is the largest city in these "highlands"—Nicaragua's elevation never gets that high though—and anchors a fertile coffee-growing region.

### TOP ITINERARY

Five days is a good length of time to see the sights of northern Nicaragua; any shorter and you'd be doing the region a disservice. León is easily reached by international bus from Honduras. Spend a day taking in the city's colonial sights, churches, and museums. You have a choice of a couple of day trips: the Pacific-coast beach at Poneloya is a favorite weekend getaway for city residents; or a visit to the ruins of León Viejo, León's original settlement, and the Momtombo volcano can be combined into one day-long excursion. Get an early morning start the next day for Matagalpa. A half-hour north of the city is the famed Selva Negra Mountain Resort, worth a visit, or even better, worth staying the night. Return to León the next day, about a two- or three-hour drive from Matagalpa, depending on traffic.

## PLANNING

### WHEN TO GO

Nicaragua's traditional lack of visitors means there aren't well-delineated high and low seasons. The selection of decent hotels is small, making reservations a good idea year-round.

This nation's climate varies greatly between regions. The central mountains, regardless of season, remain lusciously cool and agreeable all year long. As for the rest of the country, heat reigns year-round. The wet season lasts from May to November, which is referred to here as *invierno* (winter); it usually rains at least once a day (though not for very long) during these months, and is rarely a hardship. But it can come down for days at a time in October. The climate in December and January is the coolest, least humid, and least rainy. March and April can be brutally hot.

### GETTING HERE AND AROUND

Nicaragua and Honduras form part of a Central American immigration and customs union called the CA-4, along with El Salvador and Guatemala. Entry formalities are easy and land borders are open 24 hours. Time spent in Nicaragua or any of the other countries counts toward the 90-day entry you get upon arrival in Honduras.

Your own vehicle gives you the freedom to explore at will, but it is entirely possible to do Nicaragua without a car. (Remember that rental vehicles licensed in Honduras may not cross the border into Nicaragua.) Public transportation is good, if crowded and slow the farther you get off the beaten path. Tour operators can take you almost anywhere, either on scheduled excursions, or on à la carte itineraries you arrange yourself.

## BUS TRAVEL

TicaBus has service from Tegucigalpa to Matagalpa, departing daily at 9:15 AM (5 hours, $20) and from Choluteca to León. All buses are roomy and air-conditioned, and you should buy tickets one day before your departure.

Travel by public bus in northern Nicaragua seems chaotic and disorganized, but you will get where you want to go eventually. Information about schedules and bus companies is hard to come by—you generally just show up at a bus terminal and ask which buses go to your destination. Departures are frequent, usually when the vehicle fills up. *Microbuses*, minivans that seat about 15-20 people, bop around between León and other towns in the north and make many fewer stops than the large converted U.S. school buses. (They can get crowded, though.)

León's private Tierra Tour makes daily, regularly scheduled runs south to Managua and Granada, but can arrange transfers to any destination, and provides a nice, comfortable alternative to public transport.

**Bus Contacts TicaBus** (✉ *2 blocks north of church of San Juan Subtiava, León* ☎ *505/2311–6153* ✉ *½ block west of Parque Diario, Matagalpa* ☎ *505/2772–4502*). **Tierra Tour** (✉ *1 ½ blocks north of Iglesia de la Merced, León* ☎ *2315–4278* ⊕ *www.tierratour.com*). **Transnica** (✉ *½ block west of Colegio Mercantil, León* ☎ *505/2311–5219*).

## CAR TRAVEL

Directional signage is plentiful on main highways; less so off the beaten path. Streets may have names in cities, but are rarely used, and signing is almost nonexistent. (León is the surprising exception to this rule.) Your own vehicle gives you freedom to stop and go as you please: roadside stands and *miradores* (scenic lookout points) abound, and they're nearly impossible to visit passing through on a bus. Driving at night outside cities and towns is not recommended for several reasons: there is a remote possibility of robbery, but you are more likely to run into cars without headlights and unwitting two- and four-legged pedestrians on the roads.

You can rent a car in León or Matagalpa, where C$900 to C$1,500 will get you an economy vehicle with air-conditioning and a decent daily mileage allowance. Weekly rentals can be had for as little as C$3,500 and usually include unlimited mileage. Dollar has offices in León and Matagalpa; Budget has an office in Matagalpa. You must be at least 25 years old to rent a car. Your home-country license is valid here for up to one month.

GASOLINE  Gasoline sells for C$21 to C$22 per liter. Stations are plentiful in major cities such as León and Matagalpa. Fill up there if you're heading farther afield.

ROAD  Major roads in the populated western half of the country are in good
CONDITIONS  shape, but you'll need a four-wheel-drive vehicle to negotiate most smaller roads, especially during the rainy season.

**Car-Rental Agencies Budget** (✉ *Km.126, Matagalpa* ☎ *505/2772–3041* ⊕ *www.budget.com.ni*). **Dollar** (✉ *1 block south of Enitel, Matagalpa* ☎ *505/2772–4100* ⊕ *www.dollar.com.ni* ✉ *León* ☎ *505/2311–2174*).

### TAXI TRAVEL

Distances are vast in northern Nicaragua. Taxis can be hired to travel between cities. Plan on spending about C$2,000 for about half a day.

### TOUR OPERATORS

León-based Quetzaltrekkers specializes in tours of northern Nicaragua, in particular to the ruins of León Viejo and the Momotombo volcano.

**Tour Companies Quetzaltrekkers** (☎ *505/2311–6695* ⊕ *www.quetzaltrekkers. com*).

## HEALTH AND SAFETY

Stick to bottled water everywhere in Nicaragua. The intense heat and sun make replenishment with fluids and protection with sunscreen a must.

Nicaragua has Central America's lowest crime rate, a mantra the tourism industry repeats often, but in a country where many workers make the equivalent of $3 per day, you'll represent enormous wealth. Watch your things carefully. Do not accept tours from random people you meet on the street. Always go with a verifiable tour guide who is a part of a hotel or organization (with an office and phone).

The Pacific coast beaches have strong currents and undertows, although there are no warning signs or lifeguards. Nicaragua declared itself free of land mines in 2010; nevertheless, we recommend caution in off-road northern areas near the Honduran border.

León's Hospital San Vicente is the best and largest of the city's hospitals.

## MONEY MATTERS

ATMS Large and medium-size Nicaraguan cities congregate all their downtown banks on one street that everybody colloquially refers to as the *Calle de Bancos* (Bank Street). *Cajeros automáticos* (ATMs) are becoming increasingly common in Nicaragua. Branches of Banco América Central (BAC) in León and Matagalpa have red-and-gray ATMs with a lion's head symbol and accept MasterCard/Cirrus- or Visa/Plus-linked cards. (A very few of these give cash against American Express, Diners Club, and Discover cards, too.) Bancentro branches around the country operate their own CA$H network of ATMs that accept Visa/Plus cards only. Another good bet for finding a Cirrus- or Plus-linked machine is a large Esso, Shell, or Texaco gas-station convenience store on the highways heading out of León.

CURRENCY Nicaragua's currency is the córdoba, named after Spanish explorer Francisco Hernández de Córdoba, who founded León and Granada. Locals often refer to the unit of currency as a *peso*. Bills come in 10-, 20-, 50-, 100- and 500-córdoba denominations. Coins come in 1- and 5-córdoba as well as 5, 10-, 25- and 50-centavo denominations. The currency is devalued by about 1% a month against the U.S. dollar; if you think in terms of dollars, prices do remain relatively stable in the face of local devaluation and inflation. At this writing, the U.S. dollar, the only useful foreign currency here, was equal to roughly 21 córdobas. Dollars are also accepted by some large stores, hotels, restaurants, and taxi drivers—make sure the bills are in good condition, with no marks or tears—but plan on receiving change in córdobas. For payment to smaller businesses and individuals, you should plan on dealing in local currency. Change any leftover lempiras back to dollars before leaving Honduras. No one in Nicaragua will accept or exchange them.

CREDIT CARDS   Upscale hotels and restaurants accept credit cards, Visa and MasterCard being the most widely accepted, and American Express and Diner's Club, third and fourth respectively. A growing number of places can now accept the Discover card, but may not be aware that they do. Many small businesses add up to 5% to the total if you pay by credit card to offset the high fees they're charged for card transactions.

TRAVELER'S   Traveler's checks remain difficult to cash in Nicaragua. All branches
CHECKS   of Banco América Central (BAC) will cash American Express checks for a 5% commission and a long wait. Virtually no business accepts traveler's checks as payment.

## RESTAURANTS AND CUISINE

Nicaraguans favor rice and beans with meat, fish, or chicken; salads are usually made of cabbage with tomatoes and a vinaigrette-style dressing; and rice and beans usually reappear as the ubiquitous mix of the two, *gallo pinto* (literally, spotted rooster), at breakfast the next day. Two favorite dishes are *nacatamales,* corn tamales filled with chicken or pork, and *vigorón,* pork rind and cabbage served with steamed yuca. Near the coast, fresh fish is abundant and relatively cheap. It is usually served smothered in garlic (*al ajillo*) or tomato sauce (*entomatado*).

Flor de Caña, some of the best rum in the world, is produced near Chinandega: C$70 gets you a big bottle. Victoria and Toña are the two locally brewed beers. (Each beer has its own devoted fans, and a "Which is better?" question often results in passionate debate.)

If you're headed farther south in Nicaragua, Managua and Granada have seen an invasion of upscale restaurants in recent years. In the rest of the country, you'll likely eat with locals at a basic dining establishment called a *comedor* or *cafetín.* Even in the most expensive places, dining is an informal affair, and reservations are rarely required or needed.

MEALTIMES   Upscale or slightly formal restaurants usually serve lunch until 3 PM, then reopen again for dinner at 6 PM. Comedores and eating places frequented by locals are generally open all day but rarely serve an evening meal.

## HOTELS

León has a small selection of decent accommodations, but the choice of hostelry is limited in the rest of northern Nicaragua, where extremely basic *hospedajes* (lodgings) are most common. The biggest growth spurt in Nicaragua has come in smaller, medium-range, family-owned boutique hotels, where spending C$700 to C$1,200 buys you a night in some downright charming places. The reality is that there are too few hotel rooms in this part of the country to meet the growing demand. Reservations are always a good idea, no matter what the time of year.

| WHAT IT COSTS IN NICARAGUAN CÓRDOBAS | | | | | |
|---|---|---|---|---|---|
| | ¢ | $ | $$ | $$$ | $$$$ |
| RESTAURANTS | under C$70 | C$70–130 | C$131–C$175 | C$176–C$205 | over C$205 |
| HOTELS | under C$700 | C$700–C$1,200 | C$1,201–C$1,700 | C$1,701–C$2,200 | over C$2,200 |

Restaurant prices are per person for a main course at dinner. Hotel prices are for two people in a standard double room in high season.

# NORTHERN NICARAGUA

The vast, lavish geography of the northwestern lowlands and the central highlands will give you plenty to write home about. The lowlands are dotted with volcanoes—some of which are still active—that make for excellent hikes. To the west, on the sprawling beaches of the Pacific coast, lie Nicaragua's most overlooked (and underdeveloped) areas. You'll have the beaches to yourself (except during Holy Week), and the surfing here is decent year-round. León, the largest city north of Managua, pulsates with the energy emanating from Nicaragua's largest intellectual center, the Universidad Nacional Autónoma de Nicaragua. As you make your way across the prolific lowlands by way of the broken, winding highways, the stifling heat gradually diminishes. The *cordilleras* (mountain ranges) of Isabelia and Dariense tower invitingly ahead.

This coffee-growing region has historically attracted farmers who tattoo the land with a symmetrical patchwork of agricultural plots. Flocks of European settlers who immigrated here in the late 1800s left an indelible imprint: peculiar pockets of brawny, befreckled men and their families are hidden away in the deep valleys of the highest mountains. Many people make the effort to come up here just to visit the Selva Negra Mountain Resort, a 1,400-acre lot of jungly land that's blessed with an almost dizzying mixture of plants, flowers, and wildlife.

The north has always been far to the left on the political pendulum—witness León's baseball stadium, named *Héroes y Mártires* (Heroes and Martyrs) rather than simply for a well-known ball figure as elsewhere in Nicaragua. These areas were badly bruised during the revolution and Contra war years. Vestiges of these battles can still be seen today. Yet even here, most of the famous, once-ubiquitous, socialist-realist revolutionary murals have been painted over with advertisements for Pepsi and other U.S. products, a more lucrative use of the space.

## LEÓN

*93 km (56 mi) northwest of Managua.*

León means "lion" in Spanish, and the country's second largest city has always exerted a lionlike presence on Nicaraguan history. As one of Latin America's most prominent colonial cities, León played an influential role in the commercial and intellectual life of Spanish America. Some of the greatest figures in the country's literature and politics lived

# A BIT OF HISTORY: NICARAGUA

The future looks decent for Nicaragua, but then history was rarely kind to this country. Columbus claimed this territory for the Spanish crown in 1502, eventually paving the way for two major colonial settlements, both founded in 1524: Granada, on the shore of Lake Nicaragua in the south, and León, in the northern lowlands. Granada, which had access to the Atlantic via the Río San Juan, continued to prosper as a trading and commercial center, but León didn't fare as well. The longtime rivalry between intellectual, liberal León and wealthy, conservative Granada set the stage for a century and a half of turbulence.

Anastasio Somoza took control in 1935, the first of the three Somozas who would rule the country courtesy of a personal army, the Guardia Nacional (National Guard), for the next 44 years. The Somoza family appropriated for itself most of Nicaragua's prime property and commercial interests, while the country itself remained mired in poverty.

A popular revolution in 1979 toppled the Somoza dynasty and put in place the revolutionary government of Daniel Ortega and the Frente Sandinista de Liberación Nacional (Sandinista National Liberation Front), or

FSLN. The U.S. government, fearful of the Sandinistas' growing rapprochement with the Soviet bloc, supported an insurgence of *contrarevolucionarios* (Contras), supporters of the former Somoza government, keeping the country in conflict for the next decade. Exhausted by war and fed up with the nearly universally despised Sandinista military draft and curtailment of freedoms, Nicaragua voted in a series of conservative, business-backed governments in democratic elections starting in 1990.

But what goes around comes around, and Ortega and the Sandinistas were voted back into office in 2006. Ortega—his diehard fans still refer to him as Comandante Daniel—has raised eyebrows with state visits to Cuba, Iran, Libya, and Venezuela, and you'll do a double take at ubiquitous billboards showing Ortega's image. But these are not the 1980s. Ortega has taken great pains to reassure business leaders that he has no intention of dismantling post-1990 economic reforms. Nicaragua is now party to the Central American Free-Trade Agreement with the United States and a similar agreement with the European Union, inked in 2010.

or studied here, including the venerated poet Rubén Darío and such prominent Sandinistas as Sílvio Rodríguez, Tomás Borges, and FSLN founder Carlos Fonseca.

Present-day León sits 24 km (15 mi) west of its original location on the northwest shore of Lake Managua. Founded in 1524, the city was destroyed in 1609 by an earthquake caused by the eruption of nearby Volcán Momotombo. (That locale is now the site of the ruins of León Viejo—"Old León.") The survivors moved west and settled next to the village of the indigenous Subtiava people. The village still stands today, retaining much of its folklore, and León has happily incorporated those traditions as its own today.

## GETTING HERE AND AROUND

León comes close to approximating a modern city—there are street names and everything—but Leonenses, like most Nicaraguans, give directions based on distances from landmarks. Like many Nicaraguans, folks here designate "west" as *abajo* ("down"—the sun goes down, after all) and "east" as *arriba* ("up," as in the sun coming up.) Fortunately, the city is laid out

> ## THE NICAS
>
> Forget for a minute the Spanish grammatical rule about masculine words ending in *o* and feminine words ending in *a*. The invariable term *Nica*, a shortened form of *Nicaragüense*, serves as noun or adjective, no matter what is being referred to.

as a grid, with calles running east–west and avenidas north–south. The baseline is the intersection of Calle Central Rubén Darío and Avenida Central, at the northeast corner of Parque Central, in front of the cathedral. Most sights are an easy walk from Parque Central.

León's bus terminal, a dusty field adjoining a market, sits about 1 km (½ mi) northeast of downtown on 6 Calle NE, at Avenida 8 NE. Express minivans leave for various points around the region and are faster than the large converted U.S. school buses used for many routes.

León's downtown is easily navigated on foot, but for farther distances taxis are ubiquitous and inexpensive. A trip from the bus terminal to the city center runs C$15.

## MONEY MATTERS

Several banks cluster on the corner of Calle 1 Norte and Avenida 1 Oriente, one block north of the cathedral; they'll change U.S. dollars weekdays 8:30 to noon and 2 to 4, Saturday 8:30 to 11:30. Banco América Central (BAC) changes American Express traveler's checks. Find ATMs at BAC (MasterCard/Cirrus and Visa/Plus) and Bancentro (Visa/Plus only).

## VISITOR INFORMATION

The Instituto Nicaragüense de Turismo (INTUR) operates a tourist information office downtown with a helpful, friendly staff. The Oficina de Información Turística, a joint effort of the municipal government and a group of enthusiastic university students, serves as a tourist information office that keeps longer hours than INTUR's.

## ESSENTIALS

**Banks Bancentro** (⊠ *1 block north of the cathedral* ☎ *311–0991*). **Banco América Central** (*BAC* ⊠ *Esquina de los Bancos* ☎ *311–7247*).

**Emergency Services Ambulance** (☎ *505/2311–2627*). **Fire** (☎ *505/2311–2323*). **Hospital San Vicente** (⊠ *1 block south of cathedral* ☎ *505/2311–6990*). **Police** (☎ *505/2311–3137*).

**Tourist Information Instituto Nicaragüense de Turismo** (*INTUR* ⊠ *Avda. 2 NO and C. 2 NO* ☎ *505/2311–3682* ☾ *Weekdays 9–noon*). **Oficina de Información Turística** (⊠ *Avda. 2 Poniente, next to El Sesteo* ☎ *505/2311–3528* ☾ *Weekdays 8–noon and 2–6, Sat. 9–5, Sun. 9–noon*).

## EXPLORING

### TOP ATTRACTIONS

**Catedral de la Asunción.** Taking up an entire city block, León's massive cathedral is the largest church in Central America. The 1747 structure—the building was not completed until 1860—is actually the fourth church to sit on the site. Tradition holds that the architect submitted a smaller, less grandiose blueprint to the Spanish crown, fearing that Spain would nix his real intentions. Construction was funded through the sale of tombs in seven cellars lying underneath the cathedral, an option that prominent residents of the day eagerly snapped up. Despite the fierce fighting that gripped León during the 1979 revolution—Anastasio Somoza ordered the city bombed—the hardy cathedral remained intact. Inside, the high arches and heavy columns lend a feeling of indestructibility. Paintings of the Stations of the Cross by artist Antonio Sarra adorn the huge walls. Look for the tomb of poet Rubén Darío at the foot of the statue of St. Paul, to the right of the altar. A stone lion, representing the city of León, mourns atop the grave. Admission to the church itself is free; a C$40 tour—it's in Spanish only—takes you to three of the catacomb-like cellars and to the roof with its 34 domes and stupendous views of the city. ⊠ *Calle Central Rubén Darío and Avenida 1 Poniente* ☎ *No phone* 🖃 *Free; tour of roof and cellars C$40* ☺ *Mon.–Sat. 8–noon and 2–4.*

**Fodor's** Choice
★
**Centro de Arte Fundación Ortiz-Gurdián.** León holds the distinction of housing Nicaragua's finest art museum (and one of Latin America's most prominent collections). Two restored 18th century houses, across the street from each other, hold that proverbial treasure trove of colonial, modern, and contemporary art. Most are by Nicaraguan and other Latin American artists, but you'll find paintings by Picasso, Rubens, Chagall, and Rivera as well. The gallery is a project of the nearby Hotel El Convento, and should be on your "don't miss" list if you're here in León. Your admission price lets you wander the exhibits on your own. A guided tour, for now in Spanish only, costs approximately an extra nominal dollar, and is worthwhile for an added understanding of the works on display here. ⊠ *Across from San Francisco church, 2 blocks west of Parque Central* ☎ *505/2311–7225* 🖃 *C$20; free Sun.; guided tour, C$40* ☺ *Tues.–Sat. 10:30–6:30, Sun. 11–7.*

### WORTH NOTING

**Casa Popular de Cultura.** This small arts museum, with whimsical business hours—you'll just have to try your luck—contains a tiny collection of paintings by local artists. ⊠ *1 block north and 1½ blocks west of the northwest corner of Parque Central* ☎ *No phone* 🖃 *Free.*

**Centro Sandinista de Trabajadores.** The first of the Somozas met his demise at what is now the Sandinista party headquarters. There is little to see inside, but a plaque on the facade commemorates the dictator's assassination in 1956 at the hands of the poet Rigoberto López Pérez, who posed as a waiter at a government reception. (López himself was immediately shot and killed by Somoza's guards). ⊠ *1 block west and 1½ blocks north of Parque Central's northwest corner* ☎ *No phone* 🖃 *Free* ☺ *Weekdays 8–5.*

**Galería de Héroes y Mártires.** Both unabashedly political and hauntingly moving, the Gallery of Heroes and Martyrs documents in photos the history of the troubled 1970s and 1980s with a focus on 300 area young men who gave their lives fighting for the Sandinistas. The museum, with exhibits labeled in English and Spanish, is maintained by a group of their mothers. No matter what your politics, the lost youth of most of the subjects portrayed will break your heart. ✉ *1 Avda. NO and 1 C. NE* ☎ *No phone* ✇ *C$20* ☾ *Mon.–Sat. 7–5.*

**Iglesia de La Recolección.** The city's most ornate church is the 1786 La Recolección, with its dark-yellow, baroque facade and carvings depicting Christ's betrayal and crucifixion. Note the beautiful mahogany woodwork inside the church. ✉ *2½ blocks north of back of the cathedral* ☎ *No phone* ✇ *Free* ☾ *Mon.–Sat. 8–noon and 2–4.*

**Iglesia de El Calvario.** The neoclassical El Calvario has three macabre renditions of the Crucifixion and a plaque honoring five anti-Somoza protesters killed here by the National Guard in February 1979. Historians disagree on the date of the church's construction—it probably was built in the late 17th century—but all agree that it is one of the country's most beautiful houses of worship. ✉ *4 blocks from Parque Central, at the end of Calle Real* ☎ *No phone* ✇ *Free* ☾ *Mon.–Sat. 8–noon and 2–4.*

**Iglesia de San Francisco.** This 1643 rococo-style church is the birthplace of Nicaragua's Purísima (Feast of the Immaculate Conception) traditions. The facade you see is actually a 1960 reconstruction. Of course, the convent seemingly attached seamlessly to the church is the Hotel El Convento, constructed in 2000. ✉ *2 blocks west of Parque Central* ☎ *No phone* ✇ *Free* ☾ *Mon.–Sat. 8–noon and 2–4.*

**Iglesia de San Juan Bautista de Subtiava.** About 11 blocks west of Parque Central lives a community of the indigenous Subtiava people, whose ancestors were here long before Columbus arrived. Their original parish church, dating from 1698, still stands, along with the ruins of the even older church of Vera Cruz, which was destroyed by a volcanic eruption in 1835. An adjoining museum documents the history of the community. Semana Santa (Holy Week) is the most colorful time to visit, when residents create an exquisitely beautiful trail of sawdust drawings on the main streets that is then trampled by a procession carrying images of Christ's Passion. ✉ *11 blocks west of Parque Central* ✇ *Free; Museum C$40* ☾ *Daily 8:30–11:30.*

**Museo de Leyendas y Tradiciones.** Arguably León's (and Nicaragua's) quirkiest sight is this museum dedicated to the country's legends and traditions. You can learn about the country's Purísima traditions that celebrate the Feast of the Immaculate Conception as well as all manner of spirit figures that populate Nicaraguan folklore. That part is all well and good. The complex served as a notorious prison during the years of the Somoza dictatorship, however, and interspersed with the folklore displays are exhibits documenting the torture of prisoners that took place here until 1979. The juxtaposition is bizarrely fascinating and somewhat disturbing. ✉ *3 blocks south of Parque Central* ☎ *505/2311–2116* ✇ *C$20* ☾ *Tues.–Sat. 8–noon and 2–5, Sun. 8–noon.*

8

## RELIGION AND REVOLUTION

Nicaragua's major festivals commemorate faith or politics, the two aspects of its life the nation wears on its sleeve. The entire country operates at half speed during **Semana Santa,** the Holy Week preceding Easter in March or April, and closes down completely Thursday and Friday of that week. Don't plan on transacting any business that week as seemingly everyone with means leaves for vacation. León is the place to be if you're not joining the rest of the crowds who flock to the beaches. The city decorates its streets with colored sawdust designs depicting religious scenes. These are then trampled under the foot of elaborate Good Friday processions.

July 19 is **Revolution Day** in Nicaragua, celebrating the 1979 fall of the Somoza dictatorship. The Sandinistas put on rallies in most communities; León and Matagalpa host two of the largest. Supporters deck out in red-and-black Sandinista bandanas—though these days you'll see some designer jeans and Winnie-the-Pooh T-shirts among the crowd as well—listen to speeches by party leaders, sing revolutionary songs, and throw back a few beers.

The year's most joyous celebration, the **Purísima,** or Feast of the Immaculate Conception, is observed in Nicaragua on December 8, and, if you're here, makes a wonderful way to kick off your holiday season. The festivities start the night before, when crowds parade through the streets, most elaborately in León and Granada. They stop at homes, enacting the age-old ritual known as the *gritería,* shouting, *"¿Quién causa tanta alegría?"* (Who causes so much joy?) The response from those who emerge from their homes? *"¡La concepción de María!"* (The Immaculate Conception of Mary!)

**Museo y Archivo Rubén Darío.** The name Rubén Darío (1867–1916) may be fairly obscure in the English-speaking world, but throughout Nicaragua and Latin America it commands instant respect. Rubén Darío, Nicaragua's favorite son and poet laureate, became a leader of Latin American poetry's modernist movement, which rebelled against the ponderous, repetitive verse in vogue at the time. Darío was also famous for his stormy personal life, battling alcoholism, and carrying on a series of indiscreet affairs. The museum, in the house where Darío spent his boyhood, includes personal effects and a plaster death mask made shortly after the great poet died. If you're interested in Latin American literature, a visit here is a must. ⊠ *3 blocks west of the northwest corner of Parque Central* ☎ *505/2311–2388* 🖃 *Donation requested* ☉ *Tues.– Sat. 8:30–noon and 2–5, Sun. 8:30–noon.*

**Universidad Nacional Autónoma de Nicaragua.** The National Autonomous University of Nicaragua dominates the city geographically and politically. The country's largest institution of higher education was founded in 1912, and sprawls amorphously north of the city center. Though not specifically geared toward sightseeing, the UNAN's bookstores, cafés, and ubiquitous copy shops give León that college-town feel, Nicaragua style. ⊕ *www.unanleon.edu.ni.*

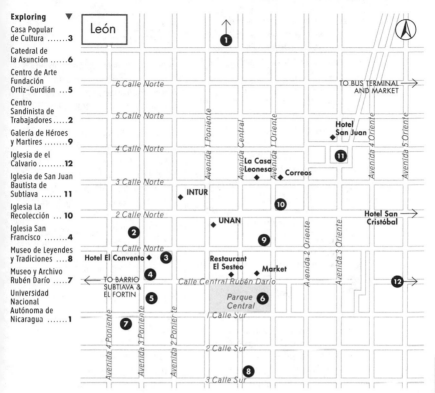

## WHERE TO EAT

Elegant dining is not León's forte, but as in any college town you'll never go hungry here. Join the throngs of university students for a quick bite or snack at the eateries dotting the city.

$ ✕ **Restaurante El Sesteo.** An indoor gallery of portraits of Nicaraguan

CAFÉ literary figures greets you at this Leonense institution, but opt for one of the pleasant outdoor tables overlooking the Parque Central instead. They make this the place to hang out for hours, late into the evening. The main dishes are a bit pricey, but the tasty ham or chicken sandwiches, amazing club sandwiches, and banana splits are all bargains. ⊠ *East side of Parque Central* ☎ *505/2311–5327* ▭ *AE, D, DC, MC, V.*

## WHERE TO STAY

$$$$ 🏨 **Hotel El Convento.** León's most sumptuous lodging was built only in

Fodor'sChoice 2000 in the style of the former San Francisco convent, and blends

★ seamlessly with the church next door. Covered interior walkways loop around a large garden and its bubbling centerpiece fountain. The owners have collected 30 years' worth of antiques that furnish the common areas and private rooms. Each tiled room has its own balcony. **Pros:** lovely furnishings; distinctive atmosphere; good restaurant. **Cons:** popular, so book ahead. ⊠ *C. Rubén Darío, 3 blocks west of cathedral* ☎ *505/2311–7053* ⊕ *www.elconventonicaragua.com* ↻ *31 rooms, 1* suite ⌂ *In-room: a/c, refrigerator, Wi-Fi. In-hotel: restaurant, room service, bar, laundry service, Internet terminal, parking (free).* ⊟ *AE, D, DC, MC, V* ⵏ⊙ⵏ *BP.*

$ ⌸ **Hotel San Crístóbal.** About 1 km (½ mi) outside the city limits on the bypass highway, the San Crístóbal is a cool, spacious alternative to the lodgings in town, but just a 10-minute taxi ride away. It opened in 2000, but is built in old Nicaragua style, around a courtyard with a central fountain. Modern tiled rooms are simply furnished with wood furniture and flowered drapes and bedspreads. The lower-floor restaurant specializes in Italian cuisine. **Pros:** quiet location; good value. **Cons:** outside town so need a car to stay here. ⊠ *Carretera Bypass, next to Tropigas* ☎ *505/ 2311–1606* ⊕ *www.sancristobalhotel.com* ⤳ *30 rooms* ⌂ *In-room: a/c, Wi-Fi. In-hotel: restaurant, room service, bar, pool, laundry service, Internet terminal, parking (free).* ⊟ *AE, MC, V* ⵏ⊙ⵏ *EP.*

> ### A NOTE ON ELECTRICITY
>
> Periodic power outages are an annoying fact of life in Nicaragua as the country struggles to upgrade its aging energy grid. (You'll learn the word for a blackout: *apagón*.) Higher-end lodgings usually have generators; smaller places may not. Ask. Remember: no electricity means no air-conditioning, no fan, and, sometimes, no water. (Electricity powers water pumps in many places here.) Restaurants that cook with gas stoves can stay open during power outages. Resign yourself to a romantic candlelight dinner if that happens.

$–$$ ⌸ **Hotel San Juan de León.** Rooms are small but comfortable with wood furniture at this lodging near the San Juan church, several blocks north of downtown. Rates include breakfast on the common upstairs balcony. For the rest of your meals, you have access to shared kitchen facilities. **Pros:** access to kitchen facilities if you want to cook; good value. **Cons:** small rooms; several blocks north of city center. ⊠ *North side of Parque San Juan* ☎ *505/2311–0547* ⊕ *www.hsanjuandeleon.com* ⤳ *20 rooms* ⌂ *In-room: a/c (some), Wi-Fi. In-hotel: restaurant, pool, laundry service, parking (free).* ⊟ *AE, D, DC, MC, V* ⵏ⊙ⵏ *CP.*

$ ⌸ **La Casa Leonesa.** An 18th-century home just north of downtown has been converted into one of León's nicest lodgings, a step down from the nearby El Convento, but a very good value. Rooms congregate around a leafy garden with a small pool, and are decorated with wrought-iron furniture, tile floors, and religious art. **Pros:** cozy rooms; good value. **Cons:** several blocks north of city center. ⊠ *3 blocks north and ¼ block east of cathedral* ☎ *505/2311–0551* ⊕ *www.casaleonesa.com* ⤳ *8 rooms* ⌂ *In-room: a/c, Wi-Fi. In-hotel: restaurant, pool, laundry service, Internet terminal.* ⊟ *AE, MC, V* ⵏ⊙ⵏ *BP.*

## NIGHTLIFE

The **Casa Popular de Cultura** (⊠ *1 block north and 1½ blocks west of the northwest corner of Parque Central*) hosts cultural events some evenings. **Tertulias Leonesas** (*León Social Gatherings*) is a weekly celebration with music and food on the Parque Central each Saturday evening from 6 to midnight.

## OUTDOOR ACTIVITIES

León-based **Quetzaltrekkers** (✉ *1½ blocks east of La Recolección church* ☎ *505/2311–6695* ⊕ *www. quetzaltrekkers.com*) leads guided excursions to many points in northern Nicaragua, including half-day tours to Volcán Momotombo that set out before dawn and also take in a visit to the ruins of León Viejo. Other reliable guides can be arranged through the INTUR office or your hotel for visits to Momotombo or León Viejo, but you'll be expected to provide a vehicle. Fully escorted excursions to these sites can also be arranged through a tour operator in Managua.

Poneloya is the favorite Leónense beach, about a half-hour west of the city on the Pacific coast.

### TALKING POLITICS

No question: Nicaraguan politics get lively, and many people here love a spirited discussion about the direction the country should take. If your Spanish is up to the task, don't be afraid to listen in, but it's best done outside the confines of the local cantina. Do let your acquaintances take the lead in the discussion, and avoid lapsing into a "This is what I think your country should do" stance; you'll be amply rewarded with some amazing insights. And U.S. citizens need not worry: despite past stormy Nicaraguan-American relations, few people here harbor any animosity against the United States.

## VOLCÁN MOMOTOMBO

*29 km (17 mi) east of León.*

The near-perfect cone of this volcano—which is best known as the subject of a famous Rubén Darío poem—rises 4,000 feet over the western shore of Lake Managua, and is visible from as far away as the capital. Access is by a bumpy dirt road (which turns muddy in the rainy season) that starts just south of the village of La Paz Centro on the León–Managua highway; look for the sign reading ORMAT MOMOTOMBO, the name of the Israeli-built geothermal plant on the volcano's lower slopes that supplies almost 10% of the country's power. To get here, take one of the buses headed toward Managua and get off at La Paz Centro. From La Paz Centro you can take one of the public-transport trucks to Puerto Momotombo. Technically, you're supposed to have a pass to venture near the power plant. A León- or Managua-based tour operator can take care of all the necessary paperwork for you if you go on one of their guided tours, a far easier option than trying to tend to those details on your own. If you plan to visit on your own, to secure a pass, visit the **Empresa Nicaragüense de Electricidad (ENEL) office** (✉ *1 block north of Casa Nazareth* ☎ *266–8756*) in Managua's Barrio Martha Quezada. The reward for your troubles, and the arduous four-hour climb, will be a stunning view of the lake and the surrounding country.

8

# LEÓN VIEJO

*24 km (15 mi) east of León.*

An interesting day trip from *new* León, the ruined city of León Viejo (Old León) was one of the first two Spanish settlements in Nicaragua. (Granada was the other.) The city was the capital of Spain's colonial province in Nicaragua until a 1610 earthquake, triggered by Volcán Momotombo, leveled it. Now that parts have been excavated—the site was not discovered until 1967, after several false leads—you can make out the cathedral and the central plaza in front of it. In 2000 León Viejo was named a UNESCO World Heritage Site—Nicaragua's first. The ruins suffered severe damage during 1998's Hurricane Mitch. Much-needed restoration is nearly complete at this writing. Your admission price includes a guided tour in Spanish only, but you will find signage in English. Most León- or Managua-based tour operators include excursions to León Viejo among their offerings. Many of the tours also take in a visit to Momotombo. ⊠ *3 km (2 mi) east of La Paz Centro, then 15 km (9 mi) northeast* ▦ *C$45* ☉ *Daily 8–4.*

# PONELOYA

*23 km (14 mi) west of León.*

One of the nicer beaches in Nicaragua, Poneloya is an easy day trip from León. The beach will be yours and yours alone during the week; weekends and holidays, especially Holy Week, are quite another story. Swimmers should be careful of the strong undertow. The seafood restaurants along the beach offer big plates of *camarones al ajillo* (garlic shrimp) for about C$100. Make the beach a day trip; you'll find only very basic accommodations here.

**GETTING HERE AND AROUND**
The road to the coast from León, although short in distance, is badly potholed. Expect the drive to take about an hour. Buses leave throughout the day from the market in León's Subtiava neighborhood.

**SAFETY**
Along this sector of Pacific coast, the waves are big and the undertow is wicked. Unless you've come here to surf, your day at the beach is best spent literally on the beach rather than in the water.

**EN ROUTE** Nicaragua has three border crossings with Honduras: Las Manos (near Ocotal) and El Espino (near Somoto)—both are north of Matagalpa and Estelí—and El Guasaule, beyond Chinandega north of León. The busy Las Manos crossing is open 24 hours a day; the others, daily 8 to 5. Get an early start and expect delays.

# MATAGALPA

*130 km (78 mi) north of Managua.*

At just over 3,300 feet, the lush mountains around workaday Matagalpa and its cool climate and reputation for hospitality have attracted large numbers of foreigners for years. In the 1800s a wave of immigrants—mostly British, German, and French—arrived and established the region's coffee plantations, forcing many of the indigenous farmers off their own land. Years later the region witnessed a more benevolent invasion of foreigners, who came during the 1980s to work on solidarity projects.

As with most of northern Nicaragua, Matagalpa's heart is staunchly Sandinista. Both Tomás Borges, the lone survivor of the group that founded the FSLN, and Carlos Fonseca, its best-known martyr, were born and raised here. The city is also known for serving one of the best cups of coffee in the country, Matagalpa Roast. You'll find few international-quality hotels and restaurants here, but the region does contain the Selva Negra Mountain Resort, arguably Nicaragua's most famous lodging, just north of Matagalpa.

### GETTING HERE AND AROUND

Matagalpa's bus depot is at the market in the southwest part of town, next to the river, about a 30-minute walk from Parque Central. A cab ride to the center should cost C$20.

You reach Matagalpa via the Interamerican Highway north from Managua. Watch for the turnoff at Sébaco, 28 km (17 mi) before Matagalpa.

### MONEY MATTERS

The city's banks cluster a half block south of the Parque Central's southeast corner. All will change cash (U.S. dollars only). Banco América Central (BAC) will change American Express traveler's checks weekdays 8:30 to 4:30 and Saturday 8 to noon. Use your Visa/Plus-affiliated card at ATMs at BAC and Bancentro. BAC's machine also accepts MasterCard/Cirrus cards.

### VISITOR INFORMATION

The Instituto Nicaragüense de Turismo (INTUR), open weekdays 8 to 12:30 and 1:30 to 5, operates a tourist information office with a helpful staff a few blocks south of downtown.

### ESSENTIALS

**Bank Information** Bancentro (✉ *Avda. de los Bancos* ☎ *505/2772–3922*). **Banco América Central** (*BAC* ✉ *1 block south of Enitel* ☎ *505/2772–5905*).

**Emergency Services** Ambulance (☎ *505/2772–2059*). **Fire** (☎ *505/2772–3167*). **Police** (☎ *505/2772–3870*).

**Tourist Information** INTUR (✉ *1 block east and ½ block north of Molagüina church* ☎ *505/2772–7060*).

### EXPLORING

Matagalpa's sole museum makes an interesting visit for fans of Nicaraguan political history. The **Museo Casa Comandante Carlos Fonseca** (✉ *1 block east of southeast corner of Parque Darío* ☎ *505/2772–3665* 🖾 *Donation requested* ☉ *Weekdays 8–noon and 2–5*) was the childhood home of Carlos Fonseca, the guiding light of the FSLN. Photographs and texts tell the story of Fonseca's life, from his childhood to his death in a skirmish with the National Guard in 1976. Its hours can be irregular.

If the anachronistic architecture of the Bavarian-style **Selva Negra Mountain Resort** doesn't charm you, then owners Eddy and Mausi Kühl will.

## ¡Beisbol sí, Fútbol no!

The most commonly played and watched sport in Latin America is *fútbol* (soccer), but Nicaraguans, always content to go their own way, couldn't care less: their passion is baseball. Soccer stadiums are few and far between, but every self-respecting town has a baseball diamond, and terms like *el pícher* and *¡esstrike!* pepper Nicaraguan Spanish. No one seems to know the reason for the "Take me out to the ball game" phenomenon here. Many attribute it to the influence of the long U.S. military occupation during the early 20th century. And instead of the song's proverbial "peanuts and Cracker Jack," you'll likely snack on *nacatamales* (dough with a filling of pork or chicken, tomatoes, rice, garlic, onions, and potatoes) and *vigorón,* (pickled cabbage, tomatoes, onions, yuca, and fried pork skins).

Nicaragua's National League (⊕ *www. lnbp.com.ni*) teams wind up for the first pitches of their opening days about the time the U.S. Major Leagues observe the World Series, and regular season championships here take place as U.S. teams are finishing their spring training. Nicaragua's November-through-April schedule gives its teams an advantage their stateside counterparts don't have: it's the dry season, so rainouts are almost nonexistent.

Denis Martínez has been Nicaragua's most venerated player ever since he made it to the U.S. Major Leagues—he was the first of 10 Nicaraguans to do so—as a pitcher, in order of appearance, for the Baltimore Orioles, Montreal Expos, Cleveland Indians, Seattle Mariners, and Atlanta Braves. (During Martínez' MLB career, sportswriters anglicized the spelling of his name to Dennis.)

After receiving a personal invitation from the Nicaraguan government to come here to grow coffee, Eddy's grandfather emigrated from Germany in 1891. More than 100 years later, Eddy still grows world-famous coffee, and his knowledge of Nicaragua's politics is infinite, as he is a personal friend of many of the country's power brokers. The owners charge C$60 if you want to visit the property, but the fee is applied toward meals or lodging. Come here for a taste of some really fresh coffee, or for the excellent hiking. The 1,500 acres surrounding the hotel house howler monkeys, sloths, minks, ocelots, wild boars, and cougars, as well as 125 species of birds and 85 varieties of orchids. Fourteen different trails wind into the cloudy mountains and around the coffee plantation, and you can even rent a horse for C$250 an hour. ⊠ *Km 140 Carretera Matagalpa–Jinotega* ☎ *505/2772–3883* ⊕ *www. selvanegra.com.*

### WHERE TO STAY

$–$$   🏨 **Selva Negra Mountain Resort.** Set in a combination private reserve and working coffee plantation, the Black Forest is arguably Nicaragua's most famous hotel. Rooms in the main house are rustic but furnished with flowered spreads and drapes. More upscale (although still a bit rustic) and expensive bungalows ($$$) have one to four bedrooms, and can accommodate two to six people. They come with private porch and spectacular views. Selva Negra also offers hostel-like accommodations next door. **Pros:** fun to stay on a working coffee plantation; owners are a wealth of information about the region. **Cons:** some rooms quite basic; need a car to stay here. ⊠ *Km 140 Carretera Matagalpa–Jinotega* ☎ *505/2772–3883* ⊕ *www.selvanegra.com* ⇆ *21 bungalows, 4 chalets, 20 dorm-style bunks* ⚭ *In-room: no a/c, no phone, no TV. In-hotel: restaurant, bar, Wi-Fi hotspot, Internet terminal, parking (free)* ▭ *AE, MC, V.*

## SPORTS AND THE OUTDOORS

HIKING The hills near Matagalpa contain some stunning scenery. One hiking trail, which begins south of town on the highway (about 60 feet south of the pedestrian bridge), climbs 600 feet to **El Calvario,** whose summit has a small shrine dedicated to the crucified Christ and a good view of the valley. An easier excursion leads to the **cemetery** south of town (about 1 km or ½ mi southwest of bus depot), where you can see the town below and visit the grave of aid worker Ben Linder, the only U.S. citizen killed during the Contra war.

8

# Side Trips to El Salvador

9

**WORD OF MOUTH**

"Think about El Salvador: smallest of the Central America countries, not many other travelers, and great waves if you like to surf."

—rpbroz

Updated by
Jeffrey Van
Fleet

El Salvador's lovely landscapes, fascinating history, and genuinely friendly people—not to mention the relative absence of foreigners—will win over new converts in the coming years. If you have the desire to experience a Central American country still untainted by tourism, you will find what you are looking for here.

The country has subtle charms that go unnoticed at first glance. Surprisingly little here is geared toward travelers, although that is slowly changing. For now, El Salvador remains a perfect destination for those with a curious spirit.

One appealing aspect of El Salvador is its diminutive size, putting the entire country within striking distance of Honduras and making it an easy add-on to your Honduran travels. The country, the smallest in Central America, is only 200 km (124 mi) long. The major roads are well paved and reasonably maintained, so trips to even the most far-flung reaches never take more than a few hours. This means that El Salvador's most beguiling sights are more accessible than you might guess. Although the country has seen most of its old-growth forests felled for timber or to make way for farms, this age of awareness about the environment—and its potential to draw tourists—has not been lost upon the powers that be, who are struggling to make up for lost time. Verdant national parks, several impressive volcanoes (some still active), and a handful of sparkling lakes are now looked at as national treasures.

You might remember the headlines coming out of El Salvador during the 1980s; they were downright grim. The country, never asking to be caught up in Cold War politics, nevertheless served as a surrogate battleground for the then-superpowers and was wracked by civil war. Those days, thankfully, are gone. Residents have put the tragedies of three decades ago behind them, and you as a visitor can, too.

San Salvador, the sprawling capital, serves as the gateway for most visitors to El Salvador. It offers the mix of good and bad found in most cities of Central America. Although it can be wretched to the eye, San Salvador also has lively markets, interesting museums, and plenty of nightlife, and is far more cosmopolitan than any urban area in Honduras. Not far from the capital are several azure lakes—Lago de Coatepeque, Lago de Ilopango, and Lago de Güija—that lure you with opportunities for boating, swimming, or just relaxing in the sun. To the east of San Salvador stretches a chain of mountains that beckon to those in search of some serious off-the-beaten-track hiking. The thinly populated northwestern region is home to national parks such as Parque Nacional Montecristo.

## TOP REASONS TO GO

**Archaeological Sites.** Although none are as grand as Copán in Honduras, El Salvador has some interesting archaeological sites where you can wander among the remnants of Mesoamerican settlements. Temples at Tazumal and San Andrés are both well worth the trip. Joya de Cerén, just a few miles from San Andrés, provides a fascinating glimpse into the daily life of ancient peoples.

**Outdoor Activities.** The upper slopes of El Salvador's string of volcanoes are irresistible for those who love the great outdoors. Since the peaks are fairly low—El Pital, the country's highest peak, rises to only 8,950 feet—easy climbs will bring you to breathtaking views. National parks such as El Imposible in the southwest, Montecristo in the northwest, and Cerro Verde between the two, are the places to go for serious hiking through a variety of terrains. Regions like Chalatenango and Morazán have trails that bring hikers through a countryside dotted with small villages. There's plenty of

opportunity for boating and other activities on lakes like Lago de Coatepeque.

**Shopping.** Markets and shops throughout the country are filled with locally produced crafts. In the village of Guatajiagua, near San Miguel, you can see local artisans making earthenware plates, jugs, and bowls the same way their ancestors did. This pottery, which is then tinted with a black dye made from seeds, is used on a daily basis in most Salvadoran homes. San Sebastián, east of San Salvador, is the place for hammocks and other woven goods. La Palma, in the north, is known for the colorful designs of artist Fernando Llort (prounounced "yort"). Other villagers now emulate Llort's childlike view of rural life. Kitschy *pícaras*, which originated in the village of Ilobasco, can be found in shops around the country. These egg-shape containers have little clay tableaux of subjects ranging from the sacred to the profane.

9

# ORIENTATION AND PLANNING

## ORIENTATION

Tiny El Salvador is about the size of the state of New Jersey, putting the entire country within easy reach of Honduras. San Salvador, the capital, sits smack-dab in the center of the country. Its international airport, which receives flights from all four of Honduras's airports, is about 45 minutes south of the capital near the coast. The country's second- and fourth-largest cities, Santa Ana and San Miguel, anchor the east and west respectively. Major roads are generally well maintained, though confusing signage and even worse maps remain a problem.

**San Salvador.** One of the isthmus's largest cities will seem downright glittering and cosmopolitan if you've arrived here from Honduras. El Salvador's sprawling capital, at the nation's geographical center, mixes developing-country grittiness with cool, upscale trendiness.

**Northern and Western El Salvador.** Diligent artisans, colonial treasures, shimmering lakes, and cloud forests make the north and west the El Salvador everyone comes to see. Yet even here, visitor numbers are still small enough that even the country's most popular destinations never feel overrun. Santa Ana, the country's second-largest city, will seem downright provincial if you've arrived directly from the capital. And that's okay, say its residents, who enjoy living in one of Central America's best-preserved colonial communities.

**Eastern El Salvador.** El Salvador's east is the least visited sector of this lesser visited country. The region has lagged behind—it was hit hard during the 1980s civil war—but with its artisanry and nature it is making a valiant effort to lure visitors. You'll likely spend time in San Miguel, if only to stock up on supplies.

## GREAT ITINERARIES

**3 Days:** Spend the first day in San Salvador after arrival from Honduras. Its major sights can easily be seen in one day. Because you'll be flying both into and out of the country via the capital, consider making this your base and taking day trips to other parts of the country. On your second day, head north to Suchitoto, a colonial-era village where beautifully preserved buildings line the cobblestone streets. On the third day, head west to Lago de Coatepeque, a beautiful lake that makes a great place to stop for lunch. Outdoors enthusiasts will want to hike up nearby Cerro Verde or Volcán Santa Ana, both in the Parque Nacional Los Volcanes.

**5 Days:** If you have a few more days to explore El Salvador, head a bit farther afield. Start with the itinerary above. On the fourth day travel west to Santa Ana, where you can stop by for a look around the central square. A cathedral and several museums are found along its edges. From Santa Ana you can spend a couple of days exploring the Ruta de las Flores, which takes you through mountain villages such as Apaneca and Juayúa.

# PLANNING

## WHEN TO GO

El Salvador greets most of its visitors during the dry season from November through April. During the wet season, which runs from May to October, it rains almost every day. Fortunately, the downpours are usually short. The best time to visit is in the very beginning or right after the end of the rainy season, when the countryside is green but the weather still manageable. Unless you're planning mountain treks, a sturdy umbrella will do fine. San Salvador and the Pacific coast are almost always hot during the day, while somewhat cooler temperatures prevail at higher elevations. March and April can be uncomfortably hot.

## GETTING HERE AND AROUND

El Salvador and Honduras form part of a Central American immigration and customs union called the CA-4, along with Nicaragua and Guatemala. Entry formalities are easy and land borders are open 24 hours. Time spent in El Salvador or any of the other countries counts toward the 90-day entry you get upon arrival in Honduras.

El Salvador has well-maintained highways, especially between the major cities. The Pan-American Highway, here called the CA-1, runs right through the middle of the country. Some smaller roads need work, but generally are passable. You can rent cars in the capital and some other cities. During the rainy season, many drivers prefer a four-wheel-drive vehicle or a pickup truck.

Salvadoran buses are of the school-bus variety (but decidedly more colorful) and are numbered according to their route. Intercity buses have their destination, along with important stops along the way, posted on the windshield. Bus travel is cheap—few trips cost more than $2. Departures on most routes are frequent, leaving every 10 to 20 minutes during the day. Buses rarely depart after sunset. Don't plan to arrive by bus "just in time" for anything, as delays are common.

### AIR TRAVEL

Many people exploring El Salvador fly into Aeropuerto Internacional El Salvador, 44 km (27 mi) south of San Salvador. This is the only commercial airport in the country. Expect a trip to the capital to take about 45 minutes.

Taca has a very good reputation. It flies between San Salvador and each of Honduras's four international airports at least twice daily.

A taxi will cost $25 from the airport to your hotel, $16 on the way back. The larger hotels, however, have shuttles waiting for flights that usually offer scheduled service several times per day for $12 to $14. Confirm in advance with your hotel to see if a shuttle coincides with your arrival; otherwise, take a taxi. Make sure you sign up with a taxi from the official booth in the arrivals terminal, rather than going along with one of the drivers that accost you, some of whom are unlicensed crooks.

**Airlines and Contacts Taca** (✉ *Multiplaza, San Salvador* ☎ *503/2267–8222*).

**Airport Information Aeropuerto Internacional El Salvador** (✉ *South of San Salvador* ☎ *503/2339–9455*).

### BUS TRAVEL

Mastering the *desvío* (highway junction) is an important skill in Salvadoran bus travel—you'll often take one bus to a desvío, and then pick up another heading to your destination. Another option is the *pickup* (pronounced PICK-a), which has been adopted by Salvadorans to mean any truck that carries passengers. If you don't mind the wind, and have a spirit of adventure, it isn't a bad way to go (and in more remote areas where buses run infrequently it may be your only option). Rates are slightly cheaper than buses.

In San Salvador, Terminal Puerto Bus is an international terminal for several bus lines, including King Quality and Transnica. Destinations include Guatemala City (five hours, $23), Tegucigalpa (seven hours, $25), and Managua (10 hours, $30). Ticabus vehicles depart from Avenida 10 Norte and Calle Concepción to and from Choluteca, Honduras.

**Bus Companies King Quality** (✉ *Blvd. del Hipódromo 415, Col. San Benito, San Salvador* ☎ *503/2271–1361*). **Ticabus** (✉ *Av. 10 Norte and C. Concepción, San Salvador* ☎ *503/2222–4808*). **Transnica** (✉ *Alameda Roosevelt and 59 Av. Sur, San Salvador* ☎ *503/2240–1212*).

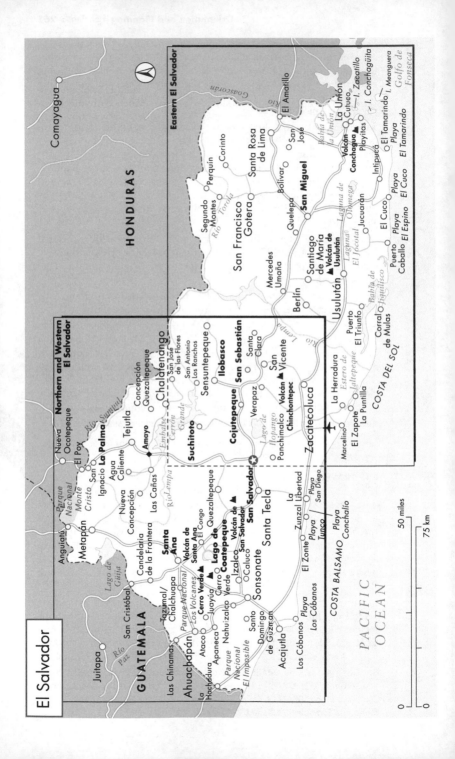

**Bus Station Terminal Puerto Bus** (✉ *Av. Juan Pablo II at Av. 19 Norte, San Salvador* ☎ *503/2222–2158*).

## CAR TRAVEL

To hit the road in El Salvador, all you need is a valid U.S. or international driver's license. You should always have evidence of your rightful possession of a car; proof of insurance isn't necessary, although it's good to have.

The capital has the standard selection of international car-rental offices. If you find yourself in need of a car in eastern El Salvador, head to San Miguel, the only place in that part of the country to rent a vehicle. You can rent cars for about $50 per day.

## TOUR OPERATORS

The Corporación Salvadoreña de Turismo (Corsatur) is the major tourist board in the country. Its office in San Salvador stocks pamphlets and maps. It's open Monday through Thursday 8 to noon and 1 to 5:30; Friday they are open from 8 to 4. SalvaNATURA is a good source for hiking information.

Good maps of El Salvador are not easily found, so keep your eyes peeled. Most official ones look like maps of Disneyland, with thick, black lines that could have been drawn with a crayon. All the more reason to go with a guide if winging it isn't your style.

AviTours offers tours throughout the country, and they offer city tours of San Salvador as well. They last four hours and cost about $25 per person.

**Tour Companies AviTours** (☎ *503/2510–7618* ⊕ *www.avitours.com.sv*).

**Tourist Information Corsatur** (✉ *Alameda Manuel Enrique Araujo and Pasaje Carbonel #1, San Salvador* ☎ *503/2243–7835* ⊕ *www.elsalvadorturismo.gob.sv*). **SalvaNATURA** (✉ *33 Av. Sur 640, Col. Flor Blanca, San Salvador* ☎ *503/2279–1515* ⊕ *www.salvanatura.org*).

## HEALTH AND SAFETY

The most common malady for visitors to El Salvador is travelers' diarrhea. The best way to avoid it is to be careful about what you eat. Don't drink the water—*agua purificada* (purified water) is available everywhere in bottles. Always order your drinks *sin hielo* (without ice). Avoid salads and fresh fruits that may have been washed in tainted water. Do sample foods from street vendors, but make sure they haven't been sitting around all day. It's a good idea to eat only what has been prepared in front of you. Prepare in advance for the possibility of becoming sick by bringing Pepto-Bismol (the chewable tablets are convenient) and Imodium (in capsules). If it doesn't blow over in a day or two, head to a doctor.

As for mosquito-borne diseases, dengue fever is much more common in El Salvador than malaria, particularly in the eastern lowlands. Socks and long pants are the best protection. Make sure your bug spray has a high DEET content. Lastly, the sun can be extremely strong, even during the rainy season. Use a good sunscreen and wear a wide-brimmed hat.

**Health Contact Centers for Disease Control and Prevention** (☎ *877/394–8747* 🖷 *888/232–3299* ⊕ *www.cdc.gov*).

## MONEY MATTERS

El Salvador completely dollarized its economy in 2001, making currency exchange a nonissue for U.S visitors. ■TIP➜ Change any leftover lempiras back to dollars before leaving Honduras; no one in El Salvador will accept or change Honduran currency. Get plenty of cash before heading from San Salvador for the countryside, as some smaller cities don't have ATMs. Credit cards are generally only accepted at big-time hotels and restaurants, mostly in the capital; elsewhere, be prepared with cash. And don't bother with traveler's checks—here, as in most of the world, they are a thing of the past.

### ATMS

Most branches of banks like CitiBank, Banco Hipotecario, and Scotiabank have ATMs that accept foreign cards. Before you leave home, make sure your PIN code has no more than four digits.

## RESTAURANTS AND CUISINE

No food is more typically Salvadoran than the *pupusa*, a fried tortilla filled with beans, cheese, and/or *chicharrón* (pork skin). A pupusa called *revuelta* has all three fillings mixed together. Delicious *pupusas de arroz* are made with rice flour and are not quite as thick; they have a certain lightness, though they are still quite filling. *Loroco*, a sprouty green local vegetable, is also a popular and interesting filling. Both are found in *pupuserías*, where they are served up with spicy tomato sauce and a vinegary pickled cabbage and carrot concoction called *curtido*. The Salvadoran version of fast food, pupusas are a good way to fill up on the cheap. An all-out breakfast here consists of eggs, beans, cheese, fried plantains, tortillas, and coffee. For lunch, expect beef, chicken, or fish with rice, beans, tortillas, perhaps fried plantains, and a small salad; chicken here is often the best option. A delicious creamy seafood soup called *mariscada* makes a satisfying dinner in the coastal regions, as does shrimp cooked in garlic or a whole fried fish. That said, most Salvadorans eat their big meal at lunchtime and stick with pupusas in the evening.

The most common drinks are *gaseosas* (sodas) and *refrescos* (fruit drinks with tons of sugar). Icy *minutas* are slushy drinks sweetened with honey—truly a godsend on a hot afternoon. ⚠ You could ask whether they are made with purified water, but the answer will often be yes to make the sale. *Licuados* are similar to minutas, but fresh fruit and sometimes milk are added. *Ponche*, usually found on the streets at festivals, is a special treat, especially after dinner on a cool evening: it's hot milk ladled from a steaming pitcher and mixed with vanilla, cinnamon, and dark rum. Omnipresent varieties of locally brewed *cerveza* (beer) include Suprema (full-bodied), Bahía (a lighter, fresher brew), and Pilsener (the lowest common denominator).

## ABOUT THE HOTELS

There's no shortage of modern hotels in San Salvador. You'll immediately recognize names of top chains such as InterContinental, Marriott, Hilton, and Crowne Plaza. Outside the capital, however, the lodgings are more modest. *Posadas* and *cabañas* are usually more upscale options, whereas *hospedajes* and *casas de huespedes* are most often lower-end lodgings; *hoteles* can be anything along the spectrum. Even in some better *hoteles,* be prepared for cold-water showers and no air-conditioning anywhere outside San Salvador. *Moteles* are almost always seedy establishments that should be avoided; they rent rooms by the hour.

| WHAT IT COSTS IN U.S. DOLLARS | | | | | |
|---|---|---|---|---|---|
| | ¢ | $ | $$ | $$$ | $$$$ |
| RESTAURANTS | under $5 | $5–$10 | $11–$15 | $16–$20 | over $20 |
| HOTELS | under $25 | $25–$75 | $76–$125 | $126–$175 | over $175 |

Restaurant prices are per person for a main course at dinner. Hotel prices are for two people in a standard double room in high season.

# SAN SALVADOR

*One hour southwest of Tegucigalpa by air, 1½ hours southeast of San Pedro Sula by air.*

Mention Tegucigalpa or San Pedro Sula to a resident of El Salvador's capital and you're likely to get a roll of the eyes and a little snicker. This is the region's big-time city, and any urban area in Honduras seems provincial by comparison. San Salvador is the city that runs the strongest economy in Central America. The fastest growing sectors of the capital are an array of upscale boutiques, foreign-fetish restaurants, and fashion-arms-race nightclubs. Although these places are the richest and hippest in the city, they are also in many ways the least Salvadoran and the most Americanized, so following the locals to their favorite new places can be a double-edged cultural sword. It is an ironic fact of life that many of the areas of San Salvador that are most authentic and interesting to tourists are often the least frequented by the local bourgeoisie.

Accordingly, financial resources are often directed away from the city's historic center, leaving it sadly neglected. Although it has some lovely old buildings, the gritty neighborhood does not make visitors feel welcome. It is crowded, noisy, and polluted and not geared toward tourists in any sense.

Some visitors are surprised to find so few older buildings in this colonial city. San Salvador has been destroyed by tremors several times since it was founded in 1525, and consequently bears hardly a trace of its heritage. In 1986 much of the capital was leveled by an earthquake that left more than 1,000 people dead. Another in 2001 caused even more damage.

**GETTING HERE AND AROUND**

Colonia San Benito is an upscale neighborhood where you can stroll among the restaurants and galleries. To the north is Colonia Escalón, where you'll find many of the city's most popular boutiques. Colonia Centroamérica has some of the city's most happening bars and clubs. More recently, the city's elite have migrated even farther from the old city center to Antiguo Cuscatlán, home to the Multiplaza and Gran Vía "lifestyle centers."

# A HISTORY OF STRUGGLE

El Salvador's natural beauty makes its history of armed conflict seem that much more tragic. Its grim past mocks its hopeful name, which in Spanish means "The Savior."

The Great Depression brought increasing political tensions to El Salvador. By the mid-20th century, the disparity between rich and poor had only grown. Agricultural exports increased tenfold in the 1960s, but the Salvadoran people ranked in the top five most undernourished populations in the world, even as the famed "fourteen families" that made up El Salvador's ruling class prospered. People pressed for change. José Napoleón Duarte, a founder of the Christian Democratic Party, won the presidency in 1972, but military leaders voided his victory. Popular protest, ranging from civil disobedience to armed insurrection, followed.

Soon after the 1980 assassination of Archbishop Oscar Romero, a leading human-rights advocate, four guerrilla organizations united under the leadership of the Frente Martí Liberación Nacional. U.S. President Ronald Reagan, wary of the success of leftists in neighboring Nicaragua, delivered unprecedented levels of aid. Instead of addressing the needs of the poverty-stricken population, the money was used to bolster the military.

In the late '80s, after rebel forces pitched battles in the heart of the capital city, negotiations began making unprecedented progress. A peace accord, mediated by the United Nations, officially ended 12 cruel years of civil war in 1992.

The last decade has brought many positive changes. The repressive Policía Nacional was disbanded and replaced by the Policía Nacional Civil, and judicial and electoral reforms were initiated. Crime is still a problem in many areas, but there are signs of progress. The country's economy is growing, foreign investment is increasing, and El Salvador has become Central America's most powerful economy. Salvadorans, eager to see their country move forward, are clearly pleased with the progress.

**AIR TRAVEL** Most people exploring this region fly into Aeropuerto Internacional El Salvador, 44 km (27 mi) south of San Salvador.

**BUS TRAVEL** Most intercity buses leave from one of the two main terminals: Terminal de Oriente serves destinations north and east of the capital, whereas Terminal de Occidente serves those to the west.

San Salvador's city bus system is dangerous. Drivers compete for customers, causing frequent accidents. Buses are crowded, resulting in pickpocketings and other crimes. ⚠ **We recommend you avoid it entirely and take taxis instead.**

**Bus Terminals Terminal de Occidente** (✉ *Av. 49 Sur and Blvd. Venezuela* ☎ *503/2223–3784*). **Terminal de Oriente** (✉ *Av. Peralta* ☎ *503/2222–0315*).

**CAR RENTAL** Most of the major rental agencies—Avis, Budget, Hertz, and Thrifty—have offices in San Salvador. A local agency worth checking into is Union.

# The Soccer War

Countries have gone to war over many things throughout history. One of the strangest disputes took place in 1969 when El Salvador and Honduras went to war for four days over a soccer game. To be sure, many underlying disputes simmered beneath the surface that year, most notably disputes over immigration and sovereignty over the Pacific coast's Gulf of Fonseca, shared by both countries and Nicaragua. Increasing levels of fighting took place during a series of World Cup qualifying matches between fans of the two countries in June and July of that year. On July 14, El Salvador's army invaded Honduras. A ceasefire was negotiated four days later, but the dispute over the gulf would not be resolved for another three decades. Of course, none of this need concern you as a visitor to either country, and today Honduras and El Salvador maintain friendly relations.

Those who are used to urban driving will find that the city's thoroughfares are relatively simple to navigate, as the capital is small. Getting around by taxis is less of a hassle, however, and cheap enough.

**Rental Agencies** Avis (⊠ *43 Av. Sur 127, Col. Flor Blanca* ☎ *503/2261–1212*). **Best** (⊠ *3 C. Poniente, Col. Escalón* ☎ *503/2298–9611*). **Budget** (⊠ *Paseo Gen. Escalón, Col. Escalón* ☎ *503/2260–4333*). **Hertz** (⊠ *9 C. Poniente at 91 Av. Norte, Col. Escalón* ☎ *503/2339–8004*). **Thrifty** (⊠ *Blvd. Orden de Malta Sur 12, Col. Santa Elena* ☎ *503/2289–2984*). **Union** (⊠ *C. Conchaga 22, Col. Santa Elena* ☎ *503/2243–8025* ⊕ *unionrentacar.com*).

TAXIS  Taxis are plentiful in San Salvador. You should always settle on a price before beginning a journey, because there are no meters. A five-minute trip should run $3 to $5, and no trip within the city should cost you more than $7.

**Taxi Companies** Acontaxis (⊠ *10 Av. Sur 2011, Col. América* ☎ *503/2270–1176*). **Radio Taxis Maranatha** (☎ *503/2289–9948*).

## TOUR OPERATORS

AviTours offers city tours of San Salvador that last four hours and cost about $25 per person.

**Tour Company** AviTours (☎ *503/2264–0146*).

## VISITOR INFORMATION

The Corporación Salvadoreña de Turismo, or Corsatur, doles out simple maps, bus schedules, and pamphlets on various points of interest. Most of the information is current, but not all of it is in English. They are open Monday through Thursday from 8 to noon and 1 to 5:30; Friday they are open from 8 to 4.

**Tourist Information** Corsatur (⊠ *Alameda Manuel Enrique Araujo and Pasaje Carbonel #1, Santa Elena* ☎ *503/2243–7835* ⊕ *www.elsalvadorturismo.gob.sv*).

## SAFETY

San Salvador is easily the most densely populated city in Central America. The official count is about 1.5 million, but that figure increases by at least half when you figure in those living in the shantytowns along its edges. There are not nearly enough jobs to go around, which means pickpocketings and other petty crimes are all too common. Be on your guard, especially in markets and other crowded places.

As in any other big city in Central America, parts of San Salvador have quite a bit of street crime. Cramped sidewalks make tourists easy targets for pickpockets. Some areas, such as El Centro, are especially dangerous. It's a good idea to take a taxi to your destination, even during the day.

As in the United States, the number for any emergency is 911. The best hospital in town, which tends to most foreign residents and locals with money, is the Hospital de Diagnóstico at Plaza Villavicencio. Less severe problems can often be handled at *laboratorios* or *clínicas*. Pharmacies are scattered throughout town. On Búlevar de los Héroes, Farmacia Internacional is open 24 hours.

**Emergency Services Emergencies** (☎ *911*). **Ambulance** (☎ *503/2223–7300*). **Fire** (☎ *503/2271–1244*). **Police** (☎ *911*).

**Hospitals Hospital de Diagnóstico** (✉ *Paseo General Escalón, 99 Av. Norte, Plaza Villavicencio* ☎ *503/2506–2000*).

## MONEY MATTERS

You'll find branches of most banks along Avenida Roosevelt in Colonia Escalón. ⚠ **We recommend not visiting banks or ATMs in the city center;** walking out, you'll be assumed to be flush with cash and an easy mark for robbery. Take out plenty of money before leaving San Salvador for the countryside, as many smaller towns don't have ATMs.

**Banks Banco de América Central (BAC)** (✉ *Paseo Escalón* ☎ *503/2254–9980* ⊕ *www*). **CitiBank** (✉ *Blvd. de los Héroes* ☎ *503/2212–2000*).

# EXPLORING

For a chaotic capital, San Salvador is surprisingly easy to navigate (at least in the center), with *avenidas* running north–south and *calles* running east–west. To make addresses easier to find, avenidas are labeled *norte* when north of the main plaza and *sur* when they are to the south (for example, Avenida 4a Norte). Ditto for calles, using *oriente* on the east side and *poniente* on the west. San Salvador takes the system one step further, placing odd-numbered avenidas west of the central plaza and even ones to the east, odd calles to the north and even to the south. Although confusing at first, this system makes orienting yourself easier, because the main plaza will always be roughly at Avenida 1 and Calle 1.

Major streets in either direction frequently change names as they cross the main square. In some cases, main streets may change names as the *colonia* (neighborhood) changes.

# San Salvador

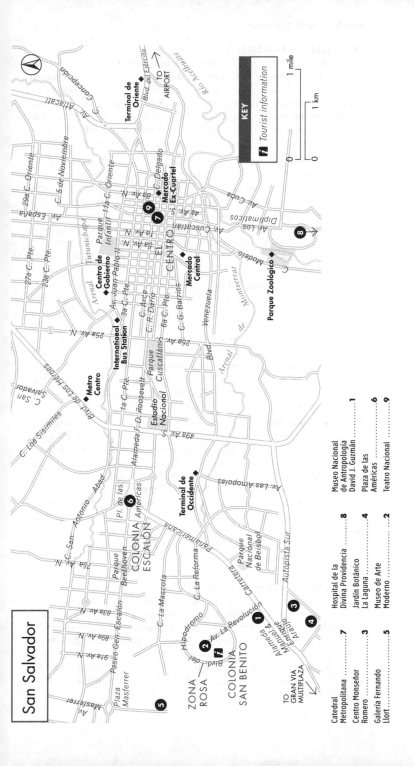

**KEY**

*i* *Tourist information*

## COLONIA SAN BENITO

Although most of the city's graceful old buildings are found in El Centro, this neighborhood is where you'll find some of the newer attractions, such as the outstanding museums dedicated to anthropology and modern art. Also here is the vibrant Zona Rosa, a stretch of Avenida del Hipódromo lined with restaurants, bars, and nightclubs. You'll probably spend most of your time in the city here in this neighborhood, in Colonia Escalón, in Colonia Centroamérica, and in Antiguo Cuscatlán.

**Centro Monseñor Romero.** In an incident that drew international outrage, a group of men broke into the rectory at the Universidad Centroaméricano José Simeón Cañas in 1989 and murdered six Jesuits, their housekeeper, and her daughter. This sobering memorial displays the victims' papers and personal items, as well as graphic photos of the murder scene. The church next door is well worth visiting, as is a small rose garden. ⊠ *C. del Mediterraneo and Av. Río Amazonas, Col. Antiguo Cusclatán* ☎ *503/2210–6675* ✎ *Free* ☉ *Weekdays 8–noon and 2–6, Sat. 8–noon.*

★ **Jardín Botánico La Laguna.** A huge collection of plants and flowers from around the world—including a 200-year-old ceiba tree, a large collection of orchids, and a bamboo forest—is found at this botanical garden, called La Laguna because it is located in the crater of an extinct volcano that was filled with water until an earthquake drained it in 1873. You don't have to be a botanist to enjoy the shady paths and babbling streams that make this park a welcome respite from the city's hustle and bustle. ⊠ *Near Universidad Centroaméricano José Simeón Cañas, Col. San Benito* ☎ *503/2243–2012* ⊕ *www.jardinbotanico.org.sv* ✎ *$1 for adults, 60¢ for children* ☉ *Tues.–Sun. 9–5:30.*

★ **Museo de Arte Moderno.** The Museum of Modern Art has become the country's most important cultural center. The 25,000-square-foot facility, consisting of a large main hall connected to three smaller galleries, is home to a permanent collection of 20th-century works by Salvadoran artists, centering around surrealist, cubist, and abstract-expressionist paintings. The smaller galleries host rotating exhibitions by national and international artists. Leaders say the museum "heralds a renaissance of cultural consciousness" for the country; by incorporating into the museum's central plaza the 70-foot Monumento de la Revolución, the museum sets itself at the center of the country's intellectual and spiritual psyche. ⊠ *End of Av. La Revolución* ☎ *503/2243–6099* ⊕ *www. marte.org.sv* ✎ *$1.50* ☉ *Tues.–Sun. 10–6.*

**Museo Nacional de Antropología David J. Guzmán.** The National Museum of Anthropology was founded in 1883 by Salvadoran scientist David Joaquín Guzmán. Stroll through the five galleries to learn about the country's cultural history. The explanatory text is only in Spanish, but it's easy to appreciate the pottery from pre-Hispanic times, the clothing of indigenous peoples, and the looms from San Sebastián. In a garden you can follow a path to a replica of a traditional wood-and-straw hut. ⊠ *Av. La Revolución* ☎ *503/2243–3927* ⊕ *www.munaelsalvador.com* ✎ *$3* ☉ *Tues.–Sun. 9–5.*

## COLONIA ESCALÓN

An upscale commercial and residential neighborhood, Colonia Escalón is west of the historic district. Along Paseo General Escalón, the neighborhood's main artery, you'll find several glitzy shopping centers.

**Galería Fernando Llort.** With much success at home and abroad, Fernando Llort (pronounced "yort") has received the most attention of any Salvadoran artist. This popular gallery sells original paintings, prints, and posters. The staff carefully packs purchases for your flight home. ⊠ *C. La Mascota and Av. Masferrer, Col. Maquilishuat* ☎ *503/2263–9206* ⊕ *www.fernando-llort.com.*

**Plaza de las Américas.** Near the beginning of Colonia Escalón is a statue called *The Savior of the World,* depicting Jesus standing on top of a globe. It sits in the center of this tree-lined park. ⊠ *Paseo General Escalón at Blvd. Constitución.*

## CENTRO HISTÓRICO

Loud, crowded, and polluted during the day and rough at night, the city's historic center is an intimidating place for visitors. Here you'll find some of the city's best-known landmarks, such as the colorful Catedral Metropolitana, but you probably won't want to spend more than a couple of hours of your trip here.

**Catedral Metropolitana.** The city's main cathedral, damaged by a series of earthquakes, was repainted by one of El Salvador's most famous artists, Fernando Llort. The facade is painted with bright solid colors, with rural motifs such as cattle, houses, corn, flowers, and butterflies. Archbishop Oscar Romero was buried here after being assassinated in 1980. You can visit his tomb in a crypt beneath the church. ⊠ *C. Oriente between Avs. Cuscatlán and 2a Sur* ☎ *503/2226–0501* ⊕ *catedraldesansalvador.blogspot.com* ✉ *Free.*

**Hospital de la Divina Providencia.** It was at the altar of this hospital's small chapel, in the middle of mass, that Archbishop Oscar Romero was gunned down by a government death squad in March 1980. The church is simple and peaceful, with a plaque near the altar commemorating the tragedy. Ask in the office to the left of the church for a tour of Romero's living quarters, where you'll find photos, books, and even the typewriter he used to compose his famous homilies. A cause for canonization of the martyred archbishop was begun in 1997 and continues to this day. ⊠ *Final C. Toluca and Av. Bernal, Col. Miramonte Poniente* ☎ *503/2260–0520* ⊕ *www.hdivinaprovidencia.org* ✉ *Free* ☉ *Weekdays 9–4, Sat. 9–2.*

**Teatro Nacional.** Dating from 1911, the elegant National Theater is one of the most recognizable landmarks in San Salvador. Huge columns line the entrance, a favorite place for vendors selling jewelry and other items. The splendid gilt-edged interior is a clue to how much wealth the coffee plantations once brought to El Salvador. ⊠ *Av. 2 Sur and C. Delgado* ☎ *503/2222–8760* ⊕ *www.sansalvador.gob.sv.*

9

# WHERE TO EAT

If you enjoy sampling *platos típicos* (typical dishes), you'll have a great time in San Salvador. Every block has at least one or two *comedores* (inexpensive eateries) serving up pupusas and other favorites. In the historic center, look for any pupusería that's clean and well kept, and you can have a filling lunch for a dollar or two. But San Salvador also has a handful of inventive restaurants where chefs apply refined techniques to local ingredients, with varying degrees of success; some are more flashy style than substance, whereas others are really worthwhile.

**$$$** ✕ **Il Bongustaio.** When Chef Roberto Sartogo brought his talents across
**Fodor'sChoice** the seas a decade ago, Florence's loss was San Salvador's gain. After
**★** cooking around town for several years, Roberto opened his own res-
ITALIAN taurant, Il Bongustaio, which is a temple to his culinary talents, to Ital-
ian tradition, and to fresh Salvadoran seafood and meats. Start with a
carpaccio of *mero* (local white fish), paper-thin and redolent of good
olive oil, or buttery strips of raw marinated salmon atop a bed of greens.
Don't miss the pastas, which might include spaghettini with picked
crabmeat; a whole fish roasted in a bed of salt; or gargantuan Salva-
doran shrimp. Service is outstanding, and the environment is sooth-
ingly elegant yet convivial, with well-dressed tables and place settings
framed by a walled-in garden. ⊠ *C. Loma Linda 327, Col. San Benito*
☎ *503/2245–1731* ⊟ *AE, D, DC, MC, V* ⊗ *Closed Sun., no lunch Sat.*

**$$** ✕ **Inka Grill.** One of San Salvador's more upscale Peruvian restaurants,
**Fodor'sChoice** Inka Grill boasts strangely addictive ceviche *peruano* (with *ají*, a pun-
**★** gent chile sauce), and they also offer, bizarrely, fried ceviche. A section
PERUVIAN of the menu entitled "Peruvian Chinese" has just that, but it might be
better just to ponder this marriage while you enjoy other parts of the
menu. Fried chicken is a good main dish, and more adventurous eaters
should try the beef hearts. Drinks are also interesting, especially *leche
de tigre,* a cocktail made from the juice of seafood ceviche. ⊠ *79 Av.
Sur, Zona Rosa* ☎ *503/2230–6060* ⊟ *AE, D, DC, MC, V.*

**$$** ✕ **Kamakura.** The traditional paper screens that decorate Kamakura are
JAPANESE a clue that you've found one of the country's best places for sushi. Sit at
simple wooden tables and chairs, at the sushi bar, or on the floor in the
private tatami room. There's also a plant-filled back room with a run-
ning fountain. The tempura is light and flaky and sometimes comes with
a pinwheel of battered lotus root. ⊠ *Av. 93 Norte 617, Col. Escalón*
☎ *503/2263–2401* ⊟ *AE, D, DC, MC, V* ⊗ *Closed Sun.*

**$$$** ✕ **La Cebichería Peruana.** San Salvador is lucky to have chef Roberto
PERUVIAN Cuadra Mora, who spent more than a decade in Peru delighting diners
with his flavorful fare. Among the top choices here is the ceviche *de
pescado* (fish marinated with lemon, garlic, onion, and cilantro) accompanied by *camote,* a delicious yellow sweet potato. The best course of
action is to order a sampling of smaller dishes—the chef will tell you his
favorites. The dining room is filled with shiny Peruvian paintings and
handicrafts, all of which are for sale. ⊠ *C. El Tanque, 99 Av. Norte and
7 C. Poniente bis130, Col. Escalón* ☎ *503/2263–2413* ⊕ *www.cafecafe.
com.sv* ⊟ *AE, D, DC, MC, V* ⊗ *No dinner Sun.*

**$** ✕ **La Hola Beto's.** You'll know this place by the wooden sailor keep-
SEAFOOD ing watch out front. Open-air tables line the rooftop deck, which is a

blessing on a breezy evening. The seafood here will trick you into thinking you are at the coast, even if the decor does not. And the sublime carpaccio of mero and salmon would fool you into thinking you were in Italy if it weren't for the relatively low prices. ⊠ *Av. Las Magnolias 230, Zona Rosa* ☎ *503/2223–6865* ⊟ *AE, D, DC, MC, V.*

**$$$** ✕ **La Pampa Argentina.** Halfway up Volcán San Salvador, this appealing ranch house has a bougainvillea-lined garden that overlooks the city, as do tables along a curtained wall of tall glass windows. At night the soft breezes and glittering lights make for a tranquil setting. Hot off the *parrilla* (grill) are tenderloin steaks weighing anywhere from 6 to 14 ounces. The service is formal and attentive. ⊠ *End of Paseo General Escalón, Col. Escalón* ☎ *503/2264–0892* ⊟ *AE, D, DC, MC, V.*

ARGENTINE

**$** ✕ **Pupusería Irma.** Though you probably won't find yourself in the gritty city center for long, this place is definitely worth a stop while you're there. Set back only a few feet from the hectic street noise, the place serves pupusas that are a welcome respite. *Pupusas de arroz* are unique, made with rice flour, and not quite as heavy as the more common *pupusas de maiz*. Interesting fillings, such as *ayote,* a sort of squash, are yet another reason to duck into this pupusería. ⊠ *1a C. Oriente and 8a Av. Norte, El Centro* ☎ *503/2271–3050* ⊟ *No credit cards.*

LATIN-AMERICAN

# WHERE TO STAY

Colonia Escalón and Colonia San Benito are home to nearly all the city's top hotels, including the Sheraton, Hilton, and Crowne Plaza. This is also a good area for restaurants. The InterContinental is nearby in Colonia Los Héroes, across from the MetroCentro, whereas the new Marriott Courtyard is the first to follow San Salvador's economic heartbeat to the Gran Vía and Multiplaza lifestyle centers, home to the city's most cutting-edge shopping and nightlife. The larger hotels, competing for guests, are quick to offer discounted rates. You may secure a corporate rate merely by showing a business card. Ask about cheaper weekend rates as well.

**$$** ▦ **Courtyard San Salvador.** As new as the Gran Vía shopping center in which it is located, Marriott is an extension of the shopping center in every sense. Aimed at the new group with money, as well as business travelers, it's a comfortable place to be. The lobby is hip and cheery, mixing bright oranges and reds with natural touches such as beiges and wood. Enjoy the proximity to San Salvador's newest nightlife scene. **Pros:** close to shopping and nightlife; good rates. **Cons:** sameness of chain hotel. ⊠ *Cs. 2 and 3, Centro de Estilo de Vida La Gran Vía, Antiguo Cuscatlán* ☎ *503/2249–3000* ⊕ *www.marriott.com* ⇆ *133 rooms* ⚭ *In-room: a/c, safe, refrigerator, Wi-Fi. In-hotel: restaurant, bar, pool, gym, laundry service, Internet terminal, parking (free)* ⊟ *AE, D, DC, MC, V.*

**$$$$** ▦ **Crowne Plaza San Salvador.** Tucked away in Colonia Escalón, this hotel is a great place to get away from the noise of the city. Off the lobby, whose vastness and lack of color make it feel a bit lonely, you'll find an interesting array of shops. The restaurant is set beside a colonnade where a waterfall drops into a pool. The main complex offers rooms

9

that are nearly identical to those in the city's other luxury hotels, but a second building behind the pool has suites that are meant for extended stays, and as such offer cheaper rates. **Pros:** can book for decent rates. **Cons:** sameness of chain hotel. ⊠ *89 Av. Norte and 11 C. Poniente, Col. Escalón* ☎ *503/2500–0700* ⊕ *www.ichotelsgroup.com* ⤳ *270 rooms, 15 suites* ⧖ *In-room: a/c, safe, kitchen (some), refrigerator (some), Wi-Fi. In-hotel: restaurant, bar, pool, spa, laundry service, Internet terminal, parking (free)* ▤ *AE, D, DC, MC, V.*

$$$$ ⊞ **Hilton Princess San Salvador.** An elegantly sloping mansard roof gives this high-rise a European flair. The interior is no less continental, with large tapestries adorning the spacious lobby, rich carpeting in the halls, and hunting prints in the rooms. Churchill's Bar, with comfortable leather sofas, adds a degree of sophistication. The formal restaurant looks out to the small pool through stately arches. There is a fine health club that offers numerous classes and free access to all guests. It has a reputation as the most luxurious hotel in the country—and deservedly so. **Pros:** decent rates for the luxury offered; nice bar and restaurant. **Cons:** lots of activity, so not a place to go if you crave solitude; pricey. ⊠ *Av. Magnolias and Blvd. del Hipódromo, Col. San Benito* ☎ *503/2268–4545* ⊕ *www.hilton.com* ⤳ *204 rooms, 4 suites* ⧖ *In-room: a/c, safe, Wi-Fi. In-hotel: restaurant, bars, pool, gym, spa, laundry service, Internet terminal, parking (free), some pets allowed* ▤ *AE, D, DC, MC, V.*

$$$ ⊞ **Holiday Inn.** This lodging has business amenities equal to those of the most expensive hotels—Internet access, business center, meeting rooms—but at half the price. Its location couldn't be more convenient for those with business at the U.S. Embassy. After you've closed the deal you can swim laps in the pool or work out in the gym. A buffet breakfast is included in some rates. **Pros:** dependable Holiday Inn experience; cheaper rates than most other chains in the capital. **Cons:** sameness of a chain hotel. ⊠ *Blvd. Santa Elena, Col. Santa Elena* ☎ *503/2500–6000* ⊕ *www.icehotelsgroup.com* ⤳ *131 rooms, 3 suites* ⧖ *In-room: a/c, safe, Wi-Fi. In-hotel: restaurant, bar, pool, laundry service, Internet terminal, parking (free)* ▤ *AE, D, DC, MC, V* ❙◎❙ *CP.*

$ ⊞ **Hotel Vista Marella.** With architecture that calls to mind the colonial period, Vista Marella is a great find: a clean, dependable, midrange hotel. Though it's marketed as a bed-and-breakfast, you don't have the feeling that you're staying in someone's home. A pleasant breakfast area, with wrought-iron chairs and tables set in a courtyard, faces a trim little pool. The simplicity of a few potted trees is cheery. **Pros:** good rates; dependable offering; nice change from the capital's megahotels. **Cons:** smallish rooms. ⊠ *C. Juan José Cañas between Avs. 81 Sur and 83 Sur, Col. Escalón* ☎ *503/2211–3432* ⊕ *www.hotelmarella.com* ⤳ *60 rooms* ⧖ *In-room: Wi-Fi. In-hotel: restaurant, bar, pool, laundry service, Wi-Fi, parking (free)* ▤ *AE, D, DC, MC, V* ❙◎❙ *CP.*

$ ⊞ **Novo Apart-Hotel.** If you're in San Salvador for an extended stay, consider the Novo Apart-Hotel. Rates are reduced if you book for 10 days or more. It's not quite like home, but it does have nice touches like fully stocked kitchens. The layout feels more like an apartment complex, but one with lush greenery all around. Relax on your terrace, which overlooks the pool and gardens dotted with statues. **Pros:** apartment-like setting feels as if you're not in a hotel; kitchens are nice quality. **Cons:** lacks some of the amenities of a larger hotel. ✉ *Av. 61 Norte, one block north of C. 1 Poniente, Col. Escalón* ☎ *503/2521–2000* ⊕ *www. novoapart-hotel.com* ⤵ *50 rooms* ♿ *In-room: a/c, kitchen, refrigerator, Wi-Fi. In-hotel: restaurant, bar, pool, gym, laundry service, Internet terminal, parking (free), some pets allowed* ⊟ *AE, D, DC, MC, V* ⍟⎮ *BP.*

$$$–$$$$   🏨 **Real San Salvador.** This high-rise in Colonia Los Héroes is considered the city's best business hotel for its large convention center and high standard of service. Rooms, with three phones and Wi-Fi, are perfect for traveling executives. Tequilas, a colorful restaurant that serves up big margaritas, is one of the best Tex-Mex spots in the city. You can relax with a cocktail in Vertigo, a sleek lobby lounge. MetroCentro, Central America's largest mall, is across the street. **Pros:** luxury experience; many business amenities. **Cons:** charges fee for Wi-Fi. ✉ *Blvd. de los Héroes and Av. Sisimiles, across from MetroCentro, Col. Los Héroes* ☎ *503/2211–3333* ⊕ *www.ichotelsgroup.com* ⤵ *222 rooms, 6 suites* ♿ *In-room: a/c, safe, refrigerator, Wi-Fi. In-hotel: 4 restaurants, room service, bars, pool, gym, laundry service, Internet terminal, parking (free)* ⊟ *AE, D, DC, MC, V.*

$$–$$$   🏨 **Sheraton Presidente San Salvador.** You're sure to feel comfortable at this hotel, which in addition to its fine rooms offers amenities like daily digests from the *New York Times*. A comfortable bar and restaurant overlook the pool and adjacent thatch-roofed bar. The hotel's unique curved shape means that all rooms have balconies, some with views of the pool and the surrounding mountains. The super-comfortable beds are an additional highlight. **Pros:** decent rates for amenities offered. **Cons:** charges fee for Wi-Fi use. ✉ *Final Av. de la Revolución, Col. San Benito* ☎ *503/2283–4000* ⊕ *www.sheraton.com* ⤵ *220 rooms, 5 suites* ♿ *In-room: a/c, safe, Wi-Fi. In-hotel: 2 restaurants, room service, bar, pool, gym, spa, laundry service, Internet terminal, parking (free)* ⊟ *AE, D, DC, MC, V.*

**9**

# NIGHTLIFE AND THE ARTS

## NIGHTLIFE

If you want to party, you'll head to one of two very different neighborhoods—Antiguo Cuscatlán, home to the luxe Multiplaza and Gran Vía "lifestyle center" shopping malls; and around Búlevar de los Héroes and Calle San Antonio Abad, in Colonia Centroamérica. The former is where you'll find the young people with lots of style and lots of cash. The latter, near the Universidad de El Salvador, has a more bohemian atmosphere.

Wednesday, Friday, and Saturday are the most popular nights for going out on the town. Dress is mostly casual. On weekends most bars get going around 11 PM and continue until 2 or 3 AM, and discos start to fill up at midnight and rock until 5 or 6 AM.

## COLONIA CENTROAMÉRICA

Part of San Salvador's top independent arts organization, **La Luna Casa y Arte** (⊠ *228 C. Berlín, Urb. Buenos Aires* ☎ *503/2260–2921* ⊕ *www. lalunacasayarte.com*) is a restaurant, bar, and performance space that hosts everything from poetry readings to film screenings to reggae dance parties. It is perhaps the city's most interesting place for drinks, with an indoor-outdoor patio and a postmodern mix of surreal and indigenous imagery. **Los Tres Diablos** (⊠ *C. San Antonio Abad 2241 and Izalco, Col. Centroamérica* ☎ *503/2225–5609*) has a bohemian bent. Inside you'll find political posters and alternative music. Look for the neon "3D" sign outside.

In the neighborhood just north of Colonia Centroamérica you'll find **El Arpa** (⊠ *Av. A 137, Col. San José* ☎ *503/2225–0429*), a surprisingly authentic place for a pint of Guinness. Indoors the decor is a tribute to the old country, but the outdoor patio is the best place to sit.

San Salvador's bohemian crowd can be found at **Poetas y Locos** (⊠ *C. Guillermo Cortez 232* ☎ *503/2261–1978*), a two-story disco bar with an impressive seafood menu; each day there is a menu of the day which might consist of *coctel de camarones* (shrimp cocktail) or *sopa de gallina* (chicken soup).

**NEED A BREAK?**

When you just can't take the heat anymore, drop into **Café la T** for a refreshing drink. It's a hippyish place, a surprising change of pace in the capital; numerous coffee concoctions dot the menu, and there are interesting lefty books to pore over while you reenergize. You're bound to see a dreadlocked backpacker or two saunter in while you sip. (⊠ *C. San Antonio Abad 2233, Col. Centroamérica* ☎ *503/2225–6219*).

## ANTIGUO CUSCATLÁN

This area includes the shopping centers of Gran Vía and Multiplaza—the place to be for nightlife. In Gran Vía a good option is **Puyas** (⊠ *Gran Vía, 2nd fl.* ☎ *503/2278–6207*), really a restaurant, but with good specials on beer. Every day from 6 to 9 PM beers are two for one.

### COLONIA SAN BENITO

**Code** (⊠ *Blvd. El Hipódromo 2–281, Col. San Benito* ☎ *503/2223–6068*) has the best dance floor in the country, which means it's always packed. Things get going late, about 1 AM.

A quieter but no less fun scene is at **Puerto Escondido** (⊠ *Blvd. El Hipódromo, Col. San Benito*), where beers abound and Latin music entertains. A ceviche menu includes many different preparations.

One of city's liveliest nightspots, **Los Rinconcitos** (⊠ *Blvd. El Hipódromo 310, Col. San Benito* ☎ *503/2298–4799*) is three bars in one—on weekends there's recorded music in the middle level and a rock band playing on the back patio. This courtyard is a great place for a drink.

## THE ARTS

**La Luna Casa y Arte** (⊠ *228 C. Berlín, Urb. Buenos Aires* ☎ *503/2260–2921* ⊕ *www.lalunacasayarte.com*), the city's top independent arts organization, has a performance space where you can see cutting-edge art, as well as films, music, dance, and poetry. Beatrice Alcaine, the young Salvadoran who runs the space from her old home, also organizes children's workshops. Check the calendar for specific events.

DANCE The **Ballet Folklórico de El Salvador** (✉ *6 Av. Norte 319, El Centro* ☎ *503/2271–2628*) performs traditional folk dances. The country's top classical and contemporary dance company is **Escuela Nacional de Danza** (✉ *1a C. Poniente 1233,* ☎ *503/2221–0972*), which performs in Teatro Presidente.

FILM San Salvador has many cinemas where you can watch movies in English with Spanish subtitles. Movie listings are posted in *El Diario de Hoy,* the country's largest newspaper. Admission is about $2. Among the best theaters in town is the **Cinemark** (✉ *Blvd. de los Héroes, Col. Miramonte* ☎ *503/2261–2001*) in the sprawling MetroCentro. **La Luna Casa y Arte** (✉ *228 C. Berlín, Urb. Buenos Aires* ☎ *503/2260–2921* ⊕ *www. lalunacasayarte.com*) hosts an independent-film series on Wednesday.

MUSIC The city has two excellent venues for classical music. The most famous classical venue is the **Teatro Nacional** (✉ *Av. 2 Sur and C. Delgado, El Centro* ☎ *503/2222–8760*), a lovely building in the city's historical center. Located in the Zona Rosa is the **Teatro Presidente** (✉ *Final Av. La Revolución, Col. San Benito* ☎ *503/2243–3407*). The well-regarded **Orquestra Sinfónica Nacional** (☎ *503/2221–2373*) got its start in 1841 as a military band. It continues to perform classical works.

THEATER The **Centro Nacional de Artes** (✉ *C. Valero Lecha, Col. San Mateo* ☎ *503/ 2298–1839*) stages plays at various theaters around the city, including the restored Teatro Nacional.

## SHOPPING

### MALLS

The shopping mecca in San Salvador, **Gran Vía** (✉ *C. Chiltiupán and Carretera Panamericana* ☎ *503/2273–8111* ⊕ *www.lagranvia.com.sv*) has just about everything you might need—clothing, jewelry, a movie theater, banks. You can spend day and night here, as there are a number of bars as well.

The midrange **MetroCentro** (✉ *Blvd. de los Héroes, Col. Miramonte* ☎ *503/2257–6000*) is one of the largest shopping centers in the city. Here you'll find two labyrinthine stories of laid-back shops where Salvadorans often come to spend an afternoon. **Basilea** (✉ *Blvd. del Hipódromo, Col. San Benito* ☎ *503/2279–0833*), a small shopping center in the Zona Rosa, caters to a fairly upscale crowd. It has a few boutiques, jewelry shops, and an art gallery. If all the shopping makes you hungry, there's also a bakery and restaurant.

### MARKETS

The rows of stalls at the **Mercado Nacional de Artesanías** (✉ *Alameda Manuel Enrique Araujo, Col. San Benito* ☎ *503/2243–2341*) are where you can find handicrafts from all over El Salvador (and some from Guatemala). This is one-stop shopping for ceramics, hammocks, and just about anything else you can imagine. It's open every day except Sunday from 8 to 5.

The huge downtown market, **Mercado Central** (⊠ *6a C. Oriente, between 23 y 27 Av. Sur, Col. La Mermeja* ☏ *No phone*). is the biggest and most colorful in the country. Pickpockets like the crowds, so be on your guard. The chaotic **Mercado Ex-Cuartel** (⊠ *Av. 8 Sur between Cs. Delgado and 1a Oriente, El Centro*) seems to go on forever. Prices here are slightly higher than in the local villages (where most of the crafts come from), but it's a great place to stop for last-minute ceramics, textiles, hammocks, and more.

## SPECIALTY SHOPS

Galería Fernando Llort is contained within a small indoor complex called **El Arbol de Dios** (⊠ *C. La Mascota and Av. Masferrer, Col. Maquilishuat* ☏ *503/2263–9165*), meaning "God's Tree." Besides the gallery, El Arbol de Dios contains a nice gift store, a framing store, and Pupusería Margoth, a small cafeteria-style eatery with a wide range of Salvadoran food. The souvenir shop is a good place to pick up vivid Llort-designed beach towels, shirts, ceramics, jewelry, and stationery. The complex is open daily 8 AM to 9 PM.

# SIDE TRIPS FROM SAN SALVADOR

An organized tour is the easiest way to take in the sights in the area around the capital. The capital's **AviTours** (☏ *503/2510–7618* ⊕ *www.avitours.com.sv*) offers tours to the sights listed below, or can put together a customized mix-and-match schedule for you. As is the case elsewhere in El Salvador, public transporation can be slow-going, although the distances themselves are short.

## LAGO DE ILOPANGO

Filling the crater of an extinct volcano, Lago de Ilopango is the country's largest and deepest lake, covering more than 120 square km (46 square mi). Along the beach is a line of stalls selling freshly fried fish. Locals will offer to take you on a half-hour boat ride to the island of Puntún. Another destination on the lake is Cerros Quemados (which means "Burned Hills"), an island created by an 1880 volcanic eruption. ⊠ *15 km (9 mi) east of San Salvador.*

## PANCHIMALCO

South of the capital lies the picturesque village of Panchimalco. Here, surrounded by lush green mountains and dramatic boulders, descendants of the indigenous Pipil people live a surprisingly traditional life. The town's tranquil cobblestone streets lead to a small but elegant colonial church. A yearly festival on the first Sunday of March features a colorful parade. ⊠ *15 km (9 mi) south of San Salvador.*

## JOYA DE CERÉN

About 1,500 years ago, Volcán Laguna Caldera erupted, depositing several yards of volcanic ash in the surrounding area, and burying a Mayan village at the base of the volcano. The perfectly preserved village—everything right down to clay urns and the food inside them—was discovered by a construction worker in 1976. The site provides an intriguing look at Mayan life, including the foods they ate, the crops they grew, and their social structure. Because there are no signs, it's best to see the site with a guide. You can view pieces unearthed here, including an ornate obsidian blade, at the anthropology museum in San Salvador. ✉ *36 km (22 mi) west of San Salvador* ☎ *No phone* ✉ *$3* ⊙ *Tues.–Sun. 9–5.*

## SAN ANDRÉS

El Salvador's second-largest archaeological site, San Andrés is a Mayan community that was inhabited between AD 600 and 900, about the same time as Tikal in Guatemala and Copán in Honduras. More than 12,000 people once made their homes in and around the city. Two plazas ringed by pyramids have been carefully excavated, though the concrete used to shore up the structures is rather ugly. An interesting museum explains the history of the site and displays clay figurines found here. A scale model of the city helps you imagine its former grandeur. The grounds are beautifully maintained, with trees set around the grass-covered terraces. Salvadorans often come here for picnics. ✉ *33 km (21 mi) west of San Salvador* ☎ *No phone* ✉ *$3* ⊙ *Tues.–Sun. 9–4:30.*

## VOLCÁN DE SAN SALVADOR

This volcano, visible from all over the region, offers excellent views of San Salvador and the entire Valle de las Hamacas. There are two craters, the most famous of which is nicknamed El Boquerón (The Big Mouth). A path leads to the bottom of the crater, where you'll find another cone, formed during an eruption in 1917. It's best to hire a guide, as robbers sometimes target hikers along this route. ✉ *11 km (7 mi) north of Santa Tecla* ☎ *No phone* ✉ *Free.*

# NORTHERN AND WESTERN EL SALVADOR

Head north or west of San Salvador and you find yourself passing through valleys carpeted in brilliant shades of green. The mild climate and fertile soil make this the country's coffee capital. The crop continues to bring in great wealth to the owners of the haciendas, but the people who live in the surrounding villages remain grindingly poor.

Toward the borders of the tiny country, you'll encounter some breathtaking scenery. In the northwest the rugged mountains near La Palma, such as Miramundo, attract hikers. In this area is El Pital, the country's highest peak.

Western El Salvador is also known for its dramatic natural beauty. South of the town of Santa Ana is Lago de Coatepeque, a beautiful blue lake hidden inside the crater of a long-dormant volcano. Rivers and scenic waterfalls draw many people to the region.

The most charming towns in western El Salvador, however, are found along the Ruta de las Flores (Route of Flowers), an informal collection of villages stretching between Sonsonate and Ahuachapán. The villages of Juayúa and Apaneca are sleepy colonial towns visited mostly by Salvadorans, meaning that the weekend is the time to go. The villages of the Ruta de las Flores are all along the same highway, so traveling between them is easy. Juayúa is the Ruta's most hospitable town in which to spend the night, but even more luxury can be found in any of several beautiful hotels along the road between the towns, some of which are converted coffee plantations. These are some of the most precious gems of El Salvador's nascent tourist industry.

## SUCHITOTO

★ *27 km (17 mi) north of San Salvador.*

Cobblestone streets lined with squat colonial buildings clustered around a pretty church make this little town enchanting. Its setting, along a huge reservoir called Lago de Suchitlán (also known as Cerrón Grande), makes it one of the most popular destinations for day-trippers from San Salvador. Lake views abound from all along the edges of Suchitoto, and boat tours of the lake are a popular activity.

Suchitoto Tours organizes inexpensive outings to wildlife preserves and other scenic sights throughout the country. NOTE: Tours run anytime, but especially on weekends.

**Tour Companies Suchitoto Tours** (✉ *Next to Telecom, Suchitoto* ☎ *503/848–3438* ⊕ *www.suchitoto-tours.com*).

In the center of town you'll find a square called **Parque San Martín,** the heart of Suchitoto. Around the bandstand are dozens of benches that are filled with locals until late in the evening. In between are a few quirky sculptures, including one that is a replica of a *tatú,* or tunnel, used as a hiding place during the civil war. More interesting pieces of public art are across the street at a restaurant called Villa Balanza. This restaurant's name refers to the scale that rests above the entrance; on one side is part of an unexploded bomb that was dropped on the city, whereas on the other is a stack of pupusas, the delicious Salvadoran street food.

The **Museo Alejandro Cotto** is housed in the residence of an eccentric man known as *el brujo de Suchitoto* (the warlock of Suchitoto). A former film director, Cotto is known for his efforts to preserve his hometown's character. He has owned the home since the early 1970s, and even remained there throughout the war, refusing to leave. After letting you in through the 300-year-old front door, Cotto proudly shows off the printing equipment owned by his father, including antique presses and blocks of metal with raised letters. A number of galleries hold his family's collection of works by top Salvadoran painters and countless portraits of Cotto; every piece has a story behind it, such as a painting personally given to Cotto by Diego Rivera while Cotto was living in Mexico. (The tour is in Spanish, so if you if you don't know the language, try to pair up with someone who could translate.) A chapel contains centuries-old wooden saints and relics. Cotto takes you down verdant paths past such antiques as a 200-year-old sugarcane juicer. The high point of the tour is a serpentine trail that leads to a magnificent view of Lago de Suchitlán. ✉ *3 Av. Norte s/n* ☎ *No phone* ☞ *$4* ⊙ *Daily 9–noon and 2–5.*

No trip to Suchitoto would be complete without having taken a boat trip on **Lago de Suchitlán,** aka Cerrón Grande. Its hazy beauty and hypnotic calmness will make you think you are traveling backward through time. Surprisingly, however, this lake was created artificially in 1974 to drive the largest hydroelectric project in El Salvador, and it is now one

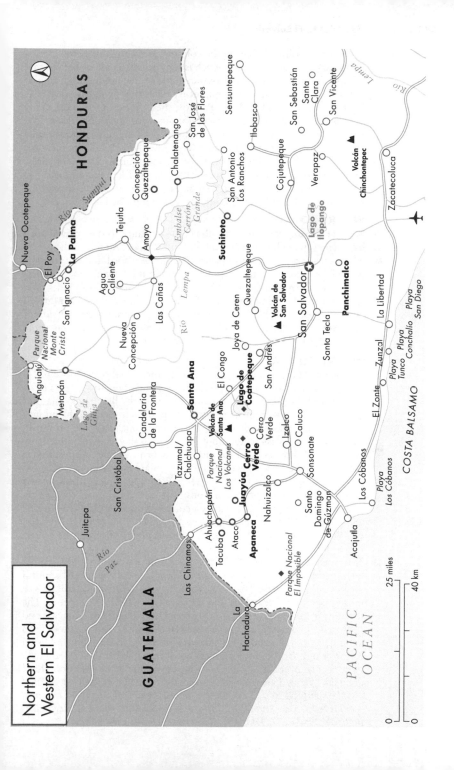

# Northern and Western El Salvador

HONDURAS

GUATEMALA

Nueva Ocotepeque

El Poy
San Ignacio
La Palma

Río Sumpul

Concepción
Quezaltepeque
Chalatenango

San José
de las Flores

Sensuntepeque

San Sebastián
Santa Clara
San Vicente

Ilobasco

Cojutepeque
Verapaz

Volcán
Chinchontepec

Zacatecoluca

Lempa

Río Lempa

Tejutla

Amayo

Agua
Caliente

Las Cañas

Embalse
Cerrón Grande

San Antonio
Los Ranchos

Suchitoto

Lago de
Ilopango

Juitcpa

San Cristóbal

Río Paz

Anguiatú

Metapán

Lago de
Güija

Parque
Nacional
Monte
Cristo

Candelaria
de la Frontera

Nueva
Concepción

Santa Ana

El Congo

Lago de
Coatepeque

Quezaltepeque

Joya de Ceren

Volcán de
San Salvador

San Salvador

Panchimalco

San Andrés

Santa Tecla

La Libertad

Las Chinamas

Tazumal/
Chalchuapa

Volcán de
Santa Ana

Parque
Nacional
Los Volcanes

Cerro
Verde

Cerro Verde

Juayúa

Ahuachapán
Tacuba
Ataco

Apaneca

Nahuizalco

Izalco

Caluco

Sonsonate

Santo
Domingo
de Guzmán

Parque Nacional
El Imposible

Acajutla

La
Hachadura

Los Cóbanos

Playa
Los Cóbanos

El Zonte

Playa
Tunco
Playa
Conchalío

Zunzal

Playa
San Diego

COSTA BALSAMO

PACIFIC
OCEAN

0    25 miles

0    40 km

Río
Lempa

of the most polluted lakes in the country, a meeting place for factory runoff and copious sewage—which is why scientists are so baffled that 150,000 or so seabirds hang out at the lake, including, according to Reuters, at least 90 species of migratory birds that fly in from places as far away as Alaska. Isla de los Pajaros, the birdiest of the lake's many islands, hums with a bizarre, cacophonous symphony of birdcalls. For $20 you can charter a boat for an hour to take you around the lake and to the Isla, past memorable flocks of low-flying birds skimming for contaminated fish. From the center of Suchitoto, it's a 10-minute drive to the shores of the lake; just follow the signs marked AL LAGO and you will reach the port. It costs $1.50 to park your car, then you arrange for your boat at the little stand on the way down to the lake.

## WHERE TO EAT

$      ✕ **Villa Balanza.** From the scale above the entrance to the prow-shaped
SALVADORAN    bar, there's much here that's symbolic and strange. A table in the tower,
★      which is decorated with antiques and artifacts, affords a beautiful view of the lake. The rest of the open-air restaurant is relaxing, and the collection of war memorabilia—bullets, mortars, and the like—provides food for thought. The menu is typically Salvadoran, like *gallina india* (grilled hen) and *mar y tierra* (surf and turf) with shrimp. ⊠ *North side of Parque San Martín* ☎ *503/2335–1408* ⊕ *www.villabalanzarestaurante. com.sv* ▤ *AE, D, DC, MC, V* ☉ *Closed Mon.*

## WHERE TO STAY

$      ⛺ **El Tejado.** This sprawling hotel-restaurant, which feels more like a resort than Suchitoto's other hotels, boasts one of the town's best overall views of the lake—you can admire it from the hammocks that dot the lawn. Also worth mentioning is the pool that seems to blend into the horizon. If you're not a guest of the hotel, but just came for lunch, you can have access to the pool for $3.25 a day. Rooms are cheery and smell of the wooden furniture. The enormous open-air restaurant ($$) serves up typical Salvadoran food—grilled meats and sopa de gallina—accompanied by that same view. **Pros:** lots of activities so never at a lack for something to do. **Cons:** can be difficult to find space on weekends; not a good choice if you crave seclusion. ⊠ *3a Av. Norte 58* ☎ *503/2335–1769* ⊕ *www.eltejadosuchtot.net* ↩ *11 rooms* ⚬ *In-room: a/c, Wi-Fi. In-hotel: restaurant, bar, pool, laundry service, Internet terminal, parking (free)* ▤ *AE, MC, V* ⦿ *CP.*

$$     ⛺ **La Posada de Suchitlán.** A quartet of villas at this century-old hacienda have private patios overlooking the lake—one of the most beautiful views in the country. The villas, set in lovely gardens, are about $10 more than the other rooms, but they are well worth the expense. The restaurant ($$–$$$) serves a fairly standard assortment of meats and *típicos*; it's more notable for the lovely lake view than for the food. If it's a hot day, try a refreshing fruit-flavored *licuado* (fruit shake) and listen to (or cringe at) the hotel's collection of exotic birds as they squawk. Note that showers don't have hot water. **Pros:** hotel and restaurant have good lake views. **Cons:** we'd like to see the exotic birds released. ⊠ *Final 4 C. Poniente* ☎ *503/2335–1064* ⊕ *www.laposada.com.sv* ↩ *11 rooms, 4 villas* ⚬ *In-room: a/c, Wi-Fi. In-hotel: restaurant, room service, parking (free)* ▤ *AE, D, DC, MC, V* ⦿ *BP.*

$   ⊡ **Las Puertas.** One of Suchitoto's newest hotels, Las Puertas has a unique location right on the town's main plaza. There are only six spectacularly comfortable, perfectly air-conditioned rooms, all of which have a view onto the square and cathedral, while their common shared terrace faces west, making it ideal for sunsets over the mountains. Facilities here—like Wi-Fi and modern TVs—are a notch above anything else in town, yet prices are eminently reasonable. Downstairs is a restaurant ($$) and bar that is one of Suchitoto's few nightlife spots. The kitchen is staffed by Suchitoto locals, who prepare interesting dishes like chicken wrapped in tobacco leaves. **Pros:** terrific rates for what's offered; central location. **Cons:** only six rooms, so reservations are essential. ⊠ *Av. 15 de Septiembre, in front of the cathedral* ☎ *503/2335–1054* ⊕ *www. laspuertassuchitoto.com* ↪ *6 suites* ⚒ *In-room: a/c, Wi-Fi. In-hotel: restaurant, pool, parking (free)* ⊟ *AE, D, DC, MC, V* ⫶◎⫶ *BP.*

$$ – $$$
Fodor's Choice
★

⊡ **Los Almendros de San Lorenzo.** Set in a 200-year-old colonial home, Los Almendros retains a stately air but throws in some hip touches, like the attractive and comfortable bar whose cutting-edge lighting might be mistaken for SoHo, not Suchitoto; it's a fun place to come for evening cocktails and meeting fellow travelers, even if you're not staying at the hotel. Rooms are cozy, and the hotel has a lounge-y living room that houses an interesting library. The restaurant ($$–$$$), brainchild of a legendary Frenchman named Pascal, has a Franco-Salvadoran menu that ranges from French onion soup to *gallo en chicha* (chicken stewed in sweet Salvadoran liquor), which you can consume as you overlook the inviting dark-blue swimming pool and courtyard greenery. Across the street is Pascal's art gallery. **Pros:** engaging owner is a wealth of information; wonderful restaurant. **Cons:** can be difficult to find space on weekends. ⊠ *4a C. Poniente,* ☎ *503/2335–1200* ⊕ *www. hotelsalvador.com* ↪ *6 rooms, 2 suites* ⚒ *In-room: a/c, no phone, refrigerator, DVD, Wi-Fi. In-hotel: restaurant, bar, pool, laundry service, Internet terminal, parking (free)* ⊟ *AE, D, DC, MC, V* ⫶◎⫶ *BP.*

## NIGHTLIFE

On weeknights head to **Bar Niceo** (⊠ *4 Av. Norte and 4 C. Poniente*), the only place that serves drinks after 10 PM on weekdays. The walls here are decorated with revolutionary posters; come in your Che Guevara T-shirt and you'll feel right at home.

On weekends, **Café los Sanchez** (⊠ *3 Av. Norte and 4 C. Poniente*) is the place to be. Dance the night away to Latin music and enjoy the beers, as that's all they serve.

For one of Suchitoto's more subdued scenes, head to **Fonda del Mirador** (⊠ *3 Av. Norte 98* ☎ *503/335–1126*), whose view is second to none. Having a beer during sunset is a safe bet here; note that if there aren't many patrons, they will close early.

Late-night drinks can be had at **Café El Harlequín** (⊠ *Barrio Santa Lucia 26* ☎ *503/325–5890*), a cute café with interesting cocktails. All tables are outdoors, and lights are strung across the area, creating a great atmosphere.

**9**

# LA PALMA

*70 km (43 mi) northwest of Concepción Quezaltepeque.*

In the shadow of El Pital, the country's highest mountain, is the little town of La Palma. That peak, as well as others nearly as high, draws hikers from around the world. From the top you can see into parts of El Salvador and Honduras.

When artist Fernando Llort moved to La Palma three decades ago, he began teaching residents his distinctive, playful style of painting. Today La Palma is famous for the dozens of workshops producing wood and ceramic goods adorned with these childlike designs. The facade of the town's little church, however, is the work of Llort himself. There isn't much to see in the town; it's just rows and rows of shops selling similar trinkets. The true draw here is the beautiful mountains, particularly the drive up to Miramundo nearby.

### GETTING HERE AND AROUND

La Palma is about 10 km (6 mi) from the border with Honduras. You can cross at El Poy quite safely, too. You must pay $3 to enter Honduras—park your car and buy the visa in a little office—and then theoretically another $3 to return to El Salvador, although if you're just popping in for the day, the border guards can be talked out of it.

### MONEY MATTERS

CitiBank in the center of town has ATMs.

**Banks CitiBank** (⊠ *C. Principal at C. La Cancha* ☎ *503/2305–9330*).

### WHERE TO STAY

$   🖃 **Hostal Miramundo.** You truly feel as if you can see the entire world laid out before you from this hotel, which is extremely popular with Salvadorans. Tiny villages of rustic but serviceable cabins are nestled amidst the towering mountains. The trek up Monte Miramundo is entertainment in itself, as you wind around hairpin turns on incredibly steep grades. (Don't attempt it without a four-wheel-drive vehicle.) Buses also travel up here, athough that can be an even more harrowing experience. Flavorful hot chocolate is a specialty. **Pros:** amazing views; get-away-from-it-all seclusion. **Cons:** difficult drive to get here; can be tough to find space on weekends. ⊠ *Cerro Miramundo* ☎ *503/230–0437* 📠 *503/729–1573* ⊕ *www.hotelmiramundo.com* ⚡ *8 rooms, 3 cabañas* ⚐ *In-hotel: restaurant, no a/c, parking (free).* ⊟ *No credit cards.*

### SHOPPING

La Palma *is* its dozens of artisans' cooperatives that produce beautiful wood and ceramic goods. The places are much more than just shops with cash registers. The folks at each all welcome you to stop for awhile and watch their works take shape, and your purchases help support the local population.

**COPAPASE.** The area's oldest and largest cooperative excels in its woodwork and Naïf paintings, and has a small museum dedicated to the history of regional arts and crafts. ⊠ *C. Principal* ☎ *2305–9376.*

**Artesanos Unidos.** Just 12 members belong to this cooperative, but Artesanos Unidos uses its small size to give a more personalized, up-close view of its fashioning of woodwork and paintings. ⊠ *C. Prinicpal* ☎ *2300–2485.*

**Asociación Semilla de Dios.** In La Palma itself is just Semilla de Dios's shop, but if you call ahead, these folks can arrange a tour of their workshops outside of town. ⊠ *C. 3 Poniente* ☎ *2335–9010.*

# SANTA ANA

*63 km (40 mi) west of San Salvador, 45 km (28 mi) south of Metapán.*

Salvadoreños call Santa Ana *la segunda ciudad,* as it's the country's second-largest city. But don't worry that this will be a smaller version of San Salvador; Santa Ana is a distant second in size. With some of the country's best-preserved pre-independence buildings, the city retains much of its past elegance and is the country's loveliest colonial city.

### GETTING HERE AND AROUND

Santa Ana's bus terminal is on 10 Avenida Sur, about 14 blocks from downtown. Buses depart San Salvador's Terminal de Occidente every 10 minutes for the 75-minute trip to Santa Ana.

### SAFETY

Santa Ana is reasonably safe, but you should take all the standard precautions you would when traveling in any foreign city.

### MONEY MATTERS

CitiBank in the center of town has ATMs.

Banks **CitiBank** (⊠ *Av. Independencia Sur at 3 C. Oriente* ☎ *503/2489–4876*).

### EXPLORING

**Parque Libertad,** at the intersection of Avenida Independencia and Calle Libertad, is marked by a graceful white bandstand.

Facing Parque Libertad is the neo-Gothic **Catedral de Santa Ana.** The ornate facade is topped by two towers. The stained glass in the rose window is broken in places, a vestige of the earthquake that devastated the region in 2001.

Facing the cathedral, the **Palacio Municipal** dates back to Santa Ana's brief stint as capital of the republic. Its neoclassical facade faces the street, but a peek inside reveals a colonial-style courtyard complete with a central fountain. Wooden balconies run around the sides.

The cream-colored **Teatro Nacional de Santa Ana,** an elegant neoclassical theater, is possibly the most remarkable piece of architecture in the country. The building, dating from 1910, is well preserved as a superb restoration returned its original grandeur. Note the depiction of Volcán de Santa Ana on the ornamental crest on the facade. It sits on the northern edge of Parque Libertad.

Next door to the Teatro Nacional is **Casino Santaneco,** built in 1896 as a private club; unlike many such buildings in Central America, it is still used as such today. Note the spiral columns that adorn the corner entrance. Ask a guard to let you inside for a peek at the polished interior. Moorish-style eight-point stars grace the woodwork of the ceiling and balconies.

**9**

On the south side of the main square is the **Museo Regional de Occidente**, a regional museum with changing exhibits dedicated to the economic, social, and cultural development of western El Salvador. Among the rotating shows you'll find some fine examples of the artifacts from the region's archaeological sites. Downstairs is a display about the country's currency. ⊠ *Av. Independencia Sur 8* ☎ *503/2441–1215* 💲 *$1 for adults, free for children* ☉ *Tues.–Sat. 8:30–noon and 1–5.*

★    The Mayan city of **Tazumal**, which means "place where people were burned" in the Q'eqchí language, is one of El Salvador's most important and best-preserved pre-Columbian sites. Although much smaller than Tikal in Guatemala or Copán in Honduras, Tazumal gives a glimpse into the lives of several indigenous civilizations dating back over 3,000 years. Archaeological evidence suggests that the city traded with communities as far away as present-day Mexico. Unfortunately, only a small part of the 5-square-km (3-square-mi) area has been excavated, although work continues on and off. Until more structures are uncovered, Tazumal's main attractions are the large pyramid and ball court. From atop the large pyramid, most likely a religious temple, you have a nice view of the town of Chalchuapa and the surrounding countryside.

A small museum displays a number of relics found at Tazumal, although many of the best ones have been taken to museums in the capital. Photos and placards relate the site's complex history and the difficult restoration process. All are in Spanish. ⊠ *13 km (8 mi) west of Santa Ana* ☎ *503/2444–0010* 💲 *$3* ☉ *Tues.–Sun. 9–5.*

## WHERE TO EAT AND STAY

The city is known for its *sorbetes,* which blend sherbet and ice cream. As you explore the city, look out for the little pushcarts run by a company called Sin Rival selling these treats. The best are *leche,* made with condensed milk, and *frutas,* made from different types of fresh fruit.

$    ✕ **El Patio.** It's worth the trip to this wonderful spot just for a taste of the
★    Salvadoran specialty called *gallo en chicha.* The sweet soup, flavored with prunes, olives, and raisins, has rooster meat in a homemade liquor made from fermented corn. Wash down your meal with a mammoth *fresco* (fruit smoothie)—try *piña* (pineapple) or *sandia* (watermelon). The restaurant, set around a cool courtyard, looks like a colonial-era ranch. ⊠ *21 C. Poniente 3 between C. Independencia and 2 Av. Sur* ☎ *503/440–4221* ▤ *AE, D, DC, MC, V* ☉ *Closed Mon.*

$    ▥ **Hotel Sahara.** This is the best hotel in the city, which isn't saying much. You'll have to put up with fluorescent lights, chipped paint, and tacky furnishings. The rooms are clean, however, and have soaring ceilings. A rooftop terrace has views of the surrounding volcanoes. **Pros:** decent rates; nice views from rooftop terrace. **Cons:** spartan rooms need a makeover. ⊠ *Av. 10 Sur and C. 3 Poniente* ☎ *503/447–8832* ⊕ *www. hotelsahara.com* 🛏 *30 rooms* ♿ *In-room: a/c, Wi-Fi. In-hotel: restaurant, laundry service, parking (free)* ▤ *AE, D, DC, MC, V* ⦿ *BP.*

# LAGO DE COATEPEQUE

*16 km (10 mi) west of Santa Ana.*

**Fodor's Choice** Set high in the mountains, Lago de Coatepeque is one of the most beau-
★ tiful sights in El Salvador. The enormous lake, set in a nearly perfectly
circular crater, covers 26 square km (16 square mi). Here you'll find
some of the best swimming in the country. The air is cool and fresh, and
the natural springs keep the water temperature remarkably comfortable.
Best of all, the lake hasn't been ruined by reckless development—in fact,
all you'll find are the dozens of lovely old homes that line the shore,
belonging primarily to Santa Ana coffee barons. The hotels, set back
from the lake, have raised terraces that let you gaze out over the water
to the looming Santa Ana and Izalco volcanoes.

### GETTING HERE AND AROUND

Though the lake lies a scant 16 km (10 mi) from Santa Ana, public
transportation can take up to an hour, especially on weekends when
you'll swear all of Santa Ana is coming out here. Buses leave Santa Ana's
main terminal every half-hour throughout the day until 4 PM. That's
also the time the last bus heads back to town.

### SAFETY

As with any locale where activities revolve around swimming, exercise
utmost caution and never swim alone. Don't plan on lifeguards here.

### MONEY MATTERS

There are no banks or ATMs here. Stock up on cash back in Santa Ana,
the closest major town.

### WHERE TO STAY

$ 🏨 **Hotel Torremolinos.** On a long dock directly above the shore, Tor-
remolinos has no real competition, which means it can get away with
slightly dingy rooms. Still, it is a wonderful spot to take in the lake's
majesty. The menu at the restaurant is typically Salvadoran, with specialties like *guapote* (bass) and shrimp-stuffed avocado. On Sunday
afternoon, dance to live Latin music while the sun sets over the mountains. **Pros:** good restaurant; bargain rates; stupendous views of lake.
**Cons:** dark rooms; can be difficult to find space on weekends. ⊠ *Lago
de Coatepeque* ☎ *503/441–6037* ⊕ *www.torremolinoslagocoatepeque.
com* 🛏 *16 rooms* ⚒ *In-room: no a/c, no phone, no TV (some). In-hotel:
restaurant, bar, parking (free)* ⊟ *AE, D, DC, MC, V* ⏐⏐ *EP.*

9

# PARQUE NACIONAL LOS VOLCANES

*8 km (5 mi) west of Lago de Coatepeque.*

As you'd expect from the name, this national park encompasses the
summits of three volcanoes—Cerro Verde, Izalco, and Santa Ana—as
well as thousands of acres of cloud forest. Easily reached from San Salvador or Santa Ana, although with some peculiarities of logistics, the
park is one of El Salvador's must-see sights.

## GETTING HERE AND AROUND

Most Salvadorans refer to the park as Cerro Verde, its former name.
■ TIP→ **When asking directions or discussing transportation arrangements, you should use the name Cerro Verde, too, for ease of communication.**

Buses directly to the park entrance depart several times a day from Santa Ana, but a car offers you the most convenience for getting here. Remember that to take advantage of the guided ranger walks, you need to be here by 11 AM.

## SAFETY

Sadly, Parque Nacional Los Volcanoes has become a popular spot for thieves. Ask a ranger to accompany you—the guided hikes are free and begin at 11, and the details they provide about the park and its wildlife can be quite interesting. ⊠ *37 km (23 mi) from Santa Ana* ▧ *$2* ☉ *Daily 8–5.*

## EXPLORING

**Cerro Verde.** The name is Spanish for "green hill," but Cerro Verde doesn't quite do justice to the towering peak that forms the centerpiece of this popular national park. This extinct volcano, with excellent views of Lago de Coatepeque, is home to a wide variety of birds; more than 125 species, including 17 types of hummingbirds, have been spotted inside the nature reserve. You can choose from several clearly marked hiking trails. The short nature trail is a pleasant stroll leading to good views of Volcán Santa Ana. Signs along the way point out unique features of the crater. The air is clean, crisp, and often chilly, so bring a jacket.

**Volcán Santa Ana.** One of the park's more serious hikes is up Volcán Santa Ana, the highest volcano in El Salvador. Also known as Lamatepec (Father Hill), this 7,757-foot peak is still active, although it hasn't erupted for decades. A hike to its crater and back takes about four hours, but the views of Volcán Cerro Verde and Volcán Izalco make it worth the effort. From the rim you'll surely get a whiff of the sulfuric lagoon inside the crater. Though long regarded as dormant, Santa Ana came to life again in 2005 and has grumbled off and on ever since. Authorities close access at the slightest whiff of peril to visitors.

**Volcán Izalco.** Hard-core hikers will want to take on the small but tough Volcán Izalco. One of the world's youngest volcanoes, the 6,396-foot mound of stone was created in 1770 when molten lava began spewing so rapidly that in less than a month the debris had piled up thousands of feet high. The pyrotechnics were so intense that they could be seen from the sea, and sailors dubbed it *El Faro del Pacífico* (The Lighthouse of the Pacific). After almost two centuries of continuous activity, Izalco suddenly went dormant in 1957. Black and utterly barren, it remains an imposing sight. The grade of the climb to the crater itself is not as daunting as it appears, but the round-trip journey involves a good three hours of strenuous hiking; the crumbling surface—two steps forward, one step back the whole way—means inexperienced hikers should think twice before accepting the challenge.

# JUAYÚA

**Fodor's** Choice ★ *30 km (18 mi) north of Sonsonate.*

The crown jewel of the Ruta de las Flores, Juayúa is the first major town you'll hit heading from Sonsonate on CA-8, and by far the most lively town along the Ruta in which to spend the night. The mountain village's colonial church and whitewashed buildings gleam in the sun. This community is best known as the home of the Cristo Negro (Black Christ), a 15th-century sculpture in the cathedral that attracts hundreds of pilgrims every year. One of the only images of Christ depicted with indigenous features, it is thought to have healing powers. The charming little village is surrounded by the fields of coffee that bring prosperity to the region. Every Saturday and Sunday, from morning until about 6 PM, the city hosts a well-known *feria gastronómica,* or food festival. The streets are lined with street vendors selling everything from gallo en chicha to delicious roast pork. Make sure to try the *riguas* (fried corn cakes with sugar). Once you try the *ponche,* you will definitely bring this recipe home with you; it's steaming hot milk mixed with rum (or tequila), cinnamon, and vanilla. Do your absolute best to time your visit with a weekend, as Juayúa's food fair is a memorable Salvadoran experience.

### GETTING HERE AND AROUND

Buses leave Santa Ana six times a day for Juayúa. Travel time is one hour. Juayúa's informal bus stop is on the town's central plaza.

### MONEY MATTERS

Juayúa has banks but no ATMs. Get cash before leaving San Salvador or Santa Ana.

### WHERE TO EAT AND STAY

$ ✕ **Casa Vieja.** Sit here amidst artisanal crafts in a verdant garden and enjoy such mainstays as the ubiquitous plato típico or *pollo encebollado* (chicken with onions). More interesting options include the quesadillas *de trigo,* a wheat tortilla stuffed with beans, cheese, and avocado. Sugary *naranjadas* (orange juice mixed with sugar) are a great way to start the day. ✉ *Avs. Daniel Coron Sur and 6 Oriente* ☎ *503/452–2599* ▤ *AE, D, DC, MC,V* ☻ *No dinner.*

$ ★ ⛺ **Hotel Anáhuac.** The people here—whether the staff or your fellow wandering travelers—will make you feel quite at home. The owner is a talented musician, and she often performs in Juayúa; don't miss it if she's playing. The staff also provides a wealth of information about the area. Rooms are pretty standard, and don't have air conditioners. Nonetheless, the garden is lovely, everything is clean, and you'll be with the right people to get to know the area. You can even take a few Spanish lessons if you have time. **Pros:** bargain rates; fun; musical owner. **Cons:** very basic rooms. ✉ *1a C. Poniente and Av. 5a Norte* ☎ *503/2469–2401* ⊕ *www.hotelanahuac.tikal.dk* ⇨ *6 rooms* ⚘ *In-room: no a/c, no phone, no TV, Wi-Fi. In-hotel: laundry service, parking (free)* ▤ *AE, MC, V* ⧎ *EP.*

9

## NIGHTLIFE

The only nightlife spot in this sleepy town is **Restaurant R & R** (⊠ *C. Merceditas Cacéres 1–4* ☎ *503/452–2083*). It's only open on Friday, Saturday, and Sunday, and there is often live music. There's easy-to-like comfort food available, too.

Another noteworthy town besides Juayúa along the Ruta de las Flores is **Nahuizalco** (⊠ *On CA-8, halfway between Sonsonate and Juayúa*), famous for its wicker workshops—a dozen or more produce baskets, chairs, tables, and other products. It's home to a large population of Pipil who came here prior to Spanish occupation. There's also a unique night market where locals buy and sell fruits and vegetables by candlelight.

# APANECA

*20 km (12 mi) west of Juayúa.*

Apaneca has the highest elevation of any major settlement in El Salvador. It is also one of the prettiest, with cobblestone streets lined with colorful houses. The surrounding countryside is spectacular, so it's no surprise that hikers come here from around the world.

## GETTING HERE AND AROUND

Apaneca and other communities on the Ruta de las Flores are served by buses that pass through from Juayúa about every 30 minutes.

## MONEY MATTERS

Apaneca has neither banks nor ATMs. Get cash in Santa Ana or San Salvador.

## EXPLORING

**Iglesia de Apaneca.** The colonial-era Iglesia de Apaneca is a bit run-down, but the twin bell towers are still pretty. Curiously, the church faces away from the main square. ⊠ *Parque Central* ☎ *No phone* ☎ *Free* ⊙ *Open for Sunday mass, irregular hours the rest of the week.*

**Finca Santa Leticia.** South of town is Finca Santa Leticia, a sprawling coffee plantation on the grounds of the Santa Leticia Mountain Resort. You can see the workings of the facility on Wednesday and Saturday mornings at 9 AM. Reserve in advance, and opt for Wednesday if your schedule permits—it's less crowded than the weekend tour. ⊠ *Km 86.5 on the Sonsonate Rd.* ☎ *503/2433–0357, 503/2298–2986 in San Salvador* ⊕ *www.coffee.com.sv* ☎ *$20.*

**Laguna de las Ninfas.** One of the area's premier bird-watching destinations is about a 45-minute hike from town, but the lake nearly dries up during the December–April dry season. Hiking here alone is not safe—a few robberies have been reported. Check with the local police in Apaneca (☎ *2433–0337*) to arrange an escort. (Yes, they are happy to do this for you; they will charge a nominal fee.) ⊠ *5 km (3 mi) northwest of Apaneca* ☎ *No phone.*

**Laguna Verde.** One of El Salvador's many volcano-crater lakes lies 7 km (4 mi) outside of town and is ringed by pine trees. As with Laguna de las Ninfas above, you should not make the hike alone, but rather arrange for an escort with the police in Apaneca (☎ *2433–0337*). ⊠ *7 km (4 mi) northeast of Apaneca* ☎ *no phone.*

## WHERE TO STAY

$ ⛺ **Hotel Alicante Apaneca.** In the shadows of a coffee plantation, you'll find this enormous hotel with an even bigger restaurant ($$–$$$) that seems as if it could house the entire population of tiny Apaneca—with room to spare. A sprawling lawn dotted with sculptures and hammocks is a great place to relax with a cocktail, as is the interestingly shaped pool. The rooms have a ski-lodge feel to them; each one has a private patio or balcony complete with comfortable wooden lounge furniture. The gargantuan restaurant offers a predictable menu of Salvadoran food. **Pros:** good restaurant; lots of activities. **Cons:** not a good bet if you crave silent seclusion. ⊠ *Km 93.5 on the Sonsonate Rd. toward Apaneca* ☎ *503/450–5651 or 503/433–0572* ⊕ *www.alicanteapaneca. com* ⤳ *26 rooms, 2 bungalows* ⚐ *In-room: no a/c, no phone. In-hotel: restaurant, pool, gym, spa, parking (free)* ▭ *AE, D, DC, MC, V* ⎮◯⎮ *CP.*

$ ⛺ **Santa Leticia Mountain Resort.** It's just outside Apaneca, but this family-run hotel's location within 230 acres of tropical hardwood forests makes it feel miles from civilization. The simply decorated rooms are crowned with ceiling beams made from lumber from the nearby farm. The restaurant ($$), La Finca, serves weekdays 9 AM to 5 PM, Saturday until 9:30 PM, and Sunday until 6 PM. The property is a fully functioning coffee plantation. Every Wednesday and Saturday they lead tours of the property in the mornings; you must reserve in advance. **Pros:** secluded atmosphere; fun to stay on a working coffee plantation. **Cons:** can get crowded on weekends. ⊠ *Km 86.5 on the Sonsonate Rd. toward Apaneca* ☎ *503/2433–0357, 503/2298–2986 in San Salvador* ⊕ *www.coffee. com.sv* ⤳ *11 rooms, 8 cabañas* ⚐ *In-room: no a/c, no phone, Wi-Fi. In-hotel: restaurant, bar, pool, parking (free)* ▭ *AE, D, DC, MC, V* ⎮◯⎮ *CP.*

### SPORTS AND THE OUTDOORS

The coolest way to explore the area is by going on the **Apaneca Canopy Tour** (☎ *503/2433–0554* ⊕ *www.elsalvadorcanopy.com*). This outfit will take you zip-lining through the forest canopy for 1½ to 2 hours.

# EASTERN EL SALVADOR

This region is extraordinarily diverse, ranging from mountain villages to charming towns to modern cities. Some areas within this region are famous for their *artesanía* (crafts), others for their outdoor activities. Eastern El Salvador rarely draws the attention of tourists, but the warm and generous spirit of its people wins the hearts of many who visit.

## SAN MIGUEL

*45 km (30 mi) east of Santiago de María.*

With over 200,000 residents, San Miguel is the fourth-largest city in the country. It has a few sights of note—the city was founded in 1530—but with each passing year, modern urban sprawl takes over more and more. As the largest metropolis in the eastern third of the country, San Miguel is more likely a place to fuel up your stomach and wallet.

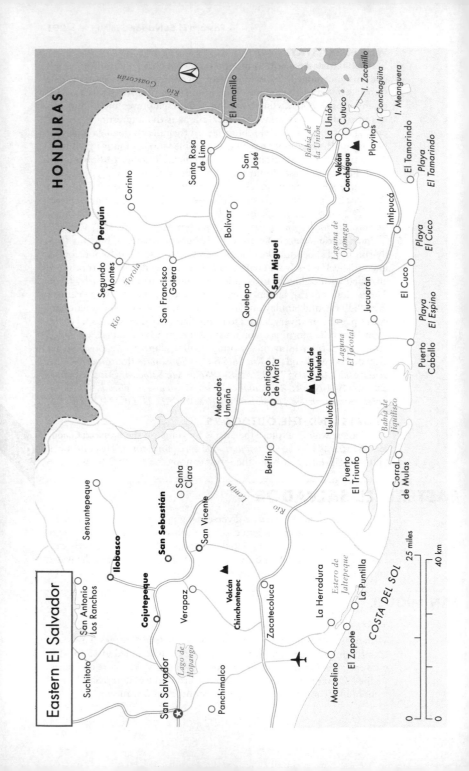

**GETTING HERE AND AROUND**

Buses leave from San Salvador's Terminal Oriente about every 15 minutes throughout the day for the two-hour trip to San Miguel. San Miguel's own bus terminal is on 6 Calle Oriente. San Miguel's Hertz is the only place in eastern El Salvador to rent a car.

**SAFETY**

Though San Miguel has nowhere near the crime problems of San Salvador, we recommend you take appropriate city precautions when visiting. Avoid handling large sums of money in public. The streets feel deserted at night, so take taxis.

**MONEY MATTERS**

CitiBank, in the center of town, has an ATM.

**ESSENTIALS**

**Banks CitiBank** (✉ *Av. Gerardo Barrios at 4 C. Pte.* ☎ *503/2678–4502*).

**Bus Terminals Terminal de Buses** (✉ *6 C. Oriente* ☎ *503/2660–2772*).

**Car Rental Hertz** (✉ *Av. Garardo Barrios 202, San Miguel* ☎ *503/2661–1691*).

## EXPLORING

**Catedral de Nuestra Señora de la Paz.** On the central Parque David J. Guzmán, the huge cathedral has a marble altar and stained-glass windows that are worth seeing. Here you'll find a statue of the Virgin Mary that is credited with saving the city from destruction during a volcanic eruption. ✉ *4 Av. Norte.*

**Antiguo Teatro Nacional.** South of the central square sits this elegant theater, a century-old building where plays are often staged from August through November. ✉ *2 C. Oriental.*

**Capilla de la Medalla Miagrosa.** About seven blocks west of the main square are the lovely gardens that house the Capilla de la Medalla Miagrosa, a chapel where a religious healer once worked miracles. ✉ *Av. 7 Norte and 4 C. Poniente.*

**Laguna de Olomega.** This lake is still the lifeblood of the many villages that dot its shoreline, which means fish is the main meal for miles around. Locals favor the tasty *guapote* (similar to bass) and the sturgeon-size tilapia. You can reach the communities around the lake, including Olomegita and La Estrachura, on passenger boats that leave at 8 AM, return at 3 PM, and leave again at 4 PM (35¢). Another nice stop is Los Cerritos, a little island where locals bake in the sun.

**Volcán Chaparrastique.** Dominating the town is this 6,986-foot volcano; it's active and last erupted in 1976. It's an intense two-hour hike to the summit from the town of La Placita; we recommend hiring a guide.

## WHERE TO EAT AND STAY

$ ✕ **Acajutla.** Great seafood dishes are served in an airy and elegant thatch-roof dining room of this San Miguel favorite that is part of a country-wide chain. ✉ *Av. Roosevelt Sur and 7 C. Poniente* ☎ *503/661–2255* ▭ *AE, D, DC, MC, V.*

SEAFOOD

¢ ✕ **Chilitas Pupusería.** At this mammoth San Miguel institution, you'll find the service lukewarm but the pupusas always piping hot. It gets crowded on weekends. ✉ *402 C. 8 Oriente* ☎ *503/2661–1176* ▭ *No credit cards.*

SALVADORAN

$ ▦ **El Mandarín.** The most comfortable accommodations in town are found here. The management is friendly and helpful, and the rooms are simple and clean. As a bonus, you can also get tasty Chinese food at the restaurant. **Pros:** friendly management; decent Chinese restaurant. **Cons:** spartan rooms. ⊠ *Av. Roosevelt Norte 407* ☎ *503/669–6969* 🖨 *503/669–7212* ➳ *51 rooms* 🛇 *In-room: a/c, Wi-Fi. In-hotel: restaurant, Internet terminal, parking (free)* ⊟ *AE, D, DC, MC, V* ⃝ *EP.*

# EASTERN VILLAGES

Distances are short and roads are good in this part of the country, but public transportation can be agonizingly slow. Your own vehicle, rented in San Salvador, is best. The capital's **AviTours** (☎ *503/2510–7618* ⊕ *www.avitours.com.sv*) has no specific Eastern El Salvador tour on offer, but can customize one for you.

## COJUTEPEQUE

*32 km (19 mi) east of San Salvador.*

The main attraction of this village is the Cerro De Pavas (Hill of Turkeys), where the **Santuario de la Virgen de Fátima** is found. The sanctuary holds a small statue, brought here from Portugal in 1949, that draws crowds of worshippers every Sunday. There's a great view of Lago Ilopango from the hill as well. The towns's famous pork sausages, spicy chorizos, and salamis garland quaint roadside stands.

## PERQUÍN

*80 km (50 mi) north of San Miguel.*

Perquín was one of the most ravaged cities in all of El Salvador during the civil war. Today the village is home to the **Museum of the Salvadoran Revolution** (☎ *503/610–6737* 🍽 *$1.20* 🕒 *Tues.–Sun. 8:30–4*).Every year on December 10th, locals in neighboring Mozonte commemorate the Mozonte Massacre, in which nearly 1,000 people were killed.

## ILOBASCO

*22 km (14 mi) north of Cojutepeque.*

This village is famous for the dozens of workshops that produce brightly colored ceramics. Along Avenida Bonilla you'll find *sorpresas,* hand-painted scenes of village life inside egg-shaped shells. (You might find depictions of randy villagers inside some.) Make sure to stop by the **Escuela de Capacitación Kiko** (⊠ *Av. Bonilla*), a ceramics school that gives tours of its facility.

## SAN SEBASTIÁN

*22 km (14 mi) south of Ilobasco, 14 km (9 mi) east of Cojutepeque.*

Festoons of colorfully dyed string hang outside storefronts in San Sebastián, famous for its textiles. Buy radiant hammocks, place mats, tablecloths, towels, blankets, and bedspreads. You are welcome to watch the weavers at work at the local textile factories. **Textiles y Funerales Duran** (⊠ *3 blocks from the plaza* ☎ *No phone*) has large, complicated looms, and weavers are happy to explain how they work.

# SPANISH VOCABULARY

| ENGLISH | SPANISH | PRONUNCIATION |
|---------|---------|---------------|

## BASICS

| | | |
|---|---|---|
| Yes/no | Sí/no | see/no |
| Please | Por favor | pore fah-**vore** |
| May I? | ¿Me permite? | may pair-**mee**-tay |
| Thank you (very much) | (Muchas) gracias | (**moo**-chas) **grah**-see-as |
| You're welcome | De nada | day **nah**-dah |
| Excuse me | Con permiso | con pair-**mee**-so |
| Pardon me | ¿Perdón? | pair-**dohn** |
| Could you tell me? | ¿Podría decirme? | po-dree-ah deh-**seer**-meh |
| I'm sorry | Lo siento | lo see-**en**-toh |
| Good morning! | ¡Buenos días! | **bway**-nohs **dee**-ahs |
| Good afternoon! | ¡Buenas tardes! | **bway**-nahs **tar**-dess |
| Good evening! | ¡Buenas noches! | **bway**-nahs **no**-chess |
| Good-bye! | ¡Adiós!/¡Hasta luego! | ah-dee-**ohss**/**ah**-stah **lwe**-go |
| Mr./Mrs. | Señor/Señora | sen-**yor**/sen-**yohr**-ah |
| Miss | Señorita | sen-yo-**ree**-tah |
| Pleased to meet you | Mucho gusto | **moo**-cho **goose**-toh |
| How are you? | ¿Cómo está usted? | **ko**-mo es-**tah** oo-**sted** |
| Very well, thank you. | Muy bien, gracias. | **moo**-ee bee-**en**, **grah**-see-as |
| And you? | ¿Y usted? | ee oos-**ted** |
| Hello (on the telephone) | Diga | **dee**-gah |

## NUMBERS

| | | |
|---|---|---|
| 1 | un, uno | oon, **oo**-no |
| 2 | dos | dos |
| 3 | tres | tress |
| 4 | cuatro | **kwah**-tro |
| 5 | cinco | **sink**-oh |
| 6 | seis | saice |

| 7 | siete | see-**et**-eh |
|---|---|---|
| 8 | ocho | **o**-cho |
| 9 | nueve | new-**eh**-vey |
| 10 | diez | dee-**es** |
| 11 | once | **ohn**-seh |
| 12 | doce | **doh**-seh |
| 13 | trece | **treh**-seh |
| 14 | catorce | ka-**tohr**-seh |
| 15 | quince | **keen**-seh |
| 16 | dieciséis | dee-**es**-ee-**saice** |
| 17 | diecisiete | dee-**es**-ee-see-**et**-eh |
| 18 | dieciocho | dee-**es**-ee-**o**-cho |
| 19 | diecinueve | **dee**-**es**-ee-new-**ev**-eh |
| 20 | veinte | **vain**-teh |
| 21 | veinte y uno/veintiuno | **vain**-te-**oo**-noh |
| 30 | treinta | **train**-tah |
| 32 | treinta y dos | train-tay-**dohs** |
| 40 | cuarenta | kwah-**ren**-tah |
| 43 | cuarenta y tres | kwah-**ren**-tay-**tress** |
| 50 | cincuenta | seen-**kwen**-tah |
| 54 | cincuenta y cuatro | seen-**kwen**-tay **kwah**-tro |
| 60 | sesenta | sess-**en**-tah |
| 65 | sesenta y cinco | sess-**en**-tay **seen**-ko |
| 70 | setenta | set-**en**-tah |
| 76 | setenta y seis | set-**en**-tay **saice** |
| 80 | ochenta | oh-**chen**-tah |
| 87 | ochenta y siete | oh-**chen**-tay see-**yet**-eh |
| 90 | noventa | no-**ven**-tah |
| 98 | noventa y ocho | no-**ven**-tah-**o**-choh |
| 100 | cien | see-**en** |
| 101 | ciento uno | see-**en**-toh **oo**-noh |

| 200 | doscientos | doh-see-**en**-tohss |
| 500 | quinientos | keen-**yen**-tohss |
| 700 | setecientos | set-eh-see-**en**-tohss |
| 900 | novecientos | no-veh-see-**en**-tohss |
| 1,000 | mil | meel |
| 2,000 | dos mil | dohs meel |
| 1,000,000 | un millón | oon meel-**yohn** |

## COLORS

| black | negro | **neh**-groh |
| blue | azul | ah-**sool** |
| brown | café | kah-**feh** |
| green | verde | **ver**-deh |
| pink | rosa | **ro**-sah |
| purple | morado | mo-**rah**-doh |
| orange | naranja | na-**rahn**-hah |
| red | rojo | **roh**-hoh |
| white | blanco | **blahn**-koh |
| yellow | amarillo | ah-mah-**ree**-yoh |

## DAYS OF THE WEEK

| Sunday | domingo | doe-**meen**-goh |
| Monday | lunes | **loo**-ness |
| Tuesday | martes | **mahr**-tess |
| Wednesday | miércoles | me-**air**-koh-less |
| Thursday | jueves | hoo-**ev**-ess |
| Friday | viernes | vee-**air**-ness |
| Saturday | sábado | **sah**-bah-doh |

## MONTHS

| January | enero | eh-**neh**-roh |
| February | febrero | feh-**breh**-roh |
| March | marzo | **mahr**-soh |
| April | abril | ah-**breel** |
| May | mayo | **my**-oh |

| June | junio | **hoo**-nee-oh |
|------|-------|----------------|
| July | julio | **hoo**-lee-yoh |
| August | agosto | ah-**ghost**-toh |
| September | septiembre | sep-tee-**em**-breh |
| October | octubre | oak-**too**-breh |
| November | noviembre | no-vee-**em**-breh |
| December | diciembre | dee-see-**em**-breh |

## USEFUL PHRASES

| | | |
|------|-------|----------------|
| Do you speak English? | ¿Habla usted inglés? | **ah**-blah oos-**ted** in-**glehs** |
| I don't speak Spanish | No hablo español | no **ah**-bloh es-pahn-**yol** |
| I don't understand (you) | No entiendo | no en-tee-**en**-doh |
| I understand (you) | Entiendo | en-tee-**en**-doh |
| I don't know | No sé | no seh |
| I am American/ British | Soy americano (americana)/ inglés(a) | soy ah-meh-ree-**kah**-no (ah-meh-ree-**kah**-nah)/in-**glehs(ah)** |
| What's your name? | ¿Cómo se llama usted? | koh-mo seh **yah**-mah oos-**ted** |
| My name is . . . | Me llamo . . . | may **yah**-moh |
| What time is it? | ¿Qué hora es? | keh **o**-rah es |
| It is one, two, three . . . o'clock. | Es la una./Son las dos, tres . . . | es la **oo**-nah/sohn lahs dohs, tress |
| Yes, please/No, thank you | Sí, por favor/No, gracias | **see** pohr fah-**vor**/no **grah**-see-us |
| How? | ¿Cómo? | **koh**-mo |
| When? | ¿Cuándo? | **kwahn**-doh |
| This/Next week | Esta semana/ la semana que entra | **es**-teh seh-**mah**-nah/lah seh-**mah**-nah keh **en** trah |
| This/Next month | Este mes/el próximo mes | **es**-teh mehs/el **proke**-see-mo mehs |
| This/Next year | Este año/el año que viene | **es**-teh **ahn**-yo/el **ahn**-yo keh vee-**yen**-ay |

| | | |
|---|---|---|
| Yesterday/today/ tomorrow | Ayer/hoy/mañana | ah-**yehr**/oy/mahn-**yah**-nah |
| This morning/ afternoon | Esta mañana/ tarde | es-tah mahn-**yah**-nah/**tar**-deh |
| Tonight | Esta noche | es-tah **no**-cheh |
| What? | ¿Qué? | keh |
| What is it? | ¿Qué es esto? | keh es **es**-toh |
| Why? | ¿Por qué? | pore **keh** |
| Who? | ¿Quién? | kee-**yen** |
| Where is . . . ? | ¿Dónde está . . . ? | **dohn**-deh es-**tah** |
| the bus stop? | la parada del autobus? | la pah-**rah**-dah del ow-toh-**boos** |
| the post office? | la oficina de correos? | la oh-fee-**see**-nah deh koh-**rreh**-os |
| the bank? | el banco? | el **bahn**-koh |
| the hotel? | el hotel? | cl oh-**tel** |
| the store? | la tienda? | la tee-**en**-dah |
| the cashier? | la caja? | la **kah**-hah |
| the museum? | el museo? | el moo-**seh**-oh |
| the hospital? | el hospital? | el ohss-pee-**tal** |
| the elevator? | el ascensor? | el ah-**sen**-sohr |
| the bathroom? | el baño? | el **bahn**-yoh |
| Here/there | Aquí/allá | ah-**key**/ah-**yah** |
| Open/closed | Abierto/cerrado | ah-bee-**er**-toh/ser-**ah**-doh |
| Left/right | Izquierda/derecha | iss-key-**er**-dah/dare-**eh**-chah |
| Straight ahead | Derecho | dare-**eh**-choh |
| Is it near/far? | ¿Está cerca/lejos? | es-**tah** **sehr**-kah/**leh**-hoss |
| I'd like . . . | Quisiera . . . | kee-see-ehr-ah |
| a room | un cuarto/una habitación | oon **kwahr**-toh/**oo**-nah ah-bee-tah-see-**on** |
| the key | la llave | lah **yah**-veh |
| a newspaper | un periódico | oon pehr-ee-**oh**-dee-koh |
| a stamp | un sello de correo | oon **seh**-yo deh koh-**reh**-oh |
| I'd like to buy . . . | Quisiera comprar . . . | kee-see-**ehr**-ah kohm-**prahr** |
| cigarettes | cigarrillos | ce-ga-**ree**-yohs |
| matches | cerillos | ser-**ee**-ohs |

| a dictionary | un diccionario | oon deek-see-oh-**nah**-ree-oh |
|---|---|---|
| soap | jabón | hah-**bohn** |
| sunglasses | gafas de sol | **ga**-fahs deh sohl |
| suntan lotion | loción bronceadora | loh-see-**ohn** brohn-seh-ah-**do**-rah |
| a map | un mapa | oon **mah**-pah |
| a magazine | una revista | **oon**-ah reh-**veess**-tah |
| paper | papel | pah-**pel** |
| envelopes | sobres | **so**-brehs |
| a postcard | una tarjeta postal | **oon**-ah tar-**het**-ah post-**ahl** |

| How much is it? | ¿Cuánto cuesta? | **kwahn**-toh **kwes**-tah |
|---|---|---|
| It's expensive/ cheap | Está caro/barato | es-**tah kah**-roh/ bah-**rah**-toh |
| A little/a lot | Un poquito/ mucho | oon poh-**kee**-toh/ **moo**-choh |
| More/less | Más/menos | mahss/**men**-ohss |
| Enough/too much/too little | Suficiente/ demasiado/ muy poco | soo-fee-see-**en**-teh/ deh-mah-see-**ah**-doh/**moo**-ee **poh**-koh |
| Telephone | Teléfono | tel-**ef**-oh-no |
| Telegram | Telegrama | teh-leh-**grah**-mah |
| I am ill | Estoy enfermo(a) | es-**toy** en-**fehr**-moh(mah) |
| Please call a doctor | Por favor llame a un medico | pohr fah-**vor ya**-meh ah oon **med**-ee-koh |

## ON THE ROAD

| Avenue | Avenida | ah-ven-**ee**-dah |
|---|---|---|
| Broad, tree-lined boulevard | Bulevar | boo-leh-**var** |
| Fertile plain | Vega | **veh**-gah |
| Highway | Carretera | car-reh-**ter**-ah |
| Mountain pass | Puerto | poo-**ehr**-toh |
| Street | Calle | **cah**-yeh |
| Waterfront promenade | Rambla | **rahm**-blah |
| Wharf | Embarcadero | em-bar-cah-**deh**-ro |

## IN TOWN

| | | |
|---|---|---|
| Cathedral | Catedral | cah-teh-**dral** |
| Church | Templo/Iglesia | **tem**-plo/ee-**glehs**-see-ah |
| City hall | Casa de gobierno | kah-sah deh go-bee-**ehr**-no |
| Door, gate | Puerta portón | poo-**ehr**-tah por-**ton** |
| Entrance/exit | Entrada/salida | en-**trah**-dah/sah-lee-dah |
| Inn, rustic bar, or restaurant | Taberna | tah-**behr**-nah |
| Main square | Plaza principal | plah-thah prin-see-**pahl** |
| Market | Mercado | mer-**kah**-doh |
| Neighborhood | Barrio | **bahr**-ree-o |
| Traffic circle | Glorieta | glor-ee-**eh**-tah |
| Wine cellar, wine bar, or wine shop | Bodega | boh-**deh**-gah |

## DINING OUT

| | | |
|---|---|---|
| Can you recommend a good restaurant? | ¿Puede recomendarme un buen restaurante? | **pweh**-deh rreh-koh-mehn-**dahr**-me oon bwehn rrehs-tow-**rahn**-teh? |
| Where is it located? | ¿Dónde está situado? | **dohn**-deh ehs-**tah** see-**twah**-doh? |
| Do I need reservations? | ¿Se necesita una reservación? | seh neh-seh-**see**-tah **oo**-nah rreh-sehr-bah-**syohn**?/ |
| I'd like to reserve a table . . . | Quisiera reservar una mesa . . . | kee-**syeh**-rah rreh-sehr-**bahr** oo-nah **meh**-sah . . . |
| for two people. | para dos personas. | **pah**-rah dohs pehr-**soh**-nahs |
| for this evening. | para esta noche. | **pah**-rah **ehs**-tah **noh**-cheh |
| for 8:00 p.m. | para las ocho de la noche. | **pah**-rah lahs **oh**-choh deh lah **noh**-cheh |
| A bottle of . . . | Una botella de . . . | **oo**-nah bo-**teh**-yah deh |
| A cup of . . . | Una taza de . . . | **oo**-nah **tah**-thah deh |

| A glass of . . . | Un vaso de . . . | oon **vah**-so deh |
|---|---|---|
| Ashtray | Un cenicero | oon sen-ee-**seh**-roh |
| Bill/check | La cuenta | lah **kwen**-tah |
| Bread | El pan | el pahn |
| Breakfast | El desayuno | el deh-sah-**yoon**-oh |
| Butter | La mantequilla | lah man-teh-**key**-yah |
| Cheers! | ¡Salud! | sah-**lood** |
| Cocktail | Un aperitivo | oon ah-pehr-ee-**tee**-voh |
| Dinner | La cena | lah **seh**-nah |
| Dish | Un plato | oon **plah**-toh |
| Menu of the day | Menú del día | meh-**noo** del **dee**-ah |
| Enjoy! | ¡Buen provecho! | bwehn pro-**veh**-cho |
| Fixed-price menu | Menú fijo o turistico | meh-**noo** **fee**-hoh oh too-**ree**-stee-coh |
| Fork | El tenedor | el ten-eh-**dor** |
| Is the tip included? | ¿Está incluida la propina? | es-**tah** in-cloo-**ee**-dah lah pro-**pee**-nah |
| Knife | El cuchillo | el koo-**chee**-yo |
| Lunch | La comida | lah koh-**mee**-dah |
| Menu | La carta, el menú | lah **cart**-ah, el meh-**noo** |
| Napkin | La servilleta | lah sehr-vee-**yet**-ah |
| Pepper | La pimienta | lah pee-me-**en**-tah |
| Please give me | Por favor déme | pore fah-**vor** **deh**-meh |
| Salt | La sal | lah sahl |
| Savory snacks | Tapas | **tah**-pahs |
| Spoon | Una cuchara | **oo**-nah koo-**chah**-rah |
| Sugar | El azúcar | el ah-**thu**-kar |
| Waiter!/Waitress! | ¡Por favor Señor/Señorita! | pohr fah-**vor** sen-**yor**/sen-yor-**ee**-tah |

# EMERGENCIES

| Look! | ¡Mire! | **mee**-reh! |
|---|---|---|
| Listen! | ¡Escuche! | ehs-**koo**-cheh! |

| Help! | ¡Auxilio!<br>¡Ayuda!<br>¡Socorro! | owk-**see**-lee-oh/<br>ah-**yoo**-dah/<br>soh-**kohr**-roh |
|---|---|---|
| Fire! | ¡Incendio! | en-**sen**-dee-oo |
| Caution!/Look out! | ¡Cuidado! | kwee-**dah**-doh |
| Hurry! | ¡Dése prisa! | **deh**-seh **pree**-sah! |
| Stop! | ¡Alto! | **ahl**-toh! |
| I need help quick! | ¡Necesito ayuda, pronto! | neh-seh-**see**-toh ah-**yoo**-dah, **prohn**-toh! |
| Can you help me? | ¿Puede ayudarme? | **pweh**-deh ah-yoo-**dahr**-meh? |
| Police! | ¡Policía! | poh-lee-**see**-ah! |
| I need a policeman! | ¡Necesito un policía! | neh-seh-**see**-toh oon poh-lee-**see**-ah! |
| It's an emergency! | ¡Es una emergencia! | ehs **oo**-nah eh-mehr-**hehn**-syah! |
| Leave me alone! | ¡Déjeme en paz! | **deh**-heh-meh ehn pahs! |
| That man's a thief! | ¡Ese hombre es un ladrón! | **eh**-seh **ohm**-breh ehs oon lah-**drohn**! |
| Stop him! | ¡Deténganlo! | deh-**tehn**-gahn-loh! |
| He's stolen my . . .<br>pocketbook.<br>wallet.<br>passport.<br>watch. | Me ha robado . . .<br>la cartera.<br>la billetera.<br>el pasaporte.<br>el reloj. | meh ah rroh-**bah**-doh . . .<br>lah kahr-**teh**-rah<br>lah bee-yeh-**teh**-rah<br>ehl pah-sah-**pohr**-teh<br>ehl rreh-**loh** |
| I've lost my . . .<br>suitcase.<br>money.<br>glasses.<br>car keys. | He perdido . . .<br>mi maleta.<br>mi dinero.<br>los anteojos.<br>las llaves de mi automóvil. | eh pehr-**dee**-doh<br>mee mah-**leh**-tah<br>mee dee-**neh**-roh<br>lohs ahn-teh-**oh**-hohs<br>lahs **yah**-behs deh mee ow-toh-**moh**-beel |

## TELLING TIME AND EXPRESSIONS OF TIME

| What time is it? | ¿Qué hora es? | keh **oh**-rah ehs? |
|---|---|---|
| At what time? | ¿A qué hora? | ah keh **oh**-rah? |
| It's . . .<br>one o'clock. | Es . . .<br>la una. | eh . . .<br>lah **oo**-nah |

| | | |
|---|---|---|
| 1:15. | la una y cuarto. | lah **oo**-nah ee **kwahr**-toh |
| 1:30. | la una y media. | lah **oo**-nah ee **meh**-dyah |
| It's . . . 1:45. | Son las . . . dos menos cuarto. | sohn lahs . . . dohs **meh**-nos **kwahr**-toh |
| two o'clock. | dos. | dohs |
| morning. | la mañana. | Lah mah-**nyah**-nah |
| afternoon | la tarde. | lah **tahr**-deh |
| It's midnight | Es media noche | ehs **meh**-dyah **noh**-cheh |
| It's noon | Es mediodía | ehs meh-dyoh-**dee**-ah |
| In a half hour | En media hora | ehn **meh**-dyah **oh**-rah |
| When does it begin? | ¿Cuándo empieza? | **kwahn**-doh ehm-**pyeh**-sah? |

## PAYING THE BILL

| | | |
|---|---|---|
| How much does it cost? | ¿Cuánto cuesta? | **kwahn**-toh **kwehs**-tah? |
| The bill, please. | La cuenta, por favor. | lah-**kwen**-tah pohr fah-**bohr** |
| How much do I owe you? | ¿Cuánto le debo? | **kwan**-toh leh **deh**-boh? |
| Is service included? | ¿La propina está incluida? | lah proh-**pee**-nah ehs-**tah** een-kloo-**ee**-dah? |
| This is for you. | Esto es para usted. | **ehs**-toh ehs pah-rah oos-**tehd** |

## GETTING AROUND

| | | |
|---|---|---|
| Do you have a map of the city? | ¿Tiene usted un mapa de la ciudad? | **tyeh**-neh oos-**tehd** oon **mah**-pah deh lah syoo-**dahd**? |
| Could you show me on the map? | ¿Puede usted indicármelo en el mapa? | **pweh**-deh oo-**stehd** een-dee-**kahr**-meh-loh ehn ehl **mah**-pah? |

| Can I get there on foot? | ¿Puedo llegar allí a pie? | **pweh**-doh yeh-**gahr** ah-**yee** ah pyeh? |
| How far is it? | ¿A qué distancia es? | ah keh dees-**tahn**-syah ehs? |
| I'm lost. | Estoy perdido(-a). | ehs-**toy** pehr-**dee**-doh(-dah) |
| Where is . . . | ¿Dónde está . . . | **dohn**-deh ehs-**tah** . . . |
| the Hotel Rex? | el hotel Rex? | ehl oh-**tehl** rreks? |
| . . . Street? | la calle . . . ? | lah **kah**-yeh . . . ? |
| . . . Avenue? | la avenida . . . ? | lah ah-beh-**nee**-dah . . . ? |
| How can I get to . . . | ¿Cómo puedo ir a . . . | **koh**-moh **pweh**-doh eer ah . . . |
| the bus stop? | la parada de autobuses? | lah pah-**rah**-dah deh ow-toh-**boo**-ses? |
| the ticket office? | la taquilla? | lah tah-**kee**-yah? |
| the airport? | el aeropuerto? | ehl ah-eh-roh-**pwehr**-toh? |
| straight ahead | derecho | deh-**reh**-choh |
| to the right | a la derecha | ah lah deh-**reh**-chah |
| to the left | a la izquierda | ah lah ees-**kyehr**-dah |
| a block away | a una cuadra | ah **oo**-nah **kwah**-drah |
| on the corner | en la esquina | ehn lah ehs-**kee**-nah |
| on the square | en la plaza | ehn lah **plah**-sah |
| facing, opposite | enfrente | ehn-**frehn**-teh |
| across | al frente | ahl **frehn**-teh |
| next to | al lado | ahl **lah**-doh |
| near | cerca | **sehr**-kah |
| far | lejos | **leh**-hohs |

## ON THE BUS

| I'm looking for the bus stop. | Estoy buscando la parada de autobuses. | ehs-**toy** boos-**kahn**-doh lah pah-**rah**-dah deh ow-toh-**boo**-sehs |
| What bus line goes . . . | ¿Qué línea va . . . | keh **lee**-neh-ah bah . . . |
| north? | al norte? | ahl **nohr**-teh? |
| south? | al sur? | ahl soor? |
| east? | al este? | ahl **ehs**-teh? |
| west? | al oeste? | ahl oh-**ehs**-teh? |

| What bus do I take to go to . . . | ¿Qué autobús tomo para ir a . . . | keh ow-toh-**boos** **toh**-moh **pah**-rah eer ah . . . |
| Can you tell me when to get off? | ¿Podría decirme cuándo debo bajarme? | poh-**dree**-ah deh-**seer**-meh **kwan**-doh **deh**-boh bah-**hahr**-meh? |
| How much is the fare? | ¿Cuánto es el billete? | **kwahn**-toh ehs ehl bee-**yeh**-teh? |
| Should I pay when I get on? | ¿Debo pagar al subir? | **deh**-boh pah-**gahr** ahl soo-**beer**? |
| Where do I take the bus to return? | ¿Dónde se toma el autobús para regresar? | **dohn**-deh seh **toh**-mah ehl ow-toh-**boos** **pah**-rah rreh-greh-**sahr**? |
| How often do the return buses run? | ¿Cada cuánto hay autobuses de regreso? | **kah**-dah **kwahn**-toh ahy ow-toh-**boo**-sehs deh rreh-**greh**-soh? |
| I would like . . . a ticket. a receipt. a reserved seat. first class. second class. | Quisiera . . . un billete. un recibo. un asiento numerado. primera clase. segunda clase. | kee-**syeh**-rah . . . oon bee-**yeh**-teh oon reh-**see**-boh oon ah-**syehn**-toh noo-meh-**rah**-doh pree-**meh**-rah **klah**-seh seh-**goon**-dah |
| a direct bus. an express bus. ticketed luggage. | un autobús directo. un autobús expreso. equipaje facturado. | **klah**-seh oon ow-toh-**boos** dee-**rehk**-toh oon ow-toh-**boos** ehks-**preh**-soh eh-kee-**pah**-heh fahk-too-**rah**-doh |

## ACCOMMODATIONS

| I have a reservation. | Tengo una reservación/ una reserva. | **tehn**-goh **oo**-nah rreh-sehr-vah-**syohn**/**oo**-nah rre-**sehr**-vah |
| I would like a room for . . . one night. two nights. | Quisiera una habitación por . . . una noche. dos noches. | kee-**syeh**-rah **oo**-nah ah-bee-tah-**syohn** pohr . . . **oo**-nah **noh**-cheh dohs **noh**-chehs |

| | | |
|---|---|---|
| a week. | una semana. | **oo**-nah seh-**mah**-nah |
| two weeks. | dos semanas. | dohs seh-**mah**-nahs |
| How much is it . . . | ¿Cuánto es . . . | **kwahn**-toh ehs . . . |
| for a day? | por día? | pohr **dee**-ah? |
| for a week? | por una semana? | pohr **oo**-nah seh-**mah**-nah? |
| Does that include tax? | ¿Incluye impuestos? | een-**kloo**-yeh eem-**pwehs**-tohs? |
| Do you have a room with . . . | ¿Tiene una habitación con . . . | **tyeh**-neh **oo**-nah ah-bee-tah-**syohn** kohn . . . |
| a private bath? | baño privado? | **bah**-nyoh pree-**bah**-doh? |
| a shower? | una ducha? | **oo**-nah **doo**-chah? |
| air-conditioning? | aire acondicionado? | **ay**-reh ah-kohn-dee-syoh-**nah**-doh? |
| heat? | calefacción? | kah-leh-fak-**syohn**? |
| television? | televisor? | teh-leh-bee-**sohr**? |
| hot water? | agua caliente? | **ah**-gwah kah-**lyehn**-teh? |
| a balcony? | balcón? | bahl-**kohn**? |
| a view facing the street? | vista a la calle? | **bees**-tah ah lah **kah**-yeh? |
| a view facing the ocean? | vista al mar? | **bees**-tah ahl mahr? |
| Does the hotel have . . . | ¿Tiene el hotel . . . ? | **tyeh**-neh ehl oh-**tehl** . . . ? |
| a restaurant? | un restaurante? | oon rrehs-tow-**rahn**-teh? |
| a bar? | un bar? | oon bahr? |
| a swimming pool? | una piscina | **oo**-nah pee-**see**-nah? |
| room service? | servicio de habitación? | sehr-**bee**-syoh deh ah-bee-tah-**syohn**? |
| a safe-deposit box? | una caja de valores/ seguridad? | **oo**-nah **kah**-hah deh bah-**loh**-rehs/ seh-goo-ree-**dahd**? |
| laundry service? | servicio de lavandería? | sehr-**bee**-syoh deh lah-vahn-deh-**ree**-ah? |
| I would like . . . | Quisiera . . . | kee-**sye**-rah . . . |
| meals included. | con las comidas incluidas. | kohn lahs koh-**mee**-dahs een-**kluee**-dahs |
| breakfast only. | solamente con desayuno. | soh-lah-**men**-teh kohn deh-sah-**yoo**-noh |
| no meals included. | sin comidas. | seen koh-**mee**-dahs |
| an extra bed. | una cama más. | **oo**-nah **kah**-mah mahs |
| a baby crib. | una cuna | **oo**-nah **koo**-nah |

308 <     **Understanding Honduras**

| | | |
|---|---|---|
| another towel. | otra toalla. | **oh**-trah **twah**-yah |
| soap. | jabón. | hah-**bohn** |
| clothes hangers. | ganchos de ropa. | **gahn**-chohs deh **rroh**-pah |
| another blanket. | otra manta. | **oh**-trah **mahn**-tah |
| drinking water. | agua para beber. | **ah**-gwah **pah**-rah beh-**behr** |
| toilet paper. | papel higiénico. | pah-**pehl** ee-**hye**-nee-koh |

| | | |
|---|---|---|
| This room is very . . . | Esta habitación es muy . . . | **ehs**-tah ah-bee-tah-**syohn** ehs muee . . . |
| small. | pequeña. | peh-**keh**-nyah |
| cold. | fría. | **free**-ah |
| hot. | caliente. | kah-**lyehn**-teh |
| dark. | oscura. | ohs-**koo**-rah |
| noisy. | ruidosa. | rruee-**doh**-sah |

| | | |
|---|---|---|
| The . . . does not work. | No funciona . . . | noh foon-**syoh**-nah |
| light | la luz. | lah loos |
| heat | la calefacción. | lah kah-leh-fahk-**syohn** |
| toilet | el baño. | ehl **bah**-nyoh |
| the air conditioner | el aire acondicionado. | ehl **ay**-reh ah-kohn-dee-syo-**nah**-doh |
| key | la llave. | lah **yah**-beh |
| lock | la cerradura | lah seh-rah-**doo**-rah |
| fan | el ventilador. | ehl **behn**-tee-lah-**dohr** |
| outlet | el enchufe. | ehl ehn-**choo**-feh |
| television | el televisor. | ehl teh-leh-bee-**sohr** |

| | | |
|---|---|---|
| May I change to another room? | ¿Podría cambiar de habitación? | poh-**dree**-ah kahm-**byar** deh ah-bee-tah-**syohn**? |

| | | |
|---|---|---|
| Is there . . . | ¿Hay . . . | ahy . . . |
| room service? | servicio de habitación? | sehr-**bee**-syoh deh ah-bee-tah-**syohn**? |
| laundry service? | servicio de lavandería? | sehr-**bee**-syoh deh lah-vahn-deh-**ree**-ah? |

## BARGAINING

| | | |
|---|---|---|
| Excuse me. | Perdón. | pehr-**dohn** |
| I'm interested in this. | Me interesa esto. | meh een-teh-**reh**-sah **ehs**-toh |
| How much is it? | ¿Cuánto cuesta? | **kwahn**-toh **kwehs**-tah? |
| It's very expensive! | ¡Es muy caro! | ehs muee **kah**-roh! |

| | | |
|---|---|---|
| It's overpriced. (It's not worth so much.) | No vale tanto. | noh **vah**-leh **tahn**-toh |
| Do you have a cheaper one? | ¿Tiene uno más barato? | **tyeh**-neh **oo**-noh mahs bah-**rah**-toh? |
| This is damaged—do you have another one? | Está dañado, ¿hay otro? | ehs-**tah** dah-**nyah**-doh, ahy **oh**-troh? |
| What is the lowest price? | ¿Cuál es el precio mínimo? | **kwahl** ehs ehl **preh**-syoh **mee**-nee-moh? |
| Is that the final price? | ¿Es el último precio? | ehs ehl **ool**-tee-moh **preh**-syoh? |
| Can't you give me a discount? | ¿No me da una rebaja? | noh meh dah **oo**-nah rreh-**bah**-hah? |
| I'll give you . . . | Le doy . . . | leh doy . . . |
| I won't pay more than . . . | No pago más de . . . | noh **pah**-goh mahs deh . . . |
| I'll look somewhere else. | Voy a ver en otro sitio. | voy ah behr ehn **oh**-troh **see**-tyoh |
| No, thank you. | No, gracias. | noh, **grah**-syahs |

## TOILETRIES

| | | |
|---|---|---|
| toiletries | objetos de baño | ohb-**jeh**-tohs deh **bah**-nyoh |
| a brush | un cepillo | oon seh-**pee**-yoh |
| cologne | colonia | koh-**loh**-nyah |
| a comb | un peine | oon **pay**-neh |
| deodorant | desodorante | dch-soh-doh-**rahn**-teh |
| diapers | desechables | deh-seh-**chah**-blehs |
| hairspray | laca | **lah**-kah |
| a mirror | un espejo | oon ehs-**peh**-hoh |
| moisturizing lotion | loción humectante | loh-**syohn** oo-mehk-**tahn**-teh |
| mouthwash | enjuague bucal | ehn-**hwah**-geh boo-**kahl** |
| nail clippers | cortaúñas | kohr-ta-**oo**-nyahs |
| nail polish | esmalte de uñas | ehs-**mahl**-teh deh **oo**-nyahs |

| nail polish remover | quitaesmalte | kee-tah-ehs-**mahl**-teh |
| --- | --- | --- |
| perfume | perfume | pehr-**foo**-meh |
| sanitary napkins | toallas sanitarias | toh-**ah**-yahs sah-nee-**tah**-ryahs |
| shampoo | champú | chahm-**poo** |
| shaving cream | crema de afeitar | **kreh**-mah deh ah-fay-**tahr** |
| soap | jabón | hah-**bohn** |
| a sponge | una esponja | **oo**-nah ehs-**pohn**-hah |
| tampons | tampones | tahm-**poh**-nehs |
| tissues | pañuelos de papel | pah-**nyweh**-lohs deh pah-**pehl** |
| toilet paper | papel higiénico | pah-**pehl** ee-**hyeh**-ee-koh |
| a toothbrush | un cepillo de dientes | oon seh-**pee**-yoh deh **dyehn**-tehs |
| toothpaste | pasta de dientes | **pahs**-tah deh **dyehn**-tehs |
| tweezers | pinzas | **peen**-sahs |

# Travel Smart
# Honduras

**WORD OF MOUTH**

"I wouldn't venture down the beach at night, leave your wallet sticking out of a pocket, or get really drunk and go home with someone you don't know, but I've avoided those scenarios and felt safe."

—Hopefulist

"The ferry between Roatán and Ceiba . . . I've taken it a few times. From Roatán to Ceiba . . . not too difficult for my stomach to handle. From Ceiba back to Roatán . . . I'll only FLY from now on!"

—roatanvortex

# GETTING HERE AND AROUND

## ▌AIR TRAVEL

Honduras sees fewer international flights than its Central American neighbors do, but the presence of four international airports here gives you a bigger selection of where to arrive and depart.

Tegucigalpa's small Aeropuerto Internacional Toncontín (TGU) receives relatively few flights for an airport serving a capital city of one million people. American flies from Miami, Continental flies from Houston, and Delta flies from Atlanta, all once daily. Taca flies from San Salvador and other Central American capitals.

San Pedro Sula's Aeropuerto Internacional Ramón Villeda Morales (SAP) is the country's largest airport. American flies from Miami, Continental flies from Houston and Newark, Delta flies from Atlanta, and Spirit Air flies from Fort Lauderdale, all daily. Taca flies from Miami and New York (JFK), as well as from San Salvador, and other Central American capitals.

La Ceiba's Aeropuerto Internacional Golosón (LCE) receives Taca flights from San Salvador. Roatan's Aeropuerto Internacional Juan Manuel Gálvez (RTB) is the country's second busiest airport. Delta flies from Atlanta and Continental flies from Houston. Taca flies from Miami, Houston, and San Salvador.

Connecting with Taca flights in San Salvador (SAL) opens up many more gateway options from North America to Honduras's four international airports. San Salvador is an efficient airport for changing flights—no immigration or customs for El Salvador if you're just connecting—and Taca has flights between SAL and Chicago, Dallas, Houston, Los Angeles, Miami, New York (JFK), Orlando, San Francisco, Toronto, and Washington Dulles.

Honduras has several domestic airlines. Taca Regional connects Tegucigalpa, San Pedro Sula, and the Bay Islands. Sosa flies between Tegucigalpa, San Pedro Sula, the Bay Islands, and Puerto Lempira. CM Airlines connects Tegucigalpa, San Pedro Sula, Roatán, and Puerto Lempira. Central American Airways flies between Tegucigalpa, San Pedro Sula, La Ceiba, and Roatán. Because the domestic airlines have no ticketing or baggage-transfer arrangements with the international carriers, it is recommended not to make an international-to-domestic transfer (or vice-versa) in the same day.

| TRAVEL TIMES FROM TEGUCIGALPA | BY AIR | BY BUS |
|---|---|---|
| To | | |
| San Pedro Sula | 45 min | 3 hrs, 30 min |
| La Ceiba | 1 hr | 6 hrs, 30 min |
| Roatán | 1 hr, 15 min | N/A |

**Airline Contacts American Airlines** (☎ 800/433–7300 ⊕ www.aa.com). **Central American Airways** (✉ Aeropuerto Internacional Toncontín ☎ 233–1614). **CM Airlines** (✉ Aeropuerto Internacional Toncontín ☎ 234–1886 ⊕ www.cmairlines.com). **Continental Airlines** (☎ 800/523—3273 ⊕ www.continental.com). **Delta Airlines** (☎ 800/221–1212 ⊕ www.delta.com). **Spirit Air** (☎ 800/772–7117 or 586/791–7300 ⊕ www.spiritair.com). **Taca Airlines** (☎ 800/221–1212 ⊕ www.taca.com). **Taca Regional** (✉ Aeropuerto Internacional Toncontín ☎ 221–1856 ⊕ www.flyislena.com).

## ▌BOAT TRAVEL

If you choose not to fly, getting to and between the Bay Islands means boat travel. MV Galaxy Wave travels twice daily in each direction between La Ceiba and Roatán. The Utila Princess II travels twice daily in each direction between La Ceiba and Utila. Bolea Express, a private speedboat service, operates twice weekly between Trujillo and Guanaja. You can arrange private boat transport between the three islands themselves. The boat trips are far cheaper than the flights, of course, but notorious at times for their rough crossings. The morning seas are calmer than the afternoon ones if you have a choice. If you are the least bit prone to motion sickness, you'll want to bring along a preventative such as Dramamine or Bonine (both are over-the-counter back home) or the prescription transdermal-scopolamine patch. Remember that you need to take the measures in advance—once seasickness starts, they are of little use—and that drowsiness is a possible side effect, especially from the tablets.

## BOAT INFO
**Ferries and Contacts** MV Galaxy Wave (✉ *Muelle de Cabotaje, La Ceiba* ☎ 443–4633 ✉ *Ferry Terminal, Roatán* ☎ 445–1795 ⊕ *www.safewaymaritime.com*). **Utila Princess II** (✉ *Muelle de Cabotaje, La Ceiba* ☎ 408–5163 ✉ *Utila Municipal Dock, Utila* ☎ 425–3390)). **Bolea Express** (✉ *Zapata dock, Bonnaca Town, Guanaja* ☎ 9944–8571).

## CRUISES
*For cruises info,* ⇨ *see Cruising to Honduras in Experience chapter.*

## ■ BUS TRAVEL

Some wise person once said, "Old school buses never die. They go to Central America." (We wish we could take credit for the observation.) Who knows? Look closely and you might just see the school bus you rode as a child converted into a mode of intercity Honduran transport. The average Honduran gets around the country by bus, and for meeting and conversing with local people, there is no better transportation mode. Bus transport includes those old school buses as well as small minivans that ply fixed routes. There's always room for one more passenger on either, and both types of service stop everywhere. Large Pullman-style buses are always more spacious and comfortable,

and make fewer stops. Opt for them on routes between larger destinations.

The highly regarded Hedman–Alas connects Tegucigalpa, San Pedro Sula, La Ceiba, Tela, Comayagua, and Copán Ruinas, as well as Guatemala City and Antigua, Guatemala. TicaBus travels to Guatemala, Nicaragua, El Salvador, Costa Rica, Panama, and Mexico. TransNica travels to Nicaragua and Costa Rica. King Quality travels to Guatemala and El Salvador.

**Bus Info** Hedman Alas (✉ *11 Av., between Cs. 13 and 14, Comayagüela* ☎ *237–7143* ⊕ *www. hedmanalas.com*). **King Quality** (✉ *Gran Central Metropolitana* ☎ *553–4547*). **TicaBus** (✉ *16 C. and 5 and 6 Avs., Comayagüela* ☎ *220–0579* ⊕ *www.ticabus.com*). **TransNica** (✉ *Blvd. Suyapa, Suyapa* ☎ *239–7933* ⊕ *www. transnica.com*).

## ■ CAR TRAVEL

Honduras is roughly the size of Ohio but not quite as easy to get around. A look at a highway map of Honduras illustrates that San Pedro Sula, in the far northwest part of the country, is oddly the hub of its highway system. Topography has dictated that fact. Highways fan out from San Pedro southwest to Copán Ruinas and the highlands, southeast to Tegucigalpa, and north and east to the Caribbean coast. If you were to drive from Tegucigalpa to Copán Ruinas, less than 200 mi as the toucan flies, you'd actually need to go via San Pedro to navigate the best route.

Seat-belt use is mandatory in Honduras. Use of cell phones and texting while driving is prohibited. Turning right at a red light is prohibited.

If the police stop you for a traffic violation, some officers are corrupt enough to solicit you for a bribe to forget about the ticket. Admittedly, many visitors do succumb to avoid the hassle especially if they know they are guilty, but we recommend not paying the officer—doing so would only contribute to the problem—and instead settling the ticket through your car-rental agency.

## GASOLINE
Although Honduras measures mostly in metrics, gasoline is sold by the *galón*, at about L70 per gallon. Most vehicles require the higher-octane *súper*. A few *autoservicio* (self-service) stations are beginning to appear in Tegucigalpa and San Pedro Sula and knock a couple of lempiras off the gallon price if you pump your own gas.

## PARKING
When you stop for the night, always ask about a secure place to leave your car. Most lodgings offer guarded parking.

## ROAD CONDITIONS
Major highways in Honduras—Tegucigalpa to San Pedro Sula, San Pedro Sula to Puerto Cortés, San Pedro Sula to La Ceiba to Trujillo, Tegucigalpa to Choluteca—are in decent shape, and you can expect to zip right along at the posted speed limit of 90 kph (about 55 mph). Even major highways will require you to slow down as they pass through urban areas and sometimes the tiniest of hamlets. Watch for the TÚMULOS signs that warn you of upcoming speed bumps. Off the major highways, secondary roads—the road from the crossroads town of La Entrada to Copán Ruinas, or from Santa Rosa de Copán to Gracias, are good examples—deteriorate and have frequent potholes. They're passable though. Always inquire about road conditions before you start out, especially during the rainy season, when landslides or flooding occasionally block passage.

Driving after dark on rural roads is never advisable. Robberies of drivers have occurred at night, but you also need to contend with pedestrians—both two- and four-legged—along the sides of the roads. When you stop anywhere for the night, always ask about a secure place to leave your car. Most lodgings offer guarded parking.

| FROM | TO | RTE./ DISTANCE |
|---|---|---|
| Tegucigalpa | San Pedro Sula | 3 hrs, 30 min |
| San Pedro Sula | Copán Ruinas | 3 hrs |
| San Pedro Sula | Puerto Cortés | 1 hr |
| San Pedro Sula | La Ceiba | 3 hrs |
| Tegucigalpa | Choluteca | 2 hrs |

## ROADSIDE EMERGENCIES
Honduras has no nationwide emergency-road-service organization à la AAA. If you are involved in any type of accident, even a minor fender bender, remain at the scene until the transit police (Policía de Tránsito) arrive to assess what happened.

**Emergency Services** Policía de Tránsito (☎ 222 nationwide).

## RULES OF THE ROAD
**Automobile Association** (*AAA* ⊕ www.aaa. com).

## CAR RENTAL
Tegucigalpa and San Pedro Sula are the best places to rent a vehicle, and both have city and airport offices of many of the major international firms. Advance, Maya, and Molinari are three highly regarded Honduran rental agencies. Vehicles are not cheap. They start at L950, or about $50 per day for the most basic four-door sedans. The minimum age to rent a car is 25.

**Local Agencies** Advance Rent-a-Car (✉ C. República de México ☎ 235-9528 ⊕ www. advancerentacar.com). **Maya** (✉ Aeropuerto Internacional Ramón Villeda Morales, San Pedro Sula ☎ 668-3168 ✉ Av. 3, between Cs. 7 and 8, San Pedro Sula ☎ 552-2670 or 552-2671). **Molinari** (✉ C. 1, between Avs. 3 and 4, San Pedro Sula ☎ 552-9999).

**Major Rental Agencies** Alamo (☎ 800/522-9696 ⊕ www.alamo.com). **Avis** (☎ 800/331-1084 ⊕ www.avis.com). **Budget** (☎ 800/472-3325 ⊕ www.budget. com). **Hertz** (☎ 800/654-3001 ⊕ www.hertz.

*com*). **National Car Rental** (☎ *800/227–7368* ⊕ *www.nationalcar.com*).

# ▮ TAXI TRAVEL

Most communities of any size have a local taxi system. They're ubiquitous and usually reasonably priced. In Tegucigalpa and San Pedro Sula, where the city bus systems are not safe for foreigners to use, and where driving your own car and finding parking can be a real a hassle, taxis are the perfect motorized alternative for getting around. In the capital and San Pedro, as well as La Ceiba, taxis should be your only option for going anywhere at night. Have your hotel call one for you if you're going out after dark. Likewise, when you're ready to call it a night, have the restaurant or nightspot call you a cab rather than you hailing one on the street after dark. It's safer that way.

In bigger cities, the taxis are regular sedan-type vehicles. In smaller towns, such as Copán Ruinas, the taxi system will be a fleet of semi-open, three-wheeled, motorized Bajaj vehicles made in India. Everyone refers to them as *tuk-tuks*. (The name echoes the sound of the engine.) They're great fun to ride in for short distances, but can be noisy and bumpy.

Taxis are not metered anywhere in Honduras. Agree on a fare when you get in. The amount is generally reasonable. Roatán taxi drivers have a reputation for overcharging tourists. Ask the friendly folks at your Roatán hotel front desk to give you the lay of the land and to tell you what reasonable fares should be.

# ESSENTIALS

## ■ ACCOMMODATIONS

Honduras offers every type of accommodation from luxury hotels to backpackers' digs. You'll find the familiar names of the international chains in Tegucigalpa and San Pedro Sula, and most of those offer a few local touches to make you feel that you're in Honduras rather than Hartford. Out-country, though, the chains are nowhere else to be found. No matter which category of lodging you select, you'll find prices to be less expensive than for corresponding offerings in the United States.

In heavily touristed locales—Copán Ruinas, the Caribbean coast, and, especially, the Bay Islands—lodgings observe high-season rates during the dry season, essentially Christmas through Easter. A second mini high season takes place during July and August, prime vacation season for North Americans and Europeans. On the topic of Christmas and Easter, expect to see much higher rates during those two weeks, both of which are prime vacation time for Hondurans as well. In the rest of the country, lodging rates remain fairly constant year-round. Hotels in Tegucigalpa and San Pedro Sula cater overwhelmingly to business travelers and, as such, often discount their rates on weekends.

Thankfully, visitor numbers to Honduras are picking up again following the double whammy of the worldwide economic slump and the country's 2009 political crisis that caused tourism to nearly evaporate the last half of that year. Many communities have only a smallish selection of decent hotels—and many midrange lodgings get booked by the many volunteer groups who come to Honduras—making reservations a good idea no matter what time of year you're here.

⇨ *Price charts can be found at the beginning of each chapter in this book.*

### APARTMENT AND HOUSE RENTALS
**Home Away** (☎ 512/493–0382 ⊕ www.homeaway.com).

### BED-AND-BREAKFASTS
**Reservation Services BedandBreakfast.com** (☎ 512/322–2710 or 800/462-2632 ⊕ www.bedandbreakfast.com). **Bed & Breakfast Inns Online** (☎ 615/868–1946 or 800/215–7365 ⊕ www.bbonline.com).

### HOSTELS
**Hostel Info Hostelling International—USA** (☎ 301/495–1240 ⊕ www.hiusa.org).

## ■ COMMUNICATIONS

### INTERNET
E-mail has become a favorite way to communicate in Honduras. Larger cities and major tourist destinations such as Roatán and Copán Ruinas have a smattering of Internet cafés, and smaller towns likely have at least one. (Some designate themselves with an @ symbol on a sign out front.) It's estimated that about half of Honduran lodgings have Wi-Fi access, called *Internet inalámbrico* in Spanish. Even if those hotels don't have wireless in their rooms, they will probably have a strong hotspot signal in their public areas. Most hotels do not charge for Internet access, but a few international chains in Tegucigalpa and San Pedro Sula do charge extra for room Wi-Fi. Those same hotels will likely also provide an Internet terminal or two for guests to use.

Computer keyboards in Honduras and Latin America are not quite the same as ones in English-speaking countries. Your biggest frustration will probably be finding the @ symbol to type an e-mail address. On a PC, you have to type ALT+164 with the NUMBERS LOCK on or some other combination. If you need to ask, it's called *arroba* in Spanish.

# LOCAL DO'S AND TABOOS

### CUSTOMS OF THE COUNTRY

Overall, Honduras is a friendly country, and people are happy to give directions, chat, and ask a question you'll hear a lot in Honduras: *¿De dónde viene Usted?* (Where are you from?). Hondurans are quite knowledgeable and proud of the history of their country, and you showing an interest goes a long way toward breaking down any barriers.

### GREETINGS

In the cities, women who know each other often greet each other with a single kiss on the cheek, whereas men shake hands. Men and women often kiss on the cheek, even when being introduced for the first time. (You as a visitor would be looked at askance if you engaged in the kissing practice, though.)

### SIGHTSEEING

To feel more comfortable, take a cue from what the locals are wearing. Except in beach towns, men typically don't wear shorts, and women don't wear short skirts on the street. Bathing suits are fine on beaches, but cover up before you head back into town. Everyone dresses conservatively to enter churches. Honduran women wearing sleeveless tops often cover their shoulders before entering a place of worship. Most churches prohibit photography of their interiors.

### OUT ON THE TOWN

Residents of big cities dress up for a night on the town, but that usually doesn't mean a jacket and tie. Dress comfortably but with a bit of style. In smaller towns, things are much more casual. Shorts will serve you for a night out only at the beach.

### LANGUAGE

Spanish is Honduras's official language. English is practically a second language— some would say almost a first language—in the Bay Islands. English on the mainland is hit or miss, however. Most people connected with the tourist industry speak some English, but the person on the street will likely know none. Honduran Spanish is known for being spoken at a faster clip than that of next-door Guatemala. You may get a lot of use out of *Repita, por favor* (Repeat, please) or *Más despacio, por favor* (Slower, please). You'll hear a few indigenous languages, too— Chortí, around Copán Ruinas; Lenca, near Gracias; and Garífuna, along the Caribbean coast and in the Bay Islands.

*Fodor's Spanish for Travelers* (available at bookstores everywhere) is an excellent way to get started.

Carrying a laptop could make you a target for thieves. Conceal your laptop in a generic bag, and keep it close to you at all times.

**Contacts Cybercafes** (⊕ *www.cybercafes.com*).

## PHONES

To call Honduras direct, dial 011 followed by the country code of 504, then the number of the party you're calling. Landline numbers have seven digits; mobile numbers have eight. There are no area codes.

### CALLING WITHIN HONDURAS

To place calls within Honduras, simply dial the seven- or eight-digit telephone number. Dial 192 for nationwide information. Public phones are everywhere, but are occasionally out of order. They function with Telecard's issued by Hondutel, the national telephone company, and are sold at many stores. Telecards come in denominations of L20, L50, and L100, and can be used from any touch-tone phone.

### CALLING OUTSIDE HONDURAS

For international calls you should dial 00, then the country code. (For example, the country code for the United States and Canada is 1.)

A reasonable option for calling home is to stop by one of the many offices of Hondutel, the national telephone company. All towns of any size have at least one, and they keep hours well into the evening. At just L2 (less than $0.10) per minute, a call to the United States is a bargain. At tourist destinations, avoid the ubiquitous blue telephones with signs that say CALL USA. Your credit card or the party you're calling back home will be socked with an enormous bill for the call.

To reach an AT&T operator, dial ☎ 800–0123. For MCI, dial ☎ 800–0122. For Sprint, dial ☎ 800–0121.

**Access Codes AT&T Direct** (☎ 800–5288). **MCI WorldPhone** (☎ 800/444–4444). **Sprint International Access** (☎ 800/793–1153).

> ### WORD OF MOUTH
>
> "Refunds on deposits anywhere on Roatán can be tough; some have clauses that allow partial refunds depending on how close to the travel date you cancel."
>
> —roatanvortex

### MOBILE PHONES

If you have a multiband phone (some countries use different frequencies than what's used in the United States) and your service provider uses the world-standard GSM network (as do AT&T, T-Mobile, Cingular, and Verizon), you can probably use your phone in Honduras. Roaming fees can be steep: 99¢ a minute is considered reasonable. It's almost always cheaper to text message than to make a call, since text messages have a very low set fee.

If you just want to make local calls, consider buying a new SIM card (note that your provider may have to unlock your phone for you to use a different SIM card) and a prepaid service plan in the destination. You'll then have a local number and can make local calls at local rates.

■**TIP➜ If you travel internationally frequently, save one of your old mobile phones or buy a cheap one on the Internet; ask your cell phone company to unlock it for you, and take it with you as a travel phone, buying a new SIM card with pay-as-you-go service in each destination.**

**Contacts Cellular Abroad** (☎ 800/287–5072 ⊕ www.cellularabroad.com) rents and sells GMS phones and sells SIM cards that work in many countries. **Mobal** (☎ 888/888–9162 ⊕ www.mobal.com) rents mobiles and sells GSM phones (starting at $49) that will operate in 190 countries. Per-call rates vary throughout the world. **Planet Fone** (☎ 888/988–4777 ⊕ www.planetfone.com) rents cell phones, but the per-minute rates are expensive.

# CUSTOMS AND DUTIES

You may bring any personal effects with you to Honduras without paying tax on them. Adult visitors may bring a maximum of 2.5 liters of alcoholic beverages and 400 cigarettes, 500 grams of tobacco, or 50 cigars tax-free.

# EATING OUT

*For information on food-related health issues, ⇨ see Health below.*

### MEALS AND MEALTIMES

Few restaurants open for breakfast (*desayuno*). For most Hondurans, lunch (*almuerzo*) is their biggest meal of the day, and that will be the case in smaller local restaurants, too. The *plato típico*, that Honduran combination of meat, tortillas, and cabbage, is lunchtime fare—served between noon and 2 PM—at most mom-and-pop places. Such places, if they open at all in the evening, will serve a lighter dinner (*cena*). Restaurants that cater mostly to tourists follow more American conventions and serve larger dinners. Restaurants tend not to serve food late into the evening, and most places start winding down their dinner service by 8 or 9 PM. Unless otherwise noted, the restaurants listed in this guide are open daily for lunch and dinner.

### RESERVATIONS AND DRESS

Almost no restaurant in Honduras is formal enough to require reservations. We only mention them specifically when reservations are essential (there's no other way you'll ever get a table) or when they are not accepted. We mention dress only when men are required to wear a jacket or a jacket and tie, but there are very few places that have such requirements.

### WINE, BEER, AND SPIRITS

Cervecería Nacional, the country's only real brewery of note, brews all major brands of Honduran beer (*cerveza*). Folks here are loyal to their brands, and the best way to start a lively conversation is to ask them what their favorite is. The lager

**WORD OF MOUTH**

"If I was looking strictly for beaches (and good food), I'd go back to Roatán."

—SusanInToronto

Imperial and the pilsner Port Royal and the darker Salva Vida are the most popular brands. Visitors to Lago de Yojoa, in the center of the country, know the local D&D Microbrewery, which offers a few distinct alternatives to the national brands. If you go out for a night on the town, the waitstaff will not clear away the bottles from your table until you're ready to leave. It helps them tally up the bill that way.

Honduras does have a tiny wine industry, but most oenophiles would turn up their noses at it. You'll likely imbibe Chilean and Argentine product if you order wine with dinner. Hondurans look on Flor de Caña, made just over the border in neighboring Nicaragua, as their favorite.

# ELECTRICITY

Honduras uses 110-volt, 60-cycle electricity, as does the United States. Most outlets take two-pronged flat plugs. Power surges can happen at inexpensive hotels. A surge protector is a necessity for any valuable appliance. Power outages happen occasionally.

# EMERGENCIES

**Foreign Embassies U.S. Embassy** (✉ *Av. La Paz, Colonia Palmira, Tegucigalpa* ☎ *236–9320; after hours: 238–5114* ⊕ *honduras.usembassy. gov*). **American Citizen Services Office** (✉ *Banco Atlántida bldg, Parque Central, San Pedro Sula* ☎ *558–1580* ⊕ *honduras. usembassy.gov/acsoffice_sps.html*).

**Hospitals and Clinics Clínica Viera** (✉ *Av. Cristobal Colón, Barrio El Centro, Tegucigalpa* ☎ *237–3160*). **Hospital del Valle** (✉ *Blvd. del Norte, Salida a Puerto Cortés, San Pedro Sula* ☎ *551–8433* ⊕ *www.hospitaldelvalle.com*).

# ▌HEALTH

Most visitors to Honduras experience nothing more serious than a mild case of traveler's diarrhea. Watch what you eat. Food from street vendors looks temptingly delicious, but unless your system is accustomed to such fare, we recommend avoiding it. Drink only bottled water or water that has been boiled for several minutes, even when brushing your teeth. Order drinks *sin hielo,* or "without ice." Mild cases of traveler's diarrhea may respond to Imodium or Pepto-Bismol, both of which can be purchased in Honduras without a prescription.

Mosquitoes are a problem in tropical areas, especially at dusk. Take along plenty of repellent containing DEET. You may not get through airport screening with an aerosol can, so take a spritz bottle or cream. Local brands of repellent are readily available in pharmacies. If you plan to spend time in the Caribbean jungle or the Mosquitía, be sure to wear clothing that covers your arms and legs, sleep under a mosquito net, and spray bug repellent in living and sleeping areas. You should also ask your doctor about antimalarial medications. Do so early, as some such medications must be started weeks before heading into a malaria zone.

Chiggers are sometimes a problem in the jungle or where there are animals. Red, itchy spots suddenly appear, most often *under* your clothes. The best advice when venturing out into chigger country is to use insect repellent and wear loose-fitting clothing. A hot, soapy bath after being outdoors also prevents them from attaching to your skin.

## MEDICAL INSURANCE AND ASSISTANCE

Consider buying trip insurance with medical-only coverage. Neither Medicare nor some private insurers cover medical expenses anywhere outside the United States. Medical-only policies typically reimburse you for medical care (excluding that related to preexisting conditions)

and hospitalization abroad, and provide for evacuation. You still have to pay the bills and await reimbursement from the insurer, though.

Another option is to sign up with a medical-evacuation assistance company. A membership in one of these companies gets you doctor referrals, emergency evacuation or repatriation, 24-hour hotlines for medical consultation, and other assistance. International SOS Assistance Emergency and AirMed International provide evacuation services and medical referrals. MedjetAssist offers medical evacuation.

**Medical Assistance Companies AirMed International** (⊕ *www.airmed.com*). **International SOS Assistance Emergency** (⊕ *www.intsos.com*). **MedjetAssist** (⊕ *www. medjetassist.com*).

**Medical-Only Insurers International Medical Group** (☎ 800/628–4664 ⊕ *www. imglobal.com*). **International SOS** (⊕ *www. internationalsos.com*). **Wallach & Company** (☎ 800/237–6615 or 540/687–3166 ⊕ *www. wallach.com*).

## SHOTS AND MEDICATIONS

No vaccinations are required to enter Honduras. It's a good idea to have up-to-date boosters for tetanus and diphtheria. A hepatitis A inoculation can prevent one of the most common intestinal infections. Those who might be around animals should consider a rabies vaccine. As rabies is a concern, most hospitals have antirabies injections. Children traveling to Honduras should have their vaccinations for childhood diseases up to date.

According to the Centers for Disease Control and Prevention (CDC), there's a limited risk of typhoid, hepatitis B, and dengue. Although a few of these you could catch anywhere, malaria is restricted to jungle areas. Dengue, for which there is no preventative vaccine, is a growing concern in Honduras. Use mosquito repellant liberally and avoid contact with pools of stagnant water. If you plan to visit remote regions or stay in Honduras for more than a month, check with the CDC's International Travelers Hot Line.

**Health Information Centers for Disease Control and Prevention** (*CDC* ☎ *877/394–8747 international travelers' health line* ⊕ *www.cdc.gov/travel*). **World Health Organization** (*WHO* ⊕ *www.who.int*).

## PRESCRIPTION AND OVER-THE-COUNTER REMEDIES

While many drugs that require a prescription back home are available over-the-counter in Honduras, exact equivalence might be a concern. Always carry your own medications with you, including those you would ordinarily take for a simple headache, as you will usually not find the same brands in the local *farmacia* (pharmacy). However, if you forgot, ask for *aspirina* (aspirin) or *acetaminofina* (acetaminophen).

## ▌HOURS OF OPERATION

Most businesses open weekdays from 9 to 5 or 6 PM, and until noon on Saturdays. The traditional midday closing is falling by the wayside in Tegucigalpa and San Pedro Sula but still holds sway in smaller communities. Banks open weekdays from 9 to 4 or 5 PM, and until noon on Saturday. Museums frequently close one day a week, often Monday.

## HOLIDAYS

New Year's Day; Easter holiday, which begins midday on Holy Thursday and continues through Easter Monday (March or April); Day of the Americas (April 14); Labor Day (May 1); Independence Day (September 15); Francisco Morazán's Birthday (October 3); Columbus Day (October 12); Honduran Army Day (October 21); Christmas.

## ▌MAIL

Mail from Honduras takes a week to 10 days to reach the United States. Letters and postcards make it just fine if posted from Tegucigalpa, San Pedro Sula, La Ceiba, or Roatán, and if they don't look like they contain anything of value. You'll pay L12 for a card or a letter up to 20 grams.

For timely delivery or valuable parcels, use FedEx, DHL, or UPS, which have offices in Tegucigalpa, San Pedro Sula, and La Ceiba. Because of the limited number of international flights, overnight service is usually not available. Plan on so-called next-day delivery, really taking three to four business days from Honduras.

## ▌MONEY

| ITEM | AVERAGE COST |
|---|---|
| Cup of Coffee | L20 |
| Glass of Wine | L80 |
| Glass of Beer | L40 |
| Sandwich | L80 |
| One-Mile Taxi Ride in Capital City | L50–L60 |
| Museum Admission | L60 |

Prices throughout this guide are given for adults. Substantially reduced fees are almost always available for children, students, and senior citizens.

## ATMS AND BANKS

Make a point to stop at an ATM (*cajero automático*) to get cash while you're in the bigger cities (Tegucigalpa, San Pedro Sula, La Ceiba, Comayagua, Santa Rosa de Copán) or important tourist destinations (Copán Ruinas, Roatán). You'll find machines at banks, large shopping malls, international airports, and gas stations. Although it may sound counterintuitive, we recommend using ATMs inside banks during opening hours. They're more secure than free-standing ATMs, and you have access to bank personnel right there if something goes wrong. If you must use a freestanding ATM, especially at night, choose one only in a well-lighted area and be aware of your surroundings.

Most branches of BAC Honduras and Banco Atlántida have ATMs that work with Visa (Plus-affiliated) or Master-Card (Cirrus-affiliated) cards. A few machines—very few—will also give cash using an American Express or Diner's Club card.

ATMs are fewer and farther between once you get out-country. Several communities—Gracias, for example—have banks but no cash machines.

**Banks BAC Honduras** (⊕ *www.bac.net*).
**Banco Atlántida** (⊕ *www.bancatlan.hn*).

## CREDIT CARDS

Throughout this guide, the following abbreviations are used: **AE**, American Express; **D**, Discover; **DC**, Diners Club; **MC**, MasterCard; and **V**, Visa.

Visa and MasterCard are the two most widely accepted credit cards, with American Express in third place. Discover has been introduced to Honduras in the past couple of years, but it is still new enough that businesses may not realize they can accept it. You may have to look at the credit-card decals on the business's window or door and point it out to the employee if Discover is shown.

Small businesses that do accept credit cards will always prefer that you pay in cash. Processors charge them high fees for credit-card transactions. The business may pass this charge onto you in the form of a surcharge on your purchase price. Conversely, it may offer a small discount if you pay in cash.

## CURRENCY AND EXCHANGE

Honduras's currency is the lempira, named for a 16th century martyred Lenca indigenous leader. (His portrait appears on the one-lempira bill.) Prices are designated L or Lps or as HNL in international currency charts. The exchange rate, which has remained fairly constant in recent years and which we use in this book, is L19 to the U.S. dollar. (When doing mental calculations, L20 to the dollar works pretty closely.)

Bills come in lempira denominations of 1 (red), 2 (purple), 5 (green), 10 (brown), 20 (green), 50 (cyan), 100 (tan), and 500 (violet). The lempira is divided into 100 centavos, with coins of 10, 20, and 50 centavos in circulation. Given the tendency of businesses to round prices up to the nearest lempira, you might never see any coins during your visit. The government has announced plans to mint 1-, 2-, 5-, and 10-lempira coins to replace the corresponding bills. At this writing, no target date has been set.

It is nearly impossible to buy or sell lempiras outside Honduras, and on the outside chance you find someone who will engage in exchange, the rates will be extremely unfavorable to you. Wait until you arrive before changing money. Conversely, try to spend or exchange those leftover lempiras before you leave Honduras, or resign yourself to saving them for your next trip.

Informal money changers with wads of bills operate anywhere that visitors congregate. Many travelers insist they are fine to deal with, but you always risk a scam or being shortchanged and run an even greater risk engaging in a cash transaction in the open on a public street. Look for more conventional means of changing money.

For the most part, Honduras is not one of those "Everybody takes dollars" destinations. U.S. dollars do circulate as practically a second currency on the Bay Islands, but much less so on the mainland. Larger tourist-oriented businesses on the mainland will accept dollars. Big hotels all over the country express their rates in dollars or the lempira equivalent. For smaller businesses on the mainland and for tipping individuals, you should deal in lempiras.

Try to be sensitive to the type of business you're dealing with when paying for purchases. While a 100-lempira bill represents only about $5 to us, a market vendor may have trouble changing it if you buy something for only L10.

### EXCHANGE RATES

Google does currency conversion. Just type in the amount you want to convert and an explanation of how you want it converted (e.g., "14 Honduran lempiras in dollars"), and then voilà. **Oanda.com** also allows you to print out a handy table with the current day's conversion rates. **XE.com** is another good currency-conversion Web site.

**Conversion sites Google** (⊕ *www.google. com*). **Oanda.com** (⊕ *www.oanda.com*). **XE.com** (⊕ *www.xe.com*).

### TIPPING

Unfortunately, Honduras offers no fixed rules to count on when tipping in restaurants. Many establishments include the tip in your final bill. If you see the word *servicio* when you get your bill, you'll have made an obligatory tip. Other places suggest a *propina voluntaria*, a voluntary tip. The bill may specify what the amount should be, or it may not. Still other places do nothing at all. In any case, 10% to 15% of the bill is a good amount to tip your waiter or waitress. Dining spots may levy a cover charge for nights when they offer live entertainment.

A tip of about L20 per day is an acceptable tip for housekeeping staff. Again, the *servicio* may be included in your final

bill at checkout. If in doubt, ask what the practice is at the hotel.

When tipping, the kind thing to do is to deal in lempiras. A tip in dollars requires the recipient to stand in line at the bank—and they're usually long lines—to change your tip into local currency.

| TIPPING GUIDELINES FOR HONDURAS | |
|---|---|
| Bartender | 10% in upscale bars |
| Bellhop | L20 per bag |
| Hotel Concierge | L100 or more, if service is performed for you |
| Hotel Doorman | $L20 if he helps you get a cab |
| Hotel Maid | L40 to L60 per day |
| Hotel Room-Service Waiter | L20, even if a service charge is added |
| Porter at Airport or Train Station | L20 per pag |
| Skycap at Airport | L20 to L40 per bag checked |
| Taxi Driver | Round up the fare to the next L20 amount, but L20 if driver helps with bags |
| Tour Guide | 10% of the cost of the tour |
| Valet Parking Attendant | L20 to L40, but only when you get your car |
| Waiter | 10%–15%; nothing additional if a service charge is added to the bill |

### TRAVELER'S CHECKS

Almost no business accepts traveler's checks for payment for purchases. Branches of BAC Honduras will exchange American Express checks for lempiras or dollars with a 2% commission.

## ▌ PACKING

Although Honduras lies solidly in the tropics, large sectors of the country will seem anything but tropical to you. Tegucigalpa and the highlands perch at altitudes of 2,000 to 4,000 feet and can feel brisk in the evening. Bring along at least a lightweight jacket and a pair of long trousers to supplement your tropical cabana wear if you plan to travel anywhere outside the Bay Islands, San Pedro Sula, and the Caribbean or Pacific coasts.

For sightseeing, casual clothing and good walking shoes are desirable and appropriate. Honduras has several colonial communities—Copán Ruinas, Santa Rosa de Copán, Gracias, and Comayagua—with cobblestone streets. They're charming, to be sure, but if you wear a flimsy pair of shoes, you'll feel every stone in the soles of your feet. Most cities don't require formal clothes, even for evenings. If you're doing business in Honduras, you'll need the same attire you would wear in U.S. and European cities: for men, suits and ties; for women, suits for day wear, and for evening, depending on the occasion— ask your host or hostess—a cocktail dress or just a nice suit with a dressy blouse.

Travel in rain-forest areas—the Caribbean coast or the Mosquitía—will require long-sleeve shirts, long pants, socks, sneakers, a hat, a light waterproof jacket, a bathing suit (if you want to swim), sunscreen, and insect repellent. You can never have too many large resealable plastic bags (bring a whole box), which are ideal for storing film, protecting official documents from rain and damp, and quarantining stinky socks.

Other useful items include a travel flashlight and extra batteries, a pocketknife with a bottle opener (put it in your checked luggage), a medical kit, binoculars, and a calculator to help with currency conversions. A sarong or light cotton blanket can have many uses: beach towel, picnic blanket, and cushion for hard seats. Most important, always travel with tissues or a roll of toilet paper as sometimes it's difficult to find in local restrooms.

# ▌PASSPORTS AND VISAS

Visitors from the United States require only a valid passport and return ticket to be issued a 90-day visa at their point of

entry into Honduras. You will be photographed at passport control. The official will keep one copy of your immigration form you were given on the plane, or at the land border. Keep the carbon copy; you'll need to present it when you leave and will pay a small fine if you lose it. Honduras is part of an immigration-and-customs union with El Salvador, Nicaragua, and Guatemala called the CA-4. Any time spent in those three neighboring countries also counts toward your 90 days in Honduras.

Honduras has stringent rules about the entry and exit of minors. Both parents or legal guardians must accompany any visitor under 18. Barring that, the absent parent(s) or guardian(s) must supply a notarized statement granting permission for their minor child to travel to Honduras. The situation comes up frequently with the large number of high school students who travel to Honduras to work with volunteer groups, accompanied by adult supervisors who are not their parents.

Make two photocopies of the data page of your passport, one for someone at home and another for you, carried separately from your passport. While sightseeing in Honduras, it's best to carry the copy of your passport and leave the original hidden in your hotel room or in your hotel's safe. If you lose your passport, call the nearest embassy or consulate and the local police.

# ■ RESTROOMS

In cities, your best bet for finding a restroom while on the go is to walk into a large hotel as if you're a guest and find the facilities. The next best thing is talking your way into a restaurant bathroom; buying a drink is a nice gesture if you do. If you're staying in a small hotel, don't throw toilet paper into the toilet—use the basket provided—as unsanitary as this may seem. Doing so can clog the antiquated plumbing. Always carry your own supply of tissues or toilet paper, just in case.

Public restrooms are usually designated as SERVICIOS SANITARIOS or, sometimes, just SANITARIOS.

**Find a Loo The Bathroom Diaries** (⊕ www. thebathroomdiaries.com) is flush with unsanitized info on restrooms the world over—each one located, reviewed, and rated.

# ■ SAFETY

Be street-smart in Honduras and trouble generally won't find you. Money belts peg you as a tourist, so if you must wear one, hide it under your clothing. If you carry a purse, choose one with a zipper and a thick strap that you can drape across your body; adjust the length so that the purse sits in front of you. Carry only enough money to cover casual spending. Keep camera bags close to your body. Note that backpacks are especially easy to grab and open secretly. Finally, avoid wearing flashy jewelry and watches.

Many streets throughout Honduras are not well lighted, so avoid walking at night, and certainly avoid deserted streets, day or night. Always walk as if you know where you're going, even if you don't.

If using your own vehicle, avoid driving on rural roads at night. It gets dark throughout Honduras between 5:30 and 6 PM year-round. Make a point to be at your destination by dark.

Use only official taxis with the company's name emblazoned on the side. Don't get into a car just because there's a taxi sign in the window, as it might be an unlicensed driver. Taxis should be your only means of getting around Tegucigalpa, San Pedro Sula, and La Ceiba after dark, even if you're going just a very short distance. Anywhere at night, you or the staff should call a taxi from your hotel or restaurant.

Do not let anyone distract you. Beware of one of the oldest tricks in the book in Central America: someone "accidentally" spills food or liquid on you and then offers to help clean it up; the spiller might have an accomplice who will walk off with your purse or your suitcase while you are distracted.

Women, especially blondes, can expect some admiring glances and perhaps a comment or two, but outright come-ons or grabbing are rare. Usually all that is needed is to ignore the perpetrator and keep walking down the street.

## GOVERNMENT INFORMATION AND ADVISORIES

**Advisories U.S. Department of State** (⊕ travel.state.gov).

# ■ TAXES

A 12% general sales tax is levied on everything except goods bought at open-air markets and street vendors. It's usually included in the advertised or posted price and should be included with food and drink. If a business offers you a discount for paying in cash, it probably means they aren't charging sales tax (and not reporting the transaction to the government). Honduras has no tax-refund scheme for foreign visitors.

In addition to the sales tax, hotels are also required to charge a 4% tourism tax. Small mom-and-pop lodgings may forego this if you pay in cash.

Departure taxes at Honduras's four international airports—Tegucigalpa, San

Pedro Sula, La Ceiba, and Roatán—are US$37.35 or L706 for international flights, and you'll pay L37.03 for domestic flights at any of the country's airports.

## ▌TIME

Honduras is on Central Standard Time (GMT-0600) year-round, with no daylight saving time observed. From November to March, Honduras is the same time as Chicago and Houston. The rest of the year, when the United States does observe daylight saving time, Honduras is the same time as Denver.

## ▌TOURS

### GUIDED TOURS

La Ruta Moskitía, based here in Honduras, can be your one-stop-shopping place for culture-adventure excursions to the sometimes-difficult-to-navigate-on-your-own Mosquitía. Tours last seven to nine days, and take you on visits to indigenous communities, but also include rafting, trekking, and animal spotting.

Mesoamerican Ecotourism Alliance (MEA) offers tours that visit Río Esteban, a Garífuna community on the Caribbean coast, with a chance to learn about women's cooperative projects and local artisan workshops. There's snorkeling, hiking, and boating on the tour operated by this Colorado-based company, too.

Mountain Travel Sobek, based in California, leads weeklong hiking tours that take in Pico Bonito National Park, and also include boating at the Cuero y Salado Reserve and a visit to the ruins at Copán.

The Michigan-based Uncommon Adventures can take you on eight-day sea-kayaking trips that originate at their own lodge in Roatán. Paddle out for day trips exploring the reef at Pigeon Cay, the island's mangrove tunnels, and other secret channels.

Honduras also figures prominently in various tour operators' multicountry trips. Overseas Adventure Travel includes

### WHAT'S IN A NAME?

Hondurans pronounce the name of their country differently than we do. The dissimilarity stems primarily from the fact than the letter *H* is always silent in Spanish. Listen for *ohn-DOO-rahs.*

visits to Copán in its 14-day "Route of the Maya" trip that takes in Belize, Guatemala, and El Salvador as well. Gap Adventures offers a similarly themed "Tikal to Copán Quest" trip that lasts for 15 days and also takes in Guatemala and El Salvador. Honduras is also a component in Gap's two monthlong tours of the entire Central American isthmus.

**Tour Operators Gap Adventures**
(☎ 888/800–4100 ⊕ www.gapadventures.com).

**La Ruta Moskitia** (☎ 406–6782 ⊕ www. larutamoskitia.com).

**Mesoamerican Ecotourim Alliance** (☎ 800/682–0504 ⊕ www.travelwithmea.com).

**Mountain Travel Sobek** (☎ 888/831–7526 ⊕ www.mtsobek.com).

**Overseas Adventure Travel** (☎ 800/493–6824 ⊕ www.oattravel.com).

**Uncommon Adventures** (☎ 866/882–5525 ⊕ www.uncommonadv.com).

## ▌TRIP INSURANCE

Comprehensive trip insurance is valuable if you're booking a very expensive or complicated trip (particularly to an isolated region) or if you're booking far in advance. Comprehensive policies typically cover trip cancellation and interruption, letting you cancel or cut your trip short because of illness, or, in some cases, acts of terrorism in your destination. Such policies might also cover evacuation and medical care. (For trips abroad you should have at least medical-only coverage. ⇨ *See Medical Insurance and Assistance under Health.*) Some also cover you for trip delays because of bad weather or mechanical problems as well as for lost or delayed luggage.

Another type of coverage to consider is financial default—that is, when your trip is disrupted because a tour operator, airline, or cruise line goes out of business. Generally you must buy this when you book your trip or shortly thereafter, and it's available to you only if your operator isn't on a list of excluded companies.

Always read the fine print of your policy to make sure that you're covered for the risks that most concern you. Compare several policies to be sure you're getting the best price and range of coverage available.

**Insurance Comparison Info** Insure My Trip (☎ *800/487–4722* ⊕ *www.insuremytrip.com*). **Square Mouth** (☎ *800/240–0369* ⊕ *www. squaremouth.com*).

**Comprehensive Insurers** Access America (☎ *800/284–8300* ⊕ *www.accessamerica.com*). **AIG Travel Guard** (☎ *800/826–4919* ⊕ *www. travelguard.com*). **CSA Travel Protection** (☎ *800/711–1197* ⊕ *www.csatravelprotection. com*). **Travelex Insurance** (☎ *888/228–9792* ⊕ *www.travelex-insurance.com*). **Travel Insured International** (☎ *800/243–3174* ⊕ *www.travelinsured.com*).

## ▌ VISITOR INFORMATION

The friendly Instituto Hondureño de Turismo in Colonia San Carlos in Tegucigalpa is worth a visit for information about the country.

**Tourist Information** Instituto Hondureño de **Turismo** (✉ *Edificio Europa, 2nd floor, Col. San Carlos* ☎ *222–2124* ⊕ *www.letsgohonduras. com*).

### ONLINE RESOURCES

The long-established English-language newspaper *Honduras Weekly* is edited in Tegucigalpa and uses correspondents from around the country. The paper publishes a Web edition with comprehensive coverage of news and the country's always-fascinating politics. It also

> INSPIRATION
>
> If you can find it, *Cabbages and Kings*, O. Henry's 1904 collection of short stories set in Honduras, details the daily life of a country beholden to the interests of multinational corporations. The author, whose real name was William Sidney Porter, fled to Honduras from embezzlement charges in the United States and penned the work while hiding out here. The book gave the world the pejorative term *banana republic*. (Yes, Honduras was the original of those.) Far more available is Paul Theroux's 1982 *The Mosquito Coast*, a tale of an American family seeking to recreate its own society in the forbidding Mosquitía. The book became a 1986 film starring Harrison Ford, Helen Mirren, and River Phoenix.

publishes some insightful travel essays to help get you in the mood for your upcoming Honduras trip.

**All About Honduras** Honduras Weekly (⊕ *www.hodurasweekly.com*).

# INDEX

# PHOTO CREDITS

8 (top), Christopher Poe/Shutterstock. 8 (bottom), Jane Sweeney/age fotostock. 9 (left), Tomasz Wojcik/ iStockphoto. 9 (right), TORRIONE Stefano/age fotostock. 10, Adalberto.H.Vega/Flickr. 11 (left), Jane Sweeney/age fotostock. 11 (right), John A. Anderson/iStockphoto. 12 (left) Holger Mette/iStockphoto. 12 (top center), Jane Sweeney/age fotostock. 12 (top right), Lauri Väin/Flickr. 12 (bottom right), Juan Irias/Wikimedia Commons. 13 (left), Richard T. Nowitz/age fotostock. 13 (top center), Anthony Clark/ Flickr. 13 (bottom center), Hjvannes/Wikimedia Commons. 13 (top right), NGerda/Wikimedia Commons. 13 (bottom right), chamo estudio/Wikimedia Commons. 14, Henryk Sadura/Shutterstock. 15 (left), Wikimedia Commons. 15 (right), Honduras Institute of Tourism. 16, Adalberto H.Vega/Flickr. 17 (left), Hacienda San Lucas. 17 (right), John Asselin/Flickr. 24, Sarah and Jason/Flickr. 25 (left), Adalberto H.Vega/Flickr. 25 (right), nichcollins/Flickr. 26, FLPA/Jurgen & Christi/age fotostock. 27, Jim Bahn/Flickr. 28, rj lerich/Shutterstock. 29 (left), Alberto Paredes/age fotostock. 29 (right), Richard T. Nowitz/age fotostock. 30, dreamtours/age fotostock. 32, wilbanks/john and carolina/Flickr. 33 (left), CCRcreations/Chris Richardson/Flickr. 33 (right), Adalberto.H.Vega/Flickr. 35 (left and right), Hacienda San Lucas. 36, Richard T. Nowitz/age fotostock. 37 (left), Wikimedia Commons. 37 (right), Richard T. Nowitz/age fotostock.

# NOTES

# ABOUT OUR WRITERS

**Maria Gallucci** is a freelance journalist and travel writer based in Mexico City. Her work has taken her to ancient ruins in Jordan, remote indigenous villages in southern Mexico, the dusty sprawl of urban Nicaragua, and to Honduras, where she researched the Caribbean Coast, Roatán and the Bay Islands, and La Mosquitía chapters for this guide. An Ohio University graduate, she has worked or written for *The Associated Press, American City Business Journals, SolveClimate News,* and Mexican publications *The News and Mexico Weekly.*

Freelance writer and pharmacist **Jeffrey Van Fleet** enjoys Wisconsin winters and Central American rainy seasons. (Most people would do it the other way around.) He is based in San Jose, Costa Rica, where he is a regular contributor to the English-language newspaper *The Tico Times,* but never misses the chance to head a couple of countries north to Honduras. Jeff has contributed to Fodor's guides to Costa Rica, Guatemala, Los Cabos & Baja, Mexico, Peru, Chile, Argentina, and Central and South America. He updated the sections on Tegucigalpa, Southern and Western Honduras, El Salvador, Nicaragua, Experience, and Travel Smart for this guide.